Cambridge Middle East Library

The Ottoman Empire and
European Capitalism, 1820–1913

Cambridge Middle East Library

The Ottoman Empire and European Capitalism, 1820–1913

Trade, investment and production

Şevket Pamuk

DEPARTMENT OF ECONOMICS
VILLANOVA UNIVERSITY

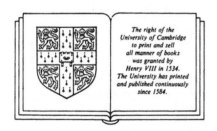

The right of the
University of Cambridge
to print and sell
all manner of books
was granted by
Henry VIII in 1534.
The University has printed
and published continuously
since 1584.

CAMBRIDGE UNIVERSITY PRESS

CAMBRIDGE
LONDON   NEW YORK   NEW ROCHELLE
MELBOURNE   SYDNEY

CAMBRIDGE UNIVERSITY PRESS
Cambridge, New York, Melbourne, Madrid, Cape Town, Singapore,
São Paulo, Delhi, Dubai, Tokyo

Cambridge University Press
The Edinburgh Building, Cambridge CB2 8RU, UK

Published in the United States of America by Cambridge University Press, New York

www.cambridge.org
Information on this title: www.cambridge.org/9780521130929

First published 1987
This digitally printed version 2010

A catalogue record for this publication is available from the British Library

Library of Congress Cataloguing in Publication data

Pamuk, Şevket,
The Ottoman empire and European capitalism, 1820–1913.
(Cambridge Middle East library)
Bibliography.
Includes index.
1. Turkey – Foreign economic relations.
2. Turkey – Commerce – History – 19th century.
3. Investments, Foreign – Turkey – History – 19th century
4. Turkey – Industries – History – 19th century.
I. Title. II. Series.
HF1583.4.P36 1987   330.956′01   86-28386

ISBN 978-0-521-33194-4 Hardback
ISBN 978-0-521-13092-9 Paperback

Contents

Illustrations

Map

Figures

Tables

Preface

Let us start by drawing the boundaries. This volume does not attempt to provide a comprehensive history of the Ottoman economy during the nineteenth century. Our purpose is twofold: (a) to examine relations between the Ottoman economy and European capitalism and the consequences of this interaction in the sphere of production; and (b) to insert this Ottoman experience into a comparative framework within the periphery of the nineteenth-century world economy.

The emphasis on the 'external' relations of the Ottoman economy does not mean that the specific path traversed by the Ottoman economy was determined only by external factors and that internal factors and structures did not play an important role. Clearly, the far-reaching social and economic transformations that the Ottoman Empire underwent during the nineteenth century were the result of complex interaction between internal and external forces. However, in the aftermath of the Industrial Revolution and the emergence of industrialized economies, we observe similar transformations in those regions of the world outside Europe, North America and Japan. For this reason, we have to search for the origins of the transformations the so-called Third World countries experienced during the nineteenth century in world capitalism as a whole. In other words, the internal dynamics of the Ottoman economy by themselves are insufficient to explain the transformation of its structure during the nineteenth century. In our initial emphasis on world economic forces in this volume, we attempt to capture the general direction of this transformation. We should hasten to add, however, that we also observe a good deal of diversity in the nineteenth-century experiences of these countries. The differences between the Ottoman case and those elsewhere in Asia or Latin America cannot be explained by reference to external factors alone. We can capture this diversity within the unity only by integrating into our analysis factors specific to Ottoman economy and society.

A second limitation of this volume concerns spatial dimensions. Frequent loss of land and population by the Ottoman Empire during the nineteenth century made it virtually impossible to undertake all our investigations within the same geographical borders. As a result, in our studies of foreign trade and external terms of trade, we followed the contracting borders of the Empire from the 1830s until World War I. On the other hand, because of the size of the Empire and the considerable differences between regions, we chose to limit some of our analyses to a smaller geographical area. In chapters on foreign investment, agriculture and the decline of handicrafts, we basically remained within the 1911 borders of the Empire, which included northern Greece, Syria, Iraq and present-day Turkey.

Outside the introductory and concluding chapters, this volume consists of two parts. In chapters 2, 3 and 4, which constitute the first part, we adopt a balance of payments framework to establish in detail and for the first time the long-term trends and fluctuations in Ottoman foreign trade, external terms of trade and funds flows arising from foreign investment. In other words, in this first part we draw a detailed map of the world economic forces faced by the Ottoman Empire during the nineteenth century. The more statistical and technical aspects of this investigation are presented in the appendices. In appendix 6, we test the internal consistency of our findings by presenting a detailed reconstruction of Ottoman international balance of payments. The emphasis in this first part is quantitative and we rely primarily on Western sources which have not been used or used only to a limited extent for this purpose. The shortcomings of some of this data are well known and, as discussed in the appendices, we have tried to make the necessary adjustments wherever possible. It should be pointed out that the amount of information that can be obtained from either published or unpublished Ottoman sources on this subject is especially limited.

In chapters 5 and 6, which constitute the second part of the volume, we move from the sphere of circulation to the sphere of production and examine the impact of the penetration of world capitalism on Ottoman agriculture and handicrafts. Rather than attempting to be comprehensive, we chose to be selective in this part. We focused on those processes that reflect most strikingly the impact of world economic forces: export orientation of agriculture, decline of handicrafts-based cotton textiles and the accompanying changes in the relations of production. These chapters also emphasize quantitative analysis and we attempt to develop new data series wherever necessary. It might be argued that by focusing on new patterns of specialization and production, we tend to ignore those parts of the Ottoman economy less affected by external forces. However, we should re-emphasize that this volume does not attempt to provide a comprehensive history of the Ottoman economy. The selections enable us to capture better the nature and direction, if not the extent, of the transformation that occurred during the nineteenth century.

The introductory and concluding chapters, on the other hand, attempt to insert the Ottoman Empire into a comparative framework. Chapter 1 develops three categories for countries in the periphery in order to account for some of the observed differences in the nineteenth-century experiences of the Third World regarding the penetration of world capitalism. Chapter 7 identifies some of the special features of the Ottoman case. It also compares various aspects of the penetration of world capitalism into the Ottoman Empire with the experiences of other medium-sized countries in the Third World by employing various indices related to foreign trade and foreign investment.

We have tried to minimize the problems of transliteration. All place names in present day Turkey and terms have been spelled according to the current Turkish usage, as in *çiftlik* or *vakıf*. For the rest, the most widely adopted usage in English was followed, as in Salonica. In order to facilitate international and intertemporal comparisons, we have used, whenever possible, British pound sterling as the unit of currency. After 1844, one pound sterling was equal to 1.10 Ottoman gold Lira.

Acknowledgements

As this project developed through the years, I have accumulated intellectual debts to a number of people. It is now a pleasure to acknowledge their assistance. At Berkeley, where parts of this volume started as a doctoral dissertation, I enjoyed the support and benefited from the criticism offered by Bent Hansen. At that stage Albert Fishlow and Jan de Vries also provided useful comments and criticism. Outside of Berkeley, I am especially grateful to Charles Issawi for encouragement and sustained interest in all stages of this work. While teaching at Ankara, I discussed many issues and benefited from the insights of Korkut Boratav and Çağlar Keyder. I also received much appreciated comments from Halil Berktay, Reşat Kasaba and Donald Quataert who read parts of the manuscript. I am indebted to the late Vedat Eldem for sharing with me his views on the Ottoman balance of payments. I would like to thank Fahri Aral who helped me in finding the cover photograph and Neyyir Kalaycıoğlu for the preparation of the index. Finally, I would like to express my gratitude to the Economics Department at Villanova University for the variety of resources it has provided in the preparation of the final manuscript.

Chapter 5 has appeared in slightly different form in another volume, *The Ottoman Empire and the World Economy*, edited by Huricihan Islamoğlu-İnan and published by Cambridge University Press (1986). Chapter 6 is an expanded version of an article that appeared in *Exploration in Economic History*. I would like to thank Academic Press for permisison to use that material here.

Chapter 1

Introduction

Internal versus external factors and the historical process

After the transition to capitalism in Europe during the sixteenth and seventeenth centuries, the European economies started expanding into other areas where pre-capitalist or non-capitalist modes of production had prevailed. For this reason, the subsequent histories of the remaining areas of the world, with the possible exception of Japan, cannot be examined solely in terms of the internal dynamics of each society. Rather, each of these countries has to be inserted into the context of the world capitalist economy and their histories have to be examined in terms of the complex interaction between internal forces such as social classes and state structures and external forces pertaining to the world economy, such as European territorial expansion, long-distance commodity trade and the logic of capital accumulation on the world scale.

During the last two centuries the world capitalist economy has been characterized by a hierarchical structure. In the nineteenth century, the upper echelons of this hierarchy were occupied by the industrialized economies of Europe, particularly of Western and Central Europe and the United States. There was a good deal of diversity within this group. However, there was also a good deal of similarity and unity between them that would justify our reference to these countries in this volume as the center of the world economy. At the lower levels of the same hierarchy were the countries on the periphery, where pre-capitalist or non-capitalist modes of production had prevailed before they came into contact with capitalist Europe. Many of these areas were pulled into the capitalist world economy as subordinate units during the nineteenth century.

Viewed from this perspective, there was undoubtedly a good deal of unity in the nineteenth-century experiences of those countries which presently constitute the Third World. There were common factors in the penetration of capitalism which affected all these economies and which will constitute the starting point of our analysis. It should also be emphasized, however, that within this unity there existed a good deal of diversity. In terms of the specific forms of interaction with the rest of the world economy and in terms of the resulting structures, the history of each country was unique.

This was because the relationship between external and internal forces formed a complex whole whose outcome did not depend solely on external dynamics. It is true that in those situations of extreme colonial dependence, local history was almost reduced to the reflection of what happened in the center country. However, colonial dependence did not encompass the entire range of experiences in the periphery of the world economy during the nineteenth century. In many cases these countries were governed by internal social classes which possessed varying degrees of independence and power *vis-à-vis* the dominant interests in the center countries. In those situations, the specific forms of interaction with the rest of the world economy and their outcome depended upon the coincidence of interests between the local dominant classes and international ones. There were also cases of clashes of interest and even short-lived challenges by the local dominant classes to the dominant international forces. At any rate, it is clear that the external forces did not produce all outcomes by themselves. For this reason, focusing solely on world economic forces or, for example, on the logic of capital accumulation on a world scale would not enable us to understand and explain the diversity of historical experiences within the present-day Third World.

This book has two basic purposes: (a) to examine some aspects and consequences of the penetration of world capitalism into the Ottoman Empire where a pre-capitalist or non-capitalist mode of production had prevailed; and (b) to insert the Ottoman case into a comparative framework within the periphery of the nineteenth century. Often, world economic forces will provide the point of departure for our analysis and we will underline the similarities between the Ottoman case and others in the present-day Third World. However, for an adequate understanding of the actual outcome, it is necessary and essential to go beyond that unity. Consequently, we will be emphasizing and examining the interaction between these world-scale forces and the local forces and structures in order to explain the historical process.

Periphery in the world economy during the nineteenth century

The Industrial Revolution transformed the economies first of Britain and later of Western Europe into mass producers of inexpensive manufactures. By the second quarter of the nineteenth century, the leading European countries were trying to establish markets for their manufactures on the one hand, and to secure cheap and abundant sources of foodstuffs and raw materials on the other. Hence, chronologically speaking, the first impact of the Industrial Revolution on the present-day Third World involved an unprecedented expansion in the volume of trade and a shift in its composition. The technological revolution in overseas transportation, coming later in the century, helped accelerate this trend.[1]

The expansion of center–periphery trade was subsequently joined by another development, export of capital from the industrialized European countries. Substantial amounts of funds were loaned to governments in Latin America, Africa and Asia. More important, greater amounts were directly invested in infrastructure, such as railroads, aimed at expanding trade. In contrast, investment in directly productive activities such as agriculture and industry remained limited until World War I.[2]

Affecting not only the sphere of circulation but also the sphere of production, the expansion of trade led to the emergence of new patterns of specialization and production on a world scale. The decline but not necessarily total destruction of pre-industrial manufacturing activities in many parts of the periphery through the competition of the products of European industry eliminated whatever existed of the complementarity of agriculture and industry in these areas. At the same time, the opportunities, real or perceived, offered by closer integration into world markets led to a shift in the patterns of production from cultivation of subsistence crops to commodity production for export.[3]

By dramatically lowering costs of transportation to the interior regions, railroads, built mostly by capital from the industrialized countries, played an important role in bringing about this shift. Typically, the railroads pulled the hinterland of a major port in a country closer to Manchester, Marseilles or Hamburg than to the adjacent hinterland of another port in the same country. While railroads were helping build national economies in Europe and the United States during the nineteenth century, they were destroying whatever existed of intra-country commodity flows in the present-day Third World.[4]

Long-term movements in the center–periphery terms of trade also helped determine the pace of this process. Shifts in the terms of trade in favor of primary commodity exports accelerated the ongoing specialization in agriculture. By making imported industrial products relatively inexpensive, these shifts also facilitated the destruction of handicrafts-based manufacturing activities.[5] On the other hand, periods of deteriorating terms of trade for the primary commodity exports represented losses for the periphery arising from specialization according to a worldwide division of labor. At the same time, they lowered the pace of the specialization process.

Since the shift in the patterns of production took place not through foreign investment in directly productive activities but through the expansion of trade, the role of merchant capital was crucial. Merchants, mostly native but frequently controlled by the foreign merchant houses and banks in the port cities, extended credit to consumers and producers to facilitate both the penetration of the products of European industry into the rural areas and the expansion of agricultural commodity production for export. During the process, merchant capital also managed to appropriate a sizeable share of the agricultural surplus.

The discussion has so far dealt with the general features of the process by which the outlying areas were pulled more strongly into the world economy and avoided an examination of the variety of paths this process took in the periphery. That each case had unique features is clearest when the analysis is extended to the relations of production in agriculture. Under which relations of production in agriculture this process would advance and to what extent these relations of production would be transformed during the process – whether, for example, commodity production for world markets would be undertaken primarily on large holdings owned by natives or by white settlers using wage labor or on large and middle holdings, with the former employing sharecroppers, or by other forms – depended on a complex set of factors. These included external factors such as the world economic and political conjuncture under which the penetration of world capitalism gained momentum. They also included factors that were at least partly external; for example, whether the country in question was formally colonized or not. Even more important in the case of agriculture, this complex set included factors specific to each country such as the historical evolution of relations of production in agriculture and more generally the nature of the existing social structures in the country, such as classes and the state.[6]

Periphery categories during the nineteenth century

This section develops a classification of the processes by which countries in the periphery were pulled into the world economy during the nineteenth century. This classification will be based on the two groups of factors emphasized earlier: those associated with the timing and nature of the penetration of world capitalism, and those specific to the country in the periphery. This classification can account for a considerable part of the observed differences in the Third World regarding the nineteenth-century penetration of world capitalism. In addition, it constitutes a convenient tool for inserting the Ottoman case into a comparative framework.

We shall offer three basic periphery categories. While these categories appear to be based on political criteria, their differences with respect to economic processes are far-reaching. The first two categories are derived from the distinction emphasized by Gallagher and Robinson in their well-known work three decades ago: formal colonies on the one hand, and those countries belonging to the 'informal empire' of an imperialist power on the other.[7] For the third category, we introduce a distinction regarding countries not formally colonized. Gallagher and Robinson had pointed out that many of these countries in the periphery ended up belonging to the informal empire of one power or another. We would argue that there were cases where conditions of inter-imperialist rivalry prevailed and the country could not be incorporated into the formal empire of any single power. We would place the Ottoman Empire in this category.

The formal colonies are the easiest to identify. The most important distinction of cases in this category was the ability of the colonizing power to intervene in the incorporation process and to use extra-economic means more directly than it could use elsewhere. Trade and investment by other industrialized countries were closed off or severely restricted. The colonial administration attempted to achieve patterns of production most beneficial to the dominant interest in the home country. This meant transforming the colony into an exporter of primary commodities and a market for the manufactures of the home country. Whenever possible, settlements by immigrants from the home country were encouraged. Finally, the collection of a variety of taxes from the local population, ostensibly in return for the costs of colonial administration (home charges), and the strict adherence by the colonial administration to regular payments on the outstanding debt resulted in large transfers of funds to the home country. In this case, local forces and structures played a more limited role in the determination of the specific historical outcome in comparison to the other two categories of periphery.[8]

The category of informal empire includes primarily those cases in Central and South America in which political power was held by an alliance of merchant capital and export-oriented landlords, both of whom favored more trade and greater specialization in agricultural production for world markets. In these cases, the opening to world capitalism proceeded under conditions of formal political independence. However, the country in question belonged to the sphere of influence of one imperialist power. In the sphere of exchange, this meant that patterns of trade and foreign investment were dominated by that center country. Although this arrangement appears to allow the imperialist power less room for direct intervention in the incorporation process, in most instances during the nineteenth century the interests of the ruling alliances in the periphery largely coincided with the dominant interests in the imperialist country.[9]

We should also emphasize, however, the relative fluidity or instability of this situation in comparison to the case of formal colonies. When the relative power of the hegemonic country was at its zenith, as was the case of Britain during the third quarter of the nineteenth century, it was difficult for lesser powers amongst the industrialized countries to carve out informal empires for themselves. On the other hand, when the situation of hegemony gave way to inter-imperialist rivalry, as happened after the 1880s, the once-hegemonic power was increasingly challenged by other industrialized countries in those areas of the world which belonged to its informal empire. In addition, within the country on the periphery those groups belonging to the local ruling alliance who had been discontented with their shares under the existing arrangements often saw in the emergence of an open competition between imperialist powers or in the ascendancy of a latecomer a chance to improve their relative positions.[10] However, conditions of informal empire did not always change in the direction of increasing rivalry. There were also cases where the hegemonic power, in order to pre-empt a challenge, formally annexed a country into its colonial empire.[11]

Our third category, penetration of world capitalism under conditions of inter-imperialist rivalry, corresponds more closely than the category of informal empire to the cases of China, Persia and the Ottoman Empire during the nineteenth century. What distinguished the third category from the category of informal empire was a different combination of internal and external factors; namely, relatively strong state structures in the country in the periphery coupled with conditions of rivalry between the major imperialist powers in order to obtain greater political and economic advantage and influence. The societies in question were often characterized by a struggle between the central bureaucracy and those social classes favoring more rapid and direct integration into the world economy, namely the merchants and export-oriented landlords. The uniqueness of these societies lay in the fact that their central bureaucracies had the upper hand in this struggle during the nineteenth century. At the same time, the central bureaucracy was strong enough *vis-à-vis* imperialist powers and/or the rivalry among those powers was such that these countries never became part of a formal or informal empire. As a result of this particular configuration of power, greater integration into the world economy could not proceed through an alliance between the dominant interests in the center countries and those social classes in the periphery whose interests lay in the same direction. Instead, this process could advance only through an accommodation between the former and the central bureaucracy.[12]

For the central bureaucracy, increasing penetration of world capitalism and the socio-economic changes it involved brought forth the possibility of loss of political power, since these processes strengthened, economically at first, those very classes which might challenge the central bureaucracy's rule. This is not to say that an accommodation between the central bureaucracy and the dominant interests in the center countries was impossible. The political, military and fiscal crises of a non-capitalist and ultimately weak central state organization provided the competing imperialist powers with frequent opportunities to advance the incorporation process. Typically, in return for its short-term political, military or financial 'support', an imperialist power obtained commercial privileges or concessions to undertake a major investment project. In due time, other powers followed through the same door.

Under these circumstances, however, penetration of world capitalism proceeded more slowly than in either the case of formal colony or that of the informal empire. Often, there were limits to the concessions offered by the central bureaucracy to the capitalists from industrialized countries. For example, they did not go so far as to allow direct intervention in the mode of production in agriculture by such means as forcible substitution of capitalist farms hiring wage laborers for petty-commodity-producing peasants. At times the central bureaucracy could offer resistance to such attempts, in part because of the maneuvering room it created by playing one imperialist power against another. In the long run, however, the tendency was clearly towards increasing penetration of world capitalism and division of the country on the periphery into spheres of influence among various imperialist powers.

The Ottoman economy before 1820

For many years, the seventeenth and eighteenth centuries have been considered a period of decline for the economy and society of the Ottoman Empire. As Owen has recently argued in the broader context of the Middle East, these interpretations were all based on the observed decline in the political power of the central state *vis-à-vis* elements in the provinces – merchants, large landlords, officials appointed from the capital city – and on the accompanying fiscal crisis.[13] At the very least, these views miss the complexity of the causal relationships between the political and fiscal strength of the central authority and the economy. Periods of decline for the state do not necessarily coincide with periods of decline for the productive forces and the economy.[14]

7

With respect to the economy, evidence for the hypothesis of decline has certainly not been well documented. For one thing, the diversity of regional experiences does not allow us to make sweeping generalizations. After rapid growth during the sixteenth century, the rural population appears to have declined in Anatolia – but not in the Balkans – between 1600 and 1800.[15] There is also information concerning a decline in handicrafts activity during the late sixteenth and seventeenth centuries.[16] On the other hand, figures indicate some increase in the volume of agricultural exports to Europe from the Balkans, Western Anatolia and Syria during the eighteenth century.[17] This increase could be a reflection of a rise in agricultural production. Or it could be a sign of a shift in the composition of agricultural output. Long-term trends in tax-farming data also suggest a shift in the composition of overall output, from handicrafts to agricultural commodity production.[18] In view of the limited and often contradictory nature of the evidence, therefore, the hypothesis of decline must be viewed with skepticism at this stage.[19]

Trends in the volume of external trade are easier to establish. Evidence from French and British archives indicates some expansion in the volume of Ottoman trade with Europe during the century up to the 1780s. However, the pace of this expansion can in no way be compared with the rates of increase of trade after the Napoleonic Wars.[20] It should also be emphasized that the share of European trade in total agricultural production or even in agricultural commodity production remained quite small until the second quarter of the nineteenth century. Around 1820, intra-regional trade within the Empire and trade with Russia and Egypt were both more important, in terms of volume, than trade with Central and Western Europe.[21]

It was above all the Balkan provinces of the Empire which participated in the early expansion of European trade.[22] It was perhaps not a coincidence that Serbia, Morea, Wallachia, Moldavia and, one might add, Egypt, areas in which merchants and large landlords stood to benefit most from greater world market orientation, were the first to secede from the Empire.[23] In contrast, in those areas which still remained within the Empire late in the nineteenth century, and above all in Anatolia, the eighteenth century brought limited changes in the way of orientation towards European markets. Around 1800, patterns of cultivation and the extent of commodity production and of export orientation in Anatolia differed dramatically from such patterns one century later.[24]

The differences between the Balkan provinces and the remaining areas of the Empire, particularly Anatolia, might need further emphasis. The sixteenth century is generally considered to have represented the zenith of the power of the central state *vis-à-vis* elements in the provinces. The following two centuries witnessed a general decline in that power.[25] It has been argued that after the dissolution of the *timar* system in the late sixteenth century, locally powerful groups, relatively free from the supervision of the central authority, responded to increasing opportunities of commodity production for European markets by carving out large estates for themselves and by escalating the exploitation of the dependent peasantry, a pattern similar to the one observed in Eastern Europe during the sixteenth century.[26]

While it is not easy to assess the extent of this transformation given the present state of the research, it should be emphasized that this argument has been developed in reference to the Balkan provinces. The extension of the argument to the rest of the Empire would be misleading. In Anatolia, where commodity production for long-distance markets remained more limited, local elements did appropriate a greater part of the surplus as the relative power of the central bureaucracy declined. However, this process was not necessarily accompanied by a transformation of the relations of production. It appears that surplus appropriation by the locally powerful groups was based on the existing organization of production. These mechanisms included greater control over the tax-gathering process in the name of the central state through *iltizam*, usury and extraction of rent payments from direct producers based on *de facto* ownership of the land, even though, with some exceptions, the central state did not recognize private property in land until the second quarter of the nineteenth century. In the meantime, small peasant production remained the basis of Anatolian agriculture.[27]

The balance of power between the central authority and the elements in the provinces shifted once more in the early decades of the nineteenth century, this time in favor of the former. The signing of the *Sened-i İttifak* in 1808 appeared to represent the zenith of the power of the provincial *ayan*, but their political fall was indeed very rapid. The 1820s and 1830s witnessed a re-centralization under the reign of Mahmud II, a trend which continued with the administrative reforms of the *Tanzimat* period and during the rest of the century. *De facto* properties of many of the big landlords were expropriated. Attempts were made to increase control over the tax-collection process. In these and other moves designed to reassert its power, the central authority owed a good deal to an effective military and administrative organization made possible by technological advances in Europe in the aftermath of the Industrial Revolution.[28]

As a result, while world capitalism penetrated into the Ottoman Empire during the nineteenth century, it was not the provincial elements, the merchants and the big landowners – whose interest lay in rapid integration into world markets – but the central bureaucracy which had the upper hand. Throughout the century, the central bureaucracy tried, on the one hand, to curb the power of the provincial groups and, on the other hand, to create some room to maneuver for itself by playing one European power off against another.[29] In turn, the European powers and capital from center countries had to deal directly and reach an accommodation with the central bureaucracy at each juncture. The specific path of the incorporation process arising from this configuration is to be examined in the remainder of this volume.

A periodization for the Ottoman economy during the nineteenth century

The discussion on pages 2–7 suggests that the penetration of world capitalism into a pre-capitalist or non-capitalist formation during the nineteenth century was not a smooth process, but occurred in waves. To an important extent, these waves corresponded to the long-term fluctuations in the levels of economic activity in the world economy and particularly in the industrialized center countries.[30] This was primarily because the long-term fluctuations in foreign trade, external terms of trade and foreign investment in an economy in the periphery were related to the long waves in economic activity in the industrialized countries. Long-term changes in the sphere of production such as patterns of production in agriculture or manufacturing activity were, in turn, closely associated with these long waves in the sphere of exchange. We should hasten to add, however, that the correspondence between long-term fluctuations in certain world economic processes in the sphere of exchange and the experience of any particular country in the periphery was not perfect. When center–periphery trade began to expand at higher rates, it did not necessarily affect all countries in the same manner. Similarly, periods of intense foreign investment in an individual country did not always coincide with big waves of European overseas investment.[31]

This section will briefly examine the history of the Ottoman economy from 1820 to World War I in terms of distinct sub-periods, particularly from the perspective of its integration into the world economy. For each sub-period we will establish the nature and direction of the world economic forces faced by the Ottoman economy and their domestic consequences. This exercise will also allow us to summarize and present in chronological order some of the basic findings of this volume. To cite an example, our examination of a number of different processes in separate chapters of this volume show that the 1840s, 1860s and finally the 1910s represented very different conjunctures for the Ottoman economy in terms of the world economic forces it faced and in terms of the stages in the incorporation process. We should also emphasize that differences between sub-periods were not limited to the economy. Economic processes were reflected strongly in the societal and political levels. In what follows we will define four distinct sub-periods.[32]

1820–53: expansion of foreign trade under British hegemony

For Ottoman society, one of the most important developments of the second quarter of the nineteenth century was the ascending power of the central government *vis-à-vis* the provincial forces and the virtual disappearance of the influence of the *ayan*. The intervention of Britain in favor of the territorial integrity of the Empire, as observed during the conflict with Mohammed Ali and Egypt, strengthened this trend towards centralization.

For the economy, this sub-period lasting until the Crimean War represents the early stage when penetration of world capitalism proceeded primarily through the expansion of foreign trade. Britain had emerged from the Industrial Revolution and the Napoleonic Wars without rivals in world markets. However, with the rise of protectionism in Continental Europe, it turned increasingly towards markets in the periphery. The Free Trade Treaty of 1838 signed between the Ottoman Empire and Britain and later with other European countries should be interpreted in this context as part of British efforts worldwide and as an arrangement that facilitated the opening of the Ottoman economy to foreign trade.

During the second quarter of the century, Ottoman foreign trade grew at unprecedented rates. As a result, agricultural commodity production for world markets expanded considerably. At the same time handicrafts-based manufacturing activities declined under the competition of industrial imports. The case of cotton textiles which we examine in chapter 6 represents the most striking example of this decline. Although the decline was slower and more limited in other branches of production, our case study reflects the general direction of the impact of imports. Another important feature of this sub-period concerns external terms of trade. As a result of the technological advances associated with the Industrial Revolution, prices of industrial products continued to fall rapidly and the terms of trade turned in favor of economies specializing in primary commodities. These movements in the terms of trade facilitated and even accelerated the shifts in the patterns of production.

One should not overstate, however, the impact of rapidly growing foreign trade on the Ottoman economy until late in the nineteenth century. It should be emphasized that in the mid-1870s the share of exports or imports did not exceed 6 to 8 per cent of total production and 12 to 15 per cent of agricultural production. Geographically speaking, the expansion of agricultural commodity production and the decline in handicrafts-based manufacturing activities remained limited to the coastal areas. As a result, the corresponding ratios were considerably higher in the coastal areas. As for economic growth, we do not have sufficient information to assess the impact of the expansion in external trade on levels of aggregate production. Despite the availability of detailed data on trade and foreign investment, we are not yet in a position to determine the general trends, particularly with respect to per capita levels of production and income during the first three-quarters of the nineteenth century.

1854–76: external borrowing and increasing financial dependence

Most of the trends that characterized the first sub-period remained in effect until the mid-1870s. The third quarter of the century was a period of expansion for the industrialized economies and for the world economy in general. The relative power of Britain *vis-à-vis* potential contenders in Western Europe reached its zenith. The doctrine of Free Trade remained supreme as Pax Britannica was established. Paralleling the growth of demand in world markets, Ottoman foreign trade continued to expand rapidly despite the cessation of the favorable trends in external terms of trade. The impact of the Crimean and American Civil Wars was felt strongly in those regions of the Empire which were opening up to world markets. The complementarity between agricultural and non-agricultural production activities was increasingly destroyed in the coastal areas of the Empire.

During the 1850s an important dimension was added to the process of incorporation of the Empire into the world capitalist economy: inflows of foreign capital through state borrowing and direct investments. Until its default in 1876, the Ottoman state borrowed heavily and under very unfavorable terms in European financial markets. During this first period of external borrowing, new capital inflows exceeded total payments on the debt. A large part of these net inflows of funds was used for military purchases abroad and for the importation of consumer goods, leading to rapid increases in the external trade deficit and making the repayment of the loans virtually impossible.

Direct foreign investment also started in the 1850s even though its volume remained limited. These investments concentrated in the construction of railroads in the coastal regions. During this mid-century period, institutional rearrangements facilitating the opening of the economy continued under the pressure of European powers. Most important among these were the transfer of the monopoly to print paper currency inside the Empire to the foreign-owned Ottoman Bank in 1863, which effectively linked the Empire to the gold standard system and the recognition, in 1866, of the rights of foreigners to purchase agricultural land.

Political historians of the Ottoman Empire usually consider the period from the declaration of *Tanzimat* in 1839 to the opening of the First Constitutional Assembly in 1876 as the *Tanzimat* period. Our findings indicate that a similar periodization can be adopted regarding the opening of the economy. The half century from the 1820s to the mid-1870s represents the first and rapid wave in the incorporation of the Empire into the world economy. In other words, the political, social and administrative arrangements which are often referred to as the *Tanzimat* reforms were accompanied by the opening of the economy to foreign trade and foreign investment. Moreover, the ground for subsequent European financial control over the Empire was also paved during this period.

1880–96: stagnation and European financial control

The mid-1870s represent a turning period in nineteenth-century Ottoman history. The years 1873–8 were a period of political, social and economic crises of extraordinary dimensions. In 1873, the crisis that engulfed the European financial markets brought to a halt exports of capital and new lending to the periphery. In 1873–4 the most severe famine of the century ravaged Central Anatolia. In 1876, the Ottoman government announced that it was ceasing all payments on its external debt. The First Ottoman Constitution was proclaimed in 1876. These events were followed by the War of 1877–8 with Russia, which ended in defeat and loss of substantial amounts of population and land for the Empire. This series of crises sharply divides the period being investigated in this volume in two. We had characterized the half century until the mid-1870s as the first and rapid wave in the incorporation of the Empire into the world economy. The period from 1880 to World War I constitutes the second wave in that process. However, at least in terms of the rate of growth of external trade, the second wave proceeded more slowly than the first.

The more favorable economic conjuncture of the third quarter of the century was rapidly reversed during the 1870s as a result of two related developments: the beginning of a long period of relative stagnation for the world economy (the 'Great Depression' of 1873–96) and the Ottoman default on the external loan payments which led to the establishment of the Ottoman Public Debt Administration in 1881. As a result, the most important characteristics of this sub-period were a slowing down in the world market orientation of the Ottoman economy and the reversal of the direction of net funds flows arising from Ottoman external borrowing.

As the rate of increase in the levels of production in the industrialized economies slowed down during the Great Depression, the rate of expansion of Ottoman foreign trade also declined. In other words, paralleling the long-term fluctuations of economic activity and demand in the center countries, we observe a relative but not absolute weakening of the commercial ties of the Ottoman Empire to the world economy. The deterioration of the external terms of trade against agricultural commodities added another unfavorable dimension to the world economic conjuncture of the period. In a related development, the rapid decline, until 1896, in international wheat prices stemming from the entry of American wheat into world markets put severe pressure on both the peasant producers and the Ottoman Treasury, as wheat imported under the Free Trade Treaties began to penetrate Ottoman markets.

Non-agricultural production activities could hardly flourish under these conditions of relative if not absolute stagnation. Our study of handicrafts-based cotton textiles shows that production levels in urban manufacturing establishments declined along with the contraction of export-related incomes and demand. In the rural areas, on the other hand, the trend towards the decline of non-agricultural activities and specialization in agriculture continued, although the pace of this long-term shift was distinctly slower than both the earlier and later periods.

For the Ottoman economy and state finances, another unfavorable aspect of this period was that after the foundation of the Ottoman Public Debt Administration, total payments on the outstanding debt began to exceed by a large margin inflows of funds due to new borrowing. The rapid decline in overall world price levels from the early 1870s to the mid-1890s increased the real burden of the outstanding debt and further exacerbated the fiscal crisis. After 1881, the fiscal crisis of the state and its financial dependence on European powers became an increasingly important factor in the opening of the economy to world capitalism and the partitioning of the Empire into spheres of influence.

In assessing the impact of the fiscal crisis on the economy, we need to take into account the deflationary consequences of the net outflows of funds abroad which reached large magnitudes. Along with net debt payments, we also observe the disappearance of the large trade deficits which had characterized the third quarter of the century. Between 1882, when debt payments started under the Ottoman Public Debt Administration, and 1903, when new borrowing regained momentum, trade deficits remained at their lowest levels of the century; there were even some years when the trade balance showed a surplus. The limited evidence we have regarding aggregate levels of production suggests that the Ottoman economy was in a general state of stagnation during this period, especially in terms of per capita levels of production and income.

Another characteristic that distinguishes the fourth quarter of the century from the third is the change in inter-imperialist power balances, the decline of British hegemony and the emergence of a worldwide rivalry between Britain, France and Germany. The Ottoman Empire was one of the areas where the conditions of rivalry were most intense. British capitalists, who generally received less support from their state apparatus, could not survive under these conditions. We observe a virtual cessation of British investments in the Ottoman Empire after the 1870s. However, Britain continued to hold the largest share in Ottoman foreign trade until World War I. Another consequence of the entry of Germany into the inter-imperialist race was the partitioning of the Ottoman Empire into spheres of influence through the construction of railroads by German and French capital during 1888–96. In addition to political and military motives, the Ottoman government was also hoping to provide a solution to its long-standing fiscal crisis by handing out railroad concessions to foreign investors. The timing of this largest wave of foreign investment in the Ottoman Empire was thus determined jointly by these internal and external forces.

Growth and inter-imperialist rivalry until World War I

In terms of economic and fiscal conditions, the mid-1890s divide the long reign of Abdulhamid II (1876–1908) into two distinct periods. After the mid-1890s we observe higher rates of growth for Ottoman foreign trade and agricultural commodity production as the world economy entered a new period of expansion. These trends in trade and production patterns were supported by favorable movements in the external terms of trade. While the first wave of expansion in foreign trade until the early 1870s had been limited to the coastal areas, this second wave, coming after the construction of railroads, extended to the regions of the interior, most notably to Central Anatolia. The limited amount of evidence we have indicates that the rate of growth of the Ottoman economy was not insignificant during the years preceding World War I.

While changes in the patterns of production accelerated along with trade, European financial control and transfer abroad of large debt payments continued. A new wave of external borrowing started in 1903. Behind this trend were increases, after a twenty-year interval, in the military expenditures of the government, changes in the conditions of European financial markets, and, finally, increasing willingness of European powers to use new lending as an instrument for gaining influence over the Ottoman Empire as conditions of rivalry intensified. After the Young Turk Revolution of 1908 fiscal revenues began to rise rapidly as the central government became more effective in its collections; however, revenues continued to lag behind expenditures and the fiscal crisis intensified.

Paralleling the new round of external borrowing, external trade deficits increased rapidly after 1903 and in the 1910s they reached record levels for the century. When examined within a balance of payments framework, it appears that these deficits were financed, in addition to new borrowing, by the revenues obtained from some invisible items, particularly by incoming money orders and tourism revenues in Palestine arising from Jewish immigration into that region.

In order to understand this period better, it would be useful to draw attention to the parallels, for the Ottoman economy and state finances, between the years preceding World War I and the 1860s and early 1870s. In both cases, the world economy was in a period of long-term expansion and Ottoman exports and imports were growing rapidly. In both periods the Ottoman state borrowed sums in the European financial markets and external trade deficits reached large magnitudes. In both instances, financial dependence was deepening and a default appeared inevitable upon the cessation of new borrowing.

However, it should also be emphasized that the similarities between the two periods are limited to these dimensions. First, by the 1910s European control over the Ottoman economy and state finances was substantially greater and the transfer abroad of large sums arising from foreign investment appeared to have gained permanence. After the foundation of the Public Debt Administration, payments on the outstanding debt remained above inflows of funds due to new borrowing. Similarly, after 1896 profit transfers arising from direct foreign investment also began to exceed new capital inflows. Second, the balances between the Great Powers had changed considerably during this century. Pax Britannica, which prevailed during the third quarter of the century, had given way to an intense rivalry between Britain, France and Germany which was going to culminate in World War I.

Third, by the 1910s the Ottoman economy had become much more open to world capitalism and its specialization in agriculture had proceeded to a much greater extent. In fact, it is difficult to talk about the Ottoman economy of the 1910s as a meaningful unit of analysis. The internal linkages of the economy had become progressively weaker throughout the century as different regions of the Empire were pulled into the divisions of labor and spheres of influence of Manchester, Hamburg and Marseilles. Far from contributing to the emergence of a national economy, the construction of railroads by foreign capital had only strengthened this tendency. In the early 1910s, close to 14 per cent of the gross national product of the Empire and more than one-fourth of net agricultural production was being exported. The ratio of imports to GNP was around 18 per cent. These ratios were substantially higher in the coastal regions. In cotton textiles more than 80 per cent of total domestic consumption of a population four-fifths of which lived in the rural areas was being imported. These statistics summarize quite well the degree of integration of the Empire into the world economy on the eve of World War I.

Chapter 2

Long-term fluctuations in Ottoman foreign trade, 1830–1913

In the aftermath of the Industrial Revolution the integration of countries in the contemporary Third World into the world economy proceeded, above all, through an unprecedented expansion of their trade with the industrializing center countries. As they were being pulled into the international division of labor, new patterns of production began to emerge in these economies. Agricultural commodity production for world markets expanded and the composition of agricultural production shifted from subsistence crops to cash crops. At the same time, a large number of manufacturing activities based on traditional handicrafts declined but did not necessarily disappear in the face of competition from industrial imports. As a result, the complementarity of agricultural and non-agricultural production activities within the framework of a peasant economy was irreversibly destroyed in the rural areas.

Ottoman foreign trade expanded at rapid rates during the nineteenth century. However, the rate of this expansion did not remain unchanged until World War I. Paralleling the long-term fluctuations in the levels of economic activity in the industrialized center countries, particularly in Western Europe, rates of growth of Ottoman foreign trade showed long-term fluctuations. This chapter will examine the extent of the century-long expansion of Ottoman foreign trade in relation to the growth of world trade and foreign trade in other countries in the periphery. We will also establish and analyze the timing of these long-term fluctuations. When taken together with long-term fluctuations in Ottoman external terms of trade and long-term swings in the flow of funds arising from foreign investment in the Ottoman Empire, these trends in the sphere of circulation should enable us to define the distinct world economic conjunctures faced by the Ottoman Empire. They will also provide new and important insights into the long-term rhythms of the process of integration into the world economy.

On the Free Trade Treaties of 1838–41

The Free Trade Treaties signed between the Ottoman Empire and Britain and subsequently with other European countries removed a number of government restrictions on Ottoman exports and imports, opening Ottoman markets and raw materials to trade with Europe. In doing so, these Treaties represented an important turning point in the integration of the Empire into the world economy. However, very often in the literature the importance of these Treaties has been overstated. These documents by themselves cannot explain the increasing specialization of the Ottoman economy in the production and exportation of primary commodities and in the importation of manufactures during the nineteenth century. These Free Trade Treaties can be best examined as a product of the world economic conditions and political balances that emerged in the aftermath of the Industrial Revolution and the Napoleonic Wars. As a prelude to examining the expansion of Ottoman foreign trade, this section will review the economic and political developments that led to the signing of these Treaties. We will also summarize the evolution of Ottoman tariff rates until World War I.[1]

By the early 1820s, Britain had completed its Industrial Revolution and, after defeating France in a series of wars, had emerged as the hegemonic power in the world economy. No country was in a position to compete with Britain in world markets. However, other European countries which had not yet completed their Industrial Revolution began to adopt protectionist policies in order to prevent the penetration of British manufactures into their markets. Under these circumstances, British merchant and industrial capital turned to the markets and raw materials in the periphery. Until mid-century, Britain signed a large number of Free Trade Treaties with countries from Latin America to China, establishing explicit alliances with export-oriented landlords and merchants wherever possible and resorting to military force wherever more subtle strategies proved unfruitful.[2]

It would have been highly unlikely for the politically, militarily and financially weak Ottoman state and its central bureaucracy to resist similar pressures from Britain and later from other European powers. In fact, the Ottoman Empire had already been forced to grant extensive commercial privileges to Russia after its defeat in the War of 1828–9.[3] In the 1830s, this agreement began to be treated by the European powers as the basis for the Treaties they would sign with the Ottoman Empire. British observers of the period were well aware of the destructive impact of such a treaty on Ottoman handicrafts.[4] For this reason, British diplomacy was waiting for a difficult conjuncture for the Ottoman central government. Given the balances of power, the signing of the Treaty was not really in doubt. Its timing, however, was going to be determined by the political developments.

The long-awaited opportunity arrived as the military power of

Mohammed Ali of Egypt began to pose a serious threat to the rule of the Ottoman central bureaucracy in Istanbul. At the same time, the state monopolies in foreign trade which Mohammed Ali had developed in order to finance his industrial and military expenditures had started to conflict with British commercial interests. Faced with the growing threat of Mohammed Ali on the one hand and the rising influence of Russia over the Empire on the other, the central government in Istanbul opted for British support. In return for opening the Ottoman economy to Free Trade, the central bureaucracy hoped to obtain long-term political and military support from Britain for the territorial integrity of the Empire.[5]

The most important article of the 1838 Treaty, which was signed during this crisis, concerned the abolition of the monopoly system in foreign trade and of the ability of the central government to impose special restrictions and additional customs duties on exports. The abolition of the state monopolies in foreign trade destroyed the fiscal foundation of Mohammed Ali's army and industrial policies. On the other hand, the elimination of extraordinary duties on exports was going to have serious long-term consequences for Ottoman state finances. Until the 1830s these additional duties had provided much-needed fiscal revenue during periods of war. Their abolition deprived the Ottoman Treasury of an important source of revenue. Fifteen years later, during the Crimean War, foreign trade could not be relied upon to generate additional revenues, and the Ottoman government was forced to start borrowing in the European financial markets.[6]

In comparison, the short-term consequences of the changes in the tariff rates brought about by the Treaties appear minor. Until 1838 both exports and imports were subject to a 3 per cent *ad valorem* duty. In addition, both domestic and foreign merchants paid 8 per cent duty on all commodities transported from one region to another within the Empire.[7] The Treaties of 1838–41 raised the tariff on exports to 12 per cent and on imports to 5 per cent. In addition, while domestic merchants were to continue paying the internal customs duty, foreign merchants were exempted from this 8 per cent. As a result, European merchants secured an important advantage over domestic competition.[8]

In the long term, the importance of the changes made during 1838–41 regarding tariff rates lay in the fact that the Ottoman government was now bound to the new arrangement, and a unilateral move towards a higher, more protective tariff structure became impossible until World War I. During the Lebanese political crisis and the fiscal crisis of 1860–1, the central bureaucracy agreed to sign a new treaty gradually reducing the duties on exports to 1 per cent, at which level they remained until

World War I. Duties on imports were raised to 8 per cent in 1861 and to 11 per cent in 1907.[9] However, the motive forcing the Ottoman government to provide other concessions to European powers in return for these rises was not the protection of domestic industry. Duties on imports remained too low to insulate domestic handicrafts, which had been hit hard and early by imports. These rises were negotiated primarily for the purpose of generating additional revenues to the hard-pressed Ottoman Treasury.

The reconstruction of Ottoman foreign trade

Official Ottoman statistics would have been the most appropriate source for a study of nineteenth-century Ottoman foreign trade. However, Ottoman foreign trade statistics began to be published only in 1878.[10] There is no evidence to indicate that trade statistics for the Empire as a whole were gathered regularly or comprehensively before this date. Moreover, as discussed in detail in a number of studies and in appendix 1, official Ottoman statistics consistently undervalued the prices of imports. Hence, they provide a misleading picture of Ottoman foreign trade, and particularly of the external trade balance.[11]

We made use of the official Ottoman statistics for the period for which they were available, especially in examining the composition of exports. However, in determining the annual magnitudes for exports and imports, we utilized the published trade statistics of virtually all the countries with which the Ottoman Empire had commercial relations. We reconstructed Ottoman foreign trade by bringing together these statistics for each year of the period 1830–1913. Since the statistics of other countries valued Ottoman exports at their own ports with c.i.f. prices, appropriate freight and insurance costs had to be subtracted from these figures in order to arrive at f.o.b. prices for Ottoman exports. Similarly, appropriate freight and insurance costs were added to the f.o.b. prices of Ottoman imports valued at foreign ports in order to arrive at c.i.f. import prices that would be more meaningful from the point of view of the Ottoman economy.[12] We converted all prices given in the currency of individual countries to British pounds sterling by using the prevailing gold standard rate of exchange.[13]

This procedure also enabled us to undertake a study of the Ottoman terms of trade. In addition, it yielded detailed information regarding the composition of Ottoman external trade. Needless to say, a reconstruction attempt of this kind and scale will have certain limitations and a number of problems. These are discussed, along with a critical evaluation of the available Ottoman statistics, in appendix 1. A detailed discussion of the

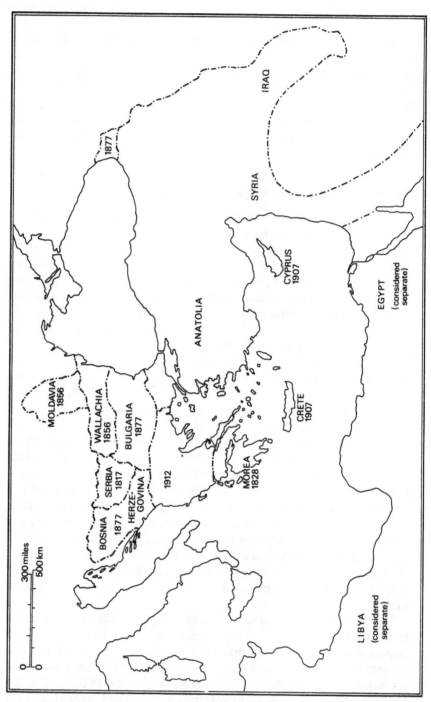

Map 1 The changing borders of the Ottoman Empire as defined for this study, 1830–1913. The dates indicate the last year for which each territory was considered as part of the Empire.

reconstruction procedure and an analysis of the commodity composition of Ottoman exports and imports are also presented in that appendix.

One issue which needs to be clarified at this stage concerns the changing borders of the Ottoman Empire. The political status of various regions changed and the Empire lost both land and population throughout the nineteenth century. Further difficulties arise from the nature of data available from the official publications of other countries. For these reasons, the borders of the Empire need to be explicitly defined for each year of the period 1830–1913. For example, the foreign trade statistics of European countries began to treat Wallachia and Moldavia as a separate entity long after they gained autonomy (1829), but long before they became formally independent. Since, to a large extent, the geographical boundaries of the Ottoman Empire as defined in these statistics had to be followed, for the purposes of this study Wallachia and Moldavia were considered part of the Empire until the end of the Crimean War (1856). Other major border changes are fairly straightforward: during 1830–1913, the Empire lost land and population basically in two periods, in 1878 as a result of the War of 1877–8 (Northern Bulgaria, Bosnia, Herzegovina) and after 1907 (Eastern Rumeli, Cyprus, Crete, Albania and Macedonia). Map 1 defines the changing borders of what has been accepted as the Ottoman Empire for the purposes of this study.

Long-term trends

The basic results of our reconstruction attempt, the estimates for annual values of exports and imports for each year of the period 1830–1913, are presented in figure 1 and table A1.1 of appendix 1. Since the estimates for the decade of the 1830s are subject to a relatively larger degree of uncertainty, we will not include them in the following discussion.

Our estimates indicate that during the three-quarters of a century following the Free Trade Treaties, total Ottoman exports measured in current prices increased more than five times, from £4.7 million to £28.4 million, while imports measured in current prices expanded six and a half times, from £5.2 million to £39.4 million, despite the contraction in geographical borders. Since the prices of the traded commodities were considerably lower on the eve of World War I than in 1840, the increases in trade volumes were actually greater. Measured in constant 1880 prices, Ottoman exports increased approximately nine times and Ottoman imports expanded approximately ten times during this period.[14]

Clearly, these figures point to an unprecedented rate of growth in Ottoman foreign trade during the nineteenth century. It should be emphasized, however, that the volume of world trade also expanded

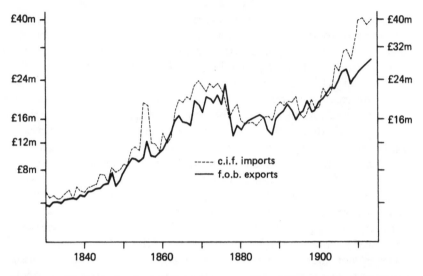

Figure 1 Ottoman foreign trade, 1830–1913 (in millions of current British pounds sterling). Note: Since logarithmic scale is used along the vertical axis, the slope of the curves gives the rate of growth. For annual values, see appendix 1, table A1.1.

rapidly in the aftermath of the Industrial Revolution, and hence the foreign trade of virtually every geographical region around the world exhibited unprecedented rates of growth during this period. Therefore, in order to insert the case of the Ottoman Empire into a comparative framework and to assess the relative performance of Ottoman foreign trade, it would have been useful to compare these estimates with rates of growth of world trade and especially with the rates of growth of foreign trade in the periphery. Such a direct comparison cannot be undertaken, however, because of the substantial loss of land and population from the Ottoman Empire during the nineteenth century. Instead, we will start with comparisons of per capita trade on the eve of World War I and later compare rates of growth of foreign trade for each sub-period of the nineteenth century.

Because of the contraction in the Empire's geographical borders, its population can be estimated to have remained roughly unchanged at 20.8 million between 1840 and 1913.[15] Hence, rates of expansion given above also approximate the increases in per capita exports and imports. However, it should be emphasized that the secession of some areas from the Empire during the century implies that, while the exchange of commodities between these areas and the rest of the Empire was not considered as external trade at the beginning of this period, it was included in the foreign trade figures at the end of the period. As a result, it is clear that the above figures understate, by a significant margin, the rate of growth of external trade of the areas remaining within the Empire in 1913. However, they also overstate, by a smaller margin, the rate of expansion of per capita external trade in those areas within the 1913 borders.[16]

After taking into account these qualifications, the rate of expansion of per capita exports from the areas within the 1913 borders of the Ottoman Empire appears to be lower than the rate of growth of exports in other parts of the world during the same period. For example, a recent study estimates that per capita exports for the world as a whole, or per capita foreign trade of the world economy, measured in constant prices, increased by eightfold between 1840 and 1900.[17] On the other hand, per capita exports from Europe as a whole, which accounted for close to 60 per cent of world trade during the nineteenth century, increased by sevenfold, measured in constant prices, between 1840 and 1913.[18] Finally, in the periphery, the rates of expansion of per capita exports in constant prices from South America and Asia were also comparable, six and a half and seven and a half times, respectively, for the period 1840–1900. Per capita exports from Africa expanded much more rapidly during this period, but their base volume in the earlier period was very low.[19]

As for the level of per capita exports, our estimates indicate that by 1913 per capita exports from the Ottoman Empire had reached £1.35. During the same year per capita exports from Europe as a whole stood at £4.45.[20] This difference is hardly surprising in view of differences in the levels of production and income. Much more meaningful in this respect would be comparisons with other economies in the periphery where income and production levels were roughly comparable to those of the Ottoman Empire. On the eve of World War I, per capita exports from the Ottoman Empire were approximately four times as high as per capita exports from Asia as a whole and twice as high as those from Africa. On the other hand, they were about half the level of per capita exports from Central America and about one-fourth of their levels from South America. It would be safe to conclude that, in terms of the degree of integration into world markets by 1913, the Ottoman Empire ranked somewhere between Asia and Africa on the one hand and Latin America on the other.[21]

Another key indicator for the degree of integration of the Empire into the world economy is the ratio of foreign trade to total production. Since no estimates are available for the value of total production in the Empire until the last quarter of the nineteenth century, we will start with the

1910s and then attempt to extend our estimates backwards in time. Vedat Eldem has made some valuable calculations regarding the 'gross national product' of the Empire during the last quarter of the century and before World War I.[22] His estimates, when used together with our estimates on foreign trade, indicate that in 1913 approximately 14 per cent of the GNP of the Empire was being exported, and the value of imports exceeded 19 per cent of GNP. Utilizing our estimates regarding the rate of growth of per capita exports and making some simple assumptions regarding changes in the levels of per capita production, we estimate that around 1880 6 to 8 per cent of the total production of the Empire was being exported. The ratio of exports to GNP in the 1840s can be estimated similarly to be around 3 to 4 per cent.[23] Considering the growth of Ottoman foreign trade before 1840, this ratio should be expected to have been quite close to 2 per cent in the early 1820s.

We also know that in 1913 foodstuffs and raw materials accounted for over 90 per cent of Ottoman exports, while approximately two-thirds of imports consisted of manufactures.[24] Taken together with the earlier estimates, these figures reveal the extent to which the Ottoman Empire had been integrated into the division of labor of the world economy by 1913. Furthermore, if we add to these rates of production for export the rates of production for urban markets within the Empire, it is not difficult to reach the conclusion that close to half of the total agricultural production in the Empire found its way to the markets.[25] Substantial regional differences and differences between crops notwithstanding, this is an important measure of the extent to which commodity production had advanced in the Ottoman Empire on the eve of World War I.

Another important development associated with the expansion of Ottoman foreign trade during the nineteenth century was the major shift in its regional distribution. Throughout the eighteenth century and until the second quarter of the nineteenth century, interregional trade within the Empire was quite significant. Those regions that remained within the Empire until the twentieth century carried on a large part of their trade with other areas of the Empire, among them Egypt, Wallachia and Moldavia, which later seceded from the Empire.[26] Starting in the second quarter of the century the axes of trade began to shift from the Near East, Eastern Europe and Central Europe sharply towards Western Europe and even beyond the Atlantic, as these latter areas steadily increased their relative importance in the world economy and the Ottoman Empire was pulled into their trade network. Similarly, during the eighteenth century most of the Ottoman trade with Europe was conducted with Central and Eastern European countries, above all with Austria and Russia. It is not clear whether the relative importance of Western Europe in Ottoman foreign trade began to rise late in the eighteenth century, but it definitely increased after the early 1830s. Austria and Russia accounted for more than 45 per cent of total Ottoman foreign trade, and the share of Western Europe was around one-third during this period. By the 1910s the total share of Austria and Russia in Ottoman foreign trade had been reduced to around 15 per cent; the share of Western Europe and the United States stood close to 60 per cent.[27]

A periodization

One of the more important results emerging from our reconstruction attempt is that the expansion of Ottoman foreign trade during the nineteenth century was not a single, continuous process, but rather occurred in long waves. We observe two long periods during which Ottoman exports and imports expanded rapidly, first during the mid-century and later in the years leading to World War I. In between was a quarter century of substantially lower rates of growth or relative stagnation for Ottoman foreign trade.

The results of this periodization are presented in tables 2.1 and 2.2. They show that after appropriate adjustments are made in trade volumes for the periodic secession of land and population from the Empire, these long-term fluctuations in the rates of growth of Ottoman exports and imports can be directly related to long-term fluctuations in the levels of economic activity in industrialized Europe and the United States. At one level this result is not very surprising, since anywhere from two-thirds to four-fifths of Ottoman foreign trade was conducted with these economies during the period under study.[28] However, this close link also indicates that the long-term fluctuations of demand for raw materials and foodstuffs in the center countries played a very important role in determining the rhythms of expansion in Ottoman foreign trade. From this long-term perspective, conditions of demand emerge as the most important single factor in the determination of these long-term fluctuations. In other words, for the century as a whole, exports emerge as the active component in Ottoman foreign trade.

This is not to say, however, that imports adjusted passively to long-term changes in the volume of exports. The results of our reconstruction also point to the existence of a virtually permanent trade deficit and long-term fluctuations in its size, suggesting that long-term changes in the volume of imports also depended upon the magnitude of the net receipts from other items of the Ottoman balance of payments.[29] In what follows we will examine the expansion of nineteenth-century Ottoman foreign trade in three sub-periods. Each one of them represents a distinct conjuncture in the integration of the Empire into the world economy.

Table 2.1. *Compound annual rates of growth of Ottoman foreign trade,*
1840–1913 (per cent)

		In current prices		In constant 1880 prices	
Sub-periods		Exports	Imports	Exports	Imports
I	1839–41 to 1852–4	5.3	5.5	5.3	6.4
II	1857–9 to 1871–3	5.0	4.9	6.2	5.2
III	1879–81 to 1897–9	1.2	0.6	2.7	2.5
IV	1897–9 to 1905–7	4.3	6.0	3.4	4.6
IIA	1857–9 to 1874–6	4.4	3.8	6.0	4.3
IVA	1897–9 to 1911–13	3.0	5.4	1.9	4.4

Table 2.2. *Compound annual rates of growth of Ottoman trade with the*
industrialized center countries,[a] 1840–1913 (per cent)

		In current prices		In constant 1880 prices	
Sub-periods		Exports	Imports	Exports	Imports
I	1839–41 to 1852–4	6.4	7.1	6.5	8.3
II	1857–9 to 1871–3	4.1	4.6	5.6	4.9
III	1879–81 to 1897–9	2.0	0.6	3.5	2.5
IV	1897–9 to 1905–7	4.2	6.2	3.4	4.8
IIA	1857–9 to 1874–6	3.6	3.4	5.8	3.8
IVA	1897–9 to 1911–13	3.1	5.7	1.9	4.7

[a]Industrial Europe and the U.S.; includes Italy for the sub-periods after 1897–9.
Sources: Tables 2.1 and 2.2: Our calculations based on appendix 1, table A1.1. For the
implicit price deflators used for the period 1854–1913, see appendix 2. The implicit price
deflators for the period before 1854 were based, with appropriate modifications, on the price
indices developed by Imlah for British exports and imports. See Imlah (1958), pp. 94–7.

1840–73: rapid expansion

Although they were divided by the Crimean War and by the secession of
Wallachia and Moldavia from the Empire, the three decades of the mid-
century represent an extended period of rapid expansion in Ottoman
foreign trade. Most of this wave of expansion coincided with the mid-

century boom in the industrial countries, and both of them came to an end in 1873, the year of the financial crises in Europe and the United States which also signalled the onset of the 'Great Depression' of 1873–96.[30]

Even though the unavailability of detailed data for the earlier period forces us to focus on the years after 1840, the beginnings of this trend of rapid growth should be traced back to the 1820s. During the eighteenth century more than half of the trade between the Levant and Western Europe, mostly an exchange of primary products for manufactures, was controlled by French merchants based in Marseilles.[31] However, by the end of the Napoleonic Wars French control over this trade had disappeared. Having completed its Industrial Revolution, Britain emerged as the leading commercial power in the Eastern Mediterranean and in many other parts of the world. Growing protectionism in the European continent during the 1820s increased the importance of Ottoman markets for Britain, and the monopolistic privileges of the Levant Company, symbols of the mercantilist era, were abolished in 1825.[32]

Exports from Britain to the Ottoman Empire excluding Egypt and Morea jumped from approximately £500,000 per year in 1816–18 to £650,000 per year in 1820–2 and to £1,729,000 in 1836–8.[33] These changes represent an annual rate of growth of over 6 per cent in current prices. The rate of expansion of the volume of this trade was even higher since the prices of manufactures and particularly of cotton textiles, by far the most important item in British exports, were declining rapidly during these decades.[34] In contrast, after the signing of the Free Trade Treaties during the period 1838–54 Ottoman imports from Britain increased at an annual rate of 3.4 per cent. Ottoman exports to Britain expanded at an average rate of 5 per cent per year during 1820–38 and later at an annual rate of 6.8 per cent during 1838–54.[35] It can be argued, therefore, that whereas British manufactures began to expand their markets in the Ottoman Empire before 1838, the opening of Ottoman primary products to trade with Britain accelerated only after the signing of the Free Trade Treaties. Evidence regarding the volume of Ottoman trade with other European countries for the period before 1840 and especially before 1830 is rather limited. It is clear, however, that this component of Ottoman foreign trade did not expand rapidly until the 1840s. It appears, then, that the rates of growth of Ottoman foreign trade were considerably higher after 1840 than in the 1820s and 1830s.

A comparison with the previous century will provide a striking illustration of the unprecedented pace of expansion in Ottoman–European trade during 1840–73. Simple calculations indicate that total European trade (imports plus exports) of the areas that constituted the Ottoman Empire during the second quarter of the nineteenth century (including Wallachia and Moldavia but excluding Egypt and Morea) expanded by about half during the half century between 1730 and 1780, at average annual rates below 1 per cent. Total value of this trade was around £3 million during the decade of the 1780s. In the next half century between 1780 and 1830, the European trade of the same areas increased by about 80–90 per cent, at annual rates below 1.5 per cent.[36] In contrast, the rate of growth of this trade jumped to over 5 per cent per year after 1840. In effect, the volume of this trade doubled every 11 to 13 years until the 1870s. The total value of Ottoman trade with indus-trialized Europe exceeded £15 million in the early 1850s and, despite the loss of Wallachia and Moldavia, reached £30 million by the early 1870s.

Our estimates also show that the rate of growth of Ottoman foreign trade and of Ottoman exports exceeded the rate of growth of world trade during 1840–73.[37] It is quite possible that Ottoman trade with the industrialized center countries expanded more rapidly than center–per-iphery trade as a whole during the same period. In view of the above evidence, it is clear that the second and third quarters of the nineteenth century represented a turning point incomparable to earlier periods in the transformation of the Ottoman economy into a supplier of primary products and an importer of manufactures. It is equally clear that the timing of this qualitative shift in trade volumes was directly associated with the Industrial Revolution and the emergence in Europe of econ-omies in need of raw materials, foodstuffs and markets for their manufactures.

On the other hand, it should also be emphasized that these high rates of growth were partly due to the relatively small trade volumes prevailing early in the century. It can be argued that this first wave until the 1870s represented the easy round of expansion after the Free Trade Treaties lifted the restrictions on exports and facilitated a shift towards export crops in the most commercialized areas of the Empire. In fact, our estimates summarized in table 2.1 indicate that the rate of growth of Ottoman trade with the industrialized center countries was highest during 1840–53, the period immediately following the signing of the Free Trade Treaties, but this rate began to decline after the Crimean War.

As for the country composition of Ottoman foreign trade during this period, Britain was by far the leading beneficiary of the Free Trade Treaties signed with virtually all of the European countries. Between the 1820s and 1870s, Britain steadily increased its share in Ottoman foreign trade, especially in the Asian provinces of the Empire. By the early 1870s, Britain accounted for about one-fourth of all Ottoman exports and one-third of all Ottoman imports. (See tables 2.3 and 2.4.)

Table 2.3. *Country distribution of Ottoman exports, 1830–1913 (per cent shares)*

Years	U.K.	France	Germany	Austria	U.K. +F+G+A	Center (Industr. Europe+ U.S.)	Russia	Periphery[d]	Av. annual value in £000 (current)
1830–2	13.3	14.3	2.1[a]	30.9	60.6	64.3	12.6	23.1	3,841
1840–2	19.8	16.6	1.9[a]	29.1	67.4	70.0	10.4	19.5	5,155
1850–2	29.1	15.8	1.1[a]	28.0	74.0	76.4	8.3	15.3	8,815
1860–2	23.5	29.9	0.5[a]	16.8	70.7	73.4	10.2	16.4	12,361
1870–2	27.2	25.3	0.4	14.3	67.2	69.4	14.7	15.9	19,431
1880–2	23.5	28.0	0.5	6.1	58.1	62.9[c]	13.6	23.5[d]	15,181
1890–2	25.9	24.5	4.3	5.9	60.6	76.1	4.2	20.7[c]	17,929
1900–2	25.9	19.2	7.2	7.8	60.1	78.3	3.9	17.8	20,299
1909–11[b]	17.9	14.1	11.4	8.0	51.4	77.0	3.9	19.2	25,890

[a]80 per cent of trade transiting through Austria.
[b]1912 was a war year.
[c]Italy, with a share of 5 to 10 per cent in Ottoman imports, is included in the center, starting in 1890.
[d]Periphery includes Italy (before 1890), Greece, Serbia, Egypt, Iran and, in the later period, Romania and Bulgaria.

Sources: Results of our reconstruction attempt based on the foreign trade statistics of other countries. For details see the text and appendix 1.

Table 2.4. *Country distribution of Ottoman imports, 1830–1913 (per cent shares)*

Years	U.K.	France	Germany	Austria	U.K. +F+G+A	Center (Industr. Europe+ U.S.)	Russia	Periphery[c]	Av. annual value in £000 (current)
1830–2	19.0	9.9	3.3[a]	16.9	49.1	52.7	31.3	16.0	4,926
1840–2	29.3	8.6	4.6[a]	22.1	64.6	67.3	16.5	16.2	5,667
1850–2	25.5	9.3	9.7[a]	26.2	70.7	74.6	13.6	11.8	9,480
1860–2	26.5	12.2	9.5[a]	17.2	65.4	67.5	11.5	20.9	12,942
1870–2	32.4	12.3	13.6	12.9	71.2	76.7	9.2	12.1	22,362
1880–2	45.2	11.8	2.4	11.8	71.2	74.9	9.7	15.4[c]	15,395
1890–2	35.9	12.4	10.3	9.8	68.4	77.5[c]	9.9	12.6[d]	19,167
1900–2	29.8	10.0	9.8	14.5	64.1	78.7	10.3	11.1	20,311
1909–11[b]	23.9	8.4	13.7	13.9	59.9	78.8	8.7	12.5	37,666

[a]80 per cent of trade transiting through Austria.
[b]1912 was a war year.
[c]Italy, with a share of 5 to 10 per cent in Ottoman exports, is included in the center starting in 1890.
[d]Periphery includes Italy (before 1890), Greece, Serbia, Egypt, Iran and, in the later period, Romania and Bulgaria.

Sources: Results of our reconstruction attempt based on the foreign trade statistics of other countries. For details see the text and appendix 1.

In the Balkan provinces, Austria benefited from its geographical proximity, despite the difficulties of competing against British manufactures, and maintained its lead. However, the share of Austria in Ottoman foreign trade declined later in the century with the secession of these areas from the Empire. France, the dominant commercial power during the eighteenth century, never regained its earlier position. In cotton textiles, the most important manufacture in Ottoman markets, French industry could not compete against British products. On the other hand, the Ottoman Empire remained an important source of raw materials and foodstuffs for the French economy. Consequently, a limited part of the large and virtually permanent trade deficits which the Ottoman Empire maintained against Britain, Austria and, later, Germany was balanced with the surplus from trade with France.[38]

Ottoman trade with Russia took place primarily to and from the Balkan provinces. While the trade with the industrialized center countries developed as an exchange of primary products for manufactures, the trade with Russia remained mostly an exchange of primary products. As such, it could not be expected to expand as rapidly as European trade did. After the Free Trade Treaties of 1838–41 extended to other European countries the commercial privileges which the 1829 Treaty of Edirne had provided for Russia, the share of Russia in Ottoman foreign trade began to decline. As large areas of the Balkans seceded from the Empire in the second half of the century, this trend continued[39] (tables 2.3 and 2.4). During the mid-century decades, Ottoman trade with Germany was conducted primarily through the Balkan provinces and in transit through Austria. Information on this trade is quite limited. It is clear, however, that the ascendancy of Germany in Ottoman foreign trade and the German–British rivalry in Ottoman markets, particularly in Anatolia, did not start until the 1880s.[40]

1879–98: Great Depression and relative stagnation in Ottoman foreign trade

Although the rapid expansion of Ottoman foreign trade came to an end in the early 1870s, the War of 1877–8 and subsequent secession of land and population from the Empire force us to start the second sub-period with the year 1879. As can be seen from map 1 and tables 2.1 and 2.2, the average rate of growth of total Ottoman exports, measured in constant 1880 prices, declined from 6.2 per cent per year during 1857–73 to 2.7 per cent in 1879–99. Similarly, the annual rate of growth of imports in constant prices declined from 5.2 per cent in 1857–73 to 2.5 per cent in 1879–99. The break with the long-term trends of the mid-century becomes even more pronounced if current prices are used. Measured in current prices, the average rate of growth of total exports declined from 5.0 per cent to 1.2 per cent per year, and the annual rate of growth of imports dropped from 4.9 per cent in 1857–73 to 0.6 per cent in 1879–99. Changes in the rates of expansion of Ottoman foreign trade with the industrialized center countries followed a similar pattern. As a result, while the volume of foreign trade continued to increase at distinctly lower rates, trade measured in current prices showed only minimal changes during these two decades.

Behind this relative stagnation of Ottoman foreign trade lies the 'Great Depression' of 1873–96. At least in part because of the Ottoman–Greek War of 1897, the upturn in Ottoman foreign trade did not come until after 1898, hence our extension of the sub-period to that year. While the extent and the manifestations of the Great Depression varied among the industrialized economies of the center, three of its basic characteristics should be emphasized here. First, for the first time in the history of the world economy, the downturn occurred simultaneously in all of the major economies. Second, for the largest industrial economies, this was not a period of absolute decline but of lower rates of increase in the levels of industrial production compared to rates in periods before and after. Third, general price levels declined rapidly and steadily until 1896.[41] Our estimates indicate that these trends were transmitted to Ottoman foreign trade. Lower rates of growth in the volume of trade were accompanied by rapidly declining prices for Ottoman exports and imports. Moreover, the slowing down of the expansion of demand for primary products in the industrialized center countries led to a greater decline in their prices in comparison to the decline in prices of manufactures. As a result, the external terms of trade turned against the Ottoman economy during this period.[42]

The country distribution of Ottoman foreign trade showed relatively little change during this period. Most important were a rise in the share of Germany, particularly in Ottoman imports, and a corresponding decline in the share of British exports. Ottoman exports to Russia also declined sharply during the 1880s, primarily because of the secession of large areas in the Balkan provinces after the War of 1877–8.

1898–1913: railroads and a new wave of expansion

With the emergence of the world economy from the Great Depression, Ottoman foreign trade entered a new period of expansion which lasted until World War I. However, since the Empire lost substantial amounts of land and population after 1908, we can extend meaningful comparison of aggregate trade figures only until 1907. Tables 2.1 and 2.2 indicate that total Ottoman exports increased at average annual rates of 4.2 per cent in current prices and at 3.4 per cent in constant prices. Total imports expanded at the rate of 6.2 per cent per year in current prices and 4.8 per cent per year in constant prices between 1898 and 1907. Trade with industrialized center countries grew at similar rates.

This rapid expansion continued despite the loss of territory after 1908. Between 1911 and 1913, the Empire lost about a quarter of its population and over 10 per cent of its land in the commercially and agriculturally more advanced European provinces, where standards of living were above average.[43] However, by 1913 the volume of exports had regained their 1907 levels, and the volume of imports exceeded 1907 levels by more than 25 per cent. As a result, the volume of Ottoman exports increased from £17.3 million in 1898 to £28.4 million in 1913; the value of imports in current prices rose from £19.8 million in 1898 to £39.4 million in 1913.

However, it should also be noted that in terms of average rates of growth the pace of this second wave of expansion did not match that of the mid-nineteenth century. While rates of growth of Ottoman foreign trade measured in constant prices averaged above 6 per cent per year during 1840–73, they remained below 3 per cent after 1880 and averaged close to 4 per cent per year after 1898. Equally important, these latter rates of expansion slightly lagged behind rates of expansion of world trade and probably of center–periphery trade for 1880–1913.[44]

Two of the reasons behind this second wave of expansion need to be emphasized. First, on the demand side, the upswing in levels of economic activity in the industrialized countries led to higher rates of growth of demand for Ottoman primary products. Paralleling this change, external terms of trade began to move in favor of the Ottoman economy.[45] As these developments increased agricultural and commercial incomes, demand for imports started to expand at a higher rate.

Second, on the supply side, railroads built by foreign capital also contributed to the more rapid expansion of Ottoman foreign trade during this period. During the 1880s the inter-imperialist struggle for markets and sources of cheap and abundant raw materials intensified with the arrival of Germany as a world power. The Ottoman Empire appeared particularly attractive to the newcomer, since it had not been incorporated into any of the existing colonial empires. Between 1888 and 1896, this Great Power rivalry led to the largest wave of railroad building in the Ottoman Empire. While German capital built railroads in Central Anatolia and Macedonia, French companies undertook the construction of new lines in Syria, Macedonia and Western Anatolia.[46] Just as these lines were being completed in the mid-1890s, the world economy was leaving the period of the 'Great Depression' behind. By reducing considerably the transportation costs between major ports and distant regions such as Central Anatolia, the railroads brought the latter closer to European industry and accelerated the expansion of agricultural commodity production for world markets in these areas.[47]

An important and related development after 1880 was the growing British–German commercial rivalry in the Ottoman Empire. As British hegemony in overseas trade began to decline in the 1880s, German capital followed an aggressive commercial policy, utilizing its superiority in iron and steel, chemicals and a few other sectors and taking advantage of support by its state apparatus and by the large banks. The Ottoman Empire was one of the areas where the rivalry was most intense and where German gains against the British and to some extent against French interests were most rapid.[48] German exports to the Ottoman Empire increased by more than 15 times during the three decades preceding World War I, exceeding £5 million by 1910. Ottoman exports to Germany increased at comparable rates, reaching over £3 million in the 1910s. Likewise, Germany's share in total Ottoman imports increased from 2.4 per cent in 1880–2 to 14.8 per cent in 1911–13 and German share in Ottoman exports rose from 0.5 per cent to 11.9 per cent during these three decades.[49] Corresponding to this trend were the declines in British and French shares in Ottoman foreign trade. (See tables 2.3 and 2.4.[50]) Nonetheless, in 1913 Britain continued to hold the largest share in Ottoman exports and imports. While railroad construction was pulling Central Anatolia and Syria into German and French spheres of influence respectively, Britain increased its trade with the Iraqi provinces of the Empire.[51] More important, in cotton textiles, which remained the most important item in Ottoman imports, Britain continued to hold the largest share despite the challenge, starting around the turn of the century, of lower-quality and inexpensive products from Italy and India.[52]

Trade, growth and factors specific to the Ottoman Empire

The previous section emphasized long-term fluctuations in conditions of demand as the most important single determinant of the rate of growth of Ottoman foreign trade. This does not mean, however, that supply side factors or developments specific to the Ottoman Empire did not play an important role in this process. We know, for example, that different regions of the Empire began to be integrated into world markets at different points in time during the nineteenth century. There also remained considerable differences between the extent to which different regions had been integrated into the world economy by 1913. Proximity to the coast and the availability of inexpensive means of transportation played an important role in this differentiation. In addition, agricultural conditions had to be suitable for the cultivation of the raw materials and foodstuffs in demand in the industrialized economies. For example, exports from Egypt, Wallachia and Moldavia began to expand rapidly as early as the 1820s and especially in the 1840s.[53] On the other hand, agricultural exports from Western Anatolia did not start to expand until the Crimean War.[54] Central Anatolia was not linked to the European markets until after the construction of the Anatolian Railway in the 1890s. Finally, in the absence of inexpensive means of transportation world market conditions had a limited impact on Eastern Anatolia until World War I.[55]

There is another, more fundamental reason why the emphasis on conditions of demand in the industrialized center countries does not imply that the Ottoman economy adjusted passively to long-term fluctuations in demand. When we examine the expansion of center–periphery trade for the nineteenth century as a whole or during any sub-period, we observe that the integration of different peripheral countries into the world economy did not proceed at even rates. The imports and exports of some countries in the periphery expanded more rapidly than those of others. As a result, over the course of the century some countries expanded their shares in the center markets at the expense of others. Clearly, such uneven rates of integration cannot be explained by reference to world economic conditions alone. Factors on the supply side, characteristics specific to each country, have to be brought into the analysis.

In the Ottoman case, the results of our reconstruction have shown that for the period 1840–1913 as a whole per capita exports from the Ottoman Empire expanded at rates close to but lower than those of per capita world trade and per capita center–periphery trade. Within this three-quarters of a century, the Ottoman–center trade grew faster than the periphery–center trade until the early 1870s, but the rate of growth of Ottoman exports lagged behind the rate of growth of total exports from the periphery after the 1870s. These aggregate figures should be treated with caution, however. They do not reveal anything about the long-term changes in the composition of demand in the industrialized center countries. We would need to know more about the rates of growth of demand in the center countries for the bundle of primary commodities exported by the Ottoman Empire in relation to the rates of growth of demand for all primary commodities. It would then be possible to separate demand and supply side factors and determine the extent to which the pace of integration of the Ottoman economy in relation to others in the periphery was affected by these long-term shifts in demand and the extent to which the relative pace of integration was due to developments specific to the Ottoman economy.

This problem can be posed more precisely in the following manner: (a) what happened from one period to the next to the share in the periphery's total exports of the commodity bundle being exported by the Ottoman Empire? and (b) given the relative performance of that bundle, what happened to the share of the Ottoman Empire in the periphery's exports of that bundle?[56]

Answers to these questions would require quite detailed world trade data on a commodity basis. Furthermore, the periodic losses of land and population from the Ottoman Empire make intertemporal comparisons of this type extremely difficult. Nonetheless, important clues to the answers to these questions can still be extracted from the foreign trade statistics of the major center countries. In what follows, we will necessarily be qualitative in view of the limited nature of our empirical investigation. Following earlier analysis, we will focus on two periods, 1840–75 and 1880–1913.

The import statistics of Britain and France indicate that the commodity bundle being exported by the Ottoman Empire expanded its share in total imports of the center countries until the 1870s. However, the same share declined significantly after 1880. Consequently, the rapid expansion of Ottoman exports during the mid-century and their stagnation after 1880 in relation to total exports from the periphery can be attributed, at least in part, to long-term changes in the composition of demand in the center.

It appears that, until the 1870s, Ottoman exports expanded their share at the expense of other exporters of the same commodities. That is, supply side factors were also behind the relatively more rapid expansion of Ottoman exports until the 1870s. On the other hand, both demand and supply side factors reversed themselves in the later period. During 1880–1913, rates of growth of Ottoman exports were unfavorably affected not only by the relatively slower rates of absorption in the center in relation to the rates of absorption of other primary commodities, but also by competition from other exporters of the same commodities.[57]

Furthermore, even if this latter trend had not occurred after 1880, it cannot be necessarily concluded that the slower rates of expansion of Ottoman exports were due to long-term shifts in demand alone. During the nineteenth century the economies in the periphery that integrated to the world markets most rapidly were also those which, for one reason or another, responded rapidly to changing conditions in demand. As a result, it would be important to determine whether there was any change in composition of Ottoman exports as the composition of demand in the center countries shifted away from the traditional export bundle of the Empire. An examination of the commodity composition of Ottoman exports shows that there was very little change in that direction after 1880. Ottoman exports continued to be quite diversified, and the share of the same eight or ten leading commodities in the total declined only slightly, from 51 per cent to 44 per cent during the three decades before World War I.[58]

In other words, for an explanation of the relative rates of growth of Ottoman exports *vis-à-vis* others in the periphery, we need to focus on factors specific to the Ottoman Empire. At this stage we can only provide an incomplete answer to this inquiry. During the earlier period 1840–73 rates of growth of Ottoman exports remained quite high, because, in addition to favorable world market conditions, this was the initial period of easy export expansion. The initial volume of exports was quite small and after the Free Trade Treaties of 1838–41 removed the earlier restrictions on exports, agricultural producers in the coastal areas shifted their production towards export crops. After 1880, the construction of railroads by foreign capital pulled regions of the interior closer to world markets and expanded agricultural exports from these areas. However, this long-term shift in the composition of output towards exports was not accompanied by a far-reaching transformation of Ottoman agriculture. Even in the more export-oriented areas of the Empire, agricultural techniques remained primitive and changed little during the century. Foreign investment remained limited to infrastructure such as railroads and ports. As a result, Ottoman exports could not maintain their share in the markets of industrialized center countries after the first round of expansion. It also appears that Ottoman agriculture was not flexible enough to respond to changes in the composition of world market demand.

Finally, we will explore briefly the possible link between high rates of expansion of foreign trade and economic growth in the Ottoman Empire during the nineteenth century. At the outset it needs to be pointed out that during most of the period under study in this volume, the ratio of exports or of foreign trade to any measure of total production in the Empire remained rather low. As a result, even under the most favorable assumptions regarding the nature and strength of this link, one would have to be cautious about relating the expansion in foreign trade to economic growth in the Empire.

Our estimates indicate that around 1840 about 3 to 4 per cent of the total production and less than 8 per cent of the agricultural production of the Empire was being exported. We also estimate that by the mid-1870s these ratios were in the ranges of 6 to 8 per cent and 12 to 15 per cent, respectively.[59] These low ratios confirm that the link between the expansion of foreign trade and economic growth was indeed very weak for the Empire as a whole until the 1870s. However, there were substantial variations between regional experiences. Western Anatolia and Northern Greece participated in the export expansion to a much greater extent than the rest of the Empire.

We have very little information regarding changes in the aggregate levels of production during this mid-century period.[60] Government estimates of expected tax collections suggest that levels of production were rising during these decades.[61] However, this was also a period of considerable growth in population, partly owing to immigration. Therefore, it is not clear whether levels of per capita production and income were rising for the Empire as a whole. It should also be emphasized that most of the destructive impact of imports of manufactures on traditional handicrafts occurred before the 1870s, at least in the important case of cotton textiles. Our study of that branch of production shows that levels of production in both urban manufacturing establishments and within the rural households declined most rapidly until the 1870s.[62]

The existence of a close and positive link between foreign trade and economic growth appears equally unlikely for the last quarter of the century, the period of the 'Great Depression'. This is not necessarily because the ratio of foreign trade to total production remained low, but because the rate of growth of exports and imports fell sharply to less than 2 per cent per year during this period. Moreover, as the rate of growth of demand for primary commodities slowed down in the industrialized economies, the terms of trade turned against the periphery. World economic forces appear to have induced stagnation, not growth, in the Ottoman Empire during the last quarter of the century.[63]

After 1898, as the levels of economic activity in the industrialized countries began to rise more rapidly, the rate of growth of Ottoman foreign trade increased as well. Consequently, the ratio of foreign trade to total production rose steadily until World War I. By 1913, approximately 14 per cent of total production and close to 20 per cent of agricultural production of the Empire was being exported. According to these estimates, then, the decade and a half before World War I emerges as the only sub-period for which a discernible and positive link can be established between foreign trade and economic growth. In fact, the only available long-term estimates regarding levels of production and income in the Empire indicates that increases in levels of production outstripped population growth during these years.[64]

Chapter 3

Ottoman terms of trade against industrialized countries, 1854–1913

This chapter will examine the long-term trends in Ottoman terms of trade against industrialized center countries from three interrelated perspectives. First, we will try to determine whether there was a secular decline in Ottoman terms of trade during the period under study, since such a movement would imply losses arising from the increasing specialization of the Ottoman economy in primary commodities for export. Second, we will establish the long-term cyclical movements in Ottoman terms of trade since these movements, along with long-term changes in Ottoman foreign trade and foreign investment in the Empire, have helped define distinct world economic conjunctures for the Ottoman economy during the nineteenth century. Third, we will emphasize that long-term cyclical movements in external terms of trade have important implications regarding the pace of the process of integration into the world economy. We would expect that, *ceteris paribus*, specialization in primary commodities for export would accelerate during periods of improving terms of trade. Similarly, periods of deteriorating terms of trade for the Ottoman Empire should be interpreted as periods of slower rates of destruction of domestic handicrafts activity and slower rates of specialization in export-oriented agriculture. The chapter ends with a discussion of the implications on the external terms of trade of one important characteristic of the Ottoman Empire during the nineteenth century: the absence of monoculture and the diversified nature of Ottoman exports.

Terms of trade and integration into the world economy

In 1949 a United Nations study was published, on the basis of which it appeared that the net barter terms of trade – the simple ratio of prices – between the primary and manufactured commodities had moved sharply in favor of the latter during the preceding three-quarters of a century. Ever since then, this secular trend has been considered a major adverse outcome for the countries in the periphery of their specialization in primary products.[1] In the next year Prebisch and Singer stated in separate articles their well-known hypothesis,[2] and an empirical and conceptual debate has followed.[3] In a recent study aimed at drawing up a balance sheet for the statistical part of the debate, Spraos has shown that the weight of the evidence presented during the last three decades does point to a deterioration of the net barter terms of trade against the primary products up to 1938, although the rate of this deterioration was probably not as high as it was first argued to be by Prebisch.[4]

As important as this secular (very long-term) trend, in our view, are the long-term cyclical movements in the manufactures–primary commodities and center–periphery terms of trade. Empirical studies in recent decades have shown that, while the net barter terms of trade of an individual country in the periphery may or may not exhibit the secular trend hypothesized by Prebisch and Singer, they are frequently subject to cyclical movements lasting as long as two decades or more in either direction.[5] From the perspective of the present study, these long-term trends need to be established, since each of them, along with the respective trends in the volume of foreign trade and in foreign investment, helped define a specific world economic conjuncture for the Ottoman Empire.

What needs to be emphasized, in addition to the gains or losses implied by movements in the terms of trade after the specialization in primary products has been established, is the role of the terms of trade during the process of integration into the world economy. After the barriers to free trade are removed by treaties or by other means, the ratio of the prices of exportable agricultural commodities to the prices of imported manufactures in the rural areas will determine the speed with which traditional agricultural crops and rural manufacturing activities will be abandoned in favor of specialization in the production of agricultural commodities for export. On the other hand, during periods of deterioration of the net barter terms of trade against the agricultural exportables, the process of destruction of the more self-sufficient nature of the rural economies may slow down or may even be reversed.[6]

In the nineteenth-century context, the terms of trade between the exported primary products and imported manufactures, measured in prices prevailing at the ports of export, could not adequately reflect the relative prices faced in the rural areas. Aside from other considerations, transportation costs between the rural areas and the ports have to be taken into account whenever physical distance to the coast and the absence of inexpensive means of transportation made these costs relatively important. Hence, the construction of a railroad into the hinterland of a major port could substantially alter the terms of trade in the rural areas by lowering the prices of imported manufactures on the one hand and raising the prices of export crops on the other, even when the terms of trade between two countries, measured in prices prevailing in the port cities of either country, remained unchanged. This change in relative prices, more than anything else, shattered the existing division of labor in the rural areas, destroyed whatever existed of intra-country commodity flows that provided the primitive beginnings of a domestic market, and induced specialization according to the division of labor of the world economy.[7]

This is not to say that the railroads solely determined the time and pace of the integration of the interior regions into the world economy. For one thing, the reduction in transportation costs brought about by the railroads could not alter the relative prices substantially if the share of transportation costs in the prices prevailing in the rural area was low, owing to either proximity to the port or the availability of some other means of inexpensive transportation, such as navigable rivers. Second, transportation costs figured only to a limited extent in the final prices of some agricultural commodities such as opium and raw wool and especially of manufactures such as textile products. Third, movements in the relative world prices of primary products and manufactures could be substantial. The movements in the center–periphery terms of trade continued to play an important role in determining the time and pace of specialization in agricultural exportables until after the previously existing activities and commodity flow networks within the periphery were destroyed.

The experience in parts of Anatolia and Syria during the American Civil War provides a case in point. The Cotton Famine in Lancashire meant sharp rises in the prices of both cotton and cotton manufactures. In those areas of Anatolia and Syria that had started specializing according to the division of labor of the world economy, two developments were observed. There was a temporary but substantial expansion of cotton production for export wherever agricultural conditions permitted. At the same time, the volume of imports of cotton textile manufactures declined as woolen cloth and cloth woven from low-quality non-exportable cotton were substituted for imported products for the duration of the Famine. It may be hypothesized that the expansion in cotton cultivation occurred in areas already producing for the world market and that a large part of it came at the expense of other export crops. This expansion was short-lived, primarily because the quality and characteristics of the cotton produced did not suit the long-term requirements of Lancashire. On the other hand, the Cotton Famine and the rise in price of imported cotton manufactures delayed the advance in destruction of rural spinning and weaving for almost a decade, especially in the non-cotton-growing regions, where agricultural incomes did not rise despite the export boom.[8]

Data and the indices

We discuss in chapter 2 and appendix 1 the problem of the absence of Ottoman statistics for the period before 1878 and the serious limitations of what is available for the period after 1878. Because of this problem, our study of Ottoman foreign trade was based on the trade statistics of most European and other countries, which provided detailed price and quantity information on these countries' trade with the Ottoman Empire.[9] Constraints on our time and resources eventually forced us to limit our examination of terms of trade to the Empire's major trading partners. The earliest date for which these data are available vary from one country to another and this has necessarily determined how far back into the nineteenth century this study could go. The countries and the periods for which data on trade with the Ottoman Empire have been utilized are the United Kingdom, 1854–1913; France, 1854–1913; Germany, 1880–1913; Austria, 1891–1913; and the United States, 1896–1913 (for Ottoman exports only; the volume of Ottoman imports throughout the nineteenth century and of Ottoman exports prior to 1896 is too small to justify their inclusion).[10]

These countries belonged to the center of the nineteenth-century world capitalist economy. Despite some differences in the composition of Ottoman imports from these countries, Ottoman trade with them was overwhelmingly an exchange of primary products for manufactures. As evidence for the later period indicates, Ottoman terms of trade with each of these countries show a fairly similar pattern.[11] A similar explanation can be given regarding Ottoman terms of trade against other industrialized countries of Europe whose share in Ottoman foreign trade was much smaller than the share of any of the five countries that are included in this study. As we point out in appendix 2, where more technical details and main results are presented, this study covers about half to three-fourths of Ottoman trade with the industrialized center countries. This coverage, in view of the scope of similar studies, is more than adequate for a terms of trade study.[12]

As for the countries of the periphery, their trade statistics began to provide price and quantity information on their trade with the Ottoman Empire only towards the end of the century. Moreover, in some cases, the best example of which is the Romanian statistics, the utilization of official prices that were not revised annually makes a terms of trade study on that basis not very meaningful. In addition, other considerations, including the smaller share of these countries in Ottoman foreign trade and limitations on our resources, have necessitated the exclusion of the Ottoman–periphery trade from this study. We also attempted to examine the Ottoman terms of trade against Russia, utilizing the annual foreign trade statistics of that country for the period 1830–1913. Russia cannot easily be categorized as a country in the periphery, and its share in Ottoman trade was not insignificant during the nineteenth century.[13] However, major data and index problems and the ambiguity of the results obtained forced us to abandon the attempt to include Russia in this study.[14]

The terms of trade concept utilized throughout the study will be the net barter terms of trade, the simple ratio of the index of export prices to the index of import prices, P_x/P_m. Since we are primarily interested in the movements of Ottoman terms of trade, the prices at the ports of other countries could not adequately reflect the movements in prices prevailing at the Ottoman ports, especially during a period of rapidly declining transportation costs such as the last quarter of the nineteenth century. Appropriate transportation and insurance costs had to be subtracted from the import prices cited in the statistics of other countries and, conversely, transportation and insurance costs had to be added to their exports to reach c.i.f. prices for Ottoman exports and f.o.b. prices for Ottoman imports. We did this by undertaking separate calculations for each country for each year. These calculations are discussed in detail in appendices 1 and 2.

It should be recognized that these efforts do not necessarily eliminate the empirical problems that might arise in a terms of trade study. As Spraos has argued recently, there might be a host of other reasons for the observed differences between prices c.i.f. port of destination reported by one country and prices f.o.b. port of origin reported by another.[15] These potential problems, along with the measures we have taken and the adjustments we have made in response, are discussed in section A1.3 of appendix 1.

Unless otherwise stated, the discussion in this chapter is based on annually linked Fisher price indices.[16] With the choice of annually linked chain indices, we could take advantage of the increasingly detailed commodity classification.[17] At this point the reader should be reminded of the impossibility of constructing a 'true index'. Both the base period weighted Laspeyres and the current period weighted Paasche are inadequate unless the purpose of the study explicitly necessitates the use of either base period weights or current period weights. While Laspeyres and Paasche can be taken as providing a range within which the 'true index' would fall, the Fisher index, by giving the geometric mean of the

45

two, provides a middle of the road answer.[18] Only under certain strong assumptions could the Fisher become the 'true index'. It should be emphasized that the over-time divergences between Laspeyres and Paasche, the so-called index drift, is not always a minor problem. In many cases, the index drift qualitatively affects the results and cannot be ignored. These problems of index construction are also discussed in greater detail in appendix 2 where the main results of the study are presented in the form of annually linked Fisher, Laspeyres and Paasche indices.

Long swings in Ottoman–center terms of trade

It will be argued in this section that the movements in Ottoman terms of trade against the industrialized center were characterized by long swings, each of which corresponded to similar long swings in the terms of trade of the industrialized center countries against the peripheral countries as a whole. Even though this correspondence was not perfect, i.e. the terms of trade of every center country did not improve each time the Ottoman terms of trade deteriorated and vice versa, we can gain major insights by examining the latter in the context of long-term movements in the center–periphery terms of trade.

If we take their level in 1880 as 100, the Ottoman terms of trade against the center countries, whose share in total Ottoman trade varied between two-thirds and four-fifths during 1854–1913,[19] declined from 134 in 1854–6 to 106 in 1911–13, a fall of 21 per cent (see figure 2 and table 3.1). This decline would have been somewhat greater, perhaps by a few percentage points, had it not been for the decline in the costs of transportation, which was more rapid than the decline in the level of prices during this sixty-year period.[20] Conversely, for the same reason, the improvement in the terms of trade of the center countries was greater than the magnitude of this adverse movement against Ottoman exports.

It might be argued that the years 1854–6 are not appropriate as the starting point of a long-term comparison, since the conjuncture of the Crimean War shifted the terms of trade sharply in favor of Ottoman exports. In fact, if the years 1858–60 are taken as the starting point, the total decline until 1913 in the Ottoman terms of trade against the center countries is reduced to 11 per cent (see table 3.1). We reach similar conclusions if simple statistical techniques are applied to these data. We applied ordinary least squares to the annual values of Fisher indices presented in figure 2 and in more detail in appendix 2, table A2.1, in order to establish the time trend for Ottoman terms of trade. When the regression is applied to 1854–1913, we observe that Ottoman terms of

Table 3.1. *Long swings in Ottoman–center terms of trade, 1854–1913*
Net barter terms of trade; Fisher price indices: 1880 = 100

Years	Ottoman–Center (1)	Primary–manufactures (2)
1854–6	113.7	114.8
1858–60	118.0	113.1
1865–6	91.0	87.3
1870–2	105.8	106.3
1888–9	85.8	89.2
1894–6	91.8	94.3
1911–13	106.0	107.9

Notes: Column 1 gives the terms of trade between Ottoman exports to the industrialized center countries and Ottoman imports from the same. Column 2 gives the terms of trade between Ottoman exports of primary commodities to the center countries and Ottoman imports of manufactures from the same.
Source: Based on the foreign trade statistics of the major European countries and the United States. Appropriate costs of transportation and insurance have been taken into account. For further details, see the text, figure 2 and appendix 2. Detailed annual indices are presented in tables A2.1 and A2.2 of the same appendix.

trade declined at an average annual rate of 0.18 per cent (approximately 2 per thousand) during this period. The time trend coefficient was statistically significant in that case. On the other hand, when the period 1854–7 is excluded from the analysis, the ordinary least squares regression indicates that Ottoman terms of trade declined at the rate of 0.0096 per cent (approximately 1 per ten thousand) per year during 1858–1913. In addition, this latter time trend coefficient was not statistically significant either at the 5 per cent or 10 per cent levels.[21] The rate of this very long-term deterioration, if any, is certainly smaller than the rate estimated by Prebisch during the early 1950s.

On the other hand, a much more striking picture emerges when changes in the respective levels of productivity are taken into account. It is widely accepted that levels of productivity increased much more rapidly in the industrial economies than in the agrarian peripheral countries during the nineteenth century. On this basis, the tendency should have been for the net barter terms of trade to move in favor of primary commodities. The fact that they did not move in favor of Ottoman exports indicates that the center countries were the prime beneficiaries of trade and of changes in the levels of productivity during this period. Rather than passing on these benefits to the Ottoman Empire

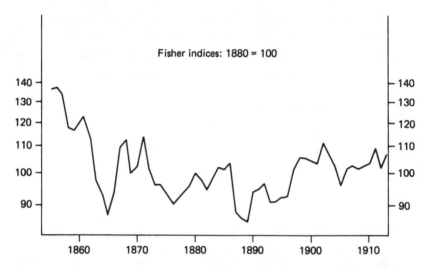

Figure 2 Ottoman terms of trade against industrialized center countries, 1854–1913. Note: Logarithmic scale is used along the vertical axis. For annual figures, see appendix 2, table A2.1.

and to the rest of the periphery in the form of lower prices, the center countries were able to retain the results of more rapid increases in the levels of productivity in the forms of higher wages and higher rates of profit.[22]

We can now turn from secular trends in Ottoman terms of trade to long-term cyclical movements. An examination of the Ottoman–center terms of trade summarized in figure 2 and table 3.1 indicates that the period until World War I can best be divided into four distinct sub-periods; 1820 to mid-1850s; 1854 to 1871; 1871 to 1896; and 1896 to 1913. We will now examine the movements in the terms of trade during each of these sub-periods not only from the perspective of gains or losses arising from the specialization in primary commodities but also in relation to their effects on the pace of that specialization process.

1820 to mid-1850s: Ottoman terms of trade against the industrializing center countries appear to have improved until the mid-1850s. At this stage of the research we have mainly indirect information regarding the period up to the Crimean War. British foreign trade statistics constitute the most important source. Imlah's well-known study shows that from 1820 to the late 1840s the movements in the British terms of trade were dominated by the rapid decline in the prices of cotton manufactures, which made up more than half of all Ottoman imports from that country.

Taking their levels in 1880 as 100, the prices of British cotton manufactures excluding yarn declined from 396 in 1819–21 to 109 in 1849–51. The decline in the price of cotton yarn was somewhat less rapid, from 221 to 84 during the same period. Of equal importance is the fact that the prices of other manufactures also declined, but did so more slowly during these decades.[23] On the other hand, the rate of decline in British domestic prices of some of the more important primary commodities exported by the Ottoman Empire was lower than the rate of decline of the prices of British exports as a whole during this period.[24] In addition, we know that the British net barter terms of trade against the rest of the world declined by about 30 per cent between 1819–21 and 1849–51.[25]

A similar rising trend in the Ottoman terms of trade against Western and Central European countries appears more than likely during this period, but it is difficult to be specific regarding its magnitude. Since these countries were in the earlier stages of industrialization and since cotton manufactures were imported primarily from Britain, it is probable that the prices of manufactures imported from these countries did not decline as rapidly as prices of imports from Britain.[26]

1854 to 1871: The choice of 1854 as the first year of this sub-period is dictated by the availability of data, particularly of import data in the British foreign trade statistics.[27] As it stands, the sub-period roughly coincides with the mid-century boom of the world economy, frequently dated as 1848 or 1850 to 1873.[28] Ottoman external trade exports plus imports also expanded exceptionally rapidly during these years, averaging over 5 per cent per annum in both constant and current prices.[29]

Ottoman–center terms of trade were affected quite strongly by two wars during this interval. The improvement in the Ottoman terms of trade during the Crimean War was due to the rapid increase in the prices of primary commodities in world markets. Combined with a high volume of demand, this situation led to a significant jump in the total value of Ottoman exports during 1856–7.[30] Only a few years after the prices of primary commodities and Ottoman external terms of trade ceased declining from their peak levels of 1856, the American Civil War began. Prices of raw cotton rose faster than the prices of cotton manufactures during the Cotton Famine.[31] However, since the share of cotton manufactures in Ottoman imports was greater than the share of raw cotton exports, the Ottoman terms of trade deteriorated until 1865.

As a result, the decade 1856 to 1865 represented a period of virtually uninterrupted decline for the Ottoman terms of trade, from 140 in 1856 to 87 in 1865, a total of 37 per cent (see figure 2). It appears that 1856 to 1865 was a period of deteriorating terms of trade for the periphery in general, a fact evidenced by the more than 20 per cent improvement in the British terms of trade.[32] An exception would be a country like Egypt, whose exports consisted almost entirely of cotton but whose imports included other commodities besides cotton manufactures.[33]

The 24 per cent improvement in the Ottoman terms of trade during 1865 to 1871 represents, more than anything else, the return of the prices of cotton manufactures to their normal levels following the American Civil War. It should also be pointed out with respect to both 1856–65 and 1865–71 that the unavailability of data from the other center countries tends to exaggerate the magnitude of the fluctuations in Ottoman terms of trade. Again, this is because Ottoman imports from the United Kingdom always had a larger share of cotton manufactures, around 70 per cent, than imports from Austria, Germany and France, which could not compete with the United Kingdom in that category.

Abstracting from the effects of these two consecutive wars, we can sum up the overall change during the sub-period 1858–60 to 1870–2 as a 10 per cent deterioration in the Ottoman–center terms of trade. It should be emphasized that total Ottoman trade and trade with the center countries, measured in both constant and current prices, doubled during these 14 years.[34] In other words, unlike the situation during the period until the 1850s, the increasing world market orientation of the Ottoman economy during the mid-century boom was not, on the whole, assisted by favorable movements in the external terms of trade.

1871 to 1896: 1871 represents a relative peak for Ottoman terms of trade. The general trend was deterioration during the next quarter century, which coincides closely with the Great Depression of 1873–96. Declining from their levels of 114 in 1871, the Ottoman–center terms of trade actually reached their trough in 1889 at 85, a decrease of 25 per cent in 18 years. They remained depressed until 1896 when, at 92, they were still 19 per cent below their levels in 1871.

The period of the Great Depression was characterized by rapidly declining prices worldwide. The prices of manufactures imported by the Ottoman Empire declined by 35 per cent between 1871 and 1896. The decline in the prices of Ottoman exports of primary commodities was even more rapid, a total of 48 per cent during the same period (see table A2.2 in appendix 2 for details).

Unlike levels of production in the 1930s, however, levels of production in the industrialized countries did not decline during the last quarter of the nineteenth century. Instead, we observe lower rates of expansion of industrial output.[35] At least in part because of this circumstance,

Ottoman trade with the center countries continued to expand during the 1880s and early 1890s, but at rates distinctly lower than those prevailing during both the mid-century boom and after 1896.[36]

1896 to 1913: With the resumption of higher rates of industrial growth in the center countries during the mid-1890s we observe a reversal of the earlier pattern of change in price levels. World price levels began to rise with the prices of primary commodities increasing faster than prices of manufactures until World War I. The prices of manufactures imports into the Ottoman Empire rose by a total of 12 per cent between 1894–6 and 1911–13. The prices of Ottoman exports of raw materials and foodstuffs increased by 28 per cent during the same period. As a result, the Ottoman–center terms of trade improved by 14 per cent between 1894–6 and 1911–13 (see table 3.1 above and table A2.2 in appendix 2).

The movements in Ottoman–center terms of trade during the Great Depression and the subsequent upswing of the world economy until World War I can be treated as another example of the 'normal' pattern of terms of trade in world trade. According to this explanation, raw materials and foodstuffs prices typically fluctuate in a wider amplitude than do the prices of manufactures. Given the respective price elasticities of supply and demand for each group of commodities, the terms of trade of a peripheral country would be expected to deteriorate during periods of depression and to improve during periods of expansion.[37] In other words, the industrialized center countries of the world economy emerge as the dominant component in this explanation of the long-term movements in center–periphery terms of trade. Furthermore, this particular pattern of the terms of trade plays an important role in the transmission of the long-term fluctuations in economic activity, of both upswings and the depressions in the industrialized center to the countries in the periphery. The behavior of the terms of trade of industrial Europe until World War I and the terms of trade of the United Kingdom during the last quarter of the nineteenth century fit this pattern. On the other hand, the 'normal' pattern cannot account for the improvement in the terms of trade of the United Kingdom during 1896–1913.[38]

What does the 'normal' pattern imply for the continuity of the process of integration into world markets? As we have noted earlier in this chapter, the movements in the terms of trade may play a significant role in that process until the destruction of the earlier pattern of specialization is completed. Since specialization of the Ottoman interior in production for world markets continued to expand but was far from being complete by 1913, because of the relatively late penetration of railroads into Anatolia, movements in the terms of trade must have had an important impact.

In other words, we would expect that the deterioration of the terms of trade against agricultural exports and the decline in the rate of expansion of their volume during the Great Depression of 1873–96 slowed down the process of specialization in export-oriented agriculture. Under these circumstances the peasant households continued to devote a larger part of their labor time to non-agricultural activities.[39] On the other hand, the shift in the terms of trade in favor of primary commodities after 1896 helped accelerate the pace of export orientation and penetration into the rural economies of imported manufactures. In short, long-term swings in Ottoman–center terms of trade, along with long-term fluctuations in the rate of expansion of the world market demand for Ottoman exports, created distinct periods of stagnation (if not depression) and expansion rather than one continuous process of integration into world markets.[40]

The composition of Ottoman exports and terms of trade

An examination of table 3.1 above reveals that the long-term movements in Ottoman–center terms of trade during the nineteenth century followed very closely the trends in the terms of trade between Ottoman exports of primary products and Ottoman imports of manufactures. This is not surprising. As appendix 1 shows, about 90 per cent of Ottoman exports in the early 1910s consisted of raw materials and foodstuffs. This share was, if anything, even higher during the earlier period. On the other hand, it appears that the share of manufactures in imports declined during the late nineteenth and early twentieth centuries. By the 1910s foodstuffs such as wheat, flour, rice, sugar and coffee made up more than one-third of Ottoman imports. Considering the volume of its imports in comparison to total world trade in manufactures and foodstuffs, we can safely treat the Ottoman Empire as a 'small country' in world trade with respect to its imports. In other words, the Ottoman economy had no influence on world prices of its imports. However, the same assumption cannot be made with respect to Ottoman exports.

One important characteristic of the composition of Ottoman exports should be re-emphasized here in relation to trends in terms of trade: even on the basis of incomplete data, it is not difficult to generalize that the share of no single commodity exceeded 15 per cent of total export revenues in any year of the period under study. It also appears that the share of the largest eight commodities in total export revenues rarely, if ever, exceeded 60 per cent.[41] As a result, Ottoman external terms of trade did not depend on the fortunes of a few commodities in world markets. This was the case primarily because patterns of cultivation in the

Ottoman Empire never approached conditions of monoculture during the nineteenth century.

Undoubtedly, the absence of monoculture was in part due to the diversity of agronomic factors and the sheer size of the Empire. However, it was also related to the fact that the Ottoman state never entirely lost its political independence to become a formal colony. Throughout the century, the central government resisted attempts by foreign capital to eliminate its fiscal base, the small peasantry. As a result, attempts by foreign capitalists to change the mode of production in agriculture and to establish large-scale farms employing wage laborers and producing for world markets proved unsuccessful.[42]

The absence of monoculture and the relative diversification of Ottoman exports do not mean that the price elasticity of demand in world markets for all Ottoman exports was close to infinity or that conditions of Ottoman supply had no bearing on the price of exports. For the period after 1880, the major export commodities were tobacco, raisins, figs, raw silk, raw wool, opium, wheat and barley. Of lesser importance, with shares of less than 5 per cent in total exports, were valonia (used as a dyestuff), hazelnuts, cotton and olive oil.[43] Ottoman shares in total world exports of many of these commodities, as revealed in an examination of the foreign trade statistics of the United Kingdom, France and Germany, were low. However, for some commodities such as tobacco, opium, goats' wool and to a lesser extent raisins, figs and valonia, Ottoman exports had a significant share in the imports of the United Kingdom and Germany. It would not be unrealistic to expect some inelasticity of demand for these commodities.

Tobacco provides the most interesting case among Ottoman exports because of both the relatively inelastic demand it faced – the Ottoman Empire being virtually the sole exporter of 'Turkish tobacco' – and the special circumstances associated with tobacco cultivation and exportation in the Empire. In 1884, the Tobacco Régie, a company founded with European capital, was granted the monopoly for the administration of tobacco cultivation, its purchase and its exportation, as well as for the manufacturing of cigarettes for domestic consumption. In return, the company agreed to pay annually a fixed sum to the Ottoman Public Debt Administration that would be transferred to the European bondholders, to set aside 8 per cent for its shareholders, and then to divide the rest of its profits among its own shareholders, the Debt Administration, and the Ottoman government.[44]

It was clear from the outset that the overriding concern of the Régie was not the expansion of tobacco exports to Europe and to the United

States but the maximization of its profits. Therefore, the policies of the Régie with respect to quantity restrictions on cultivation and pricing of exports should be expected to have resembled more the maximum revenue-oriented policies of a politically independent peripheral government in the twentieth century than the export-expansion-oriented policies followed by colonial governments during the nineteenth century.[45]

It appears that the Régie was able to use its monopoly power to increase the price of Turkish tobacco relative to other varieties in the world markets, although it is not clear to what extent other factors such as the expansion of world demand for Turkish tobacco and improvements in its quality played a part in bringing about this trend.[46] One thing is certain: the beneficiaries of the export pricing policies were not the domestic producers. The Régie exploited its monopolistic (single buyer) situation in this respect. After 1890, the average price of exports remained 20 to 50 per cent higher than the average price paid to domestic producers. Profits accruing to the Régie went primarily to the European bondholders of the Ottoman debt.[47]

The example of tobacco might demonstrate the theoretical possibility for the favorable manipulation of the terms of trade by a government free from the intervention of European powers. But that alternative certainly was not available to the Ottoman government during the nineteenth century. After the signing of the Free Trade Treaties, the Ottoman state did not have any independence with respect to commercial policy. Under pressure from European powers, *ad valorem* customs duties on imports and exports were maintained at nominally low levels, and conditions of 'open economy' prevailed until World War I.[48]

Chapter 4

Foreign capital in the Ottoman Empire, 1854–1913

Large amounts of capital from the industrialized countries were invested in the periphery during the nineteenth century. These investments can be grouped under two headings: (a) direct investments in enterprises and (b) lending to governments. During the period before World War I, most of the direct investment was placed in infrastructure such as railroads and ports rather than in production activities such as agriculture or industry. A limited amount of investment in mining would be the most important exception to this generalization. Moreover, that part of lending to governments which was used for investment rather than for meeting current expenditures also went primarily to infrastructure such as railroads. As a result, most of the foreign investment in the periphery did not directly alter the patterns of production. Rather, it facilitated the expansion of center–periphery trade through the development of infrastructure. As this trade expanded, however, the economies in the periphery were increasingly pulled into the international division of labor and patterns of production did change. Agricultural commodity production for world markets expanded and there was a general decline in handicrafts-based manufacturing activities due to competition from imported industrial products.

The examination of the role of foreign capital cannot be limited to changes in the patterns of trade and production and their consequences. We also need to establish the role played by foreign capital in the process of capital accumulation. In order to provide an answer to this inquiry, we would need to establish, at the very least, the long-term fluctuations or long-term swings in the direction and magnitude of funds flows arising from foreign investment. We would need to compare the volume of capital inflows with outflows of funds in the form of principal and interest payments and profit transfers. Such a quantitative approach will enable us to provide a more complete assessment of the role of foreign capital in the Ottoman Empire. Along with the examination of long-term fluctuations in Ottoman foreign trade and Ottoman external terms of trade, it will also help us define the distinct world economic conjunctures faced by the Ottoman Empire during different periods of the nineteenth century.[1]

This chapter adopts a balance of payments framework and establishes the long-term fluctuations in funds flows arising from foreign investment in the Ottoman Empire. We will examine Ottoman state borrowing and direct foreign investment in the Empire separately and also provide a qualitative assessment of the role of foreign capital in the transformation of the patterns of trade and production.

One of the most important features of the Ottoman case that distinguished it from others in the periphery during the nineteenth century was the existence of conditions of inter-imperialist rivalry. This chapter will also establish the long-term changes in the shares of major European powers in total foreign investment in the Ottoman Empire. When taken together with long-term changes in the shares of major European powers in Ottoman foreign trade, these quantitative trends should enable us to gain new insights into economic and political aspects of this inter-imperialist rivalry.

Foreign capital in Ottoman state borrowing, 1854–1913

The development of European financial control of the Ottoman Empire into one of the most striking forms of imperialist penetration short of *de jure* colonialism and the abundance of primary source materials as a result of that control have helped turn this subject into one of the most studied aspects of recent Ottoman history.[2] Our focus here will be somewhat different from that of most of the existing literature. We will be concerned primarily with establishing and analysing the long-term trends and fluctuations in capital inflows and debt payments arising from Ottoman external borrowing.

Behind Ottoman foreign borrowing lies the weakness of the central bureaucracy, and its inability to find a long-term solution to its long-standing fiscal crisis and budgetary deficits.[3] More than to the weakness of the underlying economy, the fiscal crisis was due to the appropriation of a large part of potential tax revenues by powerful intermediaries. Until the second quarter of the nineteenth century, frequent debasing of the coinage provided the state with additional revenues to meet its expenditures. For example, during the reign of Mahmoud II (1808–39), when frequent wars led to unusually heavy fiscal burdens, the specie content of gold coins was changed 35 times. As a result of such frequent debasing, the exchange rate or the gold equivalent of Ottoman currency declined from 23 kurus to one British pound in 1814 to 104 kurus to the pound in 1839.[4] In addition, private bankers, the so-called Galata bankers with connections in Europe, provided short-term loans to the state at high rates of interest.

By the 1840s debasing had become an ineffective and costly method for creating additional revenues for the state. High rates of inflation accompanying this process had made it clear that there were social and political limits to the rate of debasing. Moreover, the crisis of confidence and uncertainties arising from the frequent devaluations had unfavorable effects on the economy which in turn reduced tax revenues. Yet the financial needs of the central state had expanded enormously. Especially during periods of war, budget deficits were becoming so large that neither acceptable rates of debasing nor the financial reserves of the Galata bankers could close the gap.

During the 1840s European financiers, merchants and government representatives began to encourage the Ottoman government to start borrowing abroad to solve its fiscal difficulties. European bankers who would receive substantial commissions for arranging the flotation of Ottoman bonds in European financial markets stood to gain the most from Ottoman external borrowing. At the same time, Ottoman borrowing would mobilize small-scale savings in Europe and provide interest income for them. Furthermore, since the Ottoman government would use at least part of these funds for the importation of various manufactures, particularly military supplies, European lending would lead to the creation of additional demand for European industry.

Another issue that concerned European capital was the instability of the Ottoman monetary system. As long as Ottoman budgetary deficits were financed by debasing or by the printing of paper money, the fluctuations in and the uncertainty associated with the exchange rate of the Ottoman currency had an unfavorable impact on Ottoman trade with Europe. If Ottoman borrowing from European financial markets could ensure the stability of the Lira, this would, in turn, facilitate the expansion of the exchange between European manufactures and Ottoman primary products.[5]

Hence in the 1840s both fiscal difficulties and European interests created pressures on the central bureaucracy to start external borrowing. As a first step, the Galata bankers began borrowing from European banks and then passed on these short-term funds to the Ottoman government. After several attempts at formal external borrowing failed because of the hesitancy of the Ottoman bureaucracy, formal long-term borrowing in European financial markets started in 1854, as fiscal difficulties intensified even further during the Crimean War.[6]

Table 4.1 and figure 3 present the summary results of our calculations to establish the annual magnitudes of all funds flows arising from Ottoman external borrowing until World War I utilizing the data available from the debt contracts and from the records of the Ottoman

Table 4.1. *Funds flows arising from Ottoman external borrowing, 1854–1914*
Annual averages for each period in thousands of British pounds sterling

Sub-periods	Nominal value of new issues 1	Net capital inflows 2	Principal payments 3	Net capital flows 4 = 2 - 3	Interest payments 5	Total payments 6 = 3 + 5	Net funds flows 7 = 2 - 6
I 1854–75	8,300	4,660	676	3,984	2,432	3,108	1,552
IA 1854–68	2,954	2,049	300	1,749	1,027	1,327	722
IB 1869–75	19,755	10,256	1,482	8,774	5,442	6,924	3,332
II 1876–81	433	433	61	372	608	669	–236
III 1882–1913	2,217	1,783	855	928	2,893	3,748	–1,965
IIIA 1882–1901	1,315	844	662	182	2,455	3,117	–2,273
IIIB 1902–13	3,721	3,347	1,178	2,169	3,623	4,801	–1,454
1854–1914 Total	296,850	180,619	44,047	136,572	152,390	196,437	–15,818

Note: Since this table was prepared in order to calculate the international funds flows arising from the Ottoman state debt rather than to analyze Ottoman state finances, that part of the Ottoman debt held by foreigners and by its citizens inside the Ottoman Empire, Treasury bonds and short-term borrowing by the Ottoman Treasury have been excluded from the above figures. The most important components of this 'internal borrowing' were that part of the pre-1881 issues which remained within the Empire, issues of 1877 and 1906 and Treasury bonds and short-term borrowing after 1910. The large issue of 1914 is not included in columns III and IIIB.
1 British pound sterling = 1.10 Ottoman Lira. For annual figures and sources, see appendix 3, tables A3.1 and A3.2.

Public Debt Administration.[7] It appears on the basis of our calculations that Ottoman external borrowing can be best examined in two distinct periods: 1854 to 1876 and 1881 to 1913.

The most important characteristic of the first period, which lasted until the default of 1875–6, was the large volume of borrowing and the increasingly unfavorable terms of loans. Interest rates cited in the contracts were always around 4 to 5 per cent of the nominal value of the bonds.[8] However, the new issues were sold at prices far below their nominal values. The commissions of the international banks which arranged the flotation of these bonds were then subtracted from these gross revenues. Therefore, the effective rate of annual interest paid on funds that actually entered the Ottoman Treasury, a good measure of the terms of borrowing, was much higher than 4 to 5 per cent. As the condition of Ottoman finances deteriorated, net receipts of the Ottoman Treasury as a fraction of the nominal value of new issues dropped below 50 per cent. In other words, for every pound sterling that entered the Treasury, the Ottoman government began to incur a long-term debt of more than two pounds. For this reason, the effective rate of interest on external borrowing rarely fell below 10 per cent after 1860; at times it exceeded 12 per cent.[9]

For a period of constant if not declining world price levels, these effective rates of interest appear quite high. A comparison of these terms with those under which other governments borrowed in European financial markets during the same period confirms that Ottoman borrowing was secured under extraordinarily unfavorable conditions.[10] However, this should not be surprising, since Ottoman finances did not show any improvement until 1875. A large part of every new borrowing was used for meeting the payments on earlier loans. The rest went almost entirely to current expenditures, including higher levels of consumption expenditures for the palace and the purchase from Europe of a large navy.[11]

As a result, within a short period of time annual payments of interest and principal on the outstanding debt rose beyond the capacity of the Ottoman finances and the economy. Our calculations indicate that the ratio of annual debt payments to total state revenues, excluding new borrowing, escalated from 10 per cent in the early 1860s to 30 per cent in the early 1870s and to 50 per cent in the mid-1870s. Similarly, the ratio of annual debt payments to export earnings, which might be taken as a crude measure of the payment capacity of the economy, rose from 10 per cent in the early 1860s to more than 50 per cent in the mid-1870s.[12]

Despite these trends, the Ottoman government was able to borrow increasingly larger amounts in the European financial markets, albeit

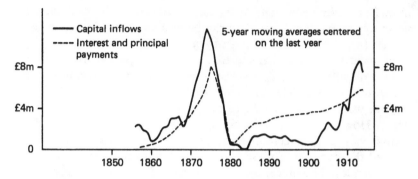

Figure 3 Funds flows arising from Ottoman foreign borrowing, 1854–1913 (in millions of British pounds sterling).

under increasingly unfavorable terms. In Europe, everyone involved seemed to benefit from this process. In Blaisdell's words, 'to allow Turkey to borrow money offered an opportunity to the speculator and financier to realize quick and easy profits and to the small investor a chance to obtain high interest'.[13] The pace of new borrowing accelerated markedly after 1868. As table 4.1 shows, the nominal value of new Ottoman borrowing had averaged close to £3 million per year during 1854–68. During this period net receipts of the Treasury arising from new borrowing had averaged £2 million per year, £1.3 million of which was used for interest and principal payments on the outstanding debt. The nominal value of new borrowing jumped more than six times to £19.8 million per year during 1869–75. The net receipts of the Treasury arising from new borrowing rose to £10.3 million per year, and payments on the outstanding debt averaged £6.9 million per year during the same period. To illustrate the extraordinary magnitudes involved after 1868, we might note that total revenues of the Ottoman state, excluding new borrowing, were estimated at no more than £18 million per year during the early 1870s.[14] In other words, the nominal value of new borrowing exceeded the estimated revenues of the central government during 1869–75.

The borrowing mania continued as long as the Ottoman government, speculators and financiers could locate new funds in the European financial markets in excess of the large annual debt payments. However, a default would be inevitable if securing new funds became more difficult. With the financial crises of 1873 in Europe and the United States, which also signalled the beginning of the Great Depression, capital exports to the periphery came to an abrupt halt.[15] After the sale in 1874 of a new issue whose flotation had been arranged earlier, new funds could not be secured. Under these circumstances, the Ottoman government announced in the fall of 1875 its decision to reduce all debt payments by half. Debt payments were stopped altogether in 1876. It should be emphasized that the Ottoman Empire was hardly alone in this respect. Close to a dozen countries in the periphery also defaulted or obtained rescheduling of their debt payments between 1872 and 1875. For these countries, fiscal and external payments difficulties constituted one of the early repercussions of the Great Depression of 1873–96.[16]

The default of 1875–6 provided European financial interests with an opportunity to establish closer control over Ottoman finance and to ensure an uninterrupted flow of funds out of the Ottoman economy towards the servicing of the debt. After a five-year period of war, uncertainty and negotiations, the Ottoman Public Debt Administration was founded in 1881. The control of some of the major sources of revenue of the state was then handed over to this Administration for payments towards the outstanding debt.[17]

The years from 1882 to 1913 constitute the second distinct period in Ottoman external borrowing. The most important characteristic of this period is the reversal in the direction of net funds flows as a result of European financial control. As table 4.1 reveals, while funds inflows from external borrowing averaged £1.8 million per year during 1882–1913, debt payments were more than twice as high at £3.7 million per year. These payments represented 20 to 30 per cent of the total revenues of the Treasury. At the same time, this close financial control reduced the risk associated with new Ottoman bond issues in European financial markets. The effective rates of interest on new borrowing remained considerably lower after 1881: they fluctuated between 5 and 7 per cent until 1910 and rose to 8 per cent after that date.[18]

The years 1882 to 1913 can be further divided into two sub-periods, 1882–1901 and 1902–13. New borrowing remained limited until 1901, but there was an acceleration in both new borrowing and in the annual debt payments after that year. On the other hand, in both sub-periods debt payments exceeded inflows of funds arising from new borrowing by a large margin.

After the foundation of the Public Debt Administration and the transfer of some of the major sources of fiscal revenue to that organization, the Ottoman central bureaucracy became hesitant about securing new loans abroad. Moreover, this early period was a relatively peaceful one for the Empire. The absence of wartime expenditures enabled the government to balance the budget with lower levels of external borrowing. On an annual basis, the level of new borrowing during 1882–1901 was lower than that of any other sub-period between 1854 and World War I. The nominal value of new Ottoman borrowing averaged £1.3 million per year during these two decades. This was about one-third of the annual averages for 1902–13 and less than one-tenth of the rate of new borrowing during 1869–75 (see column 1 in table 4.1).

Ottoman budgetary deficits began to grow once again after the turn of the century. At first, short-term borrowing from the Ottoman Bank and from other financial institutions inside the Empire increased. However, this could not delay for long higher levels of borrowing from the European markets. The increases in military expenditures further exacerbated the fiscal difficulties. By the early 1910s, Ottoman finances had returned to that stage where payments on the outstanding debt could be met only by obtaining increasingly larger amounts of new foreign loans. By most criteria, the situation resembled that of the mid-1870s. Another default did not materialize only because of the outbreak of World War I.[19]

The effects of long-term price movements on the Ottoman debt burden should also be taken into account in any long-term analysis. World prices of primary products and manufactures declined at moderate rates during 1855–73, and the rates of decline of prices accelerated during the Great Depression of 1873–96. For example, from 1855 to 1873, prices of Ottoman exports to the industrialized center countries declined by 29 per cent. From 1873 to 1896, they declined by another 41 per cent, bringing the total fall since 1855 to 58 per cent.[20] Consequently, the real amount of annual interest and principal payments that the Ottoman Treasury was obliged to pay as the result of a loan contracted in 1855 more than doubled during the next four decades. In contrast to the prices of Ottoman exports, world price levels of both primary products and manufactures rose after 1896. Between 1896 and 1913 prices of Ottoman exports to industrialized center countries increased by 27 per cent.[21] This was the only sub-period when the real burden of the Ottoman debt declined because of long-term changes in world price levels.

Foreign capital in direct investment, 1859–1913

This section attempts to estimate the magnitudes of capital flows into and profit transfers out of the Ottoman economy arising from foreign investment in all areas outside the public debt prior to World War I. We will provide estimates for these annual flows and for the foreign capital stock at different points in time, accompanied by sectoral distributions and distributions according to the country of origin.

Rather than limiting the study to the scattered estimates of the foreign capital stock by various contemporary observers, we decided to utilize firm-level data which had not been employed previously for this purpose. Available in a manual prepared by E. Pech, an employee of the Ottoman Bank, are detailed histories of all the joint-stock companies, including more than 80 which were controlled by foreign capital, operating in the Ottoman Empire in 1910.[22] Contained in the information provided in the manual are the dates and amounts of paid-in capital and debentures for each firm and the dividends. Where dividend information was incomplete, we approximated it from the average stock price of the firm for the following year by assuming a rate of return on financial capital comparable to the rates of return being realized by other firms in the same industry in the Ottoman Empire. Pech did not provide information on the country (or countries) of origin of the paid-in capital for each firm. We obtained this information from other sources. Furthermore, because of the unavailability of relevant data, we assumed that the debentures originated from the same country (or countries) as did the paid-in capital. In the environment of intense inter-imperialist rivalry over the Ottoman Empire, the capital of each European country attempted to prevent the participation of the capital of other countries in their ventures, opening projects to the capital of other countries only if the necessary funds could not be obtained in the financial markets of their own country. The political–diplomatic histories of the period abound with examples of this mode of operation. For this reason, our assumption cannot be expected to seriously bias the estimates.

In some areas, especially in commerce, mining and industry, the literature points to the presence of a considerable amount of foreign capital in companies other than those of joint-stock form. In those cases information provided by Pech was supplemented by the secondary sources. Moreover, to the extent that they were founded by foreign-owned companies already operating inside the Ottoman Empire, some of the joint-stock companies were left out of the capital flow estimate. However, these companies were included in our estimates of the sectoral distribution of foreign capital stock for the years 1888 and 1914.[23]

Another potential shortcoming of our calculations is that information on the participation of domestic capital in foreign-controlled firms, however limited this participation might have been, was unavailable in most instances. In these cases the involvement of domestic capital has been assumed to be negligible. On the basis of the secondary literature and a survey of the lists of boards of directors provided by Pech, and considering the trend that the share of domestic capital tended to diminish as company size increased, we find it highly unlikely that this bias will affect the final results by more than two to three percentage points.

Estimation of international capital flows of the past has always been a hazardous occupation. We do not claim our estimates to be free of error; however, a detailed study of the primary and secondary source materials indicates that our estimates are consistent with the foreign capital stock estimates of contemporary observers, most of which were prepared on the eve of World War I. Moreover, the utilization of detailed data on the history of individual firms has enabled us to gain major insights, for the first time, into the intertemporal fluctuations in the magnitudes of capital inflows and profit transfers and the changes over time in the country distribution of these funds flows. The results are summarized in figure 4 and tables 4.2 and 4.3. They are presented in more detail in appendix 3.[24]

Total foreign capital stock estimates presented in table 4.2 and 4.3 indicate that the volume of total direct foreign investment in the Ottoman Empire remained below the nominal value of outstanding external debt until World War I. However, between 1888 and 1914 the rate of growth of direct foreign investment was higher than the rate of growth of foreign lending to the Ottoman government. As a result, the size of foreign capital stock in direct investment increased from one-seventh of the value of outstanding foreign debt in 1888 to half of the same by 1914.

Direct foreign investment in the Ottoman Empire was concentrated in two sub-periods, as shown in figure 4. The largest wave of investment took place between 1888 and 1896. During these nine years, total foreign capital inflows arising from direct investment exceeded £30 million. This figure amounts to no less than 40 per cent of all foreign direct investment in the Empire until 1914 (see appendix 3, table A3.2 for details). Most of this capital inflow was directed towards railroad construction. A second and more limited wave of direct foreign investment occurred after 1905. During the nine-year period 1905–13, more than £17 million of foreign capital was invested in areas outside the state debt. Again, the largest share of these funds went to railroad construction. In contrast, direct foreign investment remained limited before 1875, particularly during 1876–87.

Profit transfers arising from direct foreign investment increased steadily from the early 1860s until World War I. However, because their absolute levels remained low until the 1880s and because of the large wave of direct foreign investment during 1888–96, it was only after 1896 that profit transfers began to exceed new capital inflows.

We can now examine long-term fluctuations in the direction of net funds flows arising from direct foreign investment together with those

Table 4.2. *Sectoral distribution of the foreign capital stock at the beginning of 1888*
Figures indicate sum of paid-in capital and debentures in thousands of pounds

	French	%	British	%	German	%	Other	%	Total	%	Share of sectors in the total %
Railroads	648	12.3	3,349	63.3	166	3.1	1,120	21.2	5,283	100.0	33.4
Ports	—	—	—	—	—	—	—	—	—	—	—
Utilities	87	5.9	961	65.3	—	—	424	28.2	1,472	100.0	9.3
Banking	2,500	50.0	2,500	50.0	—	—	—	—	5,000	100.0	31.6
Commerce	700	54.7	580	45.3	—	—	—	—	1,280	100.0	8.1
Industry	900	47.5	795	42.0	—	—	200	10.6	1,895	100.0	12.0
Mining	185	20.7	710	79.3	—	—	—	—	895	100.0	5.6
Total direct investment	5,020	31.7	8,895	56.2	166	1.1	1,744	11.0	15,825	100.0	100.0
Outstanding state debt in 1890 (nominal value)	44,600	37.6	27,400	23.1	13,800	11.7	32,700	27.6	118,500	100.0	

Notes: For a discussion of the procedure employed in estimating direct foreign investment, see the text.

The nominal value of new Ottoman borrowing remained substantially above the actual receipts of the Treasury during this period. However, two resettlements of the Ottoman state debt in 1881 and 1903 reduced the nominal value of the outstanding debt by approximately 40 per cent each, to the level of the actual funds received. Therefore, the figures for the nominal value of the outstanding debt given in these tables approximate closely the true magnitude of the foreign capital inflows net of principal payments. For further details of the country distribution of the state debt see tables 4.4 and 4.5.

Sources: Pech (1911) was the most important source in the estimation of direct foreign investment. For others see notes for table A3.3 in appendix 3.

Table 4.3: *Sectoral distribution of the foreign capital stock in the Ottoman Empire at the end of 1913*
Sum of paid-in capital and debentures in thousands of pounds

	French	%	British	%	German	%	Other	%	Total	%	Share of sectors in the total %
Railroads	23,247	49.6	4,588	9.8	17,248	36.8	1,785	3.8	46,868	100.0	63.1
Ports	2,206	69.1	409	12.8	576	18.1	—	—	3,191	100.0	4.3
Utilities	1,701	44.6	363	9.5	304	8.0	1,449	38.0	3,817	100.0	5.1
Banking	3,400	38.2	2,950	33.1	1,750	19.7	800	9.0	8,900	100.0	12.0
Insurance	450	81.8	100	18.2	—	—	—	—	550	100.0	0.7
Commerce	3,031	70.7	757	17.6	300	7.0	200	4.7	4,288	100.0	5.8
Industry	1,220	30.8	1,665	42.1	300	7.6	774	19.6	3,959	100.0	5.3
Mining	2,007	73.5	450	16.5	175	6.4	100	3.7	2,732	100.0	3.7
Total direct investment	37,262	50.4	11,282	15.3	20,653	27.5	5,108	6.8	74,305	100.0	100.0
Outstanding state debt (nominal value)	75,300	53.0	19,900	14.0	29,900	21.0	17,100	12.0	142,200	100.0	
Total	112,562	52.0	31,182	14.9	50,553	23.2	22,208	10.2	216,505	100.0	

For notes and sources see table 4.2.

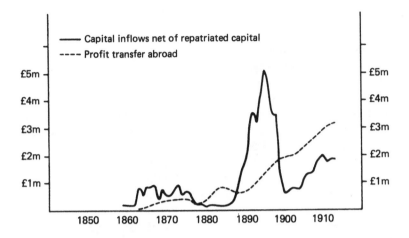

Figure 4 Funds flows arising from direct foreign investment in the Ottoman Empire, 1859–1913 (in millions of British pounds sterling). For annual figures see appendix 3, table A3.3.

arising from Ottoman external borrowing. Between 1854 and 1875, capital inflows arising from both direct and indirect foreign investment exceeded outflows of funds in the form of profit transfers and debt payments by an average of £1.9 million per year. The direction of net funds flows changed during 1876–87, at first because new capital inflows stopped and later because of large debt payments after the foundation of the Ottoman Public Debt Administration. With the large wave of direct foreign investment during 1886–96, the direction of net funds flows was reversed once again. Inflows of capital remained above outflows of funds by an average of £0.6 million per year during these nine years. Finally, during 1897–1913 debt payments and profit transfers exceeded all inflows of foreign capital by an average of £2.1 million per year. In other words, net outflows of funds were larger during the years just preceding World War I than during any other sub-period since 1854.[25]

As for the sectoral distribution of direct foreign investment, railroads, with close to two-thirds of directly invested foreign capital stock in 1914, emerge as the most important area for foreign investment after the state debt. If foreign capital invested in ports and in commerce is added to this figure, the share of investment oriented towards the expansion of trade, particularly international trade, exceeds 73 per cent of directly invested foreign capital stock. Part of the foreign capital in banking and insurance can also be included in this category. In contrast, the shares of directly productive activities such as mining and industry remained below 9 per cent of all direct foreign investment. Foreign capital in agriculture was rather insignificant until 1914.[26]

The concentration of foreign investment in the Ottoman Empire in the state debt and in railroads is in line with the basic patterns of investment during the nineteenth century exhibited by European capital around the world, particularly in the periphery. At the end of 1913, of the £3,700 million of British capital abroad around 42 per cent was invested in railroads. The share of foreign government bonds in British investment abroad was approximately 26 per cent.[27] French and German investment abroad during World War I showed a similar pattern with the exception that, because of the more active role played by the governments of these two countries in directing investment abroad, the share of foreign government bonds was considerably higher than the corresponding share in British overseas investment. Of the £1,800 million of French capital abroad in 1914, close to two-thirds was invested in foreign state debts; the railroads' share was over 15 per cent.[28] Of the £750 million of German capital invested abroad during 1880–1914, 64 per cent went to foreign government bonds while the railroads absorbed approximately 25 per cent.[29]

Railroads and their timing

Railroad construction in the Ottoman Empire will be examined in somewhat greater detail here in view of their large share in total direct foreign investment and in view of the important role they played in the incorporation of the Empire into the world economy during the nineteenth century. We will also attempt to explain the timing of the largest wave of railroad construction in the Ottoman Empire.

From the point of view of European capital, construction and operation of railroads were profitable forms of investment, especially as a result of the kilometric guarantee payments made by the Ottoman government. At the same time, they played a major role in providing inexpensive raw materials, foodstuffs and markets for manufactures to the country whose capital built and operated the railroad. When patterns of capital inflows into different regions of the Ottoman Empire are examined together with the growth of the external trade of each region, railroad construction by foreign capital emerges as one of the key developments in the partitioning of the Empire into spheres of influence among the European imperialist powers prior to World War I.

Railroad construction in a given region of the Empire led to the importation of construction equipment and rolling stock from the country whose capital owned the railroad company. The demand for the products of European iron and steel industries created by railroad construction in the peripheral countries was by no means negligible both in absolute terms and in terms of their share in the total production of these industries. After their construction, the railroads, with the help of the financial and commercial capital of the same European country, began to increase the export-oriented agricultural commodity production in the regions they penetrated. At the same time, various forms of pre-industrial manufacturing activity were being destroyed by competition from European manufactures whose prices in the regions were reduced with the arrival of the railroad. As the commercialization of agriculture and specialization in agricultural exportables proceeded, demand for European manufactured products increased further. Thus the region's trade with the European country whose capital owned the railroad company grew rapidly.[30]

In many instances, the only banks in the region were owned by the capital of the same country. The monopoly position enjoyed by the capital of that European country in extending agricultural and commercial credit and in transportation blocked commercial competition from other European powers to a large extent. At a later stage, capital from the same European country began to invest in other ventures in the region. During the nineteenth century these investments were concentrated in utilities (water, gas, electricity), in the construction of ports in those coastal cities which linked the railroads to the European country, in industry and, to some extent, in mining. This general pattern can be observed in the penetration of British capital into Western Anatolia after the construction of railroads in that region in the early 1860s, of French capital into Syria starting in the early 1890s, and of German capital into Central and Southeastern Anatolia in the 1890s with the construction of the Anatolian and later of the Baghdad Railways.[31]

Another aspect of direct foreign investment in the Ottoman Empire that needs to be explored further is the concentration of capital inflows, particularly of railroad construction in the years 1888–96. The timing of this major wave can be explained, to some extent, by international forces. It was in the second half of the 1880s that Germany, as a latecomer to inter-imperialist rivalry, began to focus on the Balkans and the Middle East. After Germany obtained a concession from the Ottoman government in 1888 to build the first part of the Baghdad Railway, French capital joined the scramble for concessions and within a short period ended up constructing a longer railway network in the Ottoman Empire than did German capital.[32]

However, in any explanation of the timing of the wave of 1888–96, domestic factors should also be emphasized. During the 1880s the

Ottoman economy and state finances began to be affected unfavorably by a series of world economic changes. The Great Depression had an unfavorable impact on Ottoman foreign trade, and the rate of growth of Ottoman exports dropped considerably after 1873. In addition, world price levels declined steadily and the terms of trade in world markets turned against exporters of primary commodities.[33] As a result, between 1880 and 1890, the receipts of the Ottoman Treasury from its two basic sources of revenue, the tithe and customs duties, actually declined. At the same time, the Ottoman Public Debt Administration had begun to control state finances. During the 1880s annual payments on the external debt averaged close to £3 million, about 20 per cent of all revenues of the Treasury.[34] Because of this control and in contrast to conditions in the third quarter of the century, the central bureaucracy was hesitant about initiating another round of external borrowing. The unfavorable conditions in the European financial markets may also have played a role in keeping new Ottoman borrowing limited during this period. Therefore, at a time when German capital and French capital were competing for railroad concessions, the central bureaucracy was searching for a long-term solution to its fiscal crisis.

Under these circumstances, railroad construction by foreign capital appeared attractive to the Ottoman central bureaucracy for a number of reasons. Most important, by reducing costs of transportation to the more distant areas, they could open up hitherto uncultivated land into agricultural production for export, thereby raising tithe and customs revenues. Second, railroads would link the remote corners of the Empire to Istanbul during times of war and peace. In addition to the obvious political and military advantages of such a network, it would strengthen the central government's hand and reduce the share of local intermediaries in the collection of tax revenues.[35]

A third potential benefit was related to developments in the international wheat markets. The rapid decline of world wheat prices after the entry of American wheat in the 1870s had led to the adoption of protectionist policies in Continental Europe. Yet, according to the Free Trade Treaties in effect, the Ottoman government could not raise its own tariffs without the consent of European powers. As a result, Ottoman exports of wheat steadily lost ground from competition of wheat from North America, Russia and elsewhere.[36] A more dramatic result was that important wheat began to increase its share in the urban markets of the Empire. The most important reason for the high domestic prices of Ottoman wheat was the absence of an adequate transportation network between wheat-growing regions of the interior, particularly Central Anatolia, and major ports and urban markets. The construction of railroads in Central Anatolia would facilitate the competition of this region's wheat in the domestic and international markets. This would also mean additional tithe revenues for the central government.[37]

In the end, however, the railroads did not provide the expected fiscal relief. An examination of tithe revenues at the province level does show that they increased more rapidly in regions with railroads.[38] However, additional payments by the government to the railroad companies in the form of kilometric guarantees far exceeded the increases in revenues. For example, total kilometric guarantee payments to the Anatolian Railway Company were in excess of £3 million during 1893–1909, while total tithe revenues collected from the major wheat-growing province of Ankara during the same period remained below this sum.[39]

Finally, we turn to an assessment of the contribution of foreign capital to the process of capital accumulation in the Empire during the nineteenth century. We have emphasized earlier that funds inflows arising from state external borrowing were not directed towards investment, but were used almost entirely to meet current expenditures. For this reason, we will focus only on direct foreign investment.

The only available estimate on the subject approximates the volume of annual gross investment in the Ottoman Empire at £17 million for the fiscal years 1907–8 and 1913–14.[40] In comparison, our estimates indicated that annual inflows of capital into the Empire arising from direct foreign investment were around £1.7 million during the same period. In other words, foreign capital is estimated to have accounted for no more than 10 per cent of gross domestic investment in the years preceding World War I. This share was probably lower in the earlier period, since direct foreign investment was more limited, except during the period 1888–96.

We also need to consider the direction and magnitude of net funds flows arising from foreign investment. Our estimates show that profit transfers abroad arising from direct foreign investment averaged £3 million per year during the decade preceding World War I, exceeding new capital inflows considerably. For the period 1859–1914 as a whole, capital inflows due to direct foreign investment exceeded profit transfers by only £0.3 million per year.[41] This evidence indicates that, at best, foreign capital did not play a major role in the process of capital accumulation in the Ottoman Empire. At worst, when we also consider funds flows rising from state external borrowing, foreign capital took away more in the form of profit transfers and debt payments than it brought into the Empire between 1854 and 1914.

In what respect, then, was direct foreign investment important? Its importance in the Ottoman Empire lies in the role it played in expanding

the trade between Ottoman agricultural products and European manufactures during the nineteenth century. As noted earlier, close to three-
fourths of all direct foreign investment in the Empire was concentrated in
railroads and other large-scale infrastructure such as ports aimed at
expanding this long-distance trade. Foreign investment in directly
productive activities such as agriculture, mining and industry remained
limited until 1914. If foreign capital had an impact on the dissolution of
the existing mode of production, that occurred indirectly, since these
investments helped change the patterns of production, pulled the
Ottoman economy more closely into the international division of labor,
and facilitated the expansion of commodity production in agriculture.

The changing shares of European powers in foreign investment

The incorporation of the Ottoman Empire into the world economy
during the nineteenth century proceeded under conditions of inter-
imperialist rivalry. In order to investigate the economic aspects of this
rivalry, it will be necessary to examine the relative shares of the Great
Powers in Ottoman external trade and in foreign investment. Having
looked at the former in chapter 2, we will establish in this section the
changes over time in the shares of Britain, France and Germany in
foreign investment in the Ottoman Empire. We will deal with external
borrowing and direct foreign investment separately. Below we discuss
some of the implications of the conditions of rivalry more generally.

External borrowing

It is difficult to give a precise account of the year-to-year changes in the
amounts of Ottoman bonds held in different European countries. An
exact record of the amounts sold in each European country at the time of
their emission is unavailable. Moreover, even those figures would be
inadequate, since Ottoman bonds changed hands from one European
country to another after their date of emission. Nevertheless, information
from several sources is still detailed enough to establish the long-term
trends in the relative shares of bondholders from different European
countries, especially for those of France, Britain and Germany.

As a crude first measure, we can establish the European stock
exchanges where the new Ottoman emissions were primarily purchased
on the date of issue. It is clear from table 4.4, where this information is
summarized, that British capital purchased most of the early issues and
remained in the market until the default of 1875–6, though its share in the

outstanding debt began to decline after the early 1860s. French capital emerged as the largest purchaser of Ottoman bonds in the 1860s and steadily increased its share after that date. There was a brief period in the early 1870s when Austrian investors entered the market. German capital, on the other hand, was not important in this period before the default.

Du Velay, reviewing the changes in the country distribution of the Ottoman debt up to the early 1870s, reaches a similar conclusion:

From the Crimean War up to the death of Lord Palmerston at the end of 1865, the English were in the first place. The first loans were emitted in England, the first Ottoman Bank was founded in London, and in Constantinople it was the English who obtained the first railroad concessions for Varna–Ruschuk, Izmir–Aydın and Kasaba-Izmir . . . [As their interest diminished,] the French immediately took their place [as the largest purchaser of the new Ottoman emissions] starting in 1866.[42]

More detailed information is available regarding the country distribution of the external debt in the period after 1881. The imposition of European financial control and the resettlement of the debt resulted in substantial changes in both its nominal amount and its servicing. In 1881, the bondholders were asked to convert the old bonds for issues in the major financial centers of Europe. A similar operation was undertaken in 1898 for the same pre-1881 debt. These two censuses provide detailed information on the changing country distribution of the pre-1881 debt. Moreover, various estimates were made in 1914 regarding the country distribution of the bondholders of the total outstanding debt in that year. These data are summarized in table 4.5. The following trends emerge from an examination of tables 4.4 and 4.5.

During 1881–98, there was a rapid decline in the volume of bonds held by British capital and their share in the total debt. This was partly due to the fact that the issues which were purchased in large amounts by British investors in the 1850s and 1860s were the first to be redeemed by the Ottoman Public Debt Administration. However, the magnitude of the decline leaves no doubt that the British were also selling some of their holdings to investors in other European countries. Moreover, the new Ottoman issues purchased by British capital during 1881–1914 remained at a minimum level.

Paralleling the decline in the British share, shares of French, German and Belgian investors increased during 1881–1914. French capital further expanded its share as the largest purchaser of the Ottoman bonds. The French–British-owned Ottoman Bank played an important role in this process. It frequently arranged the flotation of new Ottoman bonds in the European stock exchanges. More a representative of French

Table 4.4. *Ottoman bond issues and major purchasers, 1854–1914*

Date of emission	Nominal value in 000s of pounds sterling	Major purchasers in order of decreasing importance	Date of emission	Nominal value in 000s of pounds sterling	Major purchasers in order of decreasing importance
1854	3,000	B nearly all	1890	4,545	F 90%
1855	5,000	B nearly all	1891	6,317	3/4 in B: less than 1/4 in F
1858–9	5,000	B nearly all			
1860	2,037	F; none in B	1893	910	F all
1862	8,000	B nearly all	1894	1,600	G, F
1863–4	8,000	F	1894	579[a]	F, B
1865	6,000	F	1896	2,975	F 90%
1865	7,273[a]	F; B (approx. 1/4)	1903	2,160	G, F, B
1869	22,000	F	1903	1,294[a]	G all
1870	31,680	A, G, I; none in F, B	1903	1,534[a]	F, ?
1871	5,700	B, F	1904	2,500	F
1872	11,126	B, A, G (F?)	1905	2,400	G all
1873	11,465	F, B (approx. 1/4)	1908	9,080	G, F, B
1873	27,778	F	1908	4,283	F, ?
1874	40,000	F, B (approx. 1/4)	1910	1,557	F
Default			1911	909	F
1877	2,600	F 90%	1911	6,400	G
1886	6,500	F	1913	1,350	?
1888	1,471	G all	1914	20,000	F, ?

Notes: B = Britain, F = France, G = Germany, A = Austria, I = Italy.

[a]Conversion of an earlier issue. The figure given indicates the nominal value of the issue in excess of the amount prior to the conversion.

Sources: Sources cited in appendix 3, tables A3.1, A3.2; in addition, Neymarck (1908), Block (1906), Stock Exchange Official Intelligence (1908), Borsen-Enquete Kommision (1893), Deutsche Reich (1907), p. 231 and Vierteljahrshefte zur Statistik des Deutschen Reichs (1917), vol. 1, pp. 117–18. For the volume of purchases in France of each emission, see Thobie (1977), pp. 121–2.

interests than British, the Ottoman Bank spent every effort to sell the new issues in the French stock exchanges before they were offered elsewhere in Europe. On the other hand, German investors not only collected the old issues being sold by the British bondholders, but, after 1888, they began to buy the new Ottoman issues in large amounts with the help of Deutsche Bank. As a result, a large majority of the new Ottoman bond issues during 1881–1914 were floated by either French or German banks and were purchased primarily in these two countries.

Table 4.5. *Country distribution of the outstanding Ottoman debt, 1881–1914*
In millions of British pounds

	1881	%	1890	%	1898	%	1914[a]	%
France	45.0[b]	34.3	44.6	37.6	53.4	42.2	75.3[b]	53.0
Britain	43.5[b]	33.2	27.4	23.1	22.6	17.9	19.9[b]	14.0[c]
Germany	8.3	7.5	13.8	11.7	19.0	15.0	29.9[b]	21.0
Belgium	6.6	5.0	10.3	8.7	14.4	11.4	12.0	8.4
Austria	7.9	6.0	7.7	6.5	7.5	5.9		
Holland	7.0	5.3	5.3	4.5	3.5	2.8	5.1	3.6
Italy	5.4	4.1	3.2	2.7	1.0	0.8		
Turkey	7.3	5.6	6.2	5.2	5.0	4.0		
Total	131.0	100.0	118.5	100.0	126.4	100.0	142.2	100.0

[a]Since the nominal value of the outstanding pre-1881 Ottoman debt was reduced as a result of the resettlement of 1903, it was impossible to determine the magnitude of net capital flows during 1898–1914 on the basis of this table. For the latter, see table 4.1.
[b]That part of the Ottoman debt held by European financial institutions in Istanbul was included in the holdings of the respective countries to the extent these magnitudes could be determined.
[c]If the 1854, 1871 and 1877 issues which were serviced directly by the revenues of the Egyptian tribute (the tribute was sent from Cairo directly to London) and which had been subscribed almost entirely by British capital are excluded from these calculations, British share in 1914 falls to 5 per cent.

Sources: Eldem (1970), pp. 191, 266, 274 – based on Ottoman Public Debt Administration censuses, Anonymous (1919), Feis (1930), p. 320, Helfferich (1913), Commissioners of Inland Revenue (1872–1914).
We have arrived at the country distributions presented in this table by comparing the distributions presented in the sources listed above and making the necessary corrections in light of our own estimates presented in tables 4.1 and 4.4. The distributions for the years 1881, 1890 and 1898 include the issues of 1854, 1855, 1870, 1871 and 1877, which are excluded from the distribution given in Eldem (1970), as well as the issues of 1881–98 and the bonds held by the Ottoman Bank. Similarly, the issues secured on the Egyptian tribute, short-term borrowing and Treasury bonds are included in the distribution for 1914 given above. Also see Meray (1972), Set 1, vol. 3, pp. 190–1.

It should also be emphasized, however, that French capital purchased a substantially larger amount of the new Ottoman issues than did German capital during this period. New Ottoman issues had a total nominal value of £90 million during 1881–1914. Our calculations show that purchases in France accounted for £45–£50 million of this amount, whereas purchases in Germany did not exceed £20–£30 million (see table 4.4). If short-term borrowing and Treasury bonds of the early 1910s are included in these figures, total German purchases will increase only slightly, while French holdings will rise to £53–58 million. As a result of these developments, French capital held more than half of the total outstanding Ottoman debt by 1914. German capital had the second largest share with 21 per cent of the total, ahead of British capital, whose share had declined to 14 per cent from 33 per cent in 1881 (see table 4.5).

Direct foreign investment

An examination of changes over time in the country distribution of direct foreign investment reveals a similar pattern. Our estimates, presented in table A3.3 of appendix 3, show that British capital had the largest share in direct foreign investment during the 1860s and 1870s. Most of the incoming British capital was invested in Western Anatolia in the years following the construction of the Izmir–Aydın and Izmir–Kasaba railroads.[43] As late as 1888, British capital accounted for more than half of all foreign investment outside the state debt (see table 4.2). The share of British capital declined rapidly after that year. This decline was not due solely to large amounts of new investment by French and German capital and lower levels of new investment by the British. A more striking cause was that British capitalists started to sell some of the companies they owned to other European groups.[44] As a result, in the early 1880s outflows of funds in the form of profit transfers and repatriation of capital by the British began to exceed new capital inflows from Britain. The share of British capital in direct foreign investment in the Empire dropped sharply from 56 per cent in 1888 to a mere 15 per cent in 1914.

French capital, which had the second largest share in directly invested foreign capital stock in 1888 with 32 per cent, initiated a large wave of new investment during 1888–96. Railroad construction in the Syrian provinces was the most important component of this wave. By 1914, the share of French capital had risen above half in both direct foreign investment and in the external debt. As was the case with government bonds, the Ottoman Bank played an important role in the penetration of French capital into many parts of the Empire, especially after the withdrawal of British capital started.[45]

The year 1888 represents even more of a turning point for German investments in the Ottoman Empire. The share of German capital in total direct foreign investment was around 1 per cent at the beginning of that year. In 1888 a German group led by the Deutsche Bank obtained a concession for the construction of a railroad through Central Anatolia. Work on the Izmir–Ankara line started the next year. Also in 1888, the Deutsche Bank arranged for the flotation of a new Ottoman bond issue in the German financial markets in order to secure the railroad concession. During the next quarter century until World War I, German–French rivalry in the Ottoman Empire developed to a large extent in the form of a rivalry between the Deutsche Bank and the Ottoman Bank. By 1914,

German capital was holding the second largest share in foreign direct investment in the Empire with 27 per cent of the total.[46]

Trade, investment and inter-imperialist rivalry

The changing shares of major European powers in total foreign investment, along with changes in the shares of the same countries in Ottoman foreign trade, provide us with a good opportunity to focus on one important characteristic of the Ottoman Empire which distinguishes it from many other countries. During the nineteenth century a large number of countries in the periphery maintained their formal political independence. In most of these countries, political power remained with the alliance of export-oriented landlords and merchant capital. An important number of these countries, including many in Latin America, sooner or later joined the sphere of influence, or informal empire, of a single power which began to dominate the country's foreign trade and foreign investment. In contrast, in the Ottoman Empire political power remained in the hands of a relatively strong central bureaucracy whose interests did not necessarily coincide with rapid integration of the economy into world markets.[47]

As a result, the opening of the Ottoman economy during the nineteenth century into trade and investment did not proceed through an alliance of local landlords and merchants on the one hand and European capital on the other. Instead, the central bureaucracy played an important role in this process, so that at each stage of the process European interests were forced to come to terms with the central bureaucracy. In addition, partly because of the relative strength of this bureaucracy and partly because of the balance of international forces over the Empire, none of the European powers could pull the entire Empire into its own sphere of influence. While the relative position and influence of major European powers showed substantial changes over the course of the century, the Empire as a whole and especially the Ottoman state remained an arena for Great Power rivalry until World War I.

Having established the patterns of change in trade and investment shares of major European powers, we will be concerned in this section with some of the economic implications of this rivalry situation for the imperialist powers and for the Ottoman Empire.[48] For the capitalists of a European country, obtaining the support of their own state apparatus was quite important for all of their overseas ventures. However, in the presence of a relatively strong central bureaucracy and under conditions of rivalry, this support became much more essential, if not critical. In this respect, the withdrawal of British capital from the Ottoman Empire provides a good example of the relative position of a group of capitalists which did not receive an equally active and powerful backing from its state apparatus as did its competitors. The Ottoman case also provides yet another example of the decline of British hegemony on a world scale.

Until the end of the 1860s British foreign policy aimed at maintaining the territorial integrity of the Ottoman Empire. This policy had developed out of concern for preventing Russian expansion towards the Mediterranean and for keeping open the road to India, by far the most valuable piece of the British Empire. In addition, with its size and population the Ottoman Empire provided substantial opportunities for British trade and investment in the early and mid-nineteenth century. During the 1840s and even in the 1850s, the Ottoman Empire had a not insignificant share in total British foreign trade. Britain's entry into the Crimean War alongside the Ottoman Empire can be best understood in this political and economic context.[49] This official policy was no doubt instrumental in steadily increasing Britain's large share in Ottoman foreign trade until the 1870s. This policy also helped British capitalists claim the second largest share after French capital in direct foreign investment in the Ottoman Empire. However, it should also be emphasized that because of the absence of any serious challenge to British hegemony around the world during this mid-century period, the British state was not and did not need to be as active in its support of British ventures in the Ottoman Empire as the German state would be later in the century.[50]

When American exports of wheat and especially of cotton resumed after the end of the Civil War, Western Anatolia and the Danubian plains began to lose their attractiveness for British capital, which had regarded these areas as alternative sources of supply. After the opening of the Suez Canal in 1869, maintaining the territorial integrity of the Ottoman Empire became a lesser priority for Britain than gaining control of Egypt, which was now on the direct route to India.[51] In addition, as British trade with other areas of the world expanded, the Ottoman Empire rapidly lost its position as one of the more important markets for British manufactures. As a result, as early as the second half of the 1860s the British government began to waver regarding its long-standing policy towards the Ottoman Empire. This change did not become explicit until the Ottoman–Russian War of 1877–8. Nonetheless, the refusal of the British government to continue to provide guarantees for Ottoman public borrowing in European markets led small-scale British investors to move away from Ottoman bonds as early as the 1860s.[52]

Despite the shift in British policy and the decline in British lending to the Ottoman state, the decline in the British share of new direct foreign investment in the Ottoman Empire did not occur until the second half of the 1880s. By this time British power was becoming eclipsed, and French as well as German capital was challenging British interests around the world. Conditions in the Ottoman Empire became particularly difficult for British investors. The occupation of Egypt in 1882 had reduced British political influence in the Empire to its lowest point of the century. Yet, if British capitalists were to compete with their French and German counterparts under the emerging conditions of rivalry, equally active and effective support from their own state apparatus was essential. In the absence of such support, British capital began to withdraw to areas of formal and informal empire for Britain, in other words, to countries where British hegemony still prevailed and where active official support was perhaps not a *sine qua non* for survival.[53]

As for Germany, by the time this 'latecomer' had joined the race for markets and raw material sources, the most attractive areas of the world had been divided between Britain and France. Its colonies in West and East Africa did not appear to have particularly bright prospects. On the other hand, the ongoing Great Power rivalry over the Balkans and the Ottoman Empire had kept this region open for the entry of Germany. The policy of 'Drang nach Osten', which was pursued aggressively after the resignation of Bismarck, was firmly based on this assessment.[54]

The methods of penetration of British and German capital into the Ottoman Empire show distinct differences. Most British direct investment in the Empire took place under conditions of British hegemony when Pax Britannica and principles of Free Trade prevailed. On the other hand, German investments were undertaken at a time when inter-imperialist rivalry was on the rise around the world. German investors, therefore, had to rely on and benefited to a much greater extent from the support of their state apparatus than did British investors from theirs.[55] In addition, large banks and large industrial firms often acted jointly in German investment projects. Furthermore, most German investment outside the public debt concentrated on railroad construction, which was the most direct route to carving out spheres of influence inside the Ottoman Empire. By 1914, more than 80 per cent of German direct investment in the Ottoman Empire had been placed in railroad construction, whereas only 40 per cent of British direct investment and 60 per cent of French direct investment had gone to railroads (see table 4.3). As for the geographical distribution of direct investment, whereas British capital began to flow towards the Iraqi provinces of the Empire after the 1880s and French capital towards the Syrian provinces, German investments concentrated in Anatolia, the most important region for the central government in Istanbul.[56]

These differences notwithstanding, we need to examine further the reasons behind the rapid ascendancy of German influence in the Ottoman Empire, culminating in the entry of the Empire into World War I on the side of Germany. It has been hypothesized that after the 1880s a large part of French and British capital in the Ottoman Empire consisted of old investments, and that for this reason inflows of new capital remained substantially below outflows of funds in the form of interest and principal payments on the state debt and profit transfers. According to the same hypothesis, German capital was able to increase its influence over the Empire during this period by bringing in large amounts of new capital while its outflows of funds remained limited, thereby preventing another default on the external debt and relieving the pressure on the Ottoman balance of payments.[57] While it is true that British capital began to take out more than it brought in after 1880, it is difficult to say the same for the rest of this hypothesis. Our calculations, summarized in table 4.4 and appendix 3, table A3.2, show that, during the period 1882–1914, outflows of funds, namely interest and principal payments, net of new capital inflows arising from French investment in the Ottoman public debt averaged close to £500,000 per year. During the same period, German investment in the Ottoman external debt resulted in net inflows of £150,000 per year. Clearly, this small amount cannot be considered to have contributed in any significant way towards eliminating the budget deficit.

Furthermore, as table A3.3 of appendix 3 indicates, patterns of funds flows arising from direct foreign investment do not indicate a different picture for German capital in comparison to French investments. Between 1888 and 1896, inflows of new capital remained considerably above profit transfers for both French and German capital. In fact, net inflows by French investors were above those by German capital during this period. The direction of net funds flows was reversed after 1896. Profit transfers abroad exceeded new capital inflows until World War I for both French and German enterprises.

It is clear that a purely quantitative approach to this issue will be inadequate. One of the several factors that needs to be taken into account in any explanation of why French influence in the Ottoman Empire lagged so much behind that of Germany is the magnitude of French investments in Russia. In 1914, French investments abroad amounted to £1.8 thousand million, and 25 per cent of this sum was placed in Russia.[58] French investments in Russia were four times as large as French investments in the Ottoman Empire. The size of these investments inevitably affected French foreign policy, particularly policy towards the Ottoman Empire. Whenever French interests in the Ottoman Empire came into conflict with French interests in Russia, the concern for the latter determined French government policy.

One important example concerns arms sales to the Ottoman Empire. Starting in the 1890s, the German government systematically provided military equipment and training for the Ottoman army, eventually creating a strong pro-German wing within the Ottoman army.[59] Despite its considerable interests in the Ottoman Empire, France could not compete with Germany in this area. This was not necessarily due to French inferiority in the armaments industries. Rather, French supply of military equipment to the Ottoman Empire would not have been received favorably by the Russian government. Similarly, during loan negotiations immediately preceding World War I, the French government, as a result of Russian pressure, gave permission for the flotation of Ottoman bonds in the French stock exchanges on the condition that the Ottoman government would not use the revenues for military expenditures.[60] Such requests could hardly lead to greater French influence over the Ottoman bureaucracy. Therefore, despite the fact that, on purely quantitative and economic grounds, French capital inflows were greater than those of German capital and the effects of French capital on the Ottoman balance of payments were not substantially different from that of German capital, French influence in the Ottoman Empire lagged far behind that of Germany.

Chapter 5

Commodity production for world markets and relations of production in agriculture, 1840–1913

During the three-quarters of a century preceding World War I, Ottoman foreign trade, most of which was with industrialized Europe, expanded at unprecedented rates. In the second half of the nineteenth century, but especially after 1880, substantial amounts of European capital were invested in railroads and in other forms of infrastructure in the Ottoman Empire, further contributing to the expansion of that trade. These changes in the sphere of circulation had far-reaching effects on the sphere of production. Some branches of handicrafts-based manufacturing activity began to decline due to competition from industrial imports. Patterns of production in the Ottoman economy began to shift towards agricultural commodity production for world markets.

This chapter deals with some aspects of the latter process. Most important, it will examine the relations of production in Ottoman agriculture, particularly the patterns of land ownership and tenancy, and their evolution during a period of rapid expansion in commodity production. The study will be limited to the 'core' areas of the Empire, Northern Greece, Thrace and Anatolia.[1] We examine the extent and long-term rhythms of the expansion of agricultural commodity exports from the Ottoman Empire during the nineteenth century and assess the relative importance of domestic urban and European markets in the commercialization of Ottoman agriculture. Then we discuss some critical features of Ottoman agriculture and present an aggregate picture for land ownership and tenancy patterns in the Asiatic provinces during the mid-century. Finally, we analyze the impact of penetration of capitalism and expansion of commodity production on patterns of land ownership and tenancy and, more generally, on mechanisms of surplus appropriation from the direct producer on a region by region basis for the later nineteenth and early twentieth centuries.

Foreign trade and the expansion of commodity production

Long-term trends

Despite substantial losses of land and population during the century, total exports from the Ottoman Empire increased by approximately five times, measured in current prices, and by nine times, measured in constant prices, between 1840 and 1913.[2] Rates of expansion of exports from Northern Greece and Anatolia appear to be even higher: an approximately eightfold increase in current prices and an elevenfold increase in constant prices during the same period.[3] Since the share of agricultural commodities in total Ottoman exports remained high during this period, close to 90 per cent in 1913, these estimates also reflect the rate of expansion of agricultural commodity exports.[4]

We do not have equally reliable information regarding changes in the levels of agricultural production during the same period. Ottoman statistics for agricultural production do not become available until after the turn of the century. In the absence of direct measures, tithe assessment and tithe collection figures can perhaps be taken as crude measures of the long-term trends in agricultural production, but we should warn that even these tithe figures are incomplete. Although available figures start in 1863, for many years of the following half century assessment and collection statistics for many of the administrative units are simply unavailable. Nonetheless, a crude estimate regarding long-term changes in the volume of agricultural production can still be attempted. Our calculations suggest that the volume of annual gross agricultural production in the areas of the Empire under study here more than doubled between the early 1860s and World War I.[5] While this doubling represents a substantial increase in the levels of production, it also implies that the rate of growth of exports far exceeded the rate of growth of agricultural output. As a result, the share of exports in total agricultural production and in the national product rose rapidly until World War I.

There are no estimates for the 'national product' of the Ottoman Empire for the early part of this period, but an estimate for 1913 indicates that 14.1 per cent of the gross national product was being exported in that year. More important, the share of agricultural exports (excluding minerals) in net agricultural production rose from 18.4 per cent in 1889 and 17.8 per cent in 1899 to 22.3 per cent in 1910 and 26.5 per cent in 1913.[6] These ratios indicate fairly high degrees of commercialization of agriculture and of external orientation of the Ottoman economy, particularly for the later dates. However, they also hide substantial differences in the rates of marketization and exportation of different crops.

However, reviewing the century-long expansion of commodity production in Ottoman agriculture by comparing aggregates at two end points, 1840 and 1913, as we have done above, might be misleading. First, by focusing on the end points we run the risk of missing the long-term fluctuations in economic activity in the industrialized center countries and their consequences on Ottoman exports and agriculture.[7] Second, aggregate, economy-wide export rates do not reveal very much about the regionally uneven nature of the penetration of capitalism, especially in the case of the Ottoman Empire, where regional differentiation was quite pronounced even prior to the nineteenth century. Therefore, in examining the expansion of commodity production in agriculture, it would be more fruitful to pursue a line of inquiry that emphasizes both the regional differences and the long-term fluctuations in that process.

Commodity production for domestic markets

In contrast to that of the export markets, the role of the domestic market in the expansion of commodity production in agriculture was rather limited during the nineteenth century. It is difficult to determine the share of domestic markets, local or otherwise, in total agricultural production, but several observations can be made. We know that while there was some interregional trade by sea within the Empire, the volume of overland domestic trade in foodstuffs remained low until the construction of railroads. Internal trade networks were weakened even further with the construction of railroads by foreign capital, since these railroads linked the agronomically attractive areas to major ports of export and import.[8]

In the absence of substantial volumes of interregional trade, the rate of growth of the urban population and of urban markets can perhaps be taken as a rough measure for the rate of growth of agricultural commodity production for domestic markets. The population of towns with over 20,000 inhabitants in Anatolia, Northern Greece and Thrace rose from 1.4 million, or 17 per cent of the total population, in the 1830s–1840s to 3.3 million, or 22 per cent of the total population of these areas, in 1912.[9] These figures point to relatively large urban markets for the eighteenth and early nineteenth centuries but rather slow rates of urban growth during the nineteenth century. Moreover, no less than 45 per cent of the total increase was due to the growth of Istanbul, which remained dependent upon imports of foodstuffs, especially of cereals from Wallachia, Moldavia, and more recently from Russia, which lie outside the areas considered in this study.[10] Therefore, while the share of domestic urban markets in agricultural commodity production was quite high at the beginning of the nineteenth century, the rate of growth of urban markets was nowhere near the rates of expansion of agricultural exports outlined earlier. In fact, on the basis of simple calculations, we estimate that as much as three-fourths of the expansion in agricultural commodity production that took place between 1840 and 1913 in the areas included in this study was induced by world market demand.[11]

Changing composition of agricultural output

Commercialization of agriculture is usually accompanied by a shift in the composition of agricultural output from cereals and other subsistence crops towards industrial raw materials and other cash crops. However, since cereals were an important part of the expansion of commodity production in the Ottoman case, such a shift was not as pronounced as the commercialization and export orientation of agriculture. Official Ottoman statistics indicate that in 1907 88 per cent of all cultivated land in Northern Greece and Thrace was set aside for wheat, barley and other cereals. These crops accounted for 76 per cent of the total value of agricultural production excluding animal products. Similarly, in 1909 cereals covered 84 per cent of all cultivated land and accounted for 77 per cent of the value of agricultural output excluding animal products in the Anatolian provinces of the Empire.[12]

As for the composition of agricultural exports, Ottoman statistics indicate that, during the period 1878–1913, no single crop dominated exports, and only rarely did the share of any single commodity exceed 12 per cent of the value of total exports. Despite the doubling of the value of total exports from 1878 to 1913, the aggregate share of the more important commodities did not change substantially. The share of the eight most important commodities, tobacco, wheat, barley, raisins, figs, raw silk, raw wool and opium, in the total value of exports was 51 per cent during 1878–80; the same share stood at 44 per cent in 1913.[13] Similarly, the foreign trade statistics of European countries indicate that in the earlier period, 1840–78, none of these commodities had substantially larger shares in the total value of Ottoman exports.[14]

Land, labor and the state during the nineteenth century

In this section we focus on all relations of production in Ottoman agriculture except land ownership and tenancy. By relations of production we refer to a subset of all relations between economic agents that take place during the production process. More specifically, we define relations of production as the specific economic forms and mechanisms of surplus appropriation from the direct producers in a surplus-generating economy.[15] These forms and mechanisms are not limited to property relations concerning land and other means of production; they include market processes. For example, while land rent in its different pre-capitalist forms or state taxation of the direct producer constitute extra-market mechanisms of appropriating the surplus product, the unequal relations between the usurer and /or merchant and the peasant producer or wage labor in a capitalist form are mechanisms of surplus appropriation that involve market processes.[16] We should also emphasize that it would be unrealistic to expect that at a given time in a given socio-economic formation there will exist only one mechanism of surplus appropriation. While their relative importance may change over time, different extra-market and market mechanisms will coexist.

After the disintegration of the *timar* system, the Ottoman Empire had entered a period of decentralization. As the military and political power of the central government declined, the *ayan* and *derebeys* (valley lords) became increasingly powerful in the provinces. They emerged as provincial administrators and tax collectors, usurers, merchants and *de facto* owners of land tracts of *miri* (state) lands. They expanded their share of the agricultural surplus by withholding tax revenues from the government and by increasing the rates of exploitation of the direct producers. However, it is unclear to what extent they relied on their power as tax collectors, usurers and merchants, and to what extent they transformed the existing forms of agricultural organization by establishing large, semi-feudal estates (*çiftliks*) for commodity production. Undoubtedly, both processes were under way. But while we are not in a position to assess the relative importance of *çiftliks* in the Balkan provinces of the Empire, in view of the relatively low levels of commodity production we find it unlikely that they had become the dominant form in Anatolia by the late eighteenth and early nineteenth centuries. Even in the Izmir region, where commercialization of agriculture had proceeded to a greater extent than elsewhere in Anatolia, the power of the most important *ayan* derived, above all, from tax collection in agriculture and long-distance trade.[17]

One of the most important developments in the early part of the nineteenth century was the rapid change in this balance of power between the central government and the locally powerful elements. *Sened-i İttifak*, signed in 1808, represented the zenith of the power of local *ayan* and *derebeys*, but it also signaled the beginning of a centralization drive by the

Ottoman state. In the following decades, particularly between 1831 and 1837, the central government moved swiftly to destroy the economic basis of provincial opposition. In 1831 the *timar* system was formally abolished. All forms of *de facto* ownership of *miri* lands were eliminated and large estates were expropriated. Lands which reverted to the central government were then leased to *mültezim* for tax collection purposes. It is difficult to say to what extent these measures fulfilled the objectives of the central government, but there is evidence that, even in Eastern Anatolia and Northern Syria, lands in the hands of Kurdish tribal lords were confiscated, and that some were distributed to the small peasantry.[18] Later, the Land Code of 1858, enacted under pressure from European powers, recognized private ownership of land, and in 1867 ownership of land by foreign citizens was recognized. However, by this time the balance of power between Istanbul and the provinces had shifted decisively in favor of the former.[19]

Another important characteristic of nineteenth-century Ottoman agriculture was the relative proportions of labor and land, the relative scarcity of the former and the relative abundance of the latter. Following rapid increases during the sixteenth century, the population of the Anatolian countryside, but not necessarily of Northern Greece, showed a net decline between 1600 and 1800.[20] A complex set of factors – the dissolution of the *timar* system, frequent wars, heavy exploitation of the peasantry, and the general economic and fiscal crisis – contributed to this outcome.

The population of Anatolia began to grow in the nineteenth century. An important source of this trend was the immigration of large numbers of Muslims from the Caucasus and the European provinces as these areas seceded from the Empire.[21] Throughout the nineteenth century, the Ottoman central bureaucracy was very much aware that the expansion of agricultural production which constituted the primary source of fiscal revenue depended critically upon relieving the labor shortage and providing inexpensive means of transportation. Immigrants were settled along the Anatolian Railway in Eskişehir, Ankara and Konya and in agronomically favorable areas of Western Anatolia and Antalya.[22] In addition, attempts were made to settle the nomadic tribes in regions where labor shortage was particularly acute, such as the Çukurova plain.[23] Despite these policies, relative scarcity of labor, regional variations notwithstanding, continued to be an important characteristic of Ottoman agriculture until World War I.[24]

The obverse side of the same coin is the relative availability of land.[25] Throughout the nineteenth century, extensive techniques of agriculture were employed in most parts of Northern Greece and Anatolia.

Cultivated lands were left fallow every two or three years.[26] Uncultivated marginal lands were always available for 'purchase' from the state at nominal prices or in return for regular payments of tithe for ten years, particularly in areas where the absence of inexpensive forms of transportation made commodity production for long-distance markets difficult.

Under the circumstances, in areas where land had become a commodity, land prices reflected differential rents but basically excluded absolute rent. In general, land prices followed the short-term and long-term fluctuations in world market conditions for agricultural commodities. Along with the expansion of world market demand and of exports, land prices rose from 1840 until the early 1870s. They declined during the Great Depression of 1873–96, only to rise again during the subsequent upswing which continued until the outbreak of World War I.[27] The availability of marginal lands meant that, despite the relative scarcity of labor and the primitive nature of agricultural implements, substantial amounts of new land could be brought under cultivation during periods of high world market demand and favorable terms of trade. If the large increases in area under cultivation and agricultural production indicated by the official Ottoman statistics are to be believed, an explanation of these increases must include the above considerations, recent immigration and the role of the railroads.[28]

These relative proportions of land and labor tended to improve the bargaining position of the small peasant producer. Peasant households which owned a pair of oxen and the most basic implements, or those which could borrow them, cultivated their own land. When marginal land was not available, peasants sharecropped for small or large landlords. Those households which did not own a pair of oxen, frequently the most critical of the means of production, or those which were forced to sell their oxen because of poor harvests and permanent usury, offered their labor services to large landlords as sharecropping tenants. Although the landlords had the right to cancel a tenancy arrangement, evictions were infrequent.

Around the turn of the twentieth century, large landowners in the highly commercialized agricultural regions of Izmir–Aydın, Adana and Salonica began to employ imported implements and labor-saving machinery in order to reduce their dependence on relatively scarce labor.[29] However, in a social formation where marginal land was available and labor scarce, wages were bound to remain relatively high. Large farms using year-round wage laborers could not take over at the expense of simple commodity production by peasant households. If necessary, peasant households could exert much greater effort and accept much lower levels of consumption.[30] Consequently, once commodity production either by small owner-producers or by sharecropping tenants was re-established by the central government during the early part of the century, it survived until World War I.

Another factor in the survival of simple commodity production by peasant households was the central government. Throughout the century, the Ottoman state attempted to prevent the emergence of a powerful landlord class that might expand its share of the agricultural surplus at the expense of the state and even challenge the rule of the central bureaucracy.

At the same time, however, the state heavily taxed the small peasantry. Among a variety of taxes falling upon rural classes, *aşar* (tithe) as a predetermined percentage of gross agricultural product constituted the main source of fiscal revenue for the Ottoman state.[31] After the disintegration of the *timar* system, tithe revenues were auctioned off to *mültezim* (tax farmers), who not only reduced the state's share of the surplus but increased the rates of exploitation of the direct producers.[32] Despite the strengthening of the state apparatus during the nineteenth century, the tax farming system could not be abandoned until World War I, despite several state attempts in that direction.[33] Locally powerful tax collectors continued to keep a large part of the tax revenues.

After the Tanzimat Decree of 1839, the tithe was fixed at 10 per cent of the gross agricultural output, paid mostly in kind in the earlier period but increasingly in money terms later in the century. Moreover, during the years of lower agricultural prices, the tax collectors frequently demanded and received payment in cash. The 10 per cent rate was likely to increase to as much as 15 per cent whenever the fiscal crisis of the state intensified.[34] The collection of tithe along with other forms of rural taxation such as *agnam* (animal tax) meant that as much as a quarter or more of agricultural production was taxed.[35] In addition, the taxes were highly regressive, falling mostly on the unprotected small peasantry, while the large landowners were usually underassessed.[36]

Given the low levels of productivity, dependence of the harvest on weather conditions, and heavy state taxation, both the small owner-producers and the tenants were permanently indebted to usurers at interest rates ranging anywhere from 20 to 120 per cent.[37] Whatever was left after the tax collector and, in the case of the tenant, the landowner had their shares, was appropriated by the usurer.[38] The small producers frequently had to struggle to survive from one year to the next. For these peasants, capital improvements in land and implements were unheard of. At the same time, the traditional manufactures in the cities were being destroyed by competition from imported industrial commodities. Urban areas, therefore, offered no prospects of employment, and the availability of marginal lands prevented mass emigration from rural areas.[39]

During years of exceptionally poor harvests the state ensured that tax collectors arrived at the harvest place before the usurers by postponing all payments to moneylenders until the following year. Moreover, in its attempts to protect its fiscal base, the small peasant, against powerful landlords and increasing concentration of land ownership, the state issued decrees during periods of crisis to enforce the existing law against the appropriation of any owner's land because of inability to pay back debts.[40] Under these circumstances, complaints by moneylenders that the defaulting peasants were not being arrested, though infrequent, were not unheard of.[41]

Different groups dominated moneylending activities in different regions. In areas where semi-feudal relations of production and/or powerful landlords prevailed, the latter usually doubled as usurers. For the large landowners usury not only provided a means of appropriating a larger share of the surplus, but, given the relative scarcity of labor, permanent indebtedness of peasants also secured tenants for their land. On the other hand, in Central Anatolia, where small peasant ownership was dominant and in regions where production for the market had expanded to a greater degree, merchants, tax collectors and other moneylenders residing in urban centers controlled usury.[42] (For detailed descriptions of the different relations of production in Ottoman agriculture, particularly of sharecropping, fixed-rent tenancy and wage labor and for descriptions of the standards of living of the peasantry in different regions of the Empire, see appendix 4.)

Land ownership and tenancy patterns in the Asiatic provinces

There is a very important and useful survey of land ownership and tenancy patterns in the Asiatic provinces of the Ottoman Empire in the late 1860s which will serve as the starting point for our subsequent analysis. The report was prepared by the British consul in Trabzon as part of a larger, comparative study of European land tenure systems in connection with British government policies towards Ireland.[43] The date of the study, 1869, is particularly important, coming three decades after the confiscation of large land holdings, a decade after the Land Code of 1858, and towards the end of the first wave of rapid expansion of agricultural exports, which lasted until the early 1870s. In order to prepare the survey, Consul Palgrave states that he travelled extensively in Anatolia, Syria and Iraq, both 'observing and talking with the more knowledgeable people'. Clearly, the accuracy of such a survey needs to be questioned, and the approximate nature of Palgrave's figures suggests caution. Hence, in what follows we will treat Palgrave's study as a rather crude reflection of the actual patterns of ownership and tenancy.

As stated by Palgrave, the Asiatic provinces of the Ottoman Empire had a total surface area of 1,219,000 square kilometers. Fully half of this land was considered unsuitable for cultivation, and two-thirds of the remainder was occupied by forests and pastures, leaving as cultivable land a total of 21,662,000 hectares.[44] Twenty-five per cent of all cultivable land belonged to *vakıfs* (endowments) which were left relatively untouched during the 1830s. The Land Code of 1858 had reduced *miri* lands to 5 per cent of all cultivable land by 1869. The rest, or 70 per cent of all cultivable land, was *mülk*, or private property.

As table 5.1 summarizes, 75 to 82.5 per cent of all cultivable land was in small holdings ranging from 2 to 20 hectares, with the average somewhere between 6 and 8 hectares. In the study, large holdings were defined as those greater than 20 hectares, with an average of 120 hectares. Large holdings comprised 17.5 to 25 per cent of all cultivable land.

One-seventh of all *mülk* land, or 10 per cent of all cultivable land, was under large holdings, being cultivated either by labor hired on an annual basis or, in most instances, by sharecroppers (*ortakcı* or *maraba*) whose tenancy agreements were subject to renewal by the landlord every year. The remaining six-sevenths of *mülk* lands, or 60 per cent of all cultivable land, was under small holdings. One-third of these small holdings were cultivated directly by small peasant owners with an average of 6 hectares per farm. The other two-thirds of the privately owned small holdings were cultivated by small tenants either under fixed rent or, more usually, under sharecropping arrangements, at an average of 8 hectares per farm.

Of the *vakıf* and *miri* lands which together constituted 30 per cent of all cultivable land, half were small holdings of less than 20 hectares. Half of these were being cultivated by lifetime tenants whose position was 'practically equivalent to ownership of land'. The other half of the small *vakıf* and *mülk* holdings were being cultivated by sharecropper tenants. As for the large *vakıf* and *mülk* holdings, half of them were being cultivated by sharecropper tenants at an average of 8 hectares per tenant. The remaining quarter of all *vakıf* and *mülk* lands were originally in the form of large holdings, but because of various restrictions placed on them by the *Evkaf Idaresi* (Board of Endowments) had been divided up into small holdings and were being cultivated by direct producer tenants.[45]

It should be noted that according to Palgrave no less than 40 per cent of all cultivable land was being rented out by small landowners to small tenants. He does not offer any explanation for the unusually high

Table 5.1. Land ownership, land distribution, forms of tenancy and relations of production in the Asiatic provinces of the Ottoman Empire c. 1869

1	2	3	4		5
		Form of ownership			
Size of holding	Form of operation	Mülk Private property (0.70)	Vakf Endowment (0.25)	Miri State (0.05)	Form of surplus appropriation from the direct producer (in addition to state taxation, usury and merchant capital whenever applicable)
Small: 2 to 20 ha. (0.75 to 0.825)	Small peasant ownership; owners as direct producers	A (0.20) Av. 6 ha. per holding Owner/producers: 23.7%	D (0.075) Av 8 ha. per holding Tenants for life, de facto small peasant ownership Direct producers: 7.1%		A. — B. Rent payments to small owners
	Small owners to small tenants; mostly sharecropping, some fixed rent	B (0.40) Av. 8 ha. per tenant Direct producers: 37.9%	E (0.075) Av. 8 ha. per tenant Direct producers: 7.1%		C. Rent payments to large owners, wage labor D. —
Large: greater than 20 ha.; av. 120 ha. (0.175 to 0.25)	Large owners to small tenants; mostly sharecropping; some fixed rent, some year-round wage laborers; in addition 200,000 seasonal wage workers	C (0.10) Av. 8 ha. per tenant Owners: 0.6% Direct producers: 9.4%	F (0.075) Av. 8 ha. per tenant Large holdings broken up due to restrictions by Evkaf İdaresi De facto small holdings Direct producers: 7.1%		E. ⎫ Rent payments F. ⎬ to vakıf trustees G. ⎭ or to state
			G (0.075) Av. 8 ha. per tenant Direct producers: 7.1%		

Note: Figures in parentheses represent shares in total cultivable land. Percentages represent shares in total number of households in agriculture.
Source: Parliamentary Papers, Accounts and Papers (1870), 'Report on Land Tenure in (the Asiatic Provinces of) Turkey' by Consul Palgrave. For detailed descriptions of the different forms of tenancy and of wage labor, see appendix 4.

frequency of this phenomenon, but several reasons might be suggested. His category 'small' inevitably hides a good deal of differentiation among households owning, according to his definition, fewer than 20 hectares. The primitive nature of agricultural implements and techniques in nineteenth-century Ottoman agriculture set at a relatively low level the amount of land that could be cultivated by an average household using a team of oxen.[46] Holdings of small owners beyond that size had to be rented out. Similar differentiation with respect to ownership of implements and livestock might have led small tenants to cultivate additional plots without relying on hired labor.[47] Moreover, in the 'life-cycle' of a household, there will be periods of relative labor surplus – when the offspring are at working age but before they leave – and periods of labor deficiency.[48] The frequency with which the Ottoman Empire was involved in wars during the nineteenth century and the high rate of casualties inevitably compounded the scarcity of labor in rural areas, particularly of young adult males.[49] Such demographic factors may account for a good deal of the small-to-small tenancy arrangements.[50] Finally, absentee ownership by urban dwellers may have been a major factor in the relatively high frequency of these small-to-small tenancy arrangements.[51] Despite these potential explanations, we are inclined to treat this particular figure of 40 per cent with more caution than others in the same table.

After the confiscation of many of the large estates during the 1830s, sharecropping became the dominant form of tenancy in the large *mülk* lands.[52] Arrangements varied from region to region, depending upon the relative power of the landlord and the tenant, the quality of the land, and custom. In most cases the product was equally divided after government taxes and dues were paid and an allowance was made to the side which supplied the seeds, implements and livestock.[53] The length of the tenancy arrangement also depended upon the relative strength of the two sides. Particularly in areas where finding tenants was not a major problem, landlords preferred to keep the arrangement subject to renewal every year in order to extract the maximum effort and the maximum surplus from the tenants. For reasons discussed earlier, sharecropping remained the dominant form of labor organization in the large holdings until World War I.

Around mid-century a small and decreasing number of large holdings were being operated by laborers hired on an annual basis.[54] In addition, according to Palgrave's estimates, around 200,000 seasonal wage laborers were employed throughout the Asiatic provinces of the Empire in the production of cash crops, which required peak seasonal labor.[55] With increasing export orientation and increases in the production of cash

Table 5.2. *Summary distribution of land ownership and tenancy patterns,*
Asiatic provinces of the Ottoman Empire c. 1869

Type of direct producer	Reference to forms in table 5.1	Share in all direct producer households	Share of total cultivable land
Small peasant owner-producers	A, D	31.0%	27.5%
Sharecroppers, other tenants renting from small owners (small–small)	B, E, F	52.4%	55.0%
Sharecroppers, year-round wage laborers, other tenants in large holdings (small–large)	C, G	16.6%	17.5%

Source: See table 5.1.

crops such as cotton, it appears that the numbers of seasonal wage laborers began to expand, especially after the late 1890s, in the regions of Salonica, Izmir–Aydın and, in particular, Adana.

If we momentarily abstract from the distinctions between *mülk, vakıf* and *miri* lands, we can regroup the data presented in table 5.1 and arrive in table 5.2 at a more summary picture regarding the distribution of direct producers among different forms of land ownership and tenancy. This summary picture shows more clearly the dominance, in Palgrave's estimation, of small holding and small producers in the Asiatic provinces of the Empire around the middle of the nineteenth century. The early nineteenth century was a period of the strengthening of the central government, confiscation of large estates, distribution of land to small producers, a decline in the power of local notables, and a general centralization of Ottoman social formation.[56] Palgrave's report was prepared three decades after most of these changes had taken place. The long-term impact of the increasing commercialization and export orientation of agriculture on patterns of land ownership and tenancy, whatever that would be, was yet to materialize. Under these circumstances, the dominance of small holdings and small peasant producers in Anatolia and in other Asiatic provinces should not be surprising.[57]

On the other hand, however, one major theme of Palgrave's report was what he considered to be the unfavorable consequences of the confiscation of large estates and the abolition of the earlier land tenure system.

Therefore, there may well be a bias in the report towards overestimating the extent of small holding. Even if an allowance is made for this potential bias, the conclusion remains that the great majority of cultivable lands were under 'small' holdings around the mid-nineteenth century.

One important shortcoming of the Palgrave survey is its aggregate nature, which, given the substantial regional variations in land ownership and tenancy patterns and the regionally uneven nature of the penetration of capitalism into Anatolia, limits the insights it offers into the dynamics of change in Ottoman agriculture during the nineteenth century. For example, substantial regional variations should be expected in the size of 'small' and 'large' holdings, depending upon agronomical factors and the availability of irrigation.

Moreover, there is not always a one-to-one correspondence between apparent forms of tenancy and the mechanisms of surplus appropriation from the direct producer. The same tenancy relationship, for example sharecropping, between a large landowner and a small tenant may represent either semi-feudal relations of production or petty commodity production, depending upon the relative positions and power of the owner and the tenant and the nature of the relationship in the more general context of the socio-economic formation.[58] Only a region-by-region analysis of the historical evolution of relations of production and of the relative importance of commodity production will help draw the distinction between these two cases.

Regional patterns of land ownership and tenancy

As some of the relevant indicators summarized in table 5.3 indicate, agriculture in the core areas of the Ottoman Empire, namely Northern Greece, Thrace and Anatolia, showed substantial regional variations with respect to relative proportions of land and labor, agronomic factors, composition of output, and relative importance of local urban markets by the end of the nineteenth century. Equally important were regional differences in proximity to major ports, availability of inexpensive forms of transportation, and the timing of the construction of railroads by foreign capital, as well as the degree and timing of world market-induced commercialization. In this section we will examine the patterns of land ownership and tenancy in Northern Greece, Thrace and Anatolia during the nineteenth century, utilizing a framework that emphasizes the considerable differences in these variables.[59]

Our analysis will be carried out in terms of three types of regions. Region Type I includes Northern Greece and Thrace, Western Anatolia, the Eastern Black Sea Coast and the Adana region, the latter two being

Table 5.3. *Indicators of regional differentiation in Ottoman agriculture c. 1900*

Regions	Total population (millions) 1A	Labor and land — Cultivated area (thousand sq. km.) 1B	Labor and land — Rural population density (per sq. km.) 1C	Composition of agricultural output (% share of cash crops) 2	Importance of urban markets (% share of urban population) 3	Density of railroads (km per 1,000 sq. km.) 1875 4A	Density of railroads (km per 1,000 sq. km.) 1900 4B	Distribution of farm size (% of farms) — under 10 dönüms 5A	Distribution of farm size (% of farms) — 10–50 dönüms 5B	Distribution of farm size (% of farms) — over 50 dönüms 5C	Average farm size (donums) 5D
Northern Greece	1.63	4.6	310[a]	10.9	15[a]	—	—	30	52	18	19
Thrace	1.15	4.4	233	11.9	11	—	—	55	28	17	24
N. Greece and Thrace	2.78	9.0	268[a]	11.4	13	5.3	13.7	40	42	18	21
W. Anatolia/Marmara	5.20	14.9	220	18.6	37[a]	2.2	13.7	31	46	23	35
E. Black Sea	1.34	3.7	342	3.2	6	—	—	43	42	15	18
Adana	0.50	4.7	91	35.1	15	—	1.7	17	36	47	77
Central Anatolia	4.70	19.6	215	6.6	11	—	2.5	23	52	25	35
Eastern Anatolia											
Central tier	1.15	5.2	194	10.1	12	—	—	41	41	18	21
Southern tier	0.81	6.5	101	9.7	20	—	—	23	37	40	58

[a] Figure approximate.

Notes and sources:

1A Total population in 1907–9: from Güran (1978), p. 5, based on the Ottoman Agricultural Census of 1907–9. See the Ottoman Empire (1910) and (1911).

1B Land under cultivation in 1907–9: Güran (1978), p. 5, based on the Ottoman Agricultural Census.

1C Rural population/land under cultivation. Rural population has been estimated by subtracting the urban population figures derived from Issawi (1980), pp. 34–5, from column 1A.

2 The share of industrial crops and vineyards in total area under cultivation. From Güran (1978), p. 20, based on the Ottoman Agricultural Census of 1907–9.

3 Population of towns over 20,000 in 1912/Total population in 1907–9.

4A Length of railroads per 1,000 sq. km. in 1875.

4B Length of railroads per 1,000 sq. km. in 1900; both based on Eldem (1970), pp. 164–5.

5A (Farms under 10 dönüms)/(Total number of farms); 1 dönüm = 0.0913 hectare.

5B Percentage of farms between 10 and 50 dönüms.

5C Percentage of farms over 50 dönüms.

5D Average farm size in dönüms. Source for 5A–5D: Güran (1978), p. 28, based on the Ottoman Agricultural Census of 1907–9.

Definitions of regions (names of *Sancaks* and other administrative units)

Northern Greece:	Salonica, Monastir	
Thrace:	Edirne	
Western Anatolia and Marmara:	Izmit, Biga, Hüdavendigar, Aydin (Izmir)	
Eastern Black Sea Coast:	Trabzon	
Central Anatolia:	Kastamonu, Ankara, Konya, Sivas	
Eastern Anatolia, Central tier:	Erzurum, Mamuretulaziz	
Eastern Anatolia, Southern tier:	Diyarbakır, Bitlis, Van	

special cases within the broader picture. These areas were pulled into commodity production for world markets at a relatively early stage in the nineteenth century, if not earlier, and by 1913 they represented the most commercialized, export-oriented regions of the Empire. Region Type II consists of Central Anatolia, which was isolated from long-distance markets until the construction of the Anatolian Railway by German capital in the early 1890s. In the following two decades, cereal production in Central Anatolia for Istanbul and European markets expanded rapidly under small and middle peasant ownership. Region Type III includes Eastern Anatolia, with its Central and Southern tiers, both of which remained mostly isolated from the impact of world markets and the penetration of world capitalism. Small peasant ownership was relatively stronger in the Central tier, while feudal and semi-feudal relations of production dominated in Southeastern Anatolia and Northern Syria.

Eastern Anatolia

Eastern Anatolia was less affected by the world market-induced commercialization of agriculture than was any other region during the nineteenth century. Because of the absence of railroads until the early 1910s, agricultural produce of the region could not be directed towards long-distance markets on a regular basis. In years of good harvest, limited amounts of cereals were shipped by camel caravans through Aleppo to the export port of Iskenderun. The markets of Mousul, Baghdad and distant India emerged as occasional outlets for the cereals of the region only after the turn of the century.[60] However, in general, barriers posed by transportation costs isolated Eastern Anatolia from the rest of the Empire and the European markets throughout the century. Consequently, while bad harvest years led to near famine conditions, unusually good harvest years were almost equally disastrous for the small peasantry. Prices collapsed and the peasants could not pay back their debt to the usurers. A limited amount of mohair constituted the major export commodity of the region during this period.[61]

Southeastern Anatolia, including Aleppo, was the most urbanized region of Anatolia during the seventeenth and perhaps even in the eighteenth century. Although the overall population density was low and virtually no urban growth occurred during the nineteenth century, more than a fifth of the population continued to live in the medium-sized towns of the region (see table 5.3). Hence, there was a considerable amount of commodity production for local urban markets. The province of Mamuretulaziz can be singled out in this respect. In that province, small and medium-sized landowning Turkish and Armenian peasants specialized in the production of fruits, vegetables and other commercial crops for the urban markets of the region.[62]

With respect to patterns of land ownership and tenancy, the Central and Southern tiers of the region followed different paths. In the Southeastern Anatolian provinces of Diyarbakır, Bitlis and Van, the Ottoman state had recognized in the sixteenth century the autonomy of the Kurdish tribal lords in exchange for military obligations and orderly payments of tribute. The political, administrative and legal autonomy of the tribal lords and the lord–peasant bonds remained strong until the nineteenth century. The centralization attempt by the state during the 1830s resulted in the expropriation of some of the large holdings.[63] However, these measures could hardly affect the political, social and economic power of the tribal lords in the region. During the rest of the century, they benefited from a number of opportunities to acquire back their holdings.[64]

First, the Land Code of 1858 recognized the existing *de facto* distribution of land ownership, thereby making the tribal lords legal owners of large tracts of land.[65] After 1858, these landlords began to buy large amounts of *miri* land back from the state at low prices.[66] However, many of these tracts remained uncultivated because of the difficulties of finding tenants and transportation barriers against production for long-distance markets.[67] Second, the Kurdish tribal lords relied on their economic and non-economic power to secure tenants as they reduced small peasant owners to sharecropper status through usury and other means. While in other regions of the Empire the state occasionally interfered in this process in support of the small owner-producer, the centuries-long autonomy of the Kurdish tribes and lords remained unbroken during the nineteenth century.[68] Undoubtedly, a good deal of small peasant ownership did survive, given the relative proportions of land and labor in the area and the difficulties of expanding commodity production in large estates for long-distance markets. Nonetheless, the official Ottoman statistics summarized in table 5.3 confirm that by the first decade of the twentieth century, Southeastern Anatolia was second only to the Adana region in terms of inequalities in the distribution of farm size.

In the Central tier of Eastern Anatolia, which included the provinces of Erzurum and Mamuretulaziz, feudal and semi-feudal relations of production were not equally powerful. The ethnic composition of the population was distinctly different, consisting mostly of Turks and Armenians.[69] In addition, the density of population in agriculture was higher than that of the Southern tier. These factors combined with others to lead to a pattern of ownership dominated by small and middle holdings (see table 5.3). The absence of inexpensive forms of transportation limited the possibility of production for long-distance markets and the area under cultivation. Cereal shipments were undertaken only when famine prices prevailed elsewhere. While subsistence agriculture and animal husbandry dominated in Erzurum, in Mamuretulaziz, where agronomic factors were favorable, commodity production for regional markets and the cultivation of cash crops developed to a relatively high degree. In this context, state taxation and usury were the main mechanisms of surplus appropriation from the direct producer. Finally, in the period up to 1913, with the exception of Mamuretulaziz, there was virtually no improvement in the agricultural techniques and implements that had been in use in the Eastern Anatolian region for many centuries.[70]

Western Anatolia, Thrace and Northern Greece

Because of favorable agronomic conditions and proximity to major ports, agriculture along the coastal areas of Western Anatolia, Thrace and Northern Greece had been commercialized more than other regions of the Empire even before the second quarter of the nineteenth century. Salonica and Izmir were important ports of export in the eighteenth century.[71] When the Free Trade Treaties of 1838–41 took away the power of the Ottoman state to impose temporary, year-to-year restrictions on the exportation of foodstuffs and raw materials, these regions and their immediate hinterlands were first to show rapid increases in exports. The first wave of expansion of exports continued until the early 1870s, when the mid-century upswing of the world economy came to an end. The years of the Crimean and American Civil Wars were particularly important in this stretch as they generated considerable demand for primary commodities. The second wave of export expansion for these regions did not come until the end of the century, when the world economy entered another long-term upswing.[72] Along with increasing commercialization and export orientation of agriculture, raisins, tobacco, figs, cotton, raw silk and olive oil became the most important export commodities in these areas.[73]

It should also be emphasized that, in these regions, costs of transportation to the nearest ports, while by no means insignificant, did not constitute the kind of absolute barrier they were in Eastern Anatolia. The construction of railroads by European capital in the hinterland of Izmir during the early 1860s and in Thrace and Northern Greece in the early 1870s substantially reduced transportation costs, but most of the early expansion of exports in these areas had occurred before the completion of railroad construction.[74]

Prior to the second quarter of the nineteenth century, feudal obligations and feudal relations of production were not strong in Western Anatolia and Thrace despite the substantial political and economic power of the *ayans* as local administrators, tax collectors, merchants and *de facto* owners of large tracts of land. During the centralization drive of the state, the power of *ayans* was reduced, and some of their large *de facto* holdings were expropriated and distributed to the small peasantry. Hence, the expansion of commodity production for export and the penetration of foreign capital in infrastructure, trade and banking proceeded under a pattern in which small peasant owner-producers and small peasant tenants in small holdings coexisted with some large holdings. A British consular report from the Izmir area in 1863 states that 'by far the largest proportion of cultivated land is owned by peasants' in farms of 3–20 acres (1.2 to 8 hectares).[75] According to another estimate, in the province of Edirne which covered Thrace, two-thirds of all farms were under 20 hectares, and an additional 30 per cent were between 20 and 40 hectares.[76]

In contrast, large holdings and the *çiftlik* system prevailed in the Salonica and Monastir provinces of Northern Greece throughout the nineteenth century.[77] In 1859, it was estimated that three-fourths of all land in the province of Monastir was in the hands of large landlords.[78] For the province of Salonica, one estimate states that 40 per cent of all farms were larger than 200 hectares in 1863.[79] In comparison to the Western Anatolian provinces of the Empire, lord–peasant bonds were quite strong in Northern Greece. Despite the official abolition of *corvée* in the European provinces of the Empire in 1818,[80] and once more with the Tanzimat Decree of 1839,[81] it did not disappear in this area until after mid-century.[82]

Given the relative scarcity of labor, availability of marginal lands, dominance of small peasant ownership and the limited nature of capital accumulation in these regions of the Empire, transformation of large holdings into capitalist farms employing wage laborers on a year-round basis was unlikely.[83] Instead, the large landowners preferred to rent their land out to sharecropper families who represented a relatively inexpensive source of labor power, particularly for the cultivation of crops which required labor year-round.

Tenant families came from the ranks of the poor peasantry which did not have the means to cultivate marginal lands on their own.[84] Even under a tenancy arrangement, they could not, by themselves, meet the relatively large outlays associated with the cultivation of cash crops. Moreover, it was difficult for them to endure a bad harvest year if they accepted a fixed rent arrangement. Under these circumstances, sharecropping remained the most frequently adopted tenancy arrangement in Western Anatolia, Thrace and Northern Greece. Fixed rent tenancy was adopted mostly on *vakıf* lands where there was little supervision by the absentee landowners and where the tenants were relatively better off.[85]

Two different forms of sharecropping in large holdings need to be distinguished here. Sharecropping in large estates of Southeastern Anatolia represented feudal or semi-feudal relations of production where the lord–peasant bonds were quite strong and the tenant's obligations to the landlord went beyond the purely economic obligation of rent payments. On the other hand, in the Type I regions of Western Anatolia and on the Black Sea coast, where lord–peasant ties were weaker and where commodity production had expanded to a much greater extent, sharecropping represented a more limited, economic arrangement for rent payments. A careful contemporary observer draws the following picture for the Izmir area in 1890:

The mode of exploitation used by the agriculturalists changes depending upon the size of the holding. In the *çiftliks* which range from 2,000 to 18,000 dönüms, that is from 200 to 8,000 hectares, sharecropping is almost exclusively adopted except in the *kaza* [county] of Scala-Nuova [Kuşadası] where fixed rent is principally used. The sharecropper and his family provide the labor and the owner furnishes the work animals and the seed. When the time comes, they share equally without taking into account the seeds. The *çiftliks* from 500 to 2,000 *dönüms*, that is from 50 to 200 hectares, are cultivated directly by their owners with sharecropping in part. The holdings between 10 and 50 dönüms, 1 to 50 hectares, are worked directly by their owners with the help of day workers, if necessary, during harvest time.[86]

During periods of long-term expansion of the world economy, demand for agricultural exports rose rapidly and the terms of trade moved in favor of the Ottoman Empire.[87] During these periods[88] large landowners must have attempted to expand their holdings and reduce small peasant holders into sharecropper tenants. However, the limits to this process arising from the special characteristics of the Ottoman social formation need to be stressed. First, the small peasant owners were ready to exert high levels of effort and be content with very low levels of consumption which made it easier for them to retain their holdings despite the heavy burden of state taxation and the appropriation of the rest of the surplus by usurers and merchants.

Moreover, the central government attempted to support the small peasantry against large landowners by prohibiting the expropriation of the lands of defaulting owners.[89] How effectively or how frequently this law was enforced was a matter that depended upon the economic and political conjuncture and the local power of landowners.[90] However, as farm size distribution statistics summarized in table 5.3 show, small and middle owners and tenants in small holdings, heavily taxed and frequently if not permanently indebted, continued to coexist with those with large holdings and to account for a substantial part of the commodity production for export until World War I.

British attempts to establish large-scale capitalist farms should also be examined here. After the construction of the Izmir–Aydın railroad by British capital and the modification of the Ottoman Land Code in 1866 to allow for land ownership by foreigners, British citizens began to purchase substantial amounts of land and operate large, export-oriented capitalist farms in the hinterland of Izmir. According to one estimate, in the Izmir area British capitalist farmers had purchased up to one-third of all cultivable land by 1868 and most of the cultivable land by 1878.[91] These capitalists imported substantial amounts of agricultural implements and machinery for their farms.

This attempt to transform the existing mode of production by the infusion of large amounts of capital was important in its own right. Equally important, in our view, are the reasons for the unqualified failure of the British attempts at capitalist farms as well as of other colonization projects in the Ottoman Empire. In Western Anatolia, where marginal land was readily available and labor relatively scarce, the British farmers could not easily secure wage laborers for their large holdings. In the formal colonies, governments resorted to a head tax or other means in order to break up the existing mode of production, and establish wage labor whenever necessary. However, the Ottoman Empire maintained its formal political independence throughout the nineteenth century, allowing for a considerable degree of independence from the Great Powers in certain issues. In this case, the Ottoman government resisted pressures from Britain and did not attempt to separate small producers from their land, especially since the small peasantry constituted the very fiscal base of the Ottoman state.[92]

Eastern Black Sea Coast

The patterns of change in other coastal areas of Anatolia differed from those of Western Anatolia. The western half of the Black Sea Coast was not suitable for extensive cultivation. In the eastern half, Trabzon had been a major port on the transit route to Iran.[93] Agricultural commodity exports from Trabzon and to some extent Samsun expanded during the upswing of 1840–73. The secondary ports, Ordu, Giresun and Rize, emerged in the next long-term expansion from 1896 to 1913. Tobacco in the plains around Samsun and hazelnuts further to the east were the major export crops. However, the commercialization and export orientation of the region never reached levels achieved in Western Anatolia.[94]

The expropriation of large holdings during the 1830s affected the patterns of land ownership and tenancy for the rest of the century.[95] In 1863, it was reported that 100 per cent of all farms in the Trabzon area were under 4 hectares.[96] Although agricultural population density was higher in this region than anywhere else in the core areas of the Empire (see table 5.3), marginal land was still available. The relatively limited commercialization of agriculture, the labor-intensive nature of the export crops, and other reasons discussed earlier with respect to Western Anatolia prevented the re-emergence of large holdings.

Adana

The Southern Anatolian coast provides a different story. The plain of Antalya, which was to become a highly fertile and important agricultural area during the twentieth century, was sparsely populated and was not opened up to cultivation until the late 1890s when large numbers of immigrants leaving Crete after the war of 1897 were settled there.[97] In the decade preceding World War I, Italian capital became interested in the area both in terms of its agricultural potential and as an outlet for the Italian textiles industry, which was attempting to enter markets already dominated by major European powers.

Economic conditions in the plain of Adana to the east had improved considerably during the period of its occupation by Ibrahim Pasha, son of Mohammed Ali of Egypt. Irrigation projects were initiated and agriculture flourished.[98] However, with the departure of Ibrahim Pasha in 1840, security conditions in the area deteriorated, the irrigation systems were not maintained, and agricultural production declined rapidly. Improvements in irrigation and drainage systems were not attempted until the time of the American Civil War. One estimate puts the population of the entire plain, including cities and nomads, at 100,000 in 1862.[99] (Compare with the 1907 population given in table 5.3.) The last of the *derebeys* was eliminated from the area by the Ottoman army in 1864. Because of these circumstances, the worldwide cotton crisis which accompanied the American Civil War had a relatively limited impact in the plain of Adana.

With the draining of the delta, large amounts of land were opened to cultivation in the early 1870s.[100] Proximity to a port of export and the high quality of irrigated land rapidly transformed the area into one of the most export-oriented regions of Anatolia, specializing in cotton production. The subsequent evolution of land ownership and tenancy patterns owed much to the recent absence of cultivation, to settlements, and to the relative scarcity of labor in the area. As the locally powerful groups were able to claim ownership to large tracts of fertile land, securing laborers posed a serious problem from the outset. The large landowners and the state, which wanted to expand its fiscal base in the region, encouraged seasonal migration into the area during the peak cotton harvest season. More important, serious attempts were made to settle the nomadic Turkmens of the region in the agricultural lowlands.[101]

The severe drought of 1885 and the destruction of the cotton crop gave the central government the opportunity to introduce higher-quality seeds from Egypt. The commercialization of agriculture accelerated during the upswing of 1896–1913. With the arrival of the Anatolian Railway to Mersin and the purchase of the Mersin–Tarsus extension by German capital from the original British owners, the area rapidly entered the German sphere of influence.[102] The Anatolian Railway Company provided credit to landowners to adopt higher-quality seeds, import implements and machinery from Germany, and undertake irrigation investment in their large-scale farms.[103] By 1913 the plain of Adana had been transformed into the most commercialized agricultural region of the Empire, dominated by large farms cultivating cotton for export. Every harvest season, these farms employed anywhere from 50,000 to 100,000 migrant wage laborers arriving from as far away as Harput, Bitlis and Mousul.[104] (See table 5.3 for the distribution of farm size.)

Central Anatolia

The rapid expansion of commodity production in Central Anatolia started with the construction of the Anatolian railroad by German capital in the early 1890s linking Eskişehir, Konya and Ankara to Istanbul. In the earlier period, high costs of caravan transportation to Mediterranean and Black Sea ports had virtually insulated Central Anatolia from both the rest of the Empire and European markets. Only mohair and opium were shipped long distances on a regular basis.[105] The Anatolian railroad converted large areas of uncultivated dry farming land to wheat and barley production for both export and the Istanbul market, which was dependent upon imported grains from Romania, Bulgaria and Russia, and upon flour from France.[106] In 1889, Anatolian grain made up only 2 per cent of all grain received in Istanbul.[107] Within a decade of its construction, as many as 400,000 tons of cereals were being shipped annually on the railroad.[108] Novichev puts the ratio of marketization in the province of Konya at 26.4 per cent of total production for wheat and 25.5 per cent for barley in the year 1912, when total cereal shipments on the railroad did not exceed 300,000 metric tons.[109] Between a tenth and a quarter of the grain transported by rail was sent to Istanbul. In addition, a significant amount was consumed by the military units within the Empire. The construction of the Anatolian railroad did not simply reduce the imports of cereals from abroad. As much as three-quarters of the transported cereals, mostly barley, was destined for the European market.[110]

With respect to land ownership and tenancy patterns, the differences between Central Anatolia and Eastern Anatolia, particularly its Southern tier, need to be emphasized at the outset. Although the *ayan* were quite powerful in Central Anatolia during the eighteenth century, their influence was reduced, large holdings were broken up, and lord–peasant bonds were weakened during the 1830s. As a result, centuries after the dissolution of the *timar* system, the Ottoman state was able to reassert its power in the region. Because of the absence of inexpensive forms of transportation and relative scarcity of labor, large amounts of land not substantially lower in quality than those already under cultivation remained untilled until the 1890s and even after construction of the railroad. Small holdings and small peasant ownership dominated. State taxation and usury were the main mechanisms of appropriating the surplus from the direct producer.[111]

When the Anatolian Railway provided the transportation link, a shortage of labor emerged as the major obstacle in the way of expansion of cereal production in the region. To solve this problem, large numbers of immigrants from the seceding areas of the Empire, particularly from the Balkans, were settled along the railway.[112] The distribution of state lands to the immigrant families reinforced the existing small–middle owner-ship pattern.[113] The establishment of commodity-producing households in large numbers and the availability of large amounts of land made the separation of direct producers from land and the emergence of wage labor extremely difficult.[114]

Two developments of the 1880s need to be underlined here: world wheat prices continued to decline rapidly, and the long-standing historical position of Germany as a net exporter changed to one of a net importer of wheat.[115] Not coincidentally, the construction of the Anatolian railroad by German capital started towards the end of the same decade. However, given the primitive nature of agricultural techniques and the permanent indebtedness of the small peasantry, sustained increases in the volume of rail shipments and transformation of the area into a bread basket for Germany could hardly be expected. Hence, after the turn of the century, the Anatolian Railway Company was actively involved in the agriculture of the region, extending credit to middle farmers for seeds, land improvement schemes and irrigation projects.[116]

Had it not been for the outbreak of World War I, this particular form of intervention by foreign capital would have accelerated the ongoing differentiation of agricultural producers to consolidate a class of middle peasants in Central Anatolia.

Conclusion

Several important studies on nineteenth-century Ottoman agriculture in Northern Greece and Anatolia have been undertaken in recent years. [117] They have paved the way for a broader perspective on the penetration of world capitalism and its spatially uneven impact. In this chapter we undertook a region by region, comparative analysis of the dynamics of change in nineteenth-century Ottoman agriculture. The conceptual problem is a familiar one: how did the relations of production change as the economy came into contact with world capitalism, as commodity production for export increased, and as foreign investment in infrastructure and trade expanded?

Our analysis has focused on the forms of surplus appropriation from the direct producers, on the policies of the Ottoman state which heavily taxed the small peasant producers and, at the same time, attempted to support them against the emergence of a powerful class of large landowners and on the long-term rhythms of the penetration of world capitalism. Regarding the penetration of capitalism, it had already been emphasized that foreign investment and the world-market-induced expansion of commodity production did not follow an unbroken line over the course of the century. The rate of growth of the external trade of the Ottoman Empire accelerated during periods of expansion of the world economy. Similarly, foreign capital came in waves, the logic and the timing of which were closely tied to the long-term economic cycles in the capital-exporting countries and their rivalry. The complex interaction of these factors led to major regional differences in patterns of land ownership and tenancy.

We can now group direct producers in early twentieth-century Ottoman agriculture into four basic categories:

(1) Servile tenants in Southeastern Anatolia whose dependence on the landlords was not limited to economic factors;

(2) a limited number of wage laborers, mostly seasonal, who were concentrated in the most commercialized, export-oriented regions;

(3) some fixed-rent and mostly sharecropping tenants in large, middle- and small-sized holdings whose relations with the landowners did not go beyond the economic; and

(4) owner-producers in small- and middle-sized holdings.

Regional variations notwithstanding, the last two categories constituted the overwhelming majority of direct producers in Ottoman
agriculture. In other words, small peasant ownership and petty commodity production remained central characteristics of Ottoman agriculture during the nineteenth century as capitalism was beginning to
penetrate and dominate the rural areas. We would suggest, finally, that
dynamics of contemporary agrarian change in these areas of the world
cannot be fully understood without due attention to this historical legacy
– regional variation and petty commodity production.

Chapter 6

The decline and resistance of Ottoman cotton textiles, 1820–1913

In the aftermath of the Industrial Revolution in Europe, production activities in the secondary sector using pre-industrial technology were destroyed in both Europe and elsewhere. In most of Europe, the decline of handicrafts-based manufacturing activities was overshadowed by the rise of the factory system. On the other hand, it has been argued in recent years that in many areas of the Third World, from North Africa and the Middle East to South, Southeast and East Asia, the decline of employment in indigenous manufacturing activities that occurred during the nineteenth century was not compensated by a rise in the factory system equal or comparable in effect for as long as a century or more.[1]

It is also clear that, in the aftermath of the Industrial Revolution in Europe, manufacturing activities in the Third World cannot be studied in isolation. The scope and trajectory of these activities can be examined only in relation to the developments in the world market dominated by the more advanced industrial economies.[2]

In this chapter we will first attempt to reconstruct the process of decline of handicrafts and compare its magnitude with the effects of the rise of the factory system in one branch of production in the Ottoman Empire. The emphasis will be on the timing and magnitude of the changes in the levels of production and employment. However, our study also shows that, even in the case of cotton textiles, the destruction of Ottoman handicrafts was not complete. They continued to survive even a century after the beginning of competition from imports. Consequently, we will also examine the mechanisms of adaptation and resistance adopted by the different forms of indigenous production in order to gain further insights into the trajectory of manufacturing activity in the Ottoman Empire.

The choice of cotton textiles over other branches of production might require some explanation. In Britain and later elsewhere, the first wave of the Industrial Revolution brought about greater increases in productivity and more rapid declines in the prices of cotton textiles than in any other industry.[3] In the pre-industrial economies of the periphery, textiles were usually the most important branch of non-agricultural production in terms of both employment and the value of output. Hence, throughout the nineteenth century cotton textiles were by far the most important item in European exports, causing greater and more rapid destruction in the Third World than any other European industry.

In the Ottoman case, the borderline between cotton and other textiles becomes difficult to draw to the extent that some cloth products were woven using cotton and other kinds of yarn. Our quantitative estimates of imports and particularly of domestic production, given in tons, will indicate the cotton yarn content of these products. We will not deal with woolen and other textiles in this study except in reference to their size relative to cotton textiles.

The size of the Ottoman Empire and its changing borders during the nineteenth century posed important problems for the quantitative analysis undertaken in this chapter. Partly in response to these problems (which are discussed in appendix 5) we have limited the focus of this study to the 1911 borders of the Empire, Northern Greece, Thrace, Anatolia, Syria and Iraq. As a result, we deal with an area of greater geographical unity, particularly with respect to the clothing habits of the population. In contrast to the predominance of cotton textiles in these areas, in Bulgaria, for example, woolen textiles production and consumption remained relatively more important until World War I.[4]

Ottoman cotton textiles before the impact of imports

Relatively little is known about Ottoman textiles manufacturing during the seventeenth and eighteenth centuries. With respect to the seventeenth century, it has been pointed out that spinning of yarn and weaving of simple cotton cloth were in many areas predominantly rural activities carried out in close connection with the market. A recent study on Anatolia concludes that

it is very possible that there was even some kind of putting-out system in operation. At the same time, guild organization, with its possibilities of purchasing raw materials in common, may well have spread to certain settlements that remained very small in terms of population . . . About the details of organization in this branch of production we remain ignorant. Nor do we know how the weavers were affected by the upheavals of the later sixteenth century and the subsequent period, or by the export of raw materials as practiced by European traders.[5]

Available data on the trade of cotton, cotton yarn and cotton cloth allow us to obtain a fairly reliable impression of the state of manufactures in Northern Greece, Anatolia and Syria *vis-à-vis* their European counterparts during most of the eighteenth century. In the last third of the eighteenth century, these areas of the Empire were net exporters of raw cotton and of not insignificant amounts of cotton yarn from Thessaly and Macedonia. There were virtually no exports of cotton cloth to Western Europe. The extent to which this circumstance was due to the protectionist policies of European governments is not clear. Imports of cotton cloth from Europe remained limited, amounting to no more than 3 per cent of total domestic consumption.[6] In addition, some unknown amount of cotton cloth was being imported from India. Exports of cotton and partly cotton cloth to Egypt and the Northern Black Sea ports may well have equalled if not exceeded the volume of cotton cloth imports from Europe and India.[7]

The broad picture that emerges from an examination of the available evidence does not point to a flourishing, dynamic branch of production, vigorously competing in the international markets to expand its exports.[8] It is possible, in fact, that Ottoman cotton textiles experienced some decline during the eighteenth century, particularly in the European provinces.[9] On the other hand, during the last third of the eighteenth century, when the cotton industry in England was being transformed by the Industrial Revolution, and even as late as the second decade of the nineteenth century, the Empire remained self-sufficient in cotton textiles, its manufactures fully capable of supplying the domestic market, which comprised about 12 million inhabitants.[10]

In the early nineteenth century, there were considerable differences between different parts of the Empire with respect to the organization of textiles production.[11] In the urban areas of Anatolia and Syria, by far the most visible form, from the point of view of contemporary observers, was the organization of artisans around small-scale manufacturing establishments. Capital accumulation in the hands of the owners of these manufacturing establishments and the degree of differentiation among the artisans remained limited. The artisans in question can be divided into three groups.[12]

(a) the owners who employed others but who continued to work themselves;

(b) dispossessed artisans who lived in urban areas and who relied entirely on their wage income;

(c) artisans whose ties to land and rural areas had not been entirely eliminated and for whom seasonal wage incomes constituted a supplement to their rural income.

This category provided a considerable degree of fluidity and flexibility to the urban manufacturing establishments, enabling them to withstand violent fluctuations in demand.

The extent to which these establishments came under guild control varied from region to region. The influence of the guilds was strongest in Istanbul, because of the support of the state. The strength of the guilds decreased during the nineteenth century, and by the last quarter of the century guilds exerted little effective influence over the manufacturing establishments. However, the central government was reluctant to formally abolish the guilds until the twentieth century, fearing the social and political consequences of widespread unemployment of the artisans, particularly in and around the capital city.[13]

The second form of production for market was the putting-out system, about the extent of which we have limited information. It is clear that until the arrival of imported yarn merchants organized rural women for the spinning of cotton and woolen yarn. Since under pre-industrial technology spinning was a low-productivity activity in relation to weaving, one would expect that, before the arrival of industrial imports, a large proportion of the cotton yarn produced for market was spun by peasant women in their homes.[14] The extent to which weaving of simple cotton cloth and partly cotton cloth was organized under the putting-out system remains unclear.[15]

The third and last form of production, which employed basically the same technology as the first two, involved spinning and weaving activities for immediate consumption within the rural household or the village. In the context of a more or less self-sufficient rural economy, raw cotton was either produced locally in limited amounts or obtained from a nearby area.[16] Partly because of the availability of the raw material and partly because of the warm climate, cotton was about as important as wool for the daily wear of the Anatolian and Syrian peasant. This use of both wool and cotton was unlike the situation in some of the European provinces of the Empire such as Bulgaria and unlike that in pre-industrial Britain, where woolen cloth prevailed.[17] Since around 80 per cent of the Ottoman population lived in rural areas during the nineteenth century, home production of cotton and woolen textiles for immediate consumption emerges as the form of production with the largest share in the total production of textiles not only early in the nineteenth century but also in the later period, when Ottoman agriculture began to be increasingly commercialized.

In other words, the rural areas accounted for most of the cotton yarn and cloth production before the competition from European industry developed. Most of the production under the putting-out system, whatever its volume was, can also be considered a rural activity. In contrast, the urban manufacturing establishments that met the smaller, more differentiated urban demand and accounted for most of the long-distance trade, including the limited volume of exports to Egypt, were affected first and most profoundly by the offensive of European industrial products.

In the first and second quarters of the nineteenth century, urban textile manufacturing and production organized under the putting-out system to meet the urban demand was not distributed evenly around Northern Greece, Anatolia and Northern Syria.[18] While Istanbul and Bursa were important centers, the Salonica area, the Black Sea Coast, and Western and Central Anatolia do not appear as major areas of urban manufacturing activity. By far the most important concentration of urban textile manufacturing activity and probably the main use of the putting-out system existed in Northern Syria, Southeastern Anatolia, and to some extent Eastern Anatolia during both the earlier and later parts of the nineteenth century. In addition to Damascus, Hama and Humus, which were in Syria proper, Aleppo, Diyarbakır, Antep, Maraş, Urfa, Arapkir, Bitlis, Erzurum, Sivas, Amasya and Tokat, listed roughly in order of declining importance, contained substantial numbers of handlooms.

Various reasons can be offered for this spatial pattern. We will be necessarily brief and non-exhaustive. Competition from imports may have led to the decline of urban manufacturing along the Anatolian coast even before the nineteenth century. Since urban manufacturing establishments produced primarily for urban demand, the degree of urbanization was an important factor. Central and Western-Central Anatolia and the Black Sea Coast exhibited relatively low levels of urbanization until the mid-nineteenth century.[19] In contrast, outside the Istanbul region, levels of urbanization were highest during the earlier period in Southeastern Anatolia and Northern Syria. This region had historically benefited from being on a major transit trade route. It had also benefited during the eighteenth and nineteenth centuries from its proximity to Egypt, a major market for domestically produced textiles. The relative scarcity and poor quality of agricultural land and the low level of commercialization of agriculture may also have been important factors in the flourishing of manufactures in these areas.[20]

Rural household production for immediate consumption was more evenly distributed over space. Availability of raw cotton was about the only, but at times a critical, precondition. With increasing commercialization of agriculture, this form of production was bound to undergo major changes during the nineteenth century.

The self-sufficient position of the Empire in cotton textiles changed rapidly after the Napoleonic Wars under the intense competition of European industry. We will attempt to explain the resulting changes not so much in terms of legal or institutional rearrangements such as Free Trade Treaties but in terms of long-term world economic processes in the aftermath of the Industrial Revolution. It was the emergence in Europe of industrialized economies in search of markets for their manufactures and cheap and abundant sources of foodstuffs and raw materials that led to the expansion of their trade with the countries in the periphery.[21]

Nonetheless, the adverse consequences on Ottoman manufactures of the Free Trade Treaties signed after 1838 should not be underestimated. These were not limited to the lowering of the tariff rate on imports to nominally low levels until World War I. With the signing of the treaties, the *ad valorem* tariff on imports was set at 5 per cent. All exports from the Empire, among them exports of cotton cloth woven with imported yarn, were subjected to a 12 per cent *ad valorem* tariff until 1861, after which date it was gradually lowered to 1 per cent.[22]

More important, until 1870 domestically produced commodities transported over land from one part of the Empire to another were subjected to a 12 per cent internal customs duty; those transported within the Empire by sea were subject to a 4 per cent duty until 1889.[23] This system, designed to raise revenue for the central government, resulted in severe discrimination against domestic manufactures during the most critical period of decline for Ottoman cotton textiles.[24]

The reconstruction procedure

Until now, researchers have tried to assess the timing and extent of the impact of European industrial products primarily by utilizing the fragmentary and impressionistic evidence on the number of handlooms in operation in different urban areas of the Empire.[25] This data, while useful, can often be misleading because of intertemporal and inter-regional fluctuations in urban manufacturing activity, which depended, among other things, on the size of the agricultural harvest. More importantly, it is clear that most of the handicrafts-based production activity in textiles took place in the countryside.

In the absence of comprehensive, economy-wide figures, we have developed an indirect procedure for estimating the long-term changes in the level of handicrafts activity. Following a 'macro' approach, we attempted to reconstruct the decline and resistance of Ottoman cotton textiles by estimating the changes over time in the size of the domestic market for cotton textiles, the volume of imports and the level of domestic production. In this reconstruction attempt, our starting point was the foreign trade statistics of the European countries, which enabled us to draw a complete profile of Ottoman imports of cotton yarn and cotton cloth for selective intervals of the period 1820–1913 (1820–2, 1840–2,

1870–2, 1880–2, 1894–6 and 1909–11).[26] Some details of this procedure are discussed in appendix 5. In the second stage, we attempted to estimate the size of the domestic market, first for 1909–11 and then for the earlier intervals. Exports being relatively insignificant, the difference between the imports and the domestic market gave us the level of domestic production for each interval.

If we assume that yarn is not wasted in the weaving of cotton cloth, total domestic consumption and the size of the domestic market for cotton textiles can be derived from the following identity in the Ottoman context:

(1) $\quad T = M_c + M_y + H_y + F_y + E_c$

where

$T =$ domestic consumption or the size of the domestic market for cotton textiles

$M_c =$ imports of cloth

$M_y =$ imports of yarn

$H_y =$ handicrafts production of yarn

$F_y =$ domestic factory production of yarn

$E_c =$ exports of cloth

so that

(2) $\quad H_c = M_y + H_y + F_y - F_c$

where

$H_c =$ handicrafts production of cloth

$F_c =$ domestic factory production of cloth.

In other words, identity (2) indicates that, given (1), the level of domestic handicrafts weaving of cotton cloth can be indirectly measured by summing up the cotton yarn available from the three sources: imports, hand-spun yarn, and that portion of the output of the domestic factories that was not industrially woven.

All accounts of the period indicate that by the 1910s hand spinning of cotton yarn had been reduced to a very low level. Similarly, the cotton content of the exports of domestic manufactures was well below 1 per cent of the size of the domestic market for textiles.[27] As a result, the size of the domestic market in the early 1910s can be estimated primarily on the basis of the three major components in identity (1), imports of yarn and cloth and domestic factory production of yarn (see table 6.1).[28] The same framework was used to estimate the size of the domestic market and to determine the relative shares of imports and domestic production for the years 1880–2 and 1870–2. The level of pre-industrial weaving of cotton yarn was then calculated on the basis of identity (2).[29]

Carrying this reconstruction attempt further back in time, towards the first quarter of the nineteenth century, necessitated more indirect forms

Table 6.1. *Estimates of consumption and production of cotton textiles in the Ottoman Empire, 1820–1910*
Annual averages in tons

	Total population (million) 1	Population within 1911 borders (million) 2	Per capita consumption (kilograms) 3	Total consumption 4	Imports of cloth 5	Imports of yarn 6	Hand spinning of yarn 7	Handicrafts weaving 8	Industrial yarn 9	Industrial cloth 10
1820–2 I	18.5	13.5	0.90	12,150	450	150	11,550	11,700	—	—
II			1.00	13,500	450	150	12,900	13,050	—	—
III			1.10	14,850	450	150	14,250	14,400	—	—
1840–2 I	20.5	15.0	1.00	15,000	4,100	2,650	8,250	10,900	—	—
II			1.10	16,500	4,100	2,650	9,750	12,400	—	—
III			1.20	18,000	4,100	2,650	11,250	13,900	—	—
1870–2	23.0	18.5	1.52	28,050	17,300	7,750	3,000	10,750	—	—
1880–2	20.4	20.4	1.65	33,700	24,700	6,500	2,000	9,000	500	—
1894–6	22.5	22.5	1.87	42,100	26,950	11,150	1,500	14,950	2,500	200
1909–11	25.5	25.5	2.66	67,900	49,350	12,550	1,000	17,550	5,000	1,000

Notes: With the exception of column 1, all figures refer to the area within the 1911 borders of the Empire, Northern Greece, Thrace, Anatolia, Syria and Iraq.
Exports are assumed to be negligible.
All figures are rounded to the closest unit of fifty.
The underlying calculations are based on the following identities: $4 = 5 + 6 + 7 + 9$ and $8 = 6 + 7 + 9 - 10$. See text for details.
Column 9 includes industrial yarn industrially woven into cloth, given in column 10.

Sources: See text and appendix 5.

of estimation. For the period after 1870, we were able to make the assumption that hand spinning of cotton yarn had been reduced to rather low levels. However, the decades before the 1870s were exactly the period when the destruction of this activity was taking place most rapidly. We needed other means of estimating the level of hand spinning in the earlier period.

We proceeded estimating the long-term changes in per capita consumption levels of cotton textiles. Under the assumptions that all cotton yarn was woven into cloth without waste and that the cotton content of partly cotton clothes can be measured by their cotton yarn content, it can be observed from table 6.1 that between 1880–2 and 1909–11, per capita consumption of cotton textiles increased at an average rate of 1.7 per cent per annum. According to the only available estimate, Ottoman per capita GNP increased at an average rate that was slightly over 1 per cent per annum during 1899–1911.[30] Since the income elasticity of cotton textiles is expected to be relatively high in a low-income nineteenth-century economy, and since the century-long shift in patterns of demand from woolen to cotton textiles that had started in the aftermath of the Industrial Revolution was still going on,[31] these figures appear quite plausible.

How can these estimates of per capita consumption levels be extended to 1820–2, to the beginnings of the invasion of the domestic market by the products of European industry? We have virtually no information regarding changes in per capita income levels in the Empire during this earlier period. Indirectly we know that the period 1840 to 1873 was a period of rapid integration of the Empire into world markets, with rates of expansion of the Empire's external trade exceeding those of any other comparable period until World War I.[32] A recent study indicates that the real wages of common and skilled construction workers showed limited increases until the early 1870s and then a substantial jump after the War of 1877–8.[33] All in all, some limited increases in per capita income levels may have occurred after 1840, though these increases certainly were not comparable in magnitude to those estimated for the period after 1899.

Second, the rapid decline in the prices of cotton textiles that accompanied the rapid expansion of imports from Europe may have led to changes in the clothing habits of the Ottoman population, from woolen to cheaper but less durable cotton cloth. We have no way of assessing the relative magnitude of either of these effects on per capita consumption levels.[34]

Owing to this difficulty of providing reliable estimates for per capita cotton textiles consumption levels for 1820–2 and 1840–2, we chose to adopt a range for the actual levels of consumption for each of these intervals. On the basis of the considerations summarized above, we established a range of 40 to 70 per cent for the increases in per capita consumption levels between 1820 and 1870, with most of the increase occurring after 1840. Given the increases in per capita consumption levels that had been estimated for 1870–2 to 1880–2 and 1880–2 to 1909–11, these estimates lead to a range of 150 to 200 per cent increase in levels of per capita consumption of cotton textiles between 1820–2 and 1909–11.

In table 6.1 we provide three alternatives within this range. Alternative I, which represents the case of relatively lower levels of consumption in 1820–2 and 1840–2 and relatively higher rates of increase in these levels until 1870–2, sets per capita consumption of cotton textiles at 0.90 kg. per year and 1.00 kg. per year for 1820–2 and 1840–2, respectively. Since Alternative I projects relatively lower levels of domestic production activity at the early stages of decline of Ottoman textiles, it provides a lower bound for our estimates regarding the destruction and unemployment caused by the imports.

Alternative III represents the case of relatively higher levels of consumption in 1820–2 and 1840–2 and lower rates of increase of per capita consumption until 1870–2. It sets these levels at 1.10 kg. and 1.20 kg. per person per year for 1820–2 and 1840–2 respectively. By projecting relatively higher levels of domestic consumption and production in the early part of the century, Alternative III provides upper bound estimates for the impact of the imports. Finally, Alternative II depicts a middle case between I and III.

A not insignificant piece of evidence in support of our estimates comes from one of the more insightful Western observers of the Ottoman economy. Writing in the late 1820s while in search of markets for British industry, David Urquhart estimated that

In the southern provinces [of the Ottoman Empire], the poorest family of four required twenty okkes [1.275 kg. each] of uncleaned cotton and ten of wool for its yearly consumption and the manufacturing of these occupies one third of their indoor labor. The twenty okkes of uncleaned cotton will be reduced to four of manufactured or *eleven pounds* [*for a family of four*]. Of this eight pounds will consist of such stuff as they would willingly purchase if they had the means . . . Two pounds, then, for each individual [as an estimate of the size of the market for British industry], will certainly be far below the mark.[35]

Summary results

The results of our reconstruction attempt presented in table 6.1 indicate that between 1820 and World War I imports of cotton cloth and yarn into the area within the 1911 borders of the Ottoman Empire increased by over a hundredfold. Per capita imports of cotton textiles increased over fiftyfold during the same period. As a result of this massive invasion, the share of imports in total domestic consumption increased from less than 5 per cent in the 1820s to more than 80 per cent in the early 1910s.

In 1820–2, annual imports of cotton yarn and cloth into the area within the 1911 borders of the Empire, mostly from Britain, were 150 and 450 tons per annum, respectively. By 1840–2 the imports had increased by about tenfold to 2,650 and 4,100 tons per annum respectively, and their share in the domestic market exceeded 30 per cent. Within three decades, imports of cotton yarn and cloth had climbed to 7,750 and 17,300 tons per year respectively, another increase of about fourfold. By the early 1870s, imports began to account for more than 80 per cent of the total consumption of cotton textiles within the 1911 borders of the Empire.[36] Domestic production was based entirely on traditional handicrafts during this period. A few modern factories in cotton textiles were established, but they did not survive. As we will argue below, we consider the period until the mid-1870s and especially the three decades after 1840 as the decisive stage in the decline of handicrafts production in cotton textiles.[37]

Since large areas of the Ottoman Empire gained independence and since there was a considerable amount of migration from the seceding areas to the remaining areas, we do not view the results of our reconstruction attempt as sufficiently reliable for making direct comparisons between 1870–2 and 1880–2.[38] On the other hand, the period from the early 1880s to World War I was characterized by three trends. First, the rate of expansion of the domestic market was more rapid than in the earlier part of the nineteenth century. Our estimates point to an approximate doubling of total consumption during the half century between 1820 and 1870 and another doubling in the three decades until 1910. Second, we observe that the rapid expansion of the share of imports in the domestic market, which was the most important feature of the earlier period, came to a halt after the 1880s. The share of imports in total domestic consumption remained unchanged at more than 80 per cent. Third, then, levels of domestic production expanded at the same rate as the size of the domestic market and the volume of imports. Part of the increases in domestic production were due to the emergence of a limited number of 'modern' factories using imported technology, especially in cotton yarn. Equally important, while the volume of hand spinning continued to decline, the volume of hand weaving not only held its own, but approximately doubled between 1880 and World War I.

Estimation of the decline in production and employment until the 1870s

The coastal and other more commercialized areas of the Empire were first to be affected by competition from imported factory products. Contemporary observers began to describe the competition and decline in the European provinces and around Istanbul in the 1820s and 1830s.[39] By the 1840s, similar reports were providing details of the destruction and unemployment along the Anatolian and Syrian coasts, and most important, in the Bursa and Aleppo areas.[40] On the other hand, the penetration of imports into the interior of Anatolia, to such centers as Diyarbakır, Erzurum, Van and even Ankara remained limited until the early 1870s.[41] This regional differentiation is basically due to the barriers of high transportation costs in two senses of the term. First, higher transportation costs raise the prices of imported manufactures. Second, by limiting the commercialization and export orientation of agriculture, they also delayed the destruction of the more or less self-sufficient nature of rural economies, specialization in agriculture and the rise of demand for manufactures.[42]

Our calculations indicate that the decline in pre-industrial production activity in cotton textiles was most rapid during the three decades following 1840. This period started with the signing of the Free Trade Treaties between the Ottoman Empire and the European powers and coincided roughly with the long-term upswing of the world economy frequently referred to as the mid-century or Victorian boom. One unambiguous trend emerging from an examination of this period is the rapid destruction and disappearance of hand spinning of cotton yarn. According to Alternative I in table 6.1, which provides a lower bound estimate for the extent of the decline in domestic activity, the volume of domestic spinning fell from 11,550 tons per year in 1820–2, to 8,250 tons in 1840–2, to 3,000 tons in 1870–2.

We assume the average annual production of a full-time spinner working with a handloom to be about 60 kg. of cotton yarn per year.[43] In this case, the decline estimated by Alternative I corresponds to the disappearance of full-time employment for 142,500 spinners between 1820 and 1870, 60,000 of whom were displaced by imports after 1840. Since most of the hand spinning was undertaken by peasant women during the off-season, the actual number of spinners losing part-time employment was substantially larger than this figure.

According to Alternative III which, in our view, provides an upper bound estimate for the extent of the decline, the volume of domestically spun cotton yarn declined from 14,250 tons per annum in 1820–2, to 11,400 tons in 1840–2, to 3,000 tons in 1870–2. Under the assumption of 60 kg. of yarn per spinner per year, this decline corresponds to the loss of full-time employment for 187,500 spinners between 1820 and 1870, the loss of 140,000 of which occurred during the three decades after 1840.

Our estimates indicate that, in contrast to the disappearance of domestic spinning activity, a large part of the weaving existing around 1820 survived until the 1870s and beyond. According to Alternative I, cotton weaving, measured in weight terms, declined from 11,700 tons per year in 1820–2, to 10,900 tons in 1840–2, to 10,750 tons in 1870–2. If we accept average pre-industrial productivity in weaving cotton cloth as 200 kg. per person per year, this decline corresponds to the loss of full-time employment for 4,750 weavers between 1820 and 1870.[44]

According to Alternative III, which provides an upper bound estimate for the decline, the volume of weaving declined from 14,400 tons of cotton yarn per annum in 1820–2 to 13,900 tons in 1870–2. In other words, at least as much as three fourths of weaving activity appears to have survived the first wave of decline and destruction. Using 200 kg. per person per year as the average annual production, we find that these figures correspond to a loss of 18,250 full-time jobs for 18,250 weavers between 1820 and 1870. This is by no means an insignificant figure, but it is only one-tenth of the amount of unemployment created in spinning. It should also be noted that this decline, however small it may seem, occurred at a time when the size of the domestic market was doubling and imports accounted for all of the increase.

Given this sharp distinction between the unemployment effects of imports on spinning and weaving, the question inevitably arises as to why most contemporary observers of the decline referred to weaving. This apparent paradox can be explained by the fact that, while spinning was an overwhelmingly rural activity, a good part of the weaving, and certainly most of its decline until the 1870s, occurred in the urban areas. Hence the decline in this relatively small segment of Ottoman textile production was much more visible to the native and mostly Western observers.

On the basis of our reconstruction attempt, then, the total decline in full-time employment in the spinning and weaving stages of Ottoman cotton textiles during the half century after 1820 is estimated at between 147,250 and 205,750 persons. The population of the Empire within its 1911 borders averaged around 16 million during this period. Therefore, our estimates correspond to a decline of about 2 to 3 per cent of the working population in the numbers of people engaged in the secondary sector. Since the share of the secondary sector in total employment was a small fraction of any nineteenth-century economy, this decline corresponds to a major contraction of the employment provided by the secondary sector.

Before we conclude this section, we will provide a discussion of the sensitivity of our results to the key assumption regarding the levels of per capita consumption of cotton cloth in the early part of the nineteenth century. As table 6.1 indicates, if the actual per capita consumption level in 1820–2 was lower than our lower bound estimate by 0.1 kg., then our lower bound estimate for the decline in employment in the domestic spinning of cotton yarn would have to be reduced by 22,500. Similarly, our lower bound estimate for the decline in employment in the domestic weaving of cloth would then indicate that the number of full-time weavers increased slightly, by about 5 per cent, between 1820 and 1870. Conversely, if the actual per capita consumption level in 1820–2 was higher than our upper bound estimate by 0.1 kg., then our higher bound estimate for the decline in employment in spinning would have to be raised by 22,500. Similarly, our higher bound estimate for the decline in employment in weaving would then have to be raised by 6,750.

In recent studies of de-industrialization, a central question has been whether there was any decline at all in the proportion of the population engaged in secondary industry.[45] In the present context, this question can be reformulated in the following manner: which level of per capita consumption in 1820–2 would imply that the impact of imports did not lead to a decline in the proportion of the working population engaged in cotton textiles? In other words, for which level of per capita consumption in 1820–2 can we conclude that, after an allowance is made for the increase in the numbers of working population, the rapid expansion in imports met only the increase in total domestic consumption during this half century?

A simple calculation indicates that per capita consumption of cotton textiles in 1820–2 needs to be as low as 0.30 kg., one-fifth of its level in 1870–2, for Ottoman cotton textiles to have provided employment to the same proportion of the working population in 1820–2 as in 1870–2.[46] Available evidence regarding the earlier part of the nineteenth century does not point to the kind of rapid and sustained rises in the standards of living that would make a fourfold increase in per capita consumption of cotton textiles during this half century feasible, even if we accept the possibility that a large part of this increase was due to a shift in the clothing habits of the population, from the use of woolen to the use of cotton textiles.[47] For climatic and other reasons, cotton was an important, if not the most important, branch of textiles in the Ottoman Empire before the nineteenth century. The observations of contemporaries, among them David Urquhart, cited earlier, make it clear that per capita consumption levels of cotton textiles in the 1820s were three to four times higher than 0.30 kg. per year.[48] In view of the available evidence, therefore, we have to reject the hypothesis that levels of production and employment of handicrafts-based cotton textiles did not decline in the Ottoman Empire during the nineteenth century.

Employment in cotton textiles after 1880

While the numbers of people engaged in hand spinning continued to decline after 1880, there was a limited increase in the total amount of employment provided by handicrafts-based production because of increases at the weaving stage. As shown in table 6.1, home spinning of cotton yarn, which was limited to the more remote rural areas, gradually declined from about 2,000 tons per year in 1880–2 to about 1,000 tons by 1909–11. At 60 kg. of yarn per person per year, this represents a loss of full-time employment for about 16,600 rural spinners.

This loss was more than offset by the expansion of weaving. Our estimates summarized in table 6.1 indicate that between 1880–2 and 1909–11 supplies of cotton yarn available for handicrafts weaving increased by a total of 8,550 tons.[49] At an average of 200 kg. of cotton cloth per weaver per year, this represents full-time employment for an additional 42,750 urban and rural weavers. To the extent that spinning and weaving were seasonal activities, whether for wage income or for the consumption of the peasant household, the numbers of people actually affected were considerably larger in both instances.

However, it should be emphasized that these increases in the numbers of people engaged 'full-time' in handicrafts-based cotton textiles were quite limited in comparison to the decline in employment during the half century until the 1870s. This becomes particularly evident if we examine changes in the level of employment provided by this branch of production as a percentage of the population of the Empire within its 1911 borders. Our mid-point estimate represented by Alternative II indicates that in 1820–2, an equivalent of 280,250 people, or 2.1 per cent of the total population of these areas, were engaged full-time in the spinning and weaving stages of cotton textiles (see table 6.2). This fraction declined rapidly to 1.5 per cent by 1840–2 and to 0.56 per cent by 1870–2. By 1909–11 an equivalent of 104,400 people were engaged full-time in the spinning and weaving of handicrafts and they represented no more than 0.4 per cent of the total population of the Empire. As shown in table 6.2, the limited amount of employment provided by the modern cotton textile factories does not change this picture. In short, then, the numbers of people employed 'full-time' in Ottoman cotton textiles, the

Table 6.2. *'Full-time' employment in Ottoman cotton textiles as percentage of total population*

	Full-time employment			Population within 1911 borders of the Empire (millions)	Ratio of employment to population (per cent)
	Spinning 1	Weaving 2	Total 3 = 1 + 2	4	5 = 3/4
1820–2	215,000	65,250	280,250	13.5	2.08
1840–2	162,500	62,000	224,500	15.0	1.50
1870–2	50,000	53,750	103,750	18.5	0.56
1880–2	33,300	45,000	78,300	20.4	0.38
1909–11 (I)	16,650	87,750	104,400	25.5	0.41
1909–11 (II)			108,000	25.5	0.42

Notes: The underlying coefficients of average annual production for a full-time employed worker are 60 kg. of yarn in spinning and 200 kg. of cloth in weaving. 1909–11 (II) includes an estimate of employment in factories.
Source: Based on table 6.1; for the years 1820–2 and 1840–2, Alternative II of that table is used.

most important branch of production outside agriculture, declined by two-thirds between 1820 and 1913. Even more dramatically, their ratio to the total population declined by four-fifths during the same period.

World economic cycles and resistance by handicrafts

While the decline in Ottoman cotton textiles was dramatic, it was not absolute. Some handicrafts weaving survived well into the twentieth century. In this section we will discuss the interaction between different forms of pre-industrial production and their adaptation to European industry. We will also emphasize the uneven impact of long-term fluctuations in the world economy of these different forms.

By far the most important adaptation mechanism used by the handicrafts weavers was the switch to use of imported yarn in weaving. In addition to its lower price, the quality and durability of factory-produced British yarn were superior to those of the local hand-spun product.[50] In the more populous coastal areas of the Empire, imported cotton yarn began to dominate the markets at an early stage. The urban manufacturing establishments were the first to switch to the factory product, thereby cutting their ties to the rural spinners. On the other hand, home spinning survived in the more remote areas until after the turn of the century, even though imported yarn began to reach the urban markets in the interior of Anatolia in the 1830s, if not earlier.[51]

In the rural areas, the level of consumption of cotton textiles and the extent to which this consumption was met by household weaving depended upon a number of factors. First, because of the ready availability of its raw material, woolen textiles had been relatively more important within the context of a more self-sufficient rural economy. The arrival of inexpensive imports, particularly of yarn in the early period, started the shift towards cotton. This trend continued with increasing commercialization of agriculture and monetization of the rural economy. Second, standards of living did rise, to some unknown extent, particularly in the more commercialized rural areas of the Empire, and this rise was reflected in the per capita consumption levels of cotton textiles, a relatively more income elastic item.[52]

This brings us to the differentiation within the peasantry. At any point in time, the extent to which a peasant household was integrated into the long-distance markets depended upon the size of its marketable surplus. It was the peasants with middle-sized and large land holdings who purchased a larger part of their cotton textiles consumption in the form of cloth, did relatively less weaving, and even generated demand for the more differentiated products of urban manufacturing establishments.

Despite efforts by its representatives and by the representatives of the Foreign Office in the Empire, the Lancashire textiles industry could not produce the variety of cotton and partly cotton cloth patterns demanded in different parts of the Empire and elsewhere in the Middle East.[53] The survival of local preferences meant that imported yarn would be woven in rural households and especially in urban manufacturing establishments to meet this demand. The survival of the urban manufacturing establishments until World War I, in however weak a form, has to be explained to a large extent by this characteristic of the Ottoman textiles market.

We have detailed information about the urban weaving establishments in Southeastern Anatolia and Syria, the most important textile manufacturing areas of the Empire during the nineteenth century. For example, in Aleppo alone, the number of handlooms in operation weaving cotton, partly cotton and other textiles frequently reached 6,000 in the second quarter of the century.[54] In the early twentieth century, as many as 14,000 handlooms were in operation in Aleppo and in other urban areas of Southeastern Anatolia within the borders of present-day Turkey.[55] The products of this large workforce were not only sold in the local markets but shipped to the interior of Anatolia. As much as half of the total production of Aleppo was sent to Egypt.[56]

Throughout the century there was a secular tendency for urban manufacturing activity to retreat as tastes changed and as lower-priced imported cloth began to be accepted by those who had earlier preferred the local designs. On the other hand, in the medium and shorter term, the most important single determinant of the level of demand for local products was agricultural and agriculture-related incomes. This should not be surprising in an overwhelmingly agrarian economy, although most of the products of urban manufacturing establishments were consumed in the urban areas.[57]

In turn, one of the more important determinants of agricultural income levels was the level of world market demand for foodstuffs and raw materials. We observe a general decline in the volume of production by urban manufacturing establishments during the 1880s and the early 1890s when the world economy was going through a period of relative stagnation, even though the growth rate of the volume of cotton manufactures imports also declined during this period (see table 6.1). On the other hand, as world market demand for primary products began to expand at higher rates after 1896, both the volume of cotton textile imports and the level of production in the manufacturing establishments began to rise.[58]

In earlier chapters we have emphasized the fact that periods of expansion and relative stagnation of the world economy created very different conjunctures for the Ottoman economy. Here we will examine the changes in the volume of cotton textile imports from that perspective. Between 1880–2 and 1909–11 total consumption of cotton textiles in the Ottoman Empire doubled, primarily because of the 60 per cent rise in per capita consumption levels. However, this expansion took place at very different rates during periods of relative stagnation and of more rapid growth of the world economy. Our calculations presented in table 6.1 indicate that per capita consumption levels of cotton textiles increased by a total of 14 per cent between 1880–2 and 1894–6, at an average rate of 0.9 per cent per year. In contrast, they rose by a total of 40 per cent during 1894–6 to 1909–11, at an average annual rate of 2.4 per cent. The changes in the volume and composition of imports are equally striking. Between 1880–2 and 1894–6 imports of cotton cloth rose by 8 per cent only, while imports of cotton yarn increased by a total of 70 per cent. On the other hand, during 1894–6 to 1909–11, imports of cloth jumped by 85 per cent, while imports of cotton yarn grew by only 13 per cent.

As was pointed out earlier, the volume of weaving in urban manu-facturing establishments declined during the Great Depression. There-fore, we need to focus on weaving in the rural areas in order to understand the rapid growth in imports of cotton yarn until 1896. Despite the relative stagnation of the Ottoman economy during this period, exports con-tinued to rise, albeit at slower rates, and the integration of the rural areas into world markets continued. Under these circumstances it appears likely that most of the consumption was due to a shift from woolen textiles to cotton arising from increasing commercialization and not so much due to increases in income levels. Because of the relative stagnation of rural incomes, the shift towards cotton did not take the form of increased purchases of cotton cloth but proceeded through increased purchases of imported yarn, which was then woven within rural households. It appears, therefore, that the Great Depression was a critical period in the expansion of household weaving with imported yarn into the rural areas of Anatolia and Syria (see table 6.1).[59]

These long-term trends in urban manufacturing establishments and in rural areas changed rapidly after 1896. The volume of weaving in urban manufacturing establishments began to rise as agricultural and commercial incomes increased along with more rapid expansion of exports and improvements in external terms of trade. Our calculations indicate that the increases in the volume of cotton yarn imports and in domestic factory production of yarn between 1894–6 and 1909–11 roughly equalled or even remained behind the growth in the volume of urban weaving. In other words, all the additional cotton yarn that became available was consumed in the manufacturing establishments. The volume of rural household weaving did not change; it may have even declined somewhat during this period.

Can this latter trend be consistent with increases in rural income levels and in per capita consumption of cotton manufactures? In the years preceding World War I, increasing incomes accelerated the ongoing process of specialization in agriculture.[60] It is probable that, as a result, less time was allocated to non-agricultural activities in the rural areas. Lower rates of growth for imports of yarn and higher rates of growth for imports of cotton cloth can be understood in this context. With rising incomes and greater commercialization, rural households preferred to purchase more imported cloth in the marketplace rather than weaving more imported yarn at home (see table 6.1).[61]

The first factories

Chronologically overlapping with the decline and resistance of handicrafts was another process: the emergence of modern factories in cotton textiles using imported technology. This industrialization process can be examined in two distinct waves. In the second quarter of the nineteenth century and especially during the 1840s, some several dozen industrial establishments were formed under state ownership, primarily to meet military and governmental demands. Among these were at least three establishments producing cotton textiles.[62] To a large extent, this drive by the state was inspired by the industrial efforts of the Mohammed Ali administration in Egypt and its military success against Istanbul. Although their output was purchased by the military and the palace, which effectively insulated them from the competition of European imports, most of these factories collapsed within a short time. By the early 1850s very little had been left of an 'industry' producing 'cloth made in Turkey by European machinery, out of European material and by good European hands'.[63]

The second wave involved the establishment of factories by private capital under conditions of open economy, with very low rates of tariff protection. Transportation costs, availability of locally grown cotton, and low wages constituted the bases for the emergence of this industry. Not only was there virtually no support from the state until 1913, but until the last quarter of the nineteenth century many attempts to establish these factories met with resistance from the guilds.[64]

It appears that the first privately owned cotton spinning mills to remain in operation within the 1911 borders of the Empire were established in the Salonica region around 1879.[65] By the end of the 1880s, the locally produced industrial yarn dominated the market in Macedonia, but had little impact elsewhere in the Empire.[66] Cotton spinning mills in Adana, Istanbul, Izmir and elsewhere in the Empire followed. Our estimates indicate that by 1909–11 the annual production of industrial yarn, used as an input in handicrafts weaving, averaged 4,000 tons per annum, less than a quarter of the total consumption of yarn in the Empire.[67] The industrial production of cotton cloth was even more limited. In 1909–11 it averaged 1,000 tons per annum, about 2 per cent of the volume of cotton cloth imports and a share of about 1.5 per cent in total domestic consumption (see table 6.1).[68] The total volume of employment provided by these factories did not exceed several thousand in 1909–11.[69]

In short, in cotton textiles, the key industry of the Industrial Revolution, the factory system and the technology of the revolution arrived in the Ottoman Empire more than a hundred years later to an economy kept open with Free Trade Treaties. For this and other reasons the rise of modern factories in this key branch of production remained very weak. Only in the 1930s and within the context of a 'national' economy was the cotton textiles industry in Turkey going to prevail in the domestic market. The reversal of the trends in employment and production that had started with the arrival of the imports in the 1820s had taken more than a century.

Cotton textiles: a special case?

It might be argued that cotton textiles did not represent a typical case of de-industrialization. Indeed, in terms of the absolute magnitude and the rate of decline in employment, cotton textiles provide the most striking example of destruction of handicrafts-based manufacturing activity. Consequently, the limits and implications of the results of this chapter need to be carefully established. Our results do not imply that all branches of handicrafts-based production were affected to the same extent or in the same direction. Undoubtedly, in some branches of production the decline was more limited and resistance more successful. Some other branches of handicrafts may have even flourished in the face of changing world market conditions. However, it should also be emphasized that in terms of production and employment textiles occupied a very central place in the Ottoman economy during the nineteenth century. A large decline in the employment generated by this sector was bound to have a substantial impact on the total amount of employment in the secondary sector. In fact, in view of the evidence presented here, it would be difficult to argue that the share of the secondary sector in total employment in the Ottoman economy did not decline during the nineteenth century.

We should also emphasize that the case of cotton textiles has important implications for the study of the more general process of decline of handicrafts-based manufacturing activity in Third World countries. For example, in the Ottoman Empire some hand weaving survived for more than a century after the impact of imports began. The study of cotton textiles enables us to understand better the mechanisms of adaptation and resistance employed by the indigenous forms of production. Similarly, the case of cotton textiles enables us to place the experiences of different areas of the Third World into a comparative framework. For example, the results of this chapter confirm that the nineteenth-century decline of Ottoman, Indian and Chinese cotton textiles followed the same pattern in at least one important respect: allowing for differences in the extent of and the speed with which each country was integrated into world markets, the decline in the hand spinning of yarn proceeded much more rapidly and to a greater degree; on the other hand, for reasons discussed here and elsewhere, hand weaving of cloth survived for longer periods of time.[70]

The study of cotton textiles allows for other insights and comparisons as well. It is well established that clothing habits around the world changed considerably during the nineteenth century as technical progress associated with the Industrial Revolution made cotton textiles increasingly cheaper in relation to woolen and other cloth. The study of cotton textiles in this context provides important clues regarding the extent of world market integration of a nineteenth-century peripheral economy and particularly of its rural areas. Moreover, we would expect that comparisons between different peripheral countries regarding patterns of consumption, domestic production and importation of cotton textiles will also lead to important insights regarding the degree of integration of different countries into the world economy.[71]

We will end this chapter by summarizing the patterns of production and consumption of textiles in rural areas of the Ottoman Empire after a century of rapid integration into world markets. In the 1820s, the Ottoman economy was basically self-sufficient in cotton textiles with small volumes of imports and exports in both cotton and woolen textiles. It appears that, early in the nineteenth century, per capita consumption levels of cotton and woolen textiles in the areas within the 1911 borders of the Empire were comparable on a weight basis.[72] Moreover, the largest part of the production of both cotton and woolen textiles was being undertaken by rural households for consumption within the village.

By the 1910s, per capita consumption of cotton textiles had increased by more than 150 per cent and was almost three times as high as that of woolen and other cloth put together.[73] About four-fifths of the total consumption of cotton textiles was being imported. More important, our simple calculations indicate that in the 1910s Ottoman peasant households met at least two-thirds of their consumption of cotton textiles by purchasing imported cloth in the marketplace. In our view, this is as striking an indicator as any of the extent of the decline of Ottoman handicrafts in cotton textiles, the destruction of the self-sufficient nature of the rural economy, and specialization in agriculture within the context of a world economy.[74]

Chapter 7

The Ottoman case in comparative perspective

After the Industrial Revolution in Europe, those areas of the world which constitute the Third World today and where pre-capitalist or non-capitalist modes of production had prevailed came into contact with world capitalism more strongly than ever before and experienced similar economic processes. For this reason, the recent histories of these areas cannot be examined solely in terms of the internal dynamics of each society. Rather each of these countries has to be inserted into the context of a world capitalist economy and their histories need to be analyzed in terms of the complex interaction between internal and external forces.

One purpose of this volume has been to examine some aspects and consequences of the penetration of world capitalism into the Ottoman Empire. World economic forces often provided the point of departure for our analysis. Chapters 2, 3 and 4 established the long-term trends and fluctuations in Ottoman foreign trade, external terms of trade and foreign investment, thereby providing a detailed map of the world economic forces faced by the Ottoman Empire during the nineteenth century. Chapters 5 and 6 moved from the sphere of circulation to the sphere of production to examine the impact of the penetration of world capitalism on Ottoman agriculture and handicrafts.

To summarize, at the beginning of the period examined in this volume the Ottoman Empire engaged in a limited amount of trade with the rest of the world. In the early 1820s the ratio of total Ottoman exports or imports to the overall volume of production was well below 5 per cent, and was probably closer to 2 or 3 per cent.[1] During the course of the next century, Ottoman foreign trade, particularly with Western Europe, expanded rapidly. This long-term trend was facilitated by the existence of Free Trade Treaties which eliminated for the Ottoman governments the option of pursuing more independent commercial policies for protectionist or fiscal reasons.

After mid-century, European commercial penetration was accompanied by financial penetration. An intensive wave of external borrowing led to a default by the Ottoman state within two decades and to the establishment of European control over Ottoman state finances. After the turn of the century there was another wave of external borrowing, fueled by inter-imperialist rivalry over the Empire. On the eve of World War I, payments on the outstanding debt could be met only by further borrowing; another default appeared imminent.

The other form of investment in the Ottoman Empire, foreign direct investment, concentrated on infrastructure, particularly in railroads and ports. In contrast, foreign investment in production activities such as agriculture, industry or even mining remained limited. For this reason, foreign investment did not have a significant direct impact on the existing non-capitalist mode of production. Instead, foreign investment had an indirect effect on the patterns of production by facilitating the expansion of foreign trade and greater integration with world markets.

The expansion of foreign trade led, on the one hand, to increasing commercialization of agriculture and, on the other hand, to the decline of handicrafts-based activities in the secondary sector. Despite some resistance to competition from imports, it appears that the share of the secondary sector in total employment and production levels declined until the 1910s. The early beginnings of the factory system remained too weak to counteract this downward trend. By the early 1910s, specialization in agriculture had advanced considerably. According to one estimate, about 14 per cent of gross national product and one-fourth of total agricultural production were being exported on the eve of World War I. The ratio of imports to GNP was close to 18 per cent.[2] The Ottoman economy had become much more open and part of the center–periphery division of labor within the world economy.

In fact, on the eve of World War I it had become increasingly difficult to refer to the Ottoman economy as a meaningful unit of analysis. Economic linkages within the Empire continued to weaken throughout the century and various regions were gradually pulled into the divisions of labor of Manchester, Hamburg, and Marseilles. Even though formal independence was never lost, the Empire was divided into spheres of influence amongst the Great Powers of Europe. Formal partitioning was to be achieved in the aftermath of World War I.

Special characteristics of the Ottoman case

There was a good deal of unity in the nineteenth-century experiences of those countries which presently constitute the Third World. There were common factors in the penetration of capitalism which affected all these economies and the preceding overview emphasized those processes which the Ottoman case shared with many others. There existed, however, a good deal of diversity within this unity. In terms of the specific forms of interaction with the rest of the world economy and in terms of the resulting structures, the history of each country was unique. This was because the far-reaching social and economic transformations each country underwent were not due to external factors alone. The differences between the Ottoman case and those elsewhere in Asia, Latin America or North Africa cannot be explained by referring only to world economic forces. The special features of the Ottoman case can be understood only by integrating into the analysis factors specific to the Ottoman economy and society.

Any attempt to distinguish the results of the penetration of capitalism into the Ottoman Empire from other cases in the Third World has to take the political factors into account. Different parts of this volume have underlined three interrelated political characteristics of the Ottoman Empire which defined the environment under which penetration of world capitalism took place and which are essential for developing a comparative framework:

(a)   the relative strength of the central government and central bureaucracy *vis-à-vis* other social classes;

(b)   the fact that the Empire never lost its formal independence, and was never colonized;

(c)   the environment of inter-imperialist rivalry over the Empire; despite the changing balances between European Great Powers throughout the century, no one power could eliminate any of its rivals.

These interrelated political characteristics of the Ottoman case distinguish it both from formal colonies and those countries which were incorporated into the informal empire of a European power during the nineteenth century. For this reason, it will be more appropriate to examine the Ottoman case along with others in the periphery such as China and Persia in a third category, namely the category of inter-imperialist rivalry. The implications of these features on the process of penetration of capitalism into the Ottoman Empire require some elaboration.

The power balances between the central government and the local elements in the provinces had always constituted one of the most important characteristics of Ottoman economy and society. The central government, which had to contend with the increasing power of provincial forces during the seventeenth and eighteenth centuries, began to strengthen its relative position during the reign of Mahmud II. Starting in the 1830s, and continuing with the political, administrative and institutional reforms of the *Tanzimat* period, the power of the provincial *ayan* was undermined and increasing centralization was established once again as a long-term trend. The technological developments of the nineteenth century, which enabled the central government to establish a more effective army and improve the transportation and communications network, undoubtedly reinforced this trend.

At the international level, on the other hand, while the balances between the major European powers changed throughout the century, none of them was able to exclude its competitors from the Ottoman Empire. This ongoing rivalry coupled with limited but not insignificant Ottoman military strength, made it very difficult for the Great Powers to colonize or partition the Ottoman Empire. In the terminology of Western observers, the result was that the Eastern Question remained unsolved until World War I.

Under these circumstances, it would not have been very fruitful for European powers and European capital to develop alliances with those social classes such as merchants and landlords which would have been in favor of greater integration with the world economy but which had limited power *vis-à-vis* the central government. Instead, European forces had to come to terms with the central bureaucracy at every turn as they attempted to penetrate the Ottoman economy. The central bureaucracy, on the other hand, was concerned that as the economy opened to foreign capital and as agriculture became more commercialized, the power of merchants and landlords would increase and the control of the central government over the economy and society would be undermined. Throughout the century these concerns lay behind the reluctance of the central bureaucracy to encourage greater integration with world capitalism.

It can be argued that the environment of inter-imperialist rivalry provided the central government with considerable maneuvering room to play one European power off against another without becoming dependent on any single power. However, the possibilities created by the conditions of rivalry should not be exaggerated. For one thing, the degree of rivalry over the Ottoman Empire did not remain unchanged over the course of the century. It varied directly with the degree of rivalry on the world scale. It is true that conditions of rivalry intensified after the arrival of Germany on the international scene in the 1880s and 1890s. In comparison, however, the ability of the central government to play one European power off against another was much more limited earlier in the century at the height of Pax Britannica. Moreover, even under conditions of rivalry, the frequently occurring military, political and fiscal crises of the Ottoman state provided plenty of opportunities for the European Powers to obtain the necessary concessions towards greater penetration into the Ottoman economy.

This last point brings us to the fourth special characteristic of the Ottoman Empire in relation to other cases in the periphery:

(d) the military, political and especially fiscal crises of the central government were one of the key determinants of the timing and rhythms of European penetration.

A brief examination of the most important turning points in the European penetration of the Ottoman economy provides ample support for this argument. A good place to start is the Free Trade Treaty of 1838, which provided the legal and institutional framework for the expansion of trade until World War I. During the 1830s the central government was faced with major military and political crises arising from its conflict with Mohammed Ali of Egypt and possible dismemberment if not disintegration of the Empire. It agreed to sign the Treaty in order to obtain British support for the territorial integrity of the Empire. In other words, in return for British political and military support, which lasted through the Crimean War and until the 1870s, the Ottoman economy was opened to trade particularly with Britain, since the latter was virtually unrivalled in world markets at the time.

The second turning point came in the 1850s, when the central government initiated, reluctantly at first, external borrowing under the severe fiscal crisis created by the Crimean War. Within two decades, however, it became clear that, far from providing relief, external borrowing had exacerbated fiscal difficulties, leading to European control over Ottoman state finances in the 1880s.

Construction of railroads by foreign capital constitutes a third turning point in the European penetration of the Ottoman economy. In this case, as in earlier turning points, the timing was determined by military and political concerns and fiscal difficulties of the central government in addition to the pressures by European powers. In granting the extensive railroad concessions during the late 1880s the central government's fiscal aims were to improve its administrative effectiveness in the collection of taxes and to encourage the cultivation of new lands by bringing them within the reach of urban markets and major ports of export. After the completion of railroad construction, tithe collections in provinces with railroads did in fact rise faster than others. However, these increases were not sufficient to offset the kilometric guarantee payments the Ottoman government had agreed to make to foreign-owned railroad companies. In the end railroads failed to provide the much-needed fiscal relief. On the contrary, they further reduced the maneuvering room of the central government by accelerating the partitioning of the Empire into spheres of influence amongst the European powers.[3]

We now turn to the last two of the special characteristics of the

Ottoman case which need to be taken into account in placing world capitalism's penetration of the Ottoman Empire into a comparative framework.

(e) the importance of small and medium-sized peasant holdings in agriculture.

It has been argued that, in comparison to the cases of formal colony and informal empire, conditions of rivalry made it more difficult for imperialist powers to intervene directly in order to facilitate greater integration with the world economy. Conversely, conditions of rivalry enabled the central bureaucracy to maintain greater control over some areas of the economy. During the nineteenth century the most important area where the central government was able to maintain some control, and where the penetration of foreign capital remained limited, was agriculture. For the central government an agrarian structure consisting mostly of small and medium-sized holdings represented the most favorable conditions for appropriating the agricultural surplus. During the nineteenth century as well as in the earlier period, the central government supported, whenever it could, small and middle peasant holdings against large landlords both in order to preserve its fiscal base and to prevent a political challenge to its rule from the provinces.

It is not surprising, therefore, that attempts by European citizens during the nineteenth century to establish capitalist farms in Western Anatolia met with the resistance of the central government; at the very least these efforts were not supported by Istanbul.[4] Since these government policies were reinforced by certain key features of Ottoman agriculture, namely relative abundance of land, relative scarcity of labor and the primitive nature of technology, small and medium-sized holdings maintained their importance until World War I. Unlike many other countries in the periphery of the world economy during the nineteenth century, in the Ottoman Empire a large part of agricultural commodity production for world markets was undertaken by these strata of peasantry.

A similar tendency is observed in non-agricultural production activities. For political reasons the central government needed the support of the guilds and, in turn, continued to support them until their abolition early in the twentieth century. However, in comparison to agriculture, non-agricultural activities were much more conducive to economies of scale. As a result, Ottoman handicrafts declined due to competition from imported products of large-scale European industry while small-scale production in agriculture survived, although it did not flourish.

In other words, along with the penetration of world capitalism, there was a secular tendency during the nineteenth century for commodity production to expand. However, this trend was not accompanied by a similar expansion of large-scale production and wage labor. The policies of the central government were one important factor in the persistence of small-scale production in agriculture and to a lesser extent in non-agricultural production activities.

Finally, in any comparative study it is necessary to take into account that:

(f)   despite frequent loss of land and population, the nineteenth-century Ottoman state was the continuation of an empire that used to cover large territories across three continents.

Clearly, this characteristic adds a number of important political dimensions to the Ottoman case. Preceding chapters did not deal with this issue directly. It was shown, however, that being the continuation of a once powerful empire provided the nineteenth-century Ottoman economy with a number of revenue sources. As discussed in detail in appendix 6 within a balance of payments framework, most important amongst these revenue items were annual tribute payments received from Egypt and other countries, rent income from private land held in those countries which were once part of the Empire such as Egypt, and funds brought in by the large numbers of immigrants who left the seceding areas of the Empire during the nineteenth century.

A comparison of indices of trade and foreign investment

As part of our attempt to insert the nineteenth-century Ottoman case into a comparative framework, this final section will compare the degree of penetration of world capitalism into the Ottoman Empire and some special features of that process with other cases in the Third World. For this purpose a number of indices associated with foreign trade and foreign investment will be investigated.[5]

We will first establish the basic indicators of foreign trade and received foreign investment which would serve as proxies for the degree of penetration of world capitalism. Ideally, (1a) the ratio of exports or imports to GNP and (1b) the ratio of total foreign investment to GNP would be suitable for this purpose. However, since estimates of GNP are either unavailable or too crude to be reliable for most countries in the periphery for the period before World War I, less satisfactory indices such as (2a) foreign trade per capita or more simply exports per capita and (2b) foreign investment per capita will have to be employed. While these two sets of basic indicators are not identical, the second set can be used as close substitutes for the first if the variations in per capita GNP are not very large.[6]

Another basic problem is the definition of the set of countries which can be meaningfully compared with the Ottoman Empire in the nineteenth century. The discussion in this volume has broadly covered all countries in the periphery of the world economy. In any comparison of the degree and process of integration into the world economy, however, size of country emerges as an important variable that needs to be taken into account. Clearly, comparisons between the Ottoman Empire and small island economies such as Cuba or Jamaica will not be very revealing. Since the Ottoman Empire was a medium-sized country with a population of about 21 million in 1913, we decided to exclude from our sample those smaller countries in the periphery whose populations were below 4 million on the eve of World War I. Also excluded from our comparisons is sub-Saharan Africa, where European economic penetration had remained limited until late in the nineteenth century. These considerations narrowed the sample to a total of 18 countries, including the Ottoman Empire: 5 in the Middle East and North Africa, 8 in Asia, and 5 in Latin America.

Table 7.1 shows the extent to which these medium-sized and large countries had been integrated into the world capitalist economy on the eve of World War I based on indices of per capita foreign trade and per capita foreign investment. Also included in that table is a composite index for the degree of integration in which per capita foreign trade and per capita foreign investment are weighed equally and countries in the sample are then scaled in relation to the Ottoman Empire.

A number of observations can be made on the basis of table 7.1. First, it is clear that Argentina does not belong with the rest of the Third World on the eve of World War I. A comparison of per capita exports and per capita foreign investment points to a large gap between that country and others, both in Latin America and elsewhere. The gap would have been considerably smaller if it were possible to compare the share of exports in GNP and the ratio of foreign capital stock to GNP for the respective countries since per capita GNP in Argentina on the eve of World War I was anywhere from three to five times as high as those of other countries in our sample. In fact, on the eve of World War I GNP per capita in Argentina was much closer to those of Western Europe than those of other countries in Latin America. It would be more appropriate to compare Argentina until the 1920s with other countries of white settlement such as Canada and Australia.[7]

In terms of per capita indices, the two largest countries in the world on the eve of World War I, China and India, which between them accounted for close to two-thirds of the total population in the periphery, constitute the other end of the spectrum in our sample.[8] Because of their vast size,

Table 7.1. *Basic indicators for the degree of integration into the world economy of countries in the Third World on the eve of World War I*

Country	Population in 1913 (m.)	Annual per capita exports in 1910–12 (£)	Per capita foreign capital stock in 1913 (£)	Composite index of per capita exports and foreign capital (Ottoman Empire = 100.0)
Ottoman Empire	21.0	1.04	10.30	100.0
Egypt	12.0	2.63	17.25	208.6
Persia	11.5	0.62	1.74	36.2
Algeria	5.6	4.10	8.04	200.9
Morocco	5.0	0.50	7.00	60.3
Weighted average for the Middle East and North Africa		1.56	9.50	117.0
India	305.0	0.45	1.52	25.9
China	450.0	0.12	0.74	8.6
Ceylon	4.2	2.90	n.a.	—
Dutch East Indies	42.0	1.04	3.67	60.3
Philippines	9.0	1.00	2.56	52.6
French Indochina	12.5	0.74	2.48	42.2
Siam	8.4	0.83	1.55	40.5
Korea	13.5	0.23	n.a.	—
Weighted average for Asia excluding India and China		0.94	3.08	53.9
Argentina	7.6	10.33	85.53	862.0
Mexico	15.2	1.91	31.97	261.2
Brazil	24.0	2.84	18.98	214.7
Peru	4.3	1.63	10.70	124.1
Colombia	4.7	0.72	n.a.	—
Weighted average for Latin America excluding Argentina		2.23	22.70	222.0
Overall average excluding India, China and Argentina		1.44	10.16	117.2

Note: The composite index C.I. was derived in the following manner for each country:

$$\text{C.I.} = \frac{aX + bI}{a + b}$$

where a = arithmetic average of per capita foreign capital stock of the countries in the sample, in £

b = arithmetic average of per capita foreign trade of the countries in the sample, in £

X = per capita exports of the country, in £

I = per capita foreign capital stock in the country, in £

the degree of integration of these two countries into the world economy measured in per capita terms remained limited. This conclusion would not change even if indicators such as share of exports in GNP could be used, since levels of per capita GNP in these two countries appear to be comparable to or only slightly lower than levels of per capita GNP of other countries in the sample for which GNP data are available.[9] In view of these differences, the following discussion will focus mostly on the remaining 15 medium-sized countries ranging in population from 4.2 million in Ceylon to 42 million in the Dutch East Indies. As shown in table 7.1, in terms of its population in the early 1910s the Ottoman Empire was the third largest country in this group.

What broad patterns and regularities can one discern regarding degree of penetration of world capitalism into these 15 countries? First, when the smaller and the two largest countries in the periphery are excluded from the sample, the inverse correlation between size as measured by population and the degree of penetration of world capitalism ceases to be important. Second, it is clear that the degree of integration into the world economy showed major variations between different regions of the world. On the eve of World War I, Latin America was much more integrated into the world economy than other regions in the periphery. The Middle East and North Africa came second and the medium-sized countries in Asia were distinctly behind both. This simple ordering across regions would not change even if it were possible to employ the first set of indicators such as the ratio of exports to GNP or foreign investment to GNP. Even if average per capita GNP levels in Asia were lower than those in the Middle East and in Latin America, these interregional differences in per capita GNP levels were probably smaller than the interregional differences in per capita foreign trade and foreign investment levels.[10]

The Ottoman Empire fits into this broad pattern. On the eve of World

Cross multiplication ensures that foreign trade and foreign capital stock will be weighted equally. The values for each country were then scaled by letting the index for the Ottoman Empire = 100.0.

Sources for tables 7.1, 7.2, 7.3 and 7.4:
Population: *Accounts and Papers*, 'The Statistical Abstract for Foreign Countries'; *Accounts and Papers*, 'The Statistical Abstract for the Colonies' (both annual publications); McEvedy and Jones (1978).
Exports: *Accounts and Papers*, 'Commercial Reports'; *Accounts and Papers*, 'The Statistical Abstract for Foreign Countries'; *Accounts and Papers*, 'The Statistical Abstract for the Colonies'; United States, *Commercial Relations of the United States with Foreign Countries* (all annual publications); Hanson (1980), appendices A and B; Ocampo (1981).
Foreign investment: Svedberg (1978); Feis (1930), chapters 1–3; Latham (1978), pp. 51–9; Stone (1977).

War I, penetration of world capitalism into the Ottoman Empire had proceeded to a greater extent than was the case for all the medium-sized countries in Asia with the probable exception of Ceylon. On the other hand, the medium-sized countries in Latin America, with the possible exception of Colombia, had higher per capita foreign trade and foreign investment levels than the Ottoman Empire in the early 1910s. Within the Middle East, the Ottoman Empire lay somewhere between Egypt, which represented one of the more prominent examples of European economic penetration during the nineteenth century, and Persia. It should also be emphasized that in terms of both per capita exports and per capita foreign investment levels, the degree of penetration of world capitalism into the Ottoman Empire remained below the average for the 15 medium-sized countries.

This relative position of the Ottoman Empire within the periphery would not change substantially even if it were possible to employ the first set of indicators. Available evidence, admittedly crude, indicates that per capita GNP levels in the Ottoman Empire on the eve of World War I were fairly close to those of other medium-sized countries in the periphery for which estimates are available.[11]

A related question that should provide additional insights is the *rate* of integration of different countries into the world economy until World War I rather than its extent in the early 1910s. Once again, the availability of data dictates the type of indicators that can be utilized for this purpose. In the absence of foreign capital stock estimates for the earlier period, the rate of growth of per capita exports emerges as the most convenient measure for the speed with which an economy was integrated into world markets. Table 7.2 presents the rate of growth of per capita exports from the Third World countries in our sample during the half century preceding World War I. Due to limitations on data, this comparison could not be extended backwards in time.

One important trend that emerges from table 7.2 is that while Latin America was much more integrated into world markets than other regions in the periphery during the early 1860s, exports from the medium-sized countries in the Middle East, North Africa and Asia expanded more rapidly during the next half century. This was in part due to the low levels of foreign trade of this latter group of countries at the beginning of the period. However, there may be other reasons for this comparative trend, as we will consider below. As for the Ottoman Empire, its long-term rate of growth of per capita exports remained below the average for the Middle East and North Africa. This long-term rate of growth was close to but also remained below the overall average for the 15 countries. To summarize from tables 7.1 and 7.2, then, in terms

Table 7.2. *Per capita exports from medium-sized countries in the Third World, 1860–1910*
In constant 1880 British pounds sterling

Country	Annual per capita exports, 1860–2	Annual per capita exports, 1910–12	Average annual rate of growth of exports, 1860–1910 (per cent)
Ottoman Empire	0.66	1.25	1.3
Egypt	0.51	3.17	3.7
Iran	0.28	0.75	2.0
Weighted average for the Middle East			
	0.49	1.65	2.4
Algeria	0.49	4.96	4.7
Morocco	0.24	0.60	1.8
India	0.13	0.54	2.9
China	0.04	0.15	2.8
Ceylon	0.43	3.51	4.3
Dutch East Indies	0.37	1.26	2.5
French Indochina	n.a.	0.89	—
Philippines	0.41	1.21	2.2
Siam	0.26	1.00	2.7
Korea	n.a.	0.28	—
Weighted average for Asia excluding India and China			
	0.36	1.14	2.3
Argentina	1.60	12.49	4.2
Mexico	n.a.	2.31	—
Brazil	1.47	3.43	1.7
Peru	2.29	1.97	−0.3
Colombia	0.51	0.87	1.1
Weighted average for Latin America			
	1.48	3.95	2.0
Overall average excluding India, China			
	0.62	2.15	2.5

For sources see table 7.1.

of both the *degree* of integration into the world economy on the eve of World War I and the *rate* of integration during the half century until World War I, the Ottoman Empire was close to but remained below the average for the medium-sized countries in the periphery.

Size and regional location have been identified as important variables in determining the extent to which world capitalism had penetrated into a country in the periphery by the early 1910s. There still remains, however, a good deal of variation amongst medium-sized countries within each region that needs to be explained. Similarly, size and location can explain only partially the relative position of the Ottoman Empire within our sample.

One important variable that cannot be adequately examined here is the resource endowments or agronomic conditions in a country. Clearly, if the resource endowments of a country are suitable for the production of those primary commodities for which there is large demand in world markets, *ceteris paribus* per capita exports and per capita received foreign investment are likely to be higher. It is difficult, however, to go beyond this generalization here unless one is willing to undertake a major empirical project.[12]

Another variable that has been emphasized in the preceding section and earlier in this volume as an important determinant of the degree of penetration of world capitalism is the political framework, which reflects the complex interaction between political forces both internal and external to the country in the periphery. In chapter 1 we developed three categories based on political criteria for distinguishing between different cases in the periphery and, equally importantly, for the insertion of the Ottoman case into a comparative framework: formal colonies, countries that belonged to an informal empire, and countries where penetration of world capitalism proceeded under conditions of inter-imperialist rivalry.

It was argued that the first two categories provided less uncertainty and more stable conditions to both the foreign capitalists and to those internal classes in favor of greater integration with the world economy. In comparison, in the case of rivalry the tensions, on the one hand, between social classes favoring greater integration and the central bureaucracy whose political and fiscal interests were not necessarily best served by the opening of the economy and, on the other hand, the tensions between the competing imperialist powers created a more uncertain and potentially unstable environment. One hypothesis that would follow from these considerations is that the degree of penetration of world capitalism as measured by trade and investment indices is likely to be lower in the case of rivalry in comparison to the other two categories.

While our sample of 15 countries is rather small for the testing of hypotheses of this type, some observations can still be made, particularly for a more satisfactory interpretation of the comparative position of the Ottoman Empire. In Asia, if we exclude Korea, which became a colony of Japan only a few years before World War I, the country with the lowest degree of integration into the world economy was Siam. It is perhaps not surprising that Siam was also the only medium-sized country in Asia which did not belong to a formal empire and which can be best characterized as being in the rivalry category.[13]

The countries in Latin America, on the other hand, experienced similar political conditions during the nineteenth century, so that our three categories cannot be utilized to explain the variations amongst them with respect to the degree of penetration of world capitalism. With some variations these medium-sized countries belonged to the informal empire of Britain until the last quarter of the century. However, with the arrival of Germany and to some extent the United States on the scene, the dominant position of Britain began to change. All these countries experienced increasing degrees of inter-imperialist rivalry from the 1880s until World War I.

While our three categories cannot be employed for explaining the variations within Latin America, they can account for some of the differences between Latin America and medium-sized countries elsewhere in the periphery, as well as the intertemporal changes in the rate of integration of Latin American countries. As can be seen from table 7.2, in the early 1860s the per capita export indices of the Latin American countries were higher than those of countries in any other region of the Third World. During the next half century, however, as the degree of inter-imperialist rivalry increased in Latin America, the rate of growth of per capita exports from that continent dropped below those of other regions.[14] The obverse side of the same coin is that in our sample the highest rates of growth in per capita exports during the half century preceding World War I were registered by three formal colonies, Algeria, Egypt and Ceylon.

The same argument can be extended to the Middle East, where the two prominent cases of rivalry were the Ottoman Empire and Persia. As can be seen from table 7.1, in the early 1910s both of these countries had lower per capita foreign trade and foreign investment indices than did Egypt, a country of comparable size which became a colony after 1882. The degree of penetration of world capitalism into these two countries was also lower than the average for our group of medium-sized countries. Moreover, table 7.2 shows that the rate of growth of per capita exports from the Ottoman Empire and Persia during the half century preceding World War I lagged far behind that of Egypt and was also lower than the average for the medium-sized countries in the Third World.

The category of rivalry is a useful tool, therefore, for inserting the Ottoman case into a comparative framework within the Third World. However, the insights that can be obtained by the use of this category are not limited to those associated with the extent or the rate of penetration of world capitalism. The consequences of the environment of rivalry are equally clear when we go beyond the broad measures associated with the degree of integration into the world economy and examine more detailed indices.

One area where the rivalry situation brought special dimensions to the

Ottoman case concerns the behavior of foreign investment. Under the conditions of rivalry in the Ottoman Empire, lending to the government was often used by the European powers as a means of gaining influence in Istanbul. European governments often supported and occasionally provided guarantees for lending to the Ottoman state by the investors of their own country. The beginnings of European control over Ottoman finances with the establishment of the Ottoman Public Debt Administration in 1881 provided additional security to the lenders. In contrast, the uncertainties associated with and the inherent instability of the rivalry environment often discouraged direct foreign investment in the Ottoman Empire. European investors' reluctance was often compounded by the inability of the European governments to intervene directly in the sphere of production.

Some consequences of these tendencies can be followed from table 7.3. In the period before World War I, the Ottoman Empire received more per capita foreign investment in the form of lending to the state than any other medium-sized country in the periphery, with the exception of Egypt.[15] In comparison, the volume of direct foreign investment remained limited so that the share of the external debt in total foreign investment (66 per cent) was higher in the Ottoman Empire than in any medium-sized country in the periphery.

Another characteristic of the rivalry environment was the inability or limited ability of European powers to intervene directly in the sphere of production to facilitate greater integration with the world economy. In the Ottoman case one important area where the intervention of foreign capital remained limited and where the central government maintained considerable autonomy was agriculture. As has been argued, this political configuration was instrumental in the prevalence of small and medium-sized peasant holdings until World War I.

The same set of political factors helps explain another related characteristic of the Ottoman case. Table 7.4 shows that on the eve of World War I commodity exports from the Ottoman Empire were more diversified than those of any other medium-sized country in the periphery. Undoubtedly, this feature of Ottoman exports and agriculture was partly due to the diversified agronomic conditions and resource endowments of a country which covered a large geographical area. However, the inability of the European powers to intervene directly in Ottoman agriculture and transform it in the direction of monoculture and the resistance of Ottoman governments to such attempts have to be part of any satisfactory explanation of this characteristic.

These considerations inevitably lead to the link between the degree of integration into the world economy and economic growth. Does the

Table 7.3. *Composition of foreign capital stock in 1913*

Country	Total foreign investment per capita (£) $1 = 2 + 3$	Foreign direct investment per capita (£) 2	Per capita foreign investment in state debt (£) 3	Share of state in total foreign investment (per cent) $4 = 3/1$
Ottoman Empire	10.29	3.52	6.77	66
Egypt	17.25	8.92	8.33	48
Persia	1.74	n.a.	n.a.	n.a.
Algeria	8.04	n.a.	n.a.	n.a.
Morocco	7.0	n.a.	n.a.	n.a.
India	1.52	0.46	1.06	70
China	0.74	0.53	0.21	29
Ceylon	n.a.	n.a.	n.a.	n.a.
Dutch East Indies	3.67	3.43	0.24	6
Philippines	2.56	2.33	0.22	9
French Indochina	2.48	1.52	0.96	39
Siam	1.55	0.83	0.71	46
Korea	n.a.	n.a.	n.a.	n.a.
Argentina	85.53	53.95	31.58	37
Mexico	31.97	25.72	6.25	20
Brazil	18.38	12.13	6.25	34
Peru	10.70	10.23	0.47	4
Colombia	n.a.	n.a.	n.a.	n.a.
Overall average excluding India, China and Argentina				
	10.90	7.40	3.50	32

For sources see table 7.1.

Ottoman experience during the nineteenth century lend support to the view that export expansion served as an engine of growth? There is hardly any cause for optimism in this respect. At one level it can be argued that for the Ottoman Empire, and for most of the Third World countries, the foreign trade sector remained too small for high rates of growth to translate into appreciable rates of increase in the aggregate levels of production and income.[16] For the Ottoman Empire, the share of exports in total production remained below 10 per cent until the turn of the century. Under these circumstances, if the Ottoman economy experienced increases in per capita levels of production until the turn of the century – which might be the case – the primary explanation needs to be searched elsewhere. Export growth can at best be interpreted as being one of a number of factors contributing to economic growth. It should also be emphasized that, particularly during the mid-nineteenth century, the Ottoman economy experienced a long-term trend towards de-

Table 7.4. *Shares of leading commodities in total export revenues, 1910–12*

Country	Share of largest 1 (per cent)	Share of largest 3 (per cent)
Ottoman Empire	11.0	26.0
Egypt	88.9	90.9
Persia	17.4	28.8
Algeria	38.6	53.2
Morocco	18.1	37.4
India	15.9	39.0
China	19.4	39.3
Ceylon	45.2	74.0
Dutch East Indies	28.5	52.0
Philippines	36.8	85.1
French Indochina	61.8	71.7
Siam	79.7	83.3
Korea	36.3	57.5
Argentina	21.3	50.1
Mexico	28.8	56.0
Brazil	55.6	84.8
Peru	18.6	54.0
Colombia	31.0	60.4
Arithmetic average excluding India, China and Argentina	39.8	61.0

Note: Another approach for measuring the degree of concentration or diversification of the exports would have been to compute the Hirschman index, a formula that reduces the full list of a country's exports to a single number representing the degree of export concentration. See Hirschman (1945); also Hanson (1980), chapter 3. For sources see table 7.1.

industrialization caused by competition from imported manufactures. Therefore, it is possible that the expansion of foreign trade may have led to decline rather than increases in the levels of production during that earlier period.

There is a more serious potential problem in linking economic growth to patterns of specialization in primary commodity exports during the nineteenth century. Egypt provides a good case in point. The trade sector was relatively large, exports did expand rapidly and per capita levels of production did rise until World War I. In the longer term, however, Egypt paid a heavy price for its inability to develop its industry, for its exclusive reliance on the world market, and for its specialization in one crop. Levels of per capita income stagnated until the 1950s.

In conclusion, the per capita indices of foreign trade and foreign investment which have been briefly examined here indicate that the degree of integration of the Ottoman Empire into the world economy until World War I remained close to but below the average for the medium-sized countries in the Third World, above those for Asia and below those for countries in Latin America. The regional location of the Ottoman Empire and its resource endowments are some of the variables to be included in any explanation. This volume has emphasized the importance of political factors, both internal and external. On the one hand, the inability of any European power to transform the Ottoman Empire into a formal colony or incorporate it into its informal empire, and, on the other hand, the relative strength of the central bureaucracy *vis-à-vis* both the European powers and the internal classes such as merchants and landlords help explain not only the degree of integration of world capitalism but also some of the special features of that process.

The reconstruction of Ottoman foreign trade, 1830–1913

In terms of their reliability, their coverage and the period for which they are available, the official Ottoman foreign trade statistics were in-adequate for the purposes of the study presented in chapter 2. Consequently, we attempted a complete reconstruction of nineteenth-century Ottoman foreign trade, utilizing the published trade statistics of almost all the countries with which the Ottoman Empire had commercial relations. This procedure basically consisted of taking the values for exports.to the Ottoman Empire provided in the official statistics of each country and adding to them the appropriate freight and insurance costs to arrive at c.i.f. prices for Ottoman imports, and, similarly, subtracting the appropriate freight and insurance costs from Ottoman exports prices given in these statistics to arrive at f.o.b. prices valuated at Ottoman ports. In all cases, we converted prices and total values given in the currency of individual countries to British pounds sterling, using the prevailing gold standard rate of exchange. For our reconstruction, we were able to gather the foreign trade statistics, and particularly the statistics relating to imports from and exports to the Ottoman Empire of the following countries for the indicated periods: United Kingdom (1830–1913), France (1830–1913), Germany (1880–1913), Austria (1830–1913), United States (1830–1913), Russia (1830–1913), Italy (1852–1913), Belgium (1831–1913), Netherlands (1846–1913), Switzerland (1885–1913), Serbia (1878–1913), Greece (1857–76 and 1888–1913), Romania (1871–1913), Bulgaria (1880–1913), Egypt (1874–93) and Iran (1902–13).[1]

These calculations provided more reliable and more detailed information for the period 1878–1913, for which Ottoman statistics are available, and a large amount of new information for 1830–77, during which period foreign trade statistics were not collected regularly or comprehensively. Nonetheless, as anyone familiar with the construction of trade statistics would attest, our procedure is not without potential shortcomings. We start this appendix with a table presenting the annual values for Ottoman exports and imports arrived at as a result of this reconstruction. Figure 1 of chapter 2 is based on the annual figures given

Table AI.I. *Ottoman foreign trade (excluding specie), 1830–1913*
In millions of current British pounds sterling

Year	f.o.b. exports	c.i.f. imports	Year	f.o.b. exports	c.i.f. imports
1830	3.7	5.3	1873	19.2	22.4
1831	3.6	4.6	1874	21.1	23.3
1832	4.2	4.9	1875	19.0	22.1
1833	4.1	4.4	1876	23.0	19.7
1834	3.9	4.5	1877	17.4	16.4
1835	4.4	5.2	1878	13.6	18.0
1836	4.4	5.7	1879	15.0	18.9
1837	4.5	4.5	1870–9	18.6	20.8
1838	4.4	6.2			
1839	4.8	5.4	1880	14.3	15.8
1830–9	4.2	5.1	1881	15.3	15.2
			1882	15.9	15.2
1840	4.7	5.2	1883	16.3	15.3
1841	5.3	5.8	1884	16.7	15.0
1842	5.5	6.0	1885	16.9	15.8
1843	5.7	6.2	1886	16.3	16.5
1844	5.7	7.5	1887	14.0	16.6
1845	6.2	7.4	1888	13.2	16.0
1846	6.2	6.5	1889	16.3	18.5
1847	7.8	8.4	1880–9	15.5	16.0
1848	5.8	7.8			
1849	6.6	8.1	1890	17.1	19.4
1840–9	6.0	6.9	1891	17.6	18.7
			1892	19.1	19.4
1850	7.8	8.9	1893	17.7	19.3
1851	8.8	8.7	1894	15.7	20.5
1852	9.8	10.8	1895	17.1	17.4
1853	9.8	11.3	1896	17.6	16.3
1854	9.3	10.7	1897	19.9	17.7
1855	9.7	19.2	1898	17.3	19.8
1856	12.5	18.4	1899	17.6	18.0
1857	10.0	12.0	1890–9	17.7	18.6
1858	9.8	11.9			
1859	10.4	10.6	1900	19.5	18.4
1850–9	9.8	12.3	1901	20.1	21.9
			1902	21.2	20.6
1860	11.1	13.7	1903	22.5	21.6
1861	12.2	12.0	1904	22.3	27.6
1862	13.7	13.1	1905	24.1	26.1
1863	15.8	17.5	1906	26.1	30.8
1864	16.7	19.9	1907	26.6	31.3
1865	15.6	19.4	1908	23.1	28.8
1866	14.9	19.8	1909	24.5	33.3
1867	14.9	19.8	1900–9	23.0	26.0
1868	19.7	22.8			
1869	18.9	24.0	1910	26.0	39.2
1860–9	15.4	18.3	1911	27.1	40.4
			1912	27.6	35.2
1870	17.4	22.5	1913	28.4	39.4
1871	20.7	21.4	1910–13	27.3	38.6
1872	20.2	23.2			

Sources: Based on the foreign trade statistics of other countries. For details, see text and chapter I.

in table A1.1 here. In section A1.1 below, the commodity composition of Ottoman exports and imports is briefly discussed. In the second section, the deficiencies of the Ottoman statistics are evaluated. In subsequent sections of the appendix, the details of our reconstruction attempt are presented and various problems associated with this procedure are discussed.

A1.1 Observations on the composition of Ottoman foreign trade

Exports

Two characteristics of the commodity composition of Ottoman exports should be underlined. First, there was an absence throughout the nineteenth century of commodities that maintained a large share in the total value of exports. For example, the official statistics indicate that during the period 1878–1913 rarely did the share of any commodity in the total value of exports exceed 12 per cent. Second, despite the doubling of the value of total exports between 1878 and 1913, the shares in the total value of exports of the more important commodities did not change substantially. According to the Ottoman trade statistics, the share of the eight largest exports – tobacco, wheat, barley, raisins, figs, raw silk, raw wool and opium – in the total value of exports was 51 per cent during 1878–80; the share of the same eight had declined to 44 per cent by 1913. This decline was almost entirely due to the decrease in wheat exports, from 7 per cent of the total in 1878–82 to under 1 per cent in 1910–13. This fall in wheat exports occurred after 1890 and was due, at least in part, to the entry of North American wheat into world markets and the subsequent decline in world wheat prices. Tobacco was the only commodity that significantly increased its share in the total value of Ottoman exports during 1879–1913 from 6–7 per cent in 1878–80 to 11–12 per cent by 1911–13, thereby becoming the commodity with the largest share in exports. The shares of the other six largest commodities of export remained roughly unchanged during the same period. The same was true of the other Ottoman exports of lesser importance: valonia, hazelnuts, cotton and olive oil. The share of each remained under 5 per cent of the total value of exports for each year of the period 1878–1913.[2]

Relatively little can be stated with certainty regarding the earlier period. Judging from the detailed information provided in the trade statistics of other countries, it appears that the absence of commodities with large shares in total exports characteristic of the period after 1878 also existed in the period before 1878. Exports of grain, particularly wheat and barley, had higher shares in the total in the earlier period,

Table A1.2. *Composition of Ottoman exports by major commodity groups in 1911–13 (per cent)*

A	All foodstuffs	33–35
B	All raw materials	56–58
	of which minerals	2–4
	All primary products (A + B)	89–93
C	Semi-manufactures (dressed hides, etc.)	2–3
D	Manufactures (mostly woolen; carpets, etc.)	6–7

Source: Foreign trade statistics of all the other countries which had commercial relations with the Ottoman Empire. See first paragraph of appendix 1 for a complete list of the sources. The relatively large share of the category 'Miscellaneous' in the official Ottoman statistics precludes the construction of this table on the basis of the information given there.

especially during 1860–80. The same can be said about exports of raw silk. However, it is difficult to give precise shares in both cases. Another important Ottoman export commodity until 1860 was madder root, widely used as a dye in the textile industries of the center countries. The discovery in 1856 of aniline as a synthetic dyestuff quickly ended madder root's exportation around 1860. After American supplies were cut off during the American Civil War, cotton exports from Anatolia, from the plain of Adana and, more important, from the hinterland of Izmir increased sharply. In 1864, cotton exports from Anatolia reached £1,300,000, accounting for 51 per cent of all exports from the Asiatic provinces of the Ottoman Empire to the United Kingdom. Due to the cotton's poor quality, and for other reasons, exports of Anatolian cotton diminished rapidly after 1866. It averaged only around £140,000 per year during the decade of 1867–76.[3]

The composition of Ottoman exports by major commodity groups for the years 1911–13 is given in table A1.2. Like the relatively constant shares of the individual commodities in the total value of exports, the shares of the major commodity groups did not change significantly over time. Due to higher exports of cereals, a higher share for the foodstuffs should be expected for the earlier period. Another notable difference for the earlier period is lower levels of woolen manufactures, mostly carpets. Their share in total exports was below 2 per cent for the period before 1890.

Imports

The composition of Ottoman imports by major commodity groups for the years 1911–13 is summarized in table A1.3. As should be expected

151

Table A1.3. *Composition of Ottoman imports by major commodity groups in 1911–13 (per cent)*

A	All foodstuffs (grains, flour, rice, sugar, coffee, tea, etc.)	32–38
B	Various raw materials and intermediate goods (coal, petroleum, unworked metals, dyes, etc.)	6–10
C	All yarns (mostly cotton)	4
D	All manufactures of cotton, wool, silk, linen; all clothing and apparel	36–38
E	Investment goods (about half of which are railroad building materials and rolling stock)	Under 8
F	Other manufactures (including ammunition which becomes significant during periods of war)	8–10
Total manufactures (D + E + F)		56–60

Sources: Foreign trade statistics of all the countries which had commercial relations with the Ottoman Empire. See first paragraph of appendix 1 for a complete list of the sources. For a similar but rather incomplete table based on the Ottoman statistics, see Eldem (1970), p. 181.

from a peripheral economy, the share of manufactures exceeds 50 per cent. More significant, perhaps, is the large share of foodstuffs. Imports of sugar, coffee and tea are not surprising, but by 1913 the Ottoman Empire had become a net importer of grains and flour. According to the Ottoman trade statistics, imports of wheat, barley and flour exceeded exports of the same by an average of £1.5 million per year during 1910–13. By contrast, the same statistics indicate that in the early 1880s Ottoman exports of grain had approximately equalled imports of grain and flour.[4] The patterns of production and trade of cereals in different parts of the Empire are not yet known for the period before 1880. The Istanbul area had been consuming wheat transported from the Balkans and through the Danube for centuries. With the secession of some of these areas from the Empire during the nineteenth century, these commodity flows began to be treated as external trade. More important, a number of European countries chose to adopt protectionist measures in order to support domestic producers after the entry of American wheat into world markets in the 1870s. The Free Trade Treaties signed with European governments early in the century did not allow this flexibility to the Ottoman government; hence the rapid ascendancy of imported cereals in Ottoman markets. The construction of the Anatolian Railroad linking Istanbul to the wheat-growing regions of Central Anatolia did not eliminate these imports completely.[5]

A1.2 Deficiencies of the Ottoman foreign trade statistics

No information is currently available from Ottoman sources regarding Ottoman foreign trade before 1878, with the exception of estimated customs revenues for each year, which are available from the budgets that were first prepared in the 1860s. The reliability of these figures is questionable, since the early budgets were prepared primarily for window-dressing purposes in order to help the government obtain public loans in European financial markets. As for utilization of the official Ottoman trade statistics for the period after 1878, their limitations should be carefully noted.[6]

We begin with a brief discussion of three of the problems associated with the official statistics. One problem concerns the distinction between special and general trade. The statistics up to 1907 appear to provide figures only for general trade. The transit trade through the Ottoman Empire consisted mostly of European–Persian trade via Trabzon. This trade was far from negligible in the late 1870s and 1880s, especially in the direction of Persia, though it lost its importance in subsequent decades. It can be estimated that this source of error causes, for the earlier period, an upward bias of the order of 3 to 5 per cent for imports and exports.

Another deficiency of these statistics arises from their incomplete coverage. Imports and exports of tobacco until 1907 and exports of salt and wine fell under the monopoly of various agencies that were closely controlled by the Ottoman Public Debt Administration. Because these commodities were exempt from customs duties, there was no need to keep records of the value of their trade. However, since records of the annual quantities of exports were kept for each of these commodities, it is not difficult to add these items to the official Ottoman statistics. Much more serious is the exclusion of the imports of arms and ammunition, agricultural and industrial machinery and all materials for railways and factory construction. Imports of machinery and materials for factory construction were never large. On the other hand, imports of arms and ammunition and imports of material for railway construction periodically reached important magnitudes. Hence, the exclusion of these items introduces a not insignificant amount of downward bias to the Ottoman imports for some years.

Third, Ottoman foreign trade statistics present serious problems for establishing the country distribution of Ottoman foreign trade. Until 1910, the destination/country of origin definition employed in the Ottoman statistics specified the country with which trade was conducted as that from which goods were directly received or to which goods were directly sent. Thus, whenever Ottoman trade with a country was carried out via the ports of third countries, it became impossible to determine the magnitude of Ottoman trade with that country on the basis of Ottoman statistics. The most striking examples of this deficiency appear in the record of Ottoman trade with Germany, a good deal of which was shipped through the Austrian port of Trieste, and in the record of trade with the United States, most of which was shipped via French or North European ports. The Ottoman statistics seriously underestimate the Ottoman trade with both of these countries.[7] This source of error was eliminated only in 1911 when the destination/country of origin definitions employed in the Ottoman statistics were changed to refer to the country of origin of imports and to the country of final destination of exports.

Overvaluation of imports

For our purposes, the reliability of the Ottoman statistics are undermined much more seriously by the problems associated with the methods of valuation they employ. Starting with their first publication, the Ottoman trade statistics adopted a system of valuation of imports and exports based on the official lists of values established for customs purposes. The 1838–41 Free Trade Treaties signed with Britain and other European powers included the principle that the Ottoman government was to assess the fixed percentage *ad valorem* customs duties on imports and exports on the basis of lists of official prices. These lists were to be prepared only with the direct participation of the European powers and would be revised periodically in order to take into account changes in commodity prices. The first revision was made in 1850, and the next one was planned for 1855. However, the outbreak of the Crimean War necessitated the postponement of the negotiations. In subsequent years, the boom in raw material and manufactures prices brought about by the Crimean War gave Britain and other European powers sufficient incentive to resist the revision of the 1850 lists. It was only after prolonged negotiations and Ottoman concessions on related issues (customs duties on exports were to be reduced from 12 per cent to 1 per cent within eight years, while duties on imports were raised from 5 per cent to 8 per cent) that new lists based on Ottoman domestic prices were prepared in 1861.[8]

On the other hand, since world prices of both raw materials and manufactures steadily declined between 1865 and 1895, it may well be that it was subsequently the Ottoman government's turn not to show any enthusiasm about revisions in these official prices. The prices of Ottoman imports from industrial Europe declined by 18 per cent between 1860 and 1878 and by another 28 per cent between 1878 and 1895.[9] In any case, when the Ottoman foreign trade statistics began to be published in 1878, 1861 lists of official prices were still in effect.[10] These lists were used in the valuation of imports until 1882. Between 1882 and 1909, the 1861 lists continued to be considered the basis for the valuation of imports, but these lists began to be replaced by 'current' prices as negotiations with each European country began to lead to the abolition of the old official price lists.

The gradual adoption of the 'current' price system did not necessarily eliminate the potential problems of overvaluation and/or undervaluation. Until 1911 there is no explanation given in the Ottoman statistics to indicate whether these current prices were declared prices, were estimated by customs officials, or were a mixture of the two. On the basis of the reports by the U.S. consuls in Istanbul, 'estimation' of the current prices by customs officials appears to be the rule until 1909, at which time, as the Ottoman statistics indicate in 1911, the certificates of origin began to be taken as the basis for the valuation of imports.[11] Thus, there may well be an additional upwards bias in the valuation of imports if it was the case that officials were unwilling to revise their estimates frequently in a period of falling prices, as was the case until 1895. When 'current' prices are estimated by customs officials, another tendency for overvaluation arises from the revenue concerns of the state, since 8 per cent *ad valorem* duty was applied to all imports.

Undervaluation of exports

The 1909 edition of the statistics stated that valuation would be on the basis of current prices, and in 1911 the following explanation was provided: 'Export commodities are also valuated at current prices at the port of export. However, for exports subject to special tariff duties, the value is the one based on the yearly price averages.' There is no explanation in the official statistics regarding the system under which exports were valuated during the period 1883–1908. The 1861 lists may have been retained, 1859 prices on which 1861 lists were based may have been replaced gradually by more current price lists as negotiations with each European country were concluded, or Ottoman exports may have been valuated at current market prices, either as estimated by customs officials or as declared by the exporter, starting somewhere between 1883 and 1908.[12]

Therefore, it will not be possible to determine in which direction, if any, the bias of Ottoman statistics may tend with regard to the valuation of exports without our undertaking a commodity-by-commodity comparison of the unit prices given in the Ottoman statistics with those given in the statistics of the importing European countries (after making the appropriate adjustments for transportation and insurance costs). An additional comparison with the Ottoman domestic wholesale prices should also be helpful.

Table A1.4 summarizes a comparison for seven major Ottoman exports – wheat, barley, opium, valonia, raisins, olive oil and goat's wool – between the average export prices given in the Ottoman statistics and the prices given in the trade statistics of the United Kingdom under the heading 'imports from Turkey', after allowance is made for transportation and insurance costs. These figures indicate that if we are to take the British statistics and the British method of valuation as the most reliable of the contemporary statistics (and most observers agree that they were), it would not be difficult to conclude that the Ottoman statistics systematically undervalued the exports, though the magnitude of the undervaluation varied from one period to another. Similar results are obtained if we repeat these comparisons using the unit prices of imports from the Ottoman Empire given in the statistics of other European countries.

The hypothesis of the undervaluation of Ottoman exports can be further investigated by a comparison of the export prices given in the Ottoman statistics with Ottoman domestic wholesale prices. Such a comparison based on domestic 'producers' prices' was made by Vedat Eldem for the year 1913. His results show that for a group of seven major Ottoman exports weighted equally, the export prices are lower than the domestic wholesale prices by more than 25 per cent. Eldem states further that similar comparisons for the years 1907 and 1909 reveal even wider price differentials.[13]

Similar comparisons for Ottoman imports are not possible. In the Ottoman statistics, unit prices for imports are available for only the seven primary commodities (wheat, flour, barley, etc.) that together constituted no more than 20 per cent of total imports. Unit prices were not recorded for any of the imports of European manufactures. On the other hand, the available unit prices of imports provide important clues regarding the direction of the biases of the valuation system. Of the seven imported commodities for which unit prices are available, two, namely

Table A1.4. *The ratio between prices of Ottoman exports as given in the Ottoman foreign trade statistics and prices of U.K. imports from the Ottoman Empire as given in the U.K. foreign trade statistics for seven major Ottoman exports*

Years	Ottoman X prices /U.K. M prices
1881	0.74
1882	0.76
1883	0.75
1891	0.84
1892	0.89
1893	0.93
1908	0.55
1909	0.79
1910	0.95

Notes: Appropriate transportation costs are subtracted from the U.K. c.i.f. import prices to arrive at f.o.b. Ottoman export prices for both sets of figures. The commodities are weighted in proportion to the value of the trade between the two countries.
Sources: Aybar (1939) and Annual Statement of the Trade . . . of the United Kingdom, in *Parliamentary Papers, Accounts and Papers,* relevant years.

wheat and barley, are also among Ottoman exports. Unit prices are available for them in the export category as well.

In Table A1.5 a comparison is made between these commodities' import prices and export prices, as given in the official Ottoman statistics. This table shows that prices of imported wheat and barley were consistently higher than prices of exports of the same two commodities, and that the margins were quite large, exceeding 100 per cent in two cases. Although it appears unlikely, some of this price differential may be due to differences in quality. Istanbul, with its higher than average standards of living, may have been importing cereals of higher quality than cereals exported from elsewhere in the Empire. It can also be argued that some price differential should be expected if importation and exportation occur at different ports. It would be natural to expect lower prices at the ports of export, since grains are relatively abundant there, but then prices of imports of the same quality grain should not exceed the export price plus the cost of transportation. Clearly, the price differentials of the order of magnitude we are dealing with here cannot be explained entirely by quality differences and/or transportation costs.

Table A1.5. *Ratios of import to export prices of wheat and barley according to official Ottoman statistics*

Years	Wheat	Barley
1881–3	1.05	1.40
1891–3	1.23	2.10
1908–10	1.52	2.03

Source: Our calculations based on Aybar (1939).

The conclusion that either exports were undervalued or imports were overvalued, or both, is inevitable, at least in the case of these two commodities.

Contemporary observers were not unaware of the existence of these problems. For example, the U.S. Consul in Istanbul reported in 1909: 'the claim of . . . certain authorities that it is materially impossible for a country like Turkey, with little other source of income than its agricultural products, certain raw materials and the hand weaving of carpets, to purchase from 50 to 100 percent more than the nation sells . . . appear to be justified . . .; and it is only reasonable to suppose that the Turkish statistics of exports are much undervalued'.[14]

Some foreign observers went so far as to attempt to estimate the true magnitude of Ottoman exports and imports from the information provided in the statistics of all the countries with which the Ottoman Empire had commercial relations, after making the appropriate adjustments for transportation and insurance costs. The results of these studies, which were undertaken for various years during the period 1890–1913, are summarized by Eldem, and they confirm both the substantial undervaluation of exports and the overvaluation of imports.[15] These results will not be discussed further, since our reconstruction of Ottoman foreign trade represents a more thorough application of the same approach to the entire 83–year period, 1830–1913.

A1.3 The reconstruction procedure: potential pitfalls

This reconstruction was undertaken for the purpose of obtaining information more comprehensive and more reliable than that which is available from Ottoman sources. Needless to say, these results can represent only an improvement for the period before 1878, since virtually no information is available from Ottoman sources; yet it is not immediately clear whether they represent an improvement for the period 1878–1913, for which published Ottoman statistics are available. Here we will describe the measures taken to ensure that the results of this reconstruction are more reliable than the information provided by the Ottoman statistics.

Unlike the Ottoman statistics, the trade statistics of major European countries and the United States began to be published early in the nineteenth century. As the list provided at the beginning of this appendix indicates, the only significant exception is the absence of German foreign trade statistics until 1880, but the figures for Ottoman trade with Germany prior to 1880 can be obtained from the Austrian statistics on trade transiting through that country, since direct trade between German and Ottoman ports was very small. Hence, it is possible to account for at least 95 per cent of the Ottoman foreign trade for the period after 1840 on the basis of the statistics of these other countries. We estimated the rest by extrapolating backwards in time from information available for the later period. Since less information is available from the same sources on Ottoman foreign trade of the 1830s, our estimates of the total value of Ottoman imports and exports of that decade necessarily involve a greater degree of uncertainty.

At the outset one important characteristic of these foreign trade statistics needs to be emphasized: the difficulties associated with comparisons between the statistics of any two countries. More specifically, if the figures for the imports of country A from country B, as given in the statistics of country A, are compared with the figures for the exports of country B, they are frequently observed to differ by a not insignificant margin for both total trade figures and for individual commodities or commodity groups, even after transportation and insurance costs are taken into account, or, as in the case of some pairs of countries, even when all the trade takes place over the mutual land border with no transportation and insurance costs involved.[16] This disparity arises from the differences in the definitions and procedures employed in the statistics of different countries. However, as long as the sources of the disparities can be pinpointed and appropriate modifications are made accordingly, these disparities should not cast undue doubt on the accuracy of the results that are obtained from a reconstruction attempt of the kind undertaken here.

There are three potential sources of error in a reconstruction attempt of this kind:

(1) The trade statistics of different countries employed different definitions of country of origin or destination. The two definitions that were most frequently used in the nineteenth century specified the country with which trade was conducted either as 'country from which goods

were directly received, to which goods were directly sent' or as 'country of origin of imports and country of final destination of exports where they are to be consumed'.

It is clear that unless all countries adopt the same definition, there will be a discrepancy between the actual imports or exports of a country and the imports or exports estimated on the basis of the statistics of other countries. For example, let us assume exports of country A are shipped first to country B and then sent to country C, which is their final destination. If both country B and country C adopt either the first or the second definition for the country of destination, then this trade will appear as exports from country A to either country B or C, depending on which definition is used. However, if country B adopts the first definition and country C the second, then the exports from country A will appear in the statistics of both B and C. When an attempt is made to estimate the trade of country A from the statistics of B and C, these exports from A will be counted twice. Conversely, if country B adopts the second definition and country C the first, exports from country A will not appear in the statistics of either B or C. Aside from such possibilities of double counting or loss of trade, the use of the second definition by all countries would be preferable, because it would give the 'true' country distribution of trade.

Consequently, we made the appropriate adjustments in the trade data provided in the statistics of those European and Middle Eastern countries that did not adopt the second definition. To cite a more important example, the first definition was employed in the statistics of the United Kingdom. The United Kingdom's trade with Turkey as it appeared in these statistics included its trade with Iran, which transited through the Ottoman Empire. This transit trade was not insignificant, especially before the opening of the Suez Canal. Since annual estimates regarding the value of this trade are available from the reports of the British and French consuls in Trabzon, the necessary adjustments were made on the figures provided by the United Kingdom statistics.

(2) A related problem arises from the adoption of different definitions of what constitutes exports and imports; the statistics of some countries refer to special trade only, some refer only to general trade that includes transit trade, and still others make a distinction between special trade and general trade and present figures for both. If one defines the country with which trade is conducted as the country of origin of imports and the country of final destination of exports, as we did, then the only proper definition of trade would be that of special trade; utilization of the general trade figures (special trade plus transit trade) of any country would result in double counting. Therefore, our reconstruction was based entirely on

the special trade figures of each country. If special trade figures were not available, as in the case of some smaller countries in the early nineteenth century, we made adjustments on the basis of trends and on the basis of the share of transit trade in the general trade during the years for which data for both special and general trade were available.

(3) A major problem in the utilization of the foreign trade statistics of any country is that of valuation. In the nineteenth century there were two rival systems: (a) valuation by declaration and (b) valuation by official estimation. The problem with the former system arises from the difficulty of preventing underdeclaration for commodities subject to customs duty. Some undervaluation due to underdeclaration occurred even in the case of British statistics, which were usually considered the most reliable of their kind in the nineteenth century.[17] The latter method of valuation was not free of problems either. Particularly in the case of countries that did not frequently revise their official lists of values, valuation by official estimation led to divergencies from actual prices during periods of moderate or rapid price changes.

During the nineteenth century, valuation by official estimation was the rule with European statistics. Therefore, systematic undervaluation in these statistics is rather unlikely, especially in view of the downward tendency of prices during large parts of the century. Moreover, annual revision of the official values estimated, in most cases, the danger that official prices would fail to keep up with short-to-medium-term fluctuations in actual prices. However, revision of official prices was less frequent in the early part of the nineteenth century. Hence, it is difficult to follow the short-term fluctuations in unit prices and in the total value of trade from the trade statistics of the earlier period. Because of these problems of valuation and other inadequacies of the data, the results obtained in this reconstruction were not utilized for the analysis of short-run questions. Despite this shortcoming, the utilization of the statistics of European countries can only represent an improvement over the use of the Ottoman statistics with respect to inaccuracies arising from valuation.

A1.4 Estimation of transportation and insurance costs

The foreign trade returns of each country that had commercial relations with the Ottoman Empire valuated their exports to the Ottoman Empire in f.o.b. prices and their imports in c.i.f. prices. The appropriate procedure from the point of view of the Ottoman economy would be to valuate Ottoman exports to each country in f.o.b. prices and Ottoman exports in c.i.f. prices, both at Ottoman ports. The conversion from one system to the other requires the subtraction of appropriate transportation and insurance costs from the c.i.f. import prices of each country and, conversely, the addition of the appropriate transportation and insurance costs to the f.o.b. export prices of each country. We calculated these transportation and insurance costs as shares in the total value of imports and exports at the port of the country whose statistics were being utilized. Hence, once S_1 and S_2, shares of transportation and of insurance costs respectively, are estimated for the imports and exports of each country separately, the values of Ottoman exports and imports are estimated in the following manner:

(Ottoman c.i.f. imports) = (foreign f.o.b. exports) $(1 + S_1 + S_2)$
(Ottoman f.o.b. exports) = (foreign c.i.f. imports) $(1 - S_1 - S_2)$

The following formula was used to arrive at the share of transportation costs in the total value of Ottoman trade with each country:

$$\text{Share of transportation costs in the total value of trade}_{ijm} = \text{constant} \times \text{freight rate index}_{im} \times \text{distance coefficient}_j \times \text{bulk coefficient}_{jm} \times \text{price level index}_{ijm}$$

where the subscript i denotes years, j refers to different countries and m, which takes only two values, indicates whether the trade in question is Ottoman exports or imports.

During the period 1855–1913, United States and to a limited extent British consular commercial reports from the Ottoman Empire and Greece frequently provided information on the freight charges that prevailed in the transportation of various commodities between the Ottoman and Greek ports on the one hand and the North American and European ports on the other.[18] A comparison showed that the year-to-year fluctuations in these charges, as well as their long-term trends, closely followed the pattern of freight charges on a worldwide basis.[19] On the basis of this information, we decided to use in these calculations the freight rate indices developed for worldwide ocean shipping. The Cairncross indices for British incoming and outgoing freight rates for 1870–1913 were linked to Douglas North's freight rate index for United States trade from 1830 to 1870 with the help of two other indices that were also prepared by North. These were a provisional freight rate index on U.S. imports for 1860–70 and an index for shipping Black Sea wheat to Britain during 1860–70.[20] Appropriate modifications were made in these indices for periods of war in the Middle East: 1854–6, 1877–8, 1897 and 1912–13. Similarly, modifications had to be made in the index for United States imports before it could be used in this study, since the Civil War unfavorably affected freight rates in U.S. trade in the first half of the 1860s.

The freight charges in British pounds sterling for a ton of fruit from Izmir to each country during 1870–5 were used as proxy for the distance coefficient of each country. The necessity for the inclusion of a bulk coefficient in the calculation of the share of transportation costs in the total value of trade arises from the differences in the composition of Ottoman trade with each country. Clearly, the share of transportation costs in the total value of trade is not the same for wheat and for textiles. The bulk coefficients for Ottoman exports and imports were calculated after a commodity-by-commodity calculation was made of the share of transportation costs in the value of Ottoman exports to and imports from each country for the years 1860, 1890 and 1913. In most cases, the bulk coefficient was roughly the same for these three years; for those cases the bulk coefficient was assumed constant for the entire period 1860–1913. The bulk coefficient for Ottoman exports was more or less uniform across countries; it was relatively low whenever the exports to a country did not include significant amounts of grain. The variation of the bulk coefficient across countries was much larger for imports. It ranged from high values for imports from Russia (large share of wheat) and Austria (sugar) to a low value for imports from Britain, which consisted almost entirely of manufactures and primarily of textiles.

Since the prices of Ottoman exports and imports did not remain constant over this period, the share of transportation costs in the total value of trade did not simply move together with the freight rates. Therefore it becomes necessary to take into account in these calculations the changing prices of Ottoman exports and imports. For this purpose, the price indices that were constructed for the study of Ottoman external terms of trade were utilized. Separate price indices were prepared for Ottoman exports and imports to and from each major European country. The construction of these indices is discussed and the basic results are presented in chapter 3 and appendix 2.

Finally, the constant term given in the equation above is simply the scale factor required to link the product of the four coefficients discussed here to the percentage share of transportation costs in the total value of trade. As for the results of these calculations, rather than provide detailed lists for the estimated share of transportation costs in the total value of exports and imports for each year for each country, we will offer only a few examples here. We have estimated the share of transportation costs in the total value of the imports of the United Kingdom from the Ottoman

Empire at 10.39 per cent for the year 1833, 14.02 per cent for 1853, 12.31 per cent for 1873, 8.22 per cent for 1893, and 7.84 per cent for 1913. On the other hand, the share of transportation costs in the total value of French exports to the Ottoman Empire was estimated at 8.18 per cent for 1833, 6.12 per cent for 1853, 5.62 per cent for 1873, 3.31 per cent for 1893, and 4.44 per cent for 1913. The decline in these shares simply indicates that the decline in freight charges was much more rapid than the long-term decline in commodity prices during the nineteenth century.

In the absence of insurance companies to underwrite the risks involved, a good deal of Ottoman foreign trade must have gone uninsured in the early part of the nineteenth century. Nonetheless, this does not mean that no allowance should be made in our calculation for insurance costs for that period. On the contrary, it can be assumed that costs incurred by the merchants in the form of spoilage, damage to the cargo, etc., in the absence of insurance companies, was, on average, roughly equal to or somewhat lower than the insurance premium that would have been paid to the insurance companies. Under this assumption, estimates of 'insurance' costs on Ottoman foreign trade can be extended to the 1830s, decades before the date at which the majority of Ottoman foreign trade began to be covered by insurance.

The average rates of insurance as a percentage of the total value of trade paid on United States imports during 1861–1900 are available from Matthew Simon's study of the United States balance of payments.[21] In the absence of any other information on marine insurance rates in the nineteenth century, Simon's estimates were applied to the Ottoman trade with a number of modifications. Most important, it was assumed that the average insurance rates for the Ottoman–British trade in both directions was 60 per cent higher than the average rates paid on U.S. imports for the same year. We linked average rates of insurance in trade with other countries to the Ottoman–British insurance rates by assuming that relative risk in transportation costs was an increasing function of distance. To cite a few examples from our results, the share of insurance costs in the total value of Ottoman exports to the United Kingdom was estimated at 5.25 per cent in 1833, 3.89 per cent in 1853, 2.24 per cent in 1893, and 1.92 per cent in 1913.

Finally, a few words are in order regarding rates of exchange. During this reconstruction all trade values given in the statistics of various countries were converted to British pounds sterling utilizing the gold standard rates of exchange. Most of the countries in question were part of the gold standard system during the nineteenth century and adjustments in the rates of exchange were undertaken rather infrequently. As a result, the conversion of annual trade values to pounds sterling was a straightforward operation.[22]

A1.5 Further checks on the results

As the preceding discussion suggests, a large number of potential sources of error are inherent in a reconstruction attempt of this kind. Therefore, despite all the detail and care taken, it is necessary to compare the results with other information at hand. For the period before 1877 for which Ottoman statistics are not available, we have three studies that attempted to estimate the value of Ottoman exports and imports utilizing primarily the contemporary foreign trade statistics of European countries in a more simple and summary manner than was followed in our attempt. In chronological order, these studies can be found in *Accounts and Papers* (1843), MacGregor (1847) and Ubicini (1856). Each of them has a number of deficiencies, and their figures cannot be expected to match our estimates. Nonetheless, for this early part of the century, the figures given in these studies are not entirely out of line with our estimates. In addition, some of the details of these studies, such as their estimates of the Ottoman–Central European trade transiting through Austria, were useful to us in developing our own estimates of the same commodity flows.

As for the period after 1877, the reliability of our annual estimates for Ottoman exports and imports can be checked in two ways. First, the figures obtained here can be compared with those given in the official Ottoman statistics. Due to the undervaluation of exports and overvaluation of imports in the official statistics, the absolute levels of the two series cannot be expected to match. However, long-term growth, as well as annual and medium-term fluctuation of exports and imports, should be comparable in the two sets of series. This relationship can be observed in figure A1. Second, the biases of the official statistics arising, for example, from the undervaluation of exports is expected to follow a certain pattern over time. Therefore, the divergence between the results of the reconstruction attempt and the official figures should also be expected to exhibit a particular pattern. Figure A2 demonstrates strikingly the difference between the official trade balance figures and the trade balance emerging from the reconstruction attempt. Until around 1907, the reconstructed trade balance follows the official balance through its fluctuations, with a difference of £4 to £6 million. This margin can be interpreted to be due, in large part, to the undervaluation of exports and overvaluation of imports in the official statistics.

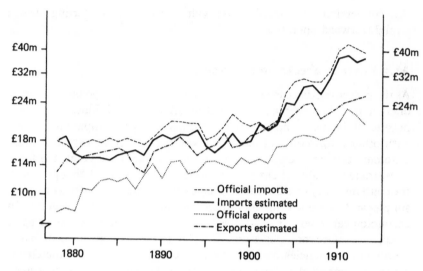

Figure A1 A comparison of the results of our reconstruction with the official Ottoman trade statistics, 1878–1913 (in millions of British pounds sterling).

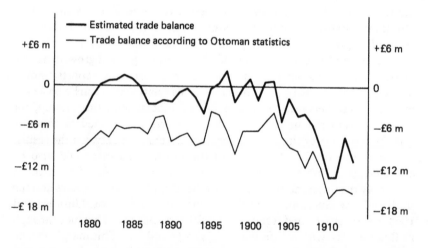

Figure A2 A comparison of the estimated Ottoman trade balance with the trade balance according to the official Ottoman statistics, 1878–1913 (in millions of British pounds sterling). Sources: Aybar (1939) and table A1.1 of this appendix.

Another procedure for checking the reliability of the results of our reconstruction attempt, at least with respect to the trade balance figures, would be to inquire whether the estimated trade deficits are consistent with a wider balance of payments picture. In fact, one of the reasons for initiating this reconstruction attempt was the observation that the trade deficits given in the official Ottoman statistics were too large to be financed by the other items of the external payments account. With the exception of the calculations by Vedat Eldem for the years 1907, 1909 and 1913, a detailed study of the Ottoman balance of payments had not been undertaken.[23] In appendix 6 we present the results of our attempt to estimate separately the basic items of the Ottoman balance of payments for each year of the period 1850–1913. Our purpose there is to check not only the reliability of our estimates for foreign trade but also of our estimates for funds flows arising from foreign investment in the Empire and to shed more light on certain aspects of the process of incorporation of the Empire into the world economy. Our balance of payments study shows that the trade deficits emerging from this reconstruction attempt could be financed by other items of the external payments account. Those balance of payments estimates show that even during the late 1890s and early in the twentieth century, when interest payments and profit transfer exceeded new inflows of foreign capital, trade deficits were financed by some of the invisible items in the external payments account. They also suggest that, for an explanation of how the growing trade deficits of the early 1910s were financed, one would have to turn to short- and medium-term commercial credits in addition to net inflows from invisibles and public borrowing.

Price indices for Ottoman foreign trade, 1854–1913

In this appendix, we present the results of our study of the Ottoman terms of trade for the period 1854–1913, which is based on the foreign trade statistics of the major European countries and, for Ottoman exports, statistics of the United States. In the first two sections of the appendix, data and index problems are discussed. The main results are presented at the end in tables A2.1 and A2.2.

A2.1 Data and their problems

Ottoman foreign trade statistics became available only after 1878. The significant biases in the valuation of both imports and exports, as well as other problems that are discussed in appendix 1, seriously limit the usefulness of these statistics for a terms of trade study for even that late period.[1] The present study was based on the volume and unit price data for Ottoman imports and exports, as given in the annual foreign trade statistics of each of the following countries for the indicated periods: the United Kingdom, 1854–1913; France, 1854–1913; Germany, 1880–1913; Austria, 1891–1913; the United States, 1896–1913 (for Ottoman exports only).[2]

The number of commodities for which price and quantity information is available varies from one period to the next and from one country to the other. In general, this number increased over time. The number of commodities with price and quantity information varied mainly between 25 and 40 for both the exports to and imports from the Ottoman Empire of each country for any given year. Taken together, these statistics provided information on about 60 commodities, for both the Ottoman imports and exports, around the mid-1850s; this number increased to about 180 for both the exports and imports by the early 1910s. It should be added that a large number of Ottoman commodity imports and exports appeared in the returns of more than one country, while some commodities may have appeared in the returns of all countries. Hence, the number of separate commodities included in any one year of this study falls considerably below the 60 to 180 range indicated above for both exports and imports.

The commodities for which both price and quantity information were available and which were included in our indices made up on average 80 to 90 per cent of the exports and imports of each country. For example, for the year 1860, for which British and French statistics were used for this study, coverage of the indices in value terms is 89 per cent of Ottoman exports to and 91 per cent of Ottoman imports from these countries. In terms of their share in total Ottoman trade, these figures represent 46 per cent of total Ottoman exports and 30 per cent of total Ottoman imports, or 63 per cent of Ottoman exports to center countries and 45 per cent of Ottoman imports from industrialized center countries. For 1913, for which British, French, German, Austrian and United States (for Ottoman exports only) statistics could be used for our price indices, the coverage in terms of value is 88 and 80 per cent respectively for the Ottoman exports to and imports from these countries. These figures represent 60 and 50 per cent respectively of total Ottoman exports and imports, or 78 per cent of Ottoman exports to and 63 per cent of Ottoman imports from the industrialized center countries.[3]

We have accepted the official returns of each country at face value, apart from instances where obvious mistakes were discovered (smuggling was not important in the Ottoman trade with these countries). As we note in appendix 1, there were two major systems of valuation in the nineteenth century: valuation by declaration and valuation on the basis of official values, which were subject to periodic revision. The United Kingdom and the United States used the declared value system, but as studies on their nineteenth-century foreign trade indicate, undervaluation was not a significant problem.[4] The other trade returns used in this study followed the official valuation method.[5] While there is no *a priori* reason to expect under- or overvaluation of trade in these returns, it is quite possible that revisions in the official value lists were not frequent enough or that they lagged behind during periods of moderate to rapid price changes. This possibility limits the use of our price indices no more and no less than it limited the indices constructed for other terms of trade studies on the nineteenth century. As long as these indices are not used for the analysis of year-to-year fluctuations, problems ensuing from imperfect methods of valuation will remain minor.

All unit prices given in the statistics were converted to British pounds sterling under the prevailing gold standard rate of exchange.[6] Since problems of undervaluation or overvaluation of the currencies in question did not exist under the gold standard, our indices are free of the exchange rate problems encountered frequently in the terms of trade studies of the post-gold standard era.

A2.2 Indices and index problems

The foreign trade statistics of the other countries gave f.o.b. prices for Ottoman imports and c.i.f. prices for Ottoman exports. The appropriate transportation and insurance costs had to be added to the f.o.b. prices of Ottoman imports, and the appropriate transportation and insurance costs had to be subtracted from the c.i.f. prices of Ottoman exports to reach c.i.f. prices for Ottoman imports and f.o.b. prices of Ottoman exports. For example, once the shares of transportation and insurance costs (t and i respectively) in total trade valuated at the foreign ports are estimated for each year, the following modifications are made in the usual computations of Laspeyres:

For f.o.b. Ottoman exports

$$\text{Laspeyres} = \frac{1 - t_1 - i_1}{1 - t_0 - i_0} \frac{(\Sigma Q_0 P_1)}{(\Sigma Q_0 P_0)}$$

For f.o.b. Ottoman imports

$$\text{Laspeyres} = \frac{1 + t_1 + i_1}{1 + t_0 + i_0} \frac{(\Sigma Q_0 P_1)}{(\Sigma Q_0 P_0)}$$

and similarly for Paasche:

where t_j = share of transportation costs in the total value of trade as valuated in the foreign port by the trade statistics of the foreign country in year j;

i_j = corresponding share of insurance costs in year j and P_j and Q_j = price and quantity at the foreign port (as given in the trade statistics of the foreign country) in year j.

The price indices computed for this study are annually linked Fisher ideal index numbers. Laspeyres and Paasche indices, which can be considered as intermediate products for the Fisher ideal, were also computed in each case and are presented along with the Fisher indices at the end of this appendix.[7] By computing chain indices with annual links we were able to take full advantage of the increasingly detailed commodity classification.

Finally, we briefly explain the reasons for the use of Fisher indices over Laspeyres and Paasche. In all price indices, including those of foreign trade, if prices and quantities are negatively correlated, Laspeyres will exceed Paasche, and in view of the identity volume times price equals value, Laspeyres quantity and price indices will both exceed corresponding Paasche indices. Conversely, when the prices and quantities are positively correlated, Laspeyres quantity and price indices will both fall short of Paasche. Since the former case is much more frequently observed, in empirical studies Laspeyres almost invariably exceeds Paasche for both price and quantity indices. With respect to foreign trade indices, it has been shown, for example, that for a small country the Laspeyres price index tends to exaggerate when applied to imports and to understate when applied to exports, whereas for Paasche the opposite is the case.[8] As a result, the terms of trade tend to be understated when calculated as the ratio between Laspeyres export and import price indices and to be exaggerated when calculated on the basis of Paasche price indices. Hence, on the basis of theoretical considerations, one can point to the potential divergence between Laspeyres and Paasche and the biases for each. The direction of these biases will depend on the direction of the price and quantity of correlation.

In either case, one thing is clear: neither Laspeyres nor Paasche can be taken as a 'true' index of what is being measured. In the absence of a 'true' index, Laspeyres and Paasche are frequently viewed as providing an upper and lower bound (not necessarily in that order) for that 'true' index. One solution has been to utilize the Fisher index, which is the geometric mean of Laspeyres and Paasche. Under certain conditions (homotheticity in both preferences and production) Fisher is not only a geometric mean but also a good proxy for a 'true' index; unfortunately, those conditions are rarely if ever satisfied.[9]

Table A2.1. Price indices for Ottoman trade with the industrialized center countries,[a] 1854–1913
1880=100

Year	Ottoman exports				Ottoman imports				Net barter terms of trade P_x/P_m		
	NCOM	LSP	PSC	FSH	NCOM	LSP	PSC	FSH	LSP	PSC	FSH
1854	44	148.7	151.6	150.1	44	101.8	140.5	120.1	146.1	107.9	125.0
1855	44	160.0	159.2	159.6	44	101.2	136.3	117.9	158.1	116.8	135.9
1856	42	173.2	165.9	169.5	45	105.7	137.7	121.0	163.9	120.5	140.1
1857	38	172.5	162.7	167.6	44	111.1	139.5	129.5	155.3	116.6	134.6
1858	46	141.9	134.6	138.2	51	105.7	131.1	117.7	134.3	102.7	117.4
1859	47	143.2	138.6	140.8	51	109.4	134.0	121.1	130.9	103.4	116.3
1860	42	152.5	145.6	149.0	51	111.9	136.9	123.8	136.2	106.3	120.3
1861	47	139.6	140.6	140.1	48	106.1	128.1	116.6	131.6	109.7	120.2
1862	48	143.6	145.8	144.7	48	118.7	138.4	128.2	121.0	105.3	112.9
1863	47	141.3	149.9	145.5	47	140.4	159.8	149.8	100.6	93.8	97.1
1864	45	144.3	153.1	148.6	47	150.7	169.7	159.9	95.7	90.2	92.9
1865	49	126.8	128.8	127.8	51	138.9	155.4	146.9	91.3	82.9	87.0
1866	53	131.9	132.1	132.0	52	134.0	149.6	141.6	98.4	88.3	93.2
1867	52	137.8	143.7	140.7	53	121.9	135.3	128.4	113.0	106.2	109.6
1868	47	131.7	135.6	133.6	51	112.6	125.1	118.7	116.9	108.3	112.6
1869	49	114.1	121.8	117.9	50	112.1	124.7	118.2	101.8	97.7	99.7
1870	48	114.6	122.5	118.5	48	109.9	122.3	115.9	104.3	100.2	102.2
1871	48	124.1	129.4	126.7	49	106.2	116.6	111.3	116.8	111.0	113.9
1872	53	119.5	123.3	121.4	53	116.4	123.7	120.0	102.7	99.6	101.2
1873	51	112.3	115.9	114.1	52	115.7	122.8	119.2	97.1	94.3	95.7
1874	50	110.2	113.8	112.0	53	113.5	119.7	116.6	97.0	95.1	96.1
1875	52	104.0	107.3	105.6	54	110.6	116.2	113.4	94.0	92.3	93.2
1876	55	98.2	100.1	99.1	50	107.9	111.7	109.8	91.0	89.7	90.3
1877	57	99.4	102.3	100.8	49	108.2	111.8	110.0	91.8	91.5	91.7
1878	56	94.4	96.4	95.4	49	100.5	102.6	101.6	94.0	93.9	93.9
1879	54	97.1	99.5	98.3	52	102.2	103.7	102.9	95.0	96.0	95.5
1880	51	100.0	100.0	100.0	54	100.0	100.0	100.0	100.0	100.0	100.0
1881	59	90.7	90.7	90.7	63	93.0	92.6	92.8	97.5	98.0	97.7
1882	58	92.4	86.3	89.3	67	95.1	94.5	94.8	97.1	91.3	94.2

	NCOM				NCOM						
1883	57	99.3	55.3	92.0	69	94.2	92.6	93.4	105.4	92.1	98.5
1884	61	98.9	84.2	91.2	65	91.0	87.8	89.4	108.6	95.9	102.0
1885	60	93.5	80.3	86.6	65	87.5	83.8	85.6	106.9	85.8	101.2
1886	68	94.0	80.4	86.9	82	85.9	81.9	83.9	109.5	98.1	103.6
1887	70	78.4	67.0	72.5	83	85.0	79.9	82.4	92.3	83.9	88.0
1888	71	76.6	64.9	70.5	84	85.2	78.6	81.8	89.9	82.6	86.2
1889	74	77.0	63.9	70.2	86	86.3	78.2	82.2	89.1	81.8	85.4
1890	85	85.7	70.4	77.7	85	88.0	77.5	82.6	97.3	90.8	94.0
1891	92	85.2	69.4	76.9	84	86.1	75.1	80.4	98.9	92.4	95.6
1892	145	83.0	67.1	74.6	121	83.2	71.9	77.4	99.7	93.3	96.5
1893	143	77.5	63.9	70.4	116	83.9	71.9	77.7	92.4	88.8	90.6
1894	146	73.7	59.9	66.5	116	79.7	67.2	73.1	92.5	89.2	90.9
1895	153	74.8	60.2	67.1	119	79.8	66.3	72.8	93.7	90.7	92.2
1896	155	75.4	59.6	67.0	123	79.7	66.0	72.5	94.6	90.3	92.4
1897	155	81.4	63.0	71.6	126	78.6	68.6	70.7	103.7	99.1	101.4
1898	152	85.5	63.9	73.9	128	77.8	62.7	69.8	109.9	102.0	105.9
1899	148	86.2	63.2	74.2	128	78.7	63.0	70.4	109.5	101.4	105.4
1900	148	88.2	64.6	75.5	126	82.7	63.4	72.4	106.6	101.8	104.2
1901	149	85.8	62.7	73.4	127	81.5	61.8	71.0	105.3	101.5	103.4
1902	147	90.0	65.2	76.6	126	49.6	59.6	68.9	113.0	109.5	111.2
1903	146	89.4	62.6	74.8	127	82.1	60.3	70.3	109.0	103.9	106.4
1904	146	89.9	60.0	73.5	123	84.8	61.5	72.2	106.1	97.6	101.8
1905	146	91.0	57.7	72.5	123	89.6	63.7	75.5	101.6	90.5	95.9
1906	126	101.0	61.5	78.8	110	92.2	65.5	77.7	109.5	93.9	101.4
1907	159	106.0	63.4	82.0	145	94.7	67.2	79.8	112.0	94.3	102.7
1908	154	101.6	59.5	77.7	147	91.5	64.3	76.7	111.1	92.6	101.4
1909	154	102.2	59.3	77.8	148	90.9	63.7	76.1	112.5	93.0	102.3
1910	151	107.3	61.2	81.0	145	94.3	65.1	78.3	113.8	94.1	103.5
1911	153	114.4	64.6	86.0	145	95.4	64.8	78.7	119.9	99.7	109.3
1912	157	113.9	62.9	84.6	148	101.3	68.3	83.2	112.4	92.0	101.7
1913	156	115.5	63.1	85.4	149	99.0	64.2	79.7	116.7	98.4	107.1

*Center countries include the United Kingdom (1854–1913), France (1854–1913), Germany (1890–1913), Austria (1891–1913) and for Ottoman exports only, the United States (1896–1913).

Abbreviations: NCOM: Number of commodities included in the price index. LSP: Laspeyres price index. PSC: Paasche price index. FSH: Fisher price index.

Table A2.2. *Price indices for commodity groups in Ottoman trade with center countries, 1854–1913*
Ottoman exports: 1880=100; Ottoman imports: 1880=100

Year	Cereals 1		Other foodstuffs 2		Raw materials 3		All primary products 4 = 1+2+3		Textiles (mostly cotton) 5		Other manufactures 6		All manufactures 7 = 5+6		Terms of trade 8 = 4/7 1880=100
	NCOM	FSH	NCOM	FSH	NCOM	FSH	NCOM	FSH	NCOM	FSH	NCOM	FSH	NCOM	FSH	
1854	8	120.8	4	96.4	28	130.1	40	146.5	9	138.8	11	137.9	20	138.3	105.9
1855	8	138.8	4	84.0	28	134.8	40	156.5	9	131.9	11	155.4	20	134.4	116.4
1856	8	119.0	4	107.5	26	160.0	38	166.3	9	134.2	11	154.5	20	136.3	122.0
1857	8	115.4	4	128.9	24	177.8	36	173.4	9	129.9	10	169.3	19	134.6	128.8
1858	8	94.7	6	117.8	29	149.5	43	145.4	9	135.1	12	150.5	21	128.1	113.5
1859	8	87.9	6	110.4	29	160.5	43	148.2	9	133.4	13	143.8	22	134.9	109.9
1860	3	116.3	6	108.9	29	164.0	38	155.1	8	131.8	14	146.1	22	133.8	115.9
1861	6	138.5	6	104.9	30	139.3	42	144.1	8	119.1	13	131.8	21	120.8	119.3
1862	6	124.0	6	101.4	31	156.5	43	149.0	8	139.0	13	138.2	21	138.6	107.5
1863	8	110.7	6	101.7	28	168.7	42	151.6	8	164.6	13	165.7	21	164.6	92.1
1864	6	104.7	6	113.3	28	176.1	40	155.1	8	180.9	12	137.8	20	173.3	89.5
1865	8	100.5	7	109.5	30	147.9	45	134.4	8	168.1	12	127.3	20	160.9	83.5
1866	11	113.6	7	108.1	30	146.6	48	137.5	8	160.6	12	126.4	20	154.5	89.0
1867	10	148.3	7	94.9	30	131.7	47	142.3	8	142.6	12	113.6	20	137.4	103.6
1868	9	134.8	7	87.3	27	135.0	43	136.5	8	130.2	11	91.5	19	123.7	110.3
1869	10	103.8	6	101.7	26	140.9	42	123.0	8	129.8	11	86.8	19	122.8	100.2
1870	12	108.6	6	91.3	25	136.6	53	123.1	7	125.0	10	89.4	17	119.0	103.4
1871	11	128.1	5	94.5	26	130.9	42	129.1	7	116.0	11	101.7	18	113.3	113.9
1872	11	117.5	6	101.1	29	126.6	46	123.3	8	122.3	13	117.5	21	121.3	101.6
1873	11	111.0	6	100.3	27	116.2	44	114.8	8	119.2	13	112.8	21	117.9	97.4
1874	10	115.2	6	97.0	28	110.8	44	113.0	8	115.1	13	130.0	21	116.5	97.0
1875	10	101.4	6	96.7	29	111.5	45	108.2	8	114.1	14	113.6	22	113.7	95.2
1876	12	88.7	6	88.7	30	108.0	48	100.1	8	110.6	10	123.9	18	111.5	89.8
1877	12	84.9	6	96.0	.30	106.0	48	98.0	8	112.3	10	110.9	18	112.2	87.3
1878	12	87.3	7	90.5	28	102.1	47	96.3	8	101.5	10	98.2	18	101.2	95.2
1879	10	95.1	7	104.6	28	94.6	45	98.6	9	105.0	12	104.3	21	105.0	93.9

Year	NCOM	Index	NCOM	Index	NCOM	Index	NCOM	Index	NCOM	Index	NCOM	Index	NCOM	Index	FSH
1880	9	100.0	6	100.0	27	100.0	42	100.0	9	100.0	13	100.0	22	100.0	100.0
1881	11	88.5	8	84.8	29	95.1	48	91.5	12	91.4	18	94.5	30	91.7	99.8
1882	10	93.1	8	86.6	29	89.7	47	89.8	13	93.9	21	111.0	34	95.3	94.2
1883	10	90.2	8	86.4	29	96.9	47	93.0	13	93.1	19	107.3	32	94.3	98.6
1884	10	84.7	10	98.6	30	95.1	50	92.9	10	89.1	18	93.5	28	89.4	103.9
1885	11	78.6	9	93.6	28	89.6	48	88.5	10	84.4	18	94.9	28	85.4	103.6
1886	14	80.7	10	99.5	29	87.4	53	88.9	15	83.0	25	94.1	40	84.0	105.8
1887	13	82.2	12	87.5	31	83.4	46	75.1	15	81.7	26	92.1	41	82.6	90.9
1888	13	79.9	12	74.9	32	81.3	57	73.0	15	79.6	26	97.7	41	81.3	89.8
1889	12	71.5	12	60.5	36	84.1	60	72.0	15	80.0	27	94.5	42	81.2	88.6
1890	15	78.5	13	63.5	40	89.5	68	79.2	15	78.6	27	85.4	42	79.0	100.3
1891	17	89.9	15	63.5	42	83.2	74	77.3	15	76.8	27	87.2	42	77.6	99.6
1892	21	92.3	20	63.9	66	77.7	107	75.2	20	74.1	43	82.0	63	74.5	100.9
1893	22	77.6	20	57.6	64	81.4	106	71.3	19	74.5	40	83.1	59	75.0	95.1
1894	23	74.1	20	54.0	64	75.4	107	66.7	19	70.6	39	81.1	58	71.5	93.2
1895	25	69.5	24	51.4	65	78.7	117	67.7	19	70.8	41	79.5	60	71.4	94.8
1896	25	72.1	24	52.9	66	74.6	115	67.4	19	71.1	46	77.2	65	71.1	94.8
1897	25	83.6	24	56.8	65	75.4	114	71.5	19	69.8	47	77.7	66	70.2	101.9
1898	24	84.0	24	63.5	63	74.8	111	73.2	20	69.1	47	75.6	67	69.2	105.8
1899	23	87.5	22	67.2	64	76.1	109	73.6	20	70.1	48	75.1	68	69.9	105.3
1900	24	79.3	22	71.9	64	78.4	110	75.2	20	74.0	47	73.5	67	72.3	104.0
1901	24	85.7	23	71.1	64	75.1	111	73.1	20	72.4	47	75.2	67	71.6	102.1
1902	24	88.7	23	72.8	64	77.7	111	75.9	20	72.2	47	73.5	67	71.1	106.8
1903	24	83.9	23	70.2	63	82.7	110	76.7	20	73.7	48	71.9	68	71.7	107.0
1904	25	82.1	23	69.5	61	79.0	109	74.0	19	74.3	47	71.5	66	72.1	102.6
1905	25	87.6	23	67.1	61	77.8	109	73.7	19	76.1	47	81.0	66	75.8	97.2
1906	24	91.2	19	71.7	56	80.4	99	79.0	14	80.3	44	83.1	58	79.4	99.4
1907	25	93.9	28	75.9	74	85.6	127	81.9	21	83.8	60	85.3	81	82.5	99.3
1908	24	103.0	28	78.8	72	77.6	124	77.0	21	80.9	60	80.6	81	79.3	97.1
1909	24	102.1	28	75.0	71	80.3	123	77.1	21	77.5	60	81.5	81	77.1	100.0
1910	25	97.1	26	76.8	71	82.4	122	81.7	21	80.5	59	76.5	80	77.7	105.1
1911	25	102.6	26	83.4	71	86.7	122	87.2	21	80.2	60	78.5	81	78.1	111.7
1912	26	102.6	26	89.5	70	87.5	122	86.0	21	82.6	60	82.5	81	80.9	106.3
1913	24	105.4	26	90.7	71	86.6	121	85.7	21	83.2	60	81.6	81	81.1	105.7

Abbreviations: NCOM: number of commodities included in the price index. FSH: Fisher price index. For sources and other details, see the text.

Estimates for funds flows arising from foreign investment in the Ottoman Empire, 1854–1913

Table A3.1. *Funds flows arising from Ottoman foreign borrowing, 1854–81*
Thousands of British pounds sterling

Years	Capital inflows from new borrowing net of commissions, etc. 1	Interest payments 2	Principal payments 3	Total payments 4 = 2 + 3
1854	2,286	—	—	—
1855	5,131	180	30	210
1856		378	32	410
1857		376	34	410
1858	3,440	375	35	410
1859		552	118	670
1860	1,233	666	144	810
1861		781	167	948
1862	5,150	771	177	948
1863	4,982	1,242	346	1,588
1864		1,702	526	2,228
1865	5,517	1,672	556	2,228
1866		2,182	735	2,917
1867	3,000[a]	2,140	777	2,917
1868		2,395	822	3,217
1869	11,555	2,346	871	3,217
1870	11,044[a]	3,633	1,240	4,873
1871	4,047	4,604	1,327	5,931
1872	4,650	4,875	1,459	6,334
1873	25,402	5,231	1,533	6,764
1874	15,091	7,824	1,895	9,719
1875		9,584	2,044	11,628
1876		480	72	552
1877	2,600	556	86	642
1878		471	9	480
1879		717	63	780
1880		714	66	780
1881		712	68	780

[a]See note at end of table A3.2.

Table A3.2. *Funds flows arising from Ottoman foreign borrowing, 1882–1913*
In thousands of British pounds sterling

Year	Capital inflows from new borrowing net of commissions, etc. 1	Debts under OPDA control			Other debts			Total		
		Interest payments 2	Principal payments 3	Total payments 4 = 2 + 3	Int. 5	Princ. 6	Total 7 = 5 + 6	Int. 8 = 2 + 5	Princ. 9 = 3 + 6	Total 10 = 4 + 7
1882		1,710	210	1,920	705	51	756	2,415	261	2,676
1883		1,447	248	1,695	703	53	756	2,150	301	2,451
1884		1,561	187	1,748	699	57	756	2,260	244	2,504
1885		1,435	236	1,671	696	60	756	2,131	296	2,427
1886	5,909	1,324	236	1,560	693	63	756	2,017	299	2,316
1887		1,307	274	1,581	985	123	1,108	2,292	397	2,689
1888	1,100	1,505	219	1,724	978	130	1,108	2,483	349	2,832
1889		1,498	256	1,754	1,044	166	1,210	2,542	422	2,964
1890	3,909	1,559	237	1,796	1,127	197	1,324	2,686	434	3,120
1891	1,272	1,243	623	1,866	1,207	229	1,436	2,450	852	3,302
1892		1,362	611	1,973	1,233	203	1,436	2,595	814	3,409
1893	612	1,377	601	1,978	1,225	211	1,436	2,602	812	3,414
1894	1,614	1,401	583	1,984	1,089	231	1,320	2,490	814	3,304
1895		1,350	582	1,932	1,285	268	1,553	2,635	850	3,485
1896	2,470	1,239	630	1,869	1,274	279	1,553	2,513	909	3,422
1897		1,079	740	1,819	1,409	306	1,715	2,488	1,046	3,534
1898		1,204	721	1,925	1,395	320	1,715	2,599	1,041	3,640
1899		1,254	693	1,947	1,380	335	1,715	2,634	1,028	3,662
1900		1,171	697	1,868	1,365	350	1,715	2,536	1,047	3,583
1901		1,236	686	1,922	1,351	332	1,683	2,587	1,018	3,605
1902	1,471	1,383	839	2,222	1,336	275	1,611	2,719	1,114	3,833
1903	5,342	1,606	644	2,250	1,455	263	1,718	3,061	907	3,968
1904	1,963	1,590	435	2,025	1,627	287	1,914	3,217	722	3,939
1905	4,237	1,621	441	2,062	1,856	329	2,185	3,477	770	4,247

Table A3.2. (cont.) *Funds flows arising from Ottoman foreign borrowing, 1882–1913*
In thousands of British pounds sterling

Year	Capital inflows from new borrowing net of commissions, etc. 1	Debts under OPDA control			Other debts			Total		
		Interest payments 2	Principal payments 3	Total payments 4 = 2 + 3	Int. 5	Princ. 6	Total 7 = 5 + 6	Int. 8 = 2 + 5	Princ. 9 = 3 + 6	Total 10 = 4 + 7
1906		1,492	569	2,061	1,894	348	2,242	3,386	917	4,303
1907		1,456	753	2,209	1,878	364	2,242	3,334	1,117	4,451
1908	12,453	1,501	765	2,266	1,867	375	2,242	3,368	1,140	4,508
1909	5,314	1,508	836	2,344	2,382	419	2,801	3,890	1,255	5,145
1910	1,354	1,390	991	2,381	2,615	503	3,118	4,005	1,494	5,499
1911	5,961	1,423	972	2,395	2,914	585	3,499	4,337	1,557	5,894
1912		1,455	852	2,307	2,925	611	3,536	4,380	1,463	5,843
1913	2,067	1,406	1,047	2,453	2,900	636	3,536	4,306	1,683	5,989

Notes to tables A3.1 and A3.2: Since these tables were prepared in order to calculate the international funds flows arising from the Ottoman state debt rather than to analyze Ottoman state finances, that part of the Ottoman debt held by its citizens inside the Ottoman Empire (primarily by Galata bankers), Treasury bonds and short-term advances to the Ottoman Treasury have been excluded. The most important of these 'internal borrowings' was that part of the pre-1881 'Umumi Borçlar' held inside the Ottoman Empire, 1881 Priority Bonds (converted in 1890, reconverted in 1906) and Treasury bonds and short-term advances after 1910. As a result, the figures provided in these tables differ from those given in Tezel (1972).

1 British pound sterling = 1.10 Ottoman Lira.

Sources: Tezel (1972), Yeniay (1964), Du Velay (1903), Suvla (1940), Corporation of Foreign Bondholders (1882–1914), Wynne (1941).

Table A3.3. *Funds flows arising from direct foreign investment in the Ottoman Empire, 1859–1913*
In thousands of British pounds sterling

Years	Total Capital inflows A	Total Repatriated capital B	Total Profit transfers C	French A	French B	French C	British A	British B	British C	German A	German B	German C	Other A	Other B	Other C
1859	1,192						1,192								
1860															
1861															
1862	100						100								
1863	2,782		155	675		74	2,107		81						
1864			258			101			157						
1865	1,375		215	437		67	938		148						
1866	200		274			97	200		177						
1867	400		326			117	400		209						
1868			356			132			224						
1869	1,794		366	480		137	50		229	1,264					
1870	320		308	160		107	160		201						
1871	300		373			149	300		224						
1872	1,500		401			154			247	1,500					
1873	769		324			116	625		208	144					
1874			384			134			208						42
1875	2,525	1,500	307	1,137		83	1,388		171					1,500	53
1876			225			40			132						53
1877			225			40			132						53
1878	125		232	100		48	25		130						53
1879	25		482			173	25		257						53
1880	600		497	50		177	550		267						53
1881	100		1,037	100		433			537						67

Table A3.3 (cont.) *Funds flows arising from direct foreign investment in the Ottoman Empire, 1859–1913*
In thousands of British pounds sterling

Years	Total — Capital inflows A	Total — Repatriated capital B	Total — Profit transfers C	French A	French B	French C	British A	British B	British C	German A	German B	German C	Other A	Other B	Other C
1882	100		1,045			441	100		537						67
1883	180		800			316	180		417						67
1884			709			266			376						67
1885	505		617	302		224	36		326	166					67
1886	395		581			204	395		305			5			67
1887	602		649	67		230	400		347			5	135		67
1888	2,085		635	1,190		208	895		348			5			74
1889	4,210	720	721	1,647	320	239	500		396	2,050		12	13	400	74
1890	2,049		857	550		254	75		471	1,424		78			54
1891	5,179		994	1,159		350			471	3,400		120	620		55
1892	4,909		1,189	3,793		400	122		459	623		255	372		76
1893	440		1,397	320		508	120		463			337			89
1894	11,437	640	1,421	9,233		528	239	640	495	1,200		317	765		83
1895	9,420		1,656	2,865		762	495		452	90		343	970		100
1896	2,045	330	1,745	990	210	773		120	459	1,055		403			110
1897	225		1,838	200		848	25		431			442			117
1898	140		2,090	40		953	100		546			441			149
1899	336		2,000	186		992			412	150		442			154
1900	1,184	365	2,078	769	100	1,042	25		416	90		468	300	265	151
1901	2,069		2,193	2,069		1,065			444			465			219
1902	838		2,258			1,145	100		468	594		469	144		179
1903			2,325			1,155			468			509			191
1904	512	385	2,346	164	90	1,277	125	295	453	168		513	180		194

1905	2,700	2,462	1,765	1,228	425	506	110	535	400	194
1906	2,925	2,688	781	1,359	159	530	1,825	557	160	242
1907	1,328	2,851	304	1,389	703	580	255	628	67	259
1908	695	2,911	446	1,390	100	632		632	149	258
1909	2,245	525 3,045	1,795	1,485	250 525	667		639	200	254
1910	3,439	3,081	1,995	1,482	189	683	1,155	639	100	277
1911	1,740	3,236	665	1,563		691	900	701	175	280
1912	1,550	3,285	1,050	1,682	150	668	200	661	150	272
1913	1,350	3,185	800	1,578	150	674	200	661	200	272

Notes: By 'repatriated capital' we refer either to the resale of a direct foreign investment in the Empire to investors from another country and the return of the initial investment to its country of origin (with incoming capital appearing under column A) or the repayment by a firm operating inside the Empire of its outstanding bonds being held in Europe. Our calculations take Into account the changing borders of the Ottoman Empire. All funds flows arising from direct foreign investment in an area which seceded from the Empire were excluded from the above estimates starting with the year after secession. In addition, all foreign investment in the principalities of Wallachia and Moldavia have been excluded from out calculations even though Romania did not gain formal independence until 1878. For a discussion of the procedure followed in obtaining these estimates, see pp. 62–64 of chapter 4.

Sources: Pech (1911) was the primary source. In addition, the following have been used: *Anonymous* (1919), U.S. Department of State Archives (1923), Verney and Dambmann (1900), 'La fortune française à l'étranger' (1902), Neymarck (1902), Kurmuş (1974), *The Stock Exchange Official Intelligence* (1908–9), Wiedenfeld (1915), Deutsche Reich, *Marineleitung, Die Marine-Vorlage* (1906), Ökçün (1972). For a detailed study of French investments in the Asiatic provinces of the Ottoman Empire during 1895–1914 based on French archival sources, see Thobie (1977).

Relations of production in agriculture and standards of living of the peasantry in the 1870s

To accompany our analysis in chapter 5, we present in this appendix excerpts from British Consular Reports. These reports were written by members of the Foreign Office in the Ottoman Empire as part of a worldwide project which attempted to provide a comparative perspective for the land tenure problem in Ireland and, at the same time, investigate the possibilities of settling the British population around the world, particularly in the periphery.

The excerpts below underline the considerable differences in relations of production and living standards that existed between different regions of the Empire; the differences between the European provinces and Anatolia become immediately apparent. However, in this appendix we do not intend to return to the topic of regional differences. That theme has been pursued in detail in chapter 5. In preparing this appendix, we gave priority to those parts of the reports which describe best the relations of production, the means of production and the living standards of the peasantry. As a result, for example, almost equal space is allocated to wage labor and sharecropping in the excerpts below, although the importance of wage laborers in Ottoman agriculture was quite limited in comparison to sharecropping. Similarly, it was estimated that about 40 per cent of all land under cultivation in the Asiatic provinces of the Empire was being cultivated by small-sized owner-producers. However, the excerpts deal with this form only indirectly. For the relative frequency of different relations of production in Ottoman agriculture during the nineteenth century, see chapter 5, tables 5.1 and 5.2.

'Muraba'lık', or sharecropping in Anatolia

Report sent by Consul Palgrave from Trabzon:[1]

The proprietor of land which he is unable or unwilling to cultivate in person, engages one or more 'muraba's', analogically tenants, really produce-partners, to do his work. The term of the engagement is invariably one calendar year, the base, equidivision of the product.

Seed, and, where requisite, beasts, implements, and so forth, are ordinarily furnished by the landlord or proprietor; who, however, at the end of the year, subtracts the equivalent of what he has thus advanced from the 'muraba's' half-share of the produce. Should, on the other hand, any of the things have been advanced by the 'muraba', he in his turn deducts the equivalent from the landlord's half-share on reckoning-day.

In regard of buildings and improvements, the rule is the same. The landlord, in most cases, supplies materials, tools, and, when work exceeding ordinary agricultural skill is required, workmen; the 'muraba' bestows his labour and superintendence. Under this arrangement no extra charge is noted against the ultimate half-shares on either side. But should, on the contrary, the landlord or the 'muraba' have contributed from his own, over and above what has just been specified, the excess is re-imbursed out of the produce-shares at the year's end.

Tithes, Government Dues, and Losses, are met in the same manner, each bearing a half.

Fixed rent tenancy and wage labor in Anatolia

Report sent by Consul Palgrave from Trabzon:[2]

... the fifth, but practically and in most instances only the eighth, tenth, or even less, of the produce value roughly estimated. This contract may have a duration of five, ten, or any number of years. Like the former, it issues not unfrequently in life tenancy.

Thirdly, 'Ijret', or day labour for daily hire. The ordinary wages for field work are 5 piastres, equal 10d. English per diem, with an oke, equal 2¾ lbs. of bread, into the bargain. Further board and lodging are not given. The earnings would be insufficient long to meet the bare life requirements of the labourer, if he had nothing else to depend on. Hence 'Ijret' is only resorted to occasionally, and to fill up a vacant gap, especially about harvest time. The mere hedger and ditcher, if he has not a field of his own, or some other means of subsistence to fall back on, soon starves or emigrates.

Sharecropping, fixed rent tenancy and wage labor in Macedonia

Report sent by Consul Wilkinson from Salonica:[3]

Agricultural laborers may be divided into three classes, all of whom are Christians, namely[4]:

1. Partner labourers, or 'ortakdjis', already alluded to. They provide

the cattle and undertake the labour and cost of cultivating the land of the owner of a farm, or 'tchiftlik', the landlord finding the seed. The produce is halved on the threshing-floor, after which the 'ortakdji's' part of the engagement is completed by his further carrying the landlord's share to the granary. Some landlords require extra labor from their 'ortakdjis' which is given on holidays; such as bringing their produce to market, or drawing firewood; as a set-off for such services the landlord grants the 'ortakdji' the use of about half an acre of land, rent-free; this arrangement is called 'paraspour'. In cases where the landlord cultivates part of his estate by means of farm-labourers, the 'ortakdji' and his family help to reap, for which service they get the usual allowance of bread, but no wages. They pay no rent for their cottages, the repairs of which, as of their stables, are at the charge of the landlord.

2. Farm-labourers, or 'ter-oglan', who are engaged by the year, and work entirely for account of the landlord. In lieu of wages they receive a stipulated quantity of grain and other necessaries, which varies with the locality. For instance, in the district of Monastir, the allowance is 15 to 17 kilos, part Indian corn and part rye ($68\frac{1}{2}$ to $77\frac{1}{2}$ English bushels), and in cash 100 piastres (15s. to 17s., according to the fluctuations of the currency); whilst in the district of Perlepe the allowance is simply 16 kilos of wheat (73 bushels), and in that of Kiuprili the landlord gives the farm-labourer 10 kilos of rye, barley, and millet ($45\frac{1}{2}$ bushels), besides 12 okes ($33\frac{1}{2}$ lbs.) of salt, half an ox-hide for sandals, half a horse-load of leeks or cabbages, and 60 to 80 piastres in money (9s. to 12s. or 13s. 6d.); sleeping-room rent-free. The same system, with slight local variations, prevails throughout the other districts of this Sandjak.

3. 'Kesemdjis'. It is difficult to find the English equivalent for this term. The nearest approach to it is 'fixed-charge-men', who resemble the 'ortakdjis' in every respect except the division of the produce, since they agree to give the landlord a certain fixed quantity of produce irrespective of the yield.

All who belong to these three classes of farm-labourers are free, on the completion of their agreement with one landlord to engage themselves to another, provided they have contracted no debts to the landlord. In such a case their position becomes one of quasi-serfage, especially when their creditor landlord, as not unfrequently happens, if he be a Mussulman, adds compound interest to the capital advanced, by which process a debt of a few pounds swells, in course of time, to such large proportions as to involve the laborer in difficulties from which the toil of a lifetime fails to extricate him. In not a few instances the debt becomes hereditary. It is not an uncommon practice for a landowner when in want of farm-labourers as fixtures upon his estate, to hire one of these unfortunate men, whose debt he pays to his former employer, and in turn becomes his creditor. All this while the labourer receives a stipulate quantity of grain in return for his work; but if his employer, in whose power he is, drives a hard bargain with him, and he happen to be burdened with a large family, the whole of his allowance scarcely suffices to keep them and himself in food, not to speak of clothing and other necessaries.

Relations of production in agriculture in Eastern Anatolia

Report sent by Consul Taylor from Erzurum:[5]

As a rule, there are no fixed yearly rents, or regular wages paid in cash; but when hired labourers are employed, a man for the six months he is alone occupied receives a suit of clothes, worth 60 piastres (10s. 10d.), and 100 maunds of wheat, worth 500 piastres (£4. 10s. 10d.). The general plan pursued by landlords is to advance the labor-seed; and should his land not be in a favourable position, or of good quality, a loan without interest, the proceeds of the harvest are, after deducting the seed-corn, then divided equally between landlord and tenant. The latter supplying all the labour for sowing, harvesting, storing, as well as the animals and implements.

It happens occasionally that a capitalist gives a certain lump sum of money down for the use of a piece of land for a stated number of years, but rents paid yearly, as in Europe, are unknown; in either case the pecuniary position of the labourers towards their employer remains the same. Families, except under the pressure of famine, never voluntarily desire to migrate from one district to the other or from their native village to a neighbouring one, although by doing so they might better their condition, the reasons being that their cottages, miserable hovels though they be, are generally their own, and that sedentary disposition common to most Easterns. This habit is so exaggerated that the majority of the inhabitants in my district have never visited either Erzurum, Diyarbakır, Van, or Harput, the chief towns in it. There is another system, but one not adopted here, although in the Diyarbakır districts where the peasants are poorer it is more general. The landlord or capitalist provides animals and seed but not the implements, together with a small loan in cash, without interest, on every quarter of seed sown; then, after deducting the seed, he takes two-thirds, and the peasant one-third, of the remainder. Under whatever system, then the land is farmed, the labourer is, as it were, in partnership, for better or worse, with his landlord; and fluctuations in prices, or inconstancy of the seasons, affect the one as much as the other, in the proportionate degrees attaching to affluence or indigence. It is, in short, a system of joint adventure, the consequences of small capitals and limited demand for home consumption or export.

Animal husbandry in Eastern Anatolia

Report sent by Consul Wilkinson from Erzurum:[6]

Pastorals: Their numbers in the Erzurum and Diyarbakir vilaiets are,

	Souls
Heads of pastoral families	109,800
Assistants taking charge of sheep	109,800
Remaining number of families	439,200
Total number of souls (in the vilaiets)	658,800

The whole of them, with few exceptions, hardly important enough to be noticed, are Moslems. During winter they live in small huts constructed of loose stone, but of a far more miserable character, if possible, than those described before, situated in low-lying valleys. Their flocks and horses are penned and tethered in similar but larger buildings communicating with the dwelling chamber, as in other villages already noticed. In spring and summer they migrate to the hills in their or adjacent districts, where they live in spacious goathair or woollen tents. Their food is the same as that of the agricultural class, consisting of bread, boorghul, and all the preparations derived from milk; with them, also, meat is rarely used, unless travellers of consequence alight at their homes, when it is the invariable custom to kill a lamb or sheep or more, as the occasion requires. They certainly are distinguished by a rough hospitality, though at the same time in their migrations, they are the most notorious thieves possible. Their furniture is rather better than that of the other classes, inasmuch as their females manufacture good carpets, with which every family is provided, in addition to fine felts. Their condition, taking food, dwellings, clothing, and universal ignorance as criterions, would justly warrant me in classing them in the lowest scale; but it is a well-known and established fact, that among the labouring classes generally they solely are rich and well to do. The habits, position, and manner of life peculiar to these people enable them to trick or totally evade the tax farmer, while the same causes operate to relieve them from the usual four days' corvee every adult male is bound to give the State yearly, as also the pressure of Government officers and soldiers, who in travelling about the district, or in changing quarters from one town to the other, exercise such tyranny towards, and occasion so great expenses to, the sedentary populations. It is this class alone that, contributing the least to the Treasury, and having no more expenses than the agriculturalist, absorbs at the same time all the cash remittances to these parts, from other places in Turkey and from Europe, for cattle, sheep, horses, wool, and butter. None are so poor as not to possess a few sheep or goats, sufficient with their earnings as shepherds, to maintain a family in the rude state they are accustomed to live, while the more prosperous (opulent capitalists rather than labourers, and so not to be considered here) can count their flocks by thousands.

Living conditions of the Anatolian peasant

Report sent by Consul Palgrave from Trabzon:[7]

Average Conditions:
... Let us now select an average peasant, whether proprietor or tenant, and let us give him the average allowance of arable land, namely, 4 dunems [?], about 8 English acres, according to East Anatolian measurement. More than this his rude implements will not permit him to cultivate to advantage. The market value of an acre of land hereabouts is, if for ploughing, 300 piastres (£21. 10s.) on an ordinary estimate; if for planting, about 130 piastres (£11. 1s. 8d.).

The materials of the peasant's cottage, wood, stone or unbaked brick, according to the district, cost him little or nothing, and the construction itself is in part done by his own labour and that of his friends, and is so far gratis. Still much remains towards completion that exceeds mere peasant skill; and the total expense of the dwelling generally reaches 2,000 or even 3,000 piastres (£16. 13s. 4d. to £25). Cottages to let are things unheard of in the country villages.

A barn requires for its construction about 1,000 piastres (£8. 6s. 8d.), and when once built may, like the house, last from twenty to thirty years.

A pair of oxen, here used for drawing the plough, as horses are in England, costs from 700 to 1,000 piastres (£5. 16s. 8d. to £9. 13s. 4d.). The two animals taken together have hardly the strength of one English beast. Buffaloes are preferred where they can be had; the pair costs about 1,400 piastres (£11. 13s. 4d.). A pack-horse too, is indispensable for conveying field-produce to market; the price is from 450 to 800 piastres (£3. 15s. to £6. 13s. 4d.). Agricultural implements and house furniture represent a value of about 2,400 piastres (£20) additional.

It would be almost superfluous to say that every grown-up peasant of these lands is married. His daily food for himself and his family comes to about 3 piastres (6d. English); thus much being spent on purchase, the remaining and the greater part is the produce of his own ground. A complete suit of clothes costs about 200 piastres (£1. 13s. 4d.), and lasts from two to three years.

The quality of these several articles comes next under consideration. The cottage is fairly clean, especially if its inhabitants are Mahometan, and is much more spacious than the dwelling of the town artizan. Regularly it has three rooms, one for sleeping, one for sitting in, and one for cooking; but it is a cottage that no English labourer would wish to live in. Glass is unknown; the roof, made of wooden shingles in the coast region, of earth if in the interior, is far from water-tight, and the walls let in wind and rain everywhere. Drains there are none, not even when the villages are close built; but the lowness of the cottages, combined with the free access of air, renders the ill results less serious than might have been anticipated.

The peasant's food is mostly vegetable, and in great measure the produce of his own ground. Maize bread in the littoral districts, and brown bread, in which rye and barley are largely mixed for the inland provinces, form nine-tenths of a coarse but not unwholesome diet. This is varied occasionally with milk, curds, cheese, and eggs; the more so if the household happens to possess a cow and barn-door fowls. Dried meat or fish are rare but highly esteemed luxuries. Water is the only drink.

The women of the family join freely in field-labour, and so do the children as soon as their age and strength permit. Many villages are provided with schools; but the profit of the schooling is, like the cost, little or nothing.

Liabilities of the agricultural population

These are regular, or incidental.

Of the first kind is taxation. For a complete examination of this subject, and the details of the burden under which the rural classes are crushed, I must once more beg to refer to the statements made in preceding Reports. On the present occasion it is enough to say that the average amount levied yearly by the Ottoman Government in Anatolia on each country householder, taking land-owners, tenants, and labourers or whatever degree together, the more with the less, cannot be estimated under 240 piastres (£2 English) per head per annum.[8]

Seed is a regular though indirect expense, being reserved from the last year's crop. Horse-keep costs little, for the animal seldom gets anything except what he picks up for himself when grazing; but his shoes and other equipments have to be bought and renewed. Analogous outlays occur for the oxen, buffaloes, and whatever other stock is kept; and when the peasant, as often happens, adds to his regular occupations a little wood carrying, charcoal burning, and the like.

This is the place to add a word or two on the debt cancer, that corrodes the agricultural population of these provinces through and through. That every small landed proprietor, and almost every tenant, whether 'muraba' or other, is and must be deep in debt, will appear as a natural consequence on considering the balances, a little further on, the result of which we now so far anticipate.[9] Now, debt in Anatolia, where no banking or other respectable credit system exists, means the falling into the hands of an usurious money-lender, commonly an Armenian, whose most moderate rate of loan is 24 per cent., more often 48 per cent., sometimes 60 per cent., and all this at compound interest. It is true, however, that the peasant borrower has rarely to repay the capital, having been already sold out of stock, land, and house to meet the interest.

Regarding the second class of liabilities, namely, the incidental or extraordinary, such as, sooner or later, befall the peasant through sickness or accident to himself, to some member of his family, to his horse, his oxen, or the life, nothing need here be added to what has been already said for analogous cases among the town workmen. Poorer even than they, the countryman has little in hand for the present, and absolutely no provision at all for the future; nor, as may easily be imagined, are the villagers better off in matter of medical or surgical assistance than their brethren of the towns, unless, indeed, that they enjoy a greater immunity from the visits of quacks and imposters.

Under the same head come lastly the various contingencies to which husbandmen as such are specially exposed, namely, droughts, floods, bad harvests, blights, excessive snows, untimely frosts, and the like. All these find the Anatolian peasant wholly unprepared. In the old days of the Ottoman Empire public calamities of the sort were met by a corresponding diminution of taxes, or even a total exemption from them for a time. But the existing fiscal administration takes account of none of these things, and admits of no relaxation.

Quality of work

Everything connected with field labour is yet at its simplest and most primitive expression. The wooden plough here used is merely a crooked stick, shod with iron at the point, such as may still be seen in some remote corners of Europe; an implement, in a word, for scratching the soil, not for ploughing it. Next comes a wooden spade, or a two-pronged fork for turning up the clods; then a harrow, which is nothing but a hurdle of wattle twigs; these, with a sickle of the rudest description that tears up more than it cuts, and a clumsy iron hatchet, are the chief items on the list. Sowing is done by hand and broadcast; threshing, like that of biblical Palestine, is the work of oxen or horses, who partly trample out the grain, partly crush it from the ear by dragging over it a heavy hob-nailed board, on which a boy is seated to give it additional weight. Winnowing here means just tossing up the chaff and the grain together against the breeze.

Manure is seldom employed, never systematically, nor is it properly spread and dug into the ground. Of subsoil draining, a process which the nature of the surface strata in most places hereabouts, and the conditions of the climate, would render eminently useful, no one has so much as heard. Nor is there any established system of rotation in the crops; the land, when overtaxed, is left to lie fallow for one or more years, and then tilled exactly as before.

Lastly, the cultivation of vines, olives, and fruit trees in these districts consists almost wholly in letting them grow just as nature wills, without pruning, cleaning, clipping, binding, or even so much as turning the earth about their stems. Grafting is the only horticultural art known or practised.

The clothing of peasants in Macedonia

Report sent by Consul Wilkinson in Salonica:[10]

A feature of the labouring classes which deserves special notice is, that with the exception of the indebted farm-labourers, both men and women are well clothed. Their shirts and drawers are manufactured at home, of cotton-twist (from England) which the women weave into substantial cloth. Their outer clothing is of stout, black or brown woollen stuff, which, as well as their thick woollen socks, is also home-made. The head is protected by a woollen, red skull-cap, over which the men twist a white or black cotton turban. The females' head-dress is also warm, and over it they wear a white cotton kerchief fastened round the neck and bosom. The women's cotton clothing is elaborately embroidered in brilliant colours with home-dyed wool. Sandals of raw buffalo-hide are worn on working-days, and those who can afford the luxury wear red leather shoes on holidays. There are few who have not a holiday suit that lasts them their lifetime. In winter the men wear sheepskin overcoats with the wool inside.

The reconstruction of Ottoman textile imports, 1820–1913

A5.1 Estimation of textile imports

This section presents the details of our reconstruction of nineteenth-century Ottoman textile imports. The results of this reconstruction have been utilized for a study of the decline and resistance of handicrafts production in cotton textiles presented in chapter 6. Although we were primarily interested in cotton yarn and cloth, we have also estimated the volume of imports of woolen and other (silk, linen, etc.) textiles for a comparison of the relative magnitudes involved.

As we explain in more detail in appendix 1, Ottoman foreign trade statistics are not available for the period before 1878. The official statistics for 1878–1913 are of limited value for our purposes since, in addition to problems of valuation, commodity classification of imports is inadequate.[1] The residual category 'other commodities' frequently accounts for as much as 40 per cent of the total value of imports. Consequently, we attempted to reconstruct Ottoman textile imports using the annual foreign trade statistics of the European and other countries with which the Ottoman Empire had commercial relations during the nineteenth century. Official Ottoman statistics were then used as an additional source to check the accuracy of some of our results.

In the first stage, textile exports to the Ottoman Empire from each of these countries were added up on a commodity basis for each year of the selected intervals, 1820–2, 1840–2, 1870–2, 1894–6, and 1909–11. The changing borders of the Empire were defined in the same manner as in the reconstruction of Ottoman foreign trade discussed in chapter 2. The problems encountered at this stage were basically the same as those met during our reconstruction of the aggregate imports and exports.[2]

Statistics on Ottoman trade with Germany before 1880, which was conducted mostly with the European provinces of the Empire and which transited through Austria, could be derived only from the sources of the latter country. We could only approximate the commodity composition of this trade in textiles by examining the structure of imports from Germany after 1880.

There was a similar problem with the composition of Austrian exports until 1891, since no breakdown was given in the Austrian statistics within the category of textile products. Again, the composition of Austrian exports after 1891 was used as the basis for estimating the composition of the earlier trade. It should be noted, however, that during the period until 1891, the share of imports from Germany and Austria in the cotton textile imports of the Empire was relatively small. Their combined share did not exceed 10 per cent at any time.[3] Moreover, since most of this trade was with the European provinces of the Empire, which are not directly included in this study, the potential error associated with these approximations is even smaller.

Another potential problem was associated with imports of cotton yarn from India, which expanded rapidly after the turn of the twentieth century. While we did not have access to Indian foreign trade statistics, we relied on the Ottoman Industrial Census of 1913 which indicates that imports from India accounted for 21 per cent of total imports of cotton yarn in 1913.[4]

The most serious potential problem of this stage was related to the foreign trade statistics of the country that accounted for as much as three-fourths of the cotton textile imports of the Empire, Britain. Unlike the trade statistics of other countries, British exports of cloth were given primarily in units of length (yards), with an additional 5 to 10 per cent given by value only.[5] In the absence of any information regarding the method of measurement of length used by British customs officials or coefficients for conversion of yards of cotton and woolen cloth into units of weight, we decided to estimate the prices of imports of cloth from Britain on a per ton basis by utilizing the prices of cloth imported from other European countries. In estimating the relative prices of British cotton and woolen cloth *vis-à-vis* imports from other countries for 1909–11, we made use of the following information: most important for cotton cloth, the per ton price of British cotton yarn in relation to the per ton prices of cotton yarn imports from other countries, the data for all of which are available from the respective foreign trade statistics; assessments in consular reports and from secondary sources regarding the quality of the British products *vis-à-vis* other imports; and relative shares of the products of each country in the Ottoman markets for cotton and woolen cloth separately. For example, we knew from consular reports and secondary sources that British cotton cloth products were lower priced and addressed the mass market much more than did products from Austria and Germany. On the other hand, the share of Britain declined in the face of competition from even lower priced Italian and Indian products after the turn of the century.

Table A5.1. *Estimated relative prices of imports of British textiles*
F.o.b. prices per ton; for 1909–11

	Cotton yarn	Cotton cloth	Ratio of cotton yarn to cotton cloth	Woolen cloth
Italy	100	100	100	100
Austria	122	144	118	88
Germany	143	135	94	68
Britain	111	118 (est.)	106 (est.)	98 (est.)

Source: The official foreign trade statistics of the respective countries.

We derived from this procedure a yards per ton coefficient for British exports of cotton and woolen cloth for 1909–11, which we then applied to British exports in all of our selected intervals to arrive at estimates of their volume in tons. The reliability of our estimate for cotton cloth was then broadly checked in the following manner: the statistics of each European country provided a cotton cloth/cotton yarn price ratio on a per ton basis for each of our selected intervals (see table A5.1). We found that the cloth/yarn ratios for one ton of British cotton textiles derived from our estimates of British cloth prices were well within the range spanned by the price ratios of major European exporters for each of the selected intervals.

Another useful way of checking the reliability of our estimate for cotton cloth would have been to compare the share, in units of weight, of British cotton cloth in total Ottoman imports that we estimated for 1913 with the share cited in the Ottoman foreign trade statistics for the same year. The inadequate nature of the commodity classification in the Ottoman statistics does not allow for such a comparison for cotton cloth.

However, we were able to undertake a similar comparison for Ottoman imports of cotton yarn. Our estimates based on the statistics of other countries indicated shares of 34 per cent and 30 per cent, respectively, for Britain and Italy in Ottoman imports of cotton yarn, all measured in units of weight for the year 1913. The Ottoman statistics give shares of 32 per cent and 28 per cent respectively for the same shares. As for the volume of total imports of cotton yarn, our estimates were within 1 per cent of the figure given in the official Ottoman statistics for the year 1913.[6] Needless to say, such comparisons increased considerably our confidence in the procedure we employed.[7] Again, the inadequate nature of the commodity classification in the Ottoman statistics does not allow for such a comparison for cotton cloth.

The Ottoman Empire periodically lost territory and population during the nineteenth century.[8] Clothing habits (most important among them the option of cotton vs. woolen clothing) and production patterns showed considerable variations between the seceding and remaining areas. In addition, there was a considerable amount of trade between these areas in certain textile products.[9] To attempt intertemporal comparisons regarding per capita imports and levels of domestic production by redefining the geographical borders of the Empire as they changed throughout the century would have posed major empirical problems. In order to minimize these problems, we decided to limit the study to the area within the 1911 borders of the Empire. Once this choice was made, it became necessary, for the period before 1880, to reduce the volumes of imports, which were originally estimated for the entire Empire, to those of this smaller area. (Borders of the Empire as we defined them in this volume for the purposes of its foreign trade changed very little between 1880 and 1911. See the discussion in chapter 2.) These calculations were carried out by utilizing estimated population figures for all of the regions in question and some crude measures regarding per capita consumption and import levels for each region.[10]

One assumption was still essential for estimating the early nineteenth-century levels of domestic production within the 1911 borders of the Empire, namely that in the early part of the century the internal cotton textiles trade of the Empire between those areas that seceded before 1911 and the rest of the Empire was small enough to be ignored. In this respect we know, for example, that inland trade in woolen textiles from Bulgaria to Anatolia and to the rest of the Empire was quite important before 1880. However, we have not come across any evidence indicating that there was a comparable volume of internal trade in cotton textiles between the seceding and remaining areas of the Empire. The results of this second stage of our reconstruction are summarized in tables A5.2 and A5.3.

A5.2 On woolen textiles

The reconstruction of nineteenth-century consumption and domestic production patterns for woolen textiles would have been important for this study for several reasons. First, the relative position of the domestic cotton textiles within the framework of Ottoman textiles in general needed to be assessed. Second, determining the extent of decline in other branches would have provided a better perspective on the decline and destruction in cotton textiles. Third, long-term changes in per capita consumption of woolen textiles might have thrown considerable light on the extent to which the increase in per capita consumption of cotton

Table A5.2. *Ottoman imports of cotton textiles, 1820–1910*
Annual averages in tons

	Cotton cloth			Cotton yarn		
Years	Total imports of the Empire A	Shares of major exporters B %	Imports of the area within 1911 borders C	Total imports of the Empire A	Shares of major exporters B %	Imports of the area within 1911 borders C
1820–2	585	U.K. 55	450	185	U.K. 70	150
1840–2	5,100	U.K. 68	4,100	3,335	U.K. 79	2,650
1870–2	20,300	U.K. 73	17,300	9,100	U.K. 76	7,750
1880–2	24,700	U.K. 87	24,700	6,500	U.K. 84	6,500
1894–6	26,950	U.K. 81	26,950	11,150	U.K. 76 Italy 5	11,150
1909–11	49,350	U.K. 58 Italy 21 Austria 6 Germany 6	49,350	12,550	Italy 37 U.K. 36 India 16 Austria 7	12,550

Sources: Foreign trade statistics of other countries. For details see text.

Table A5.3. *Ottoman imports of woolen and other textiles, 1820–1910*
Annual averages in tons

| Year | Woolen cloth | | | Woolen yarn | | Other cloth (silk, linen, etc.) | |
	Total imports of the Empire A	Shares of major exporters B %	Imports of the area within 1911 borders C	Total imports A	Major exporters B %	Total imports of the Empire A	Imports of the area within 1911 borders B
1820–2	330	Austria 45 France 30	265	—	—	50	40
1840–2	900	Austria 45 France 20	720	—	—	100	80
1880–2	2,800	U.K. 33 Austria 32 France 13	2,800	—	—	200	200
1894–6	4,750	Austria 24 U.K. 21 Germany 19	4,750	—	—	400	400
1909–11	8,000	Germany 30 U.K. 22 Austria 15	8,000	400	U.K. 65	1,000	1,000

Sources: Foreign trade statistics of other countries. For details see text.

textiles was due to the price effects, i.e. more rapid decline in the prices of cotton textiles in comparison to the prices of woolen textiles after the Industrial Revolution.

However, we have very limited information regarding nineteenth-century Ottoman woolen textiles. It is clear that the impact of imports was neither as rapid nor as dramatic as it was in cotton textiles. Since rural hand spinning of cotton yarn disappeared relatively rapidly, we have been able to estimate the level of domestic weaving for the period after 1880 primarily by reconstructing the volume of imported yarn. In woolen textiles, rural hand spinning of yarn and weaving of cloth continued to account for a very large part of domestic production and consumption until World War I. As a result, estimating the per capita levels of either domestic production or consumption for any part of the nineteenth century is very difficult in the absence of information on the rural economy.

On the basis of estimates for the 1910s of the domestic production of raw wool, the volume of exports of raw wool and the volume of raw wool consumed in the weaving of carpets and other uses, one might reach the approximate figure of 10,000 tons for the volume of hand-spun woolen yarn that was woven into cloth. This would mean that in the early 1910s domestic production levels in woolen textiles were still comparable to, but not as high as, those of cotton textiles (see table 6.1 in chapter 6 for production and consumption levels in cotton textiles). If we add to this figure the volume of imports given in table A5.3 (over 8,000 tons) and the output of the domestic factories, we reach a total of about 20,000 tons as the level of consumption of woolen textiles within the 1911 borders of the Empire. In terms of weight, this is less than one-third of the total consumption of cotton textiles in the same areas of the Empire in the 1910s. These estimates also confirm the conclusion that European industrial products failed to capture the mass market in woolen textiles. Whereas imports accounted for over 80 per cent of the domestic market in cotton textiles, their share in the woolen textiles market was around 40 per cent in the 1910s.

It is very difficult to extend these figures to earlier periods. It is clear, however, that per capita consumption of woolen textiles did not show the kind of rapid increases exhibited by cotton textiles during 1820–1913. If anything, one might conjecture that the shift away from woolen textiles arising from lower prices of cotton products (price effect) was roughly matched by the rises in the standards of living of the Ottoman peasantry (income effect) during this century. If this was the case, then (a) per capita consumption of woolen textiles remained roughly unchanged between 1820 and 1913; and (b) consumption and domestic production levels of woolen and cotton textiles in the 1820s were roughly comparable (see table 6.1 in chapter 6).

Finally, just to give an idea of the relative orders of magnitude, we will offer a crude estimate for the level of consumption and production of silk, linen and other kinds of cloth in 1909–11. In table A5.3 we estimate the level of imports in this category at 40 tons for 1820–2 and 1,000 tons for 1909–11 for the area within the 1911 borders of the Empire. We also estimate the annual domestic production of silk, linen and all other cloth at 3,000 tons per year for 1909–11, indicating an average per capita consumption of 0.15 kg. per person per year.[11]

An essay on the international balance of
payments of the Ottoman Empire, 1830–1913

The basic purpose of this study is to better understand the world economic forces and their influences on the Ottoman Empire during the nineteenth century. The relative importance of different processes and different forces did not necessarily remain unchanged during this period. Penetration of world capitalism into the Empire may have proceeded primarily through trade in one period, while public loans may have become important in the next. Direct investment or a combination of any of these three mechanisms may have played the leading role in yet another period. Typically, then, we would expect the Ottoman international balance of payments to exhibit long swings, corresponding to the long-term shifts in the direction and magnitude of payments flows arising from foreign trade and foreign investment.[1] Furthermore, we would expect that the relations with the world economy of each country in the periphery would include certain special features. For example, the fact that the Ottoman Empire had covered, for centuries, a vast area across three continents brought special dimensions to its relations with the world economy during the nineteenth century. A reconstruction of the Ottoman balance of payments, separately for each year, will enable us to establish and analyze these long swings. In other words, it will facilitate a better understanding of the roles played by foreign trade, foreign investment and these special features during different periods as the Empire was being incorporated into the world economy. It will also enable us to gain important and fresh insights into the complex set of world economic forces or the world economic conjunctures faced by the Ottoman Empire during different periods of the nineteenth century.

A second purpose of this study is to check, once more, the reliability of our estimates of Ottoman foreign trade and of funds flows arising from foreign investment in the Empire. The results of our reconstruction of Ottoman foreign trade have been presented in chapter 2 and in greater detail in appendix 1. Similarly, our estimates for capital inflows, debt payments and profits transfers arising from state external borrowing and from direct foreign investment in the Empire have been presented in chapter 4 and appendix 3. Despite all the care taken in these estimation procedures, it is difficult to judge the accuracy and reliability of the estimates in the absence of previous studies. For example, for the period 1900–13, our estimates of the three basic items, the trade balance, funds flows arising from external borrowing and funds flows arising from direct foreign investment, point to fairly large Ottoman deficits, the sum of which could not have been entirely financed by bullion and specie outflows. Does this result point to an error in our estimates, or is it possible that these large deficits were financed by net revenues from other items of the balance of payments? It was these considerations, as well as the estimation of the invisible items *per se*, that motivated us to undertake this admittedly somewhat speculative exercise. The reader should be warned at the outset not to expect the same high degree of confidence on all of the following estimates.

In the next section we discuss briefly the relative accuracy and reliability of our estimates for Ottoman exports and imports and of funds flows arising from foreign investment in the Empire. The estimation of the other items of the balance of payments are described in section A6.2. Subsequently, we assess the internal consistency of our estimates. In the last section we summarize the results and attempt to establish the long swings in the nineteenth-century Ottoman balance of payments. Annual estimates for each item of the Ottoman balance of payments are presented at the end of the appendix in table A6.4.

The only other studies of the Ottoman balance of payments were undertaken by A. Biliotti and V. Eldem for the years 1907, 1909 and 1913.[2] A good part of our estimates is based on the same sources as those of Eldem, and, as will become clear below, this study owes a good deal to the earlier work of Biliotti and Eldem.

A6.1 On the relative accuracy of different items

Major historical studies involving the reconstruction of the balance of payments of a country proceed by first estimating separately all items including bullion and specie flows, except payment flows based on capital movements, and then by 'closing' the system by pointing out that net payment flows based on international capital flows were equal to the residual necessary to balance the annual payments accounts.[3] The estimated capital stock abroad and/or the estimated total foreign indebtedness are then periodically compared with other independent estimates of these magnitudes to check the reliability of the reconstruction. However, since the available data for a reconstruction of the Ottoman balance of payments allowed for more reliable estimates of the flows arising from capital movements than of net bullion and specie flows, a somewhat different procedure was followed in this study. Each item of the balance of payments with the exception of bullion and specie flows was estimated separately. Since a surplus in the balance of payments would imply bullion and specie inflow and a deficit would mean bullion and specie outflow, the cumulative surplus or deficit indicated by our estimates was then checked periodically against those Ottoman statistics that show the amount of gold and silver coins minted from bullion and foreign coins during different periods. As we will show below, in the Ottoman case there are good reasons for using these statistics as an approximate measure for the net inflow of specie.

Since the commodity trade figures are by far the most important item, their accuracy is essential. The availability of official Ottoman foreign trade statistics for the period after 1878 allows a comparison of our estimates of the total exports and imports with those given in the official statistics. The most important divergence between the two sets of data is that our estimates point to significantly smaller trade deficits. As we explain in detail in appendix 1, this difference is due to the persistent undervaluation of exports and overvaluation of imports in the official statistics. As contemporary observers were aware and as our estimates for the other items of the balance of payments confirm, the deficits indicated by the official Ottoman foreign trade statistics are too large to be explained in terms of the other items of payments account.

It is difficult to talk with the same degree of confidence about our estimates of total exports and imports for the period before 1878. The difficulties related to the estimation of the Ottoman–Austrian trade and the virtually complete absence of previous estimates for the total imports and exports inevitably reduce the confidence one can place on these estimates.

By comparison, the other two major items, payments flows arising from Ottoman public borrowing and from foreign direct investment, probably constitute the most accurate items of the reconstructed balance of payments. Since the amounts and the actual payments schedules of the Ottoman loans are public knowledge, there is little room for uncertainty in that case. Similarly, the availability of detailed data on the firm level allows for the calculation of reasonably accurate estimates for direct foreign investment, repatriation of capital and profit transfer flows.[4]

In comparison, the amount of uncertainty associated with our estimates of the invisible items is greater. The difficulty there arises not only from the absence of previous estimates for these items (with the exception of the estimates of Biliotti and Eldem, whose calculations are limited to the period immediately preceding World War I), but also from the relative absence of data that could be utilized to make accurate estimates for the earlier period.[5] The derivation of our estimates for the invisible items is discussed below. At present one can only hope that future research will build on and improve our estimates.

A6.2 Estimation of invisible items

Freight receipts

An Ottoman merchant marine fleet was virtually non-existent for the entire period under study. A small number of low tonnage ships carried the coastal trade; they could not operate beyond the Black Sea, the Aegean and the Eastern Mediterranean. However, since Ottoman exports and imports are estimated f.o.b. and c.i.f. respectively, a credit item should still be included in the balance of payments for that small portion of Ottoman foreign trade that was carried by Ottoman ships. Aside from the annual statistics provided by British and U.S. consular reports on the tonnage and nationality of the commercial ships entering and leaving each Ottoman port (a classification by destination/port of origin and nationality is never provided), no information is available regarding the size of the Ottoman merchant marine fleet or the share of the Ottoman foreign trade it transported. Therefore, proceeding with the following, inevitably somewhat arbitrary, set of assumptions appeared to be the most realistic course to follow.

We assumed that 15 per cent of the Ottoman trade (imports and exports) with Russia, 20 per cent of the trade with Romania, 25 per cent of the trade with Egypt, 25 per cent of the trade with Greece and 5 per cent of the trade with Austria and Italy was carried in Ottoman ships. The Ottoman ships carried no part of the Ottoman trade with Western and Northwestern Europe and the United States; they did not operate between third countries.

Our calculations of Ottoman freight receipts for various years of the period 1830–1913 on the basis of these assumptions and on the basis of the share of transportation costs in total trade discussed in appendix 1 led to the conclusion that freight receipts constituted a relatively minor item in the Ottoman balance of payments. Consequently, and owing to the rather arbitrary nature of our assumptions, we decided not to present separate estimates of freight receipts for each year. Instead, a single figure for each decade, which approximates the results of our calculations, is presented in table A6.4.

Another potential credit item in the balance of payments is receipts from marine insurance. However, the absence of Ottoman insurance companies, large or small, eliminates that possibility.

Revenues from land held in other countries

Ottoman citizens owned large amounts of land in countries that were once part of the Ottoman Empire. Annual revenues from these holdings were regularly sent to Istanbul and elsewhere in the Ottoman Empire where the owners lived. It is possible, for example, to calculate the amount of land in Egypt held by Ottoman citizens from the publications of the Egyptian Ministry of Finance.[6] Similarly, Ottoman citizens had large holdings of land in Cyprus, Crete and Rhodes, and, during certain periods, in those Balkan countries that had seceded from the Empire. It has been difficult to estimate the annual revenue to Ottoman citizens from these holdings. Biliotti has suggested the figure of 1 million Ottoman Liras (£900,000) for the year 1907. In the absence of additional information, the figure has been adopted by Eldem, with the qualification that it probably represents a lower bound.[7]

We kept that figure. In extending it backwards in time to cover the entire period 1830–1913, we took several considerations into account. First, until the 1870s most of these revenues were probably obtained from land in Egypt, and land rents in Egypt must have risen in the 1860s during and after the Cotton Famine. Also, after Cyprus and most of the Balkans left the Ottoman Empire, revenues from these areas should have started to appear in the balance of payments. Finally, periods of war must have substantially reduced the inflow of revenue from land owned abroad.

Tourism revenues

Again, there is very little information available on this item. Biliotti estimates the net annual revenues at 0.5 million Ottoman Liras (£450,000) but·in view of other information this figure appears too low.[8] Eldem cites an Ottoman statistic indicating the presence of 129,000 foreigners in Istanbul during 1914 (probably counting those living in *and* those passing through Istanbul). On the basis of expenditures of £9 per person per year for half of that population, who are assumed to be tourists, and considering the rest of the country, he arrives at a figure of 1 million Ottoman Liras (£900,000) for tourism revenues in 1914. Another estimate is given by A. Ruppin, who made a detailed study of the Syrian region (including Palestine). Ruppin claims that the transportation, lodging and food expenditures alone of the tourists in that region reached £1.8 million per year during the period immediately preceding World War I. He states that tourists left an additional £400,000 per year to various religious institutions in Syria and Palestine.[9] Clearly, there are enormous discrepancies among the various estimates; the former two appear to be biased, since they ignore or at least strongly underestimate the revenues in Syria and Palestine.

In order to roughly check the figures provided by these three authors, we tried to arrive at our own estimates based on the statistic of 129,000 foreigners either living in or passing through Istanbul in 1914. Our calculations differ from those of Eldem primarily in the amount of expenditure per person. Let us assume that of the 129,000 foreigners only a quarter were tourists and that the others earned their income in Istanbul. Again assuming that every three out of four tourists entering the Ottoman Empire passed through Istanbul in any given year, we conclude that there were approximately 40,000 tourists in the Ottoman Empire as a whole. Considering the vast area the Empire covered and the enormous interest Europeans had begun to show in various regions, especially Palestine, this figure does not appear too high.

In his study of the balance of payments of the United States for 1860–1900, Matthew Simon estimates the average per capita daily expenditure of American tourists in Europe at £1.5 during 1897–1900.[10] This figure excludes all transportation costs and expenditures on sundry items and luxury goods, which were not insignificant, since only the relatively wealthy could travel abroad. Thus, even if we assume that basic daily expenditures in the Middle East were only about a third of what they were in Europe, once we consider expenditures for transportation, sundries and luxury goods and add the effects of the worldwide upward swing in prices from 1897–1900 to 1913, we can approximate the average per capita daily expenditures of tourists in the Middle East at around £1 for the year 1913. For an average length of stay of 60 days – Simon assumes 50 to 60 days for U.S. tourists in Europe, excluding the ocean voyage – this means total expenditures of £2,400,000 for 40,000 tourists. If nothing else, this simple calculation does point to the plausibility of Ruppin's estimates for Syria and Palestine and indicates that there is substantial understatement in Eldem's and especially in Biliotti's figures.

Then there is the problem of extending these estimates backwards in time. If Ruppin's estimates are reliable, and we are assuming that they have at least the correct order of magnitude, a very large part of the total Ottoman revenues owing to tourism must have come from Syria and Palestine. Accounts of the European Jewish emigration to Palestine indicate that the number of migrants began to pick up in the decade of the 1890s, reaching new heights with every passing year.[11] We assumed that the number of European tourists visiting Syria and Palestine each year after 1880 is a function of the cumulative number of Jewish and German immigrants arriving at this region since 1880. (For the annual numbers of these immigrants see table A6.1 below.)

Since evidence points to a sharp rise in the numbers of incoming tourists after the turn of the century, something like a threshold effect appears to be working here. Hence we chose to estimate the annual revenue from tourism, including the donations of the tourists to religious institutions, as being proportional to the square of the number of recent immigrants (after 1880) rather than being a linear function of the same figure. Our estimates of tourism revenues net of expenditures by the Ottoman government and citizens abroad for the period before 1880 are necessarily very crude; it is very difficult to be more precise without conducting a detailed investigation of this issue.

Immigrants' funds

The nineteenth and early twentieth centuries witnessed an almost uninterrupted flow of immigrants into the Ottoman Empire, primarily from lands that were once part of the Empire. The magnitudes of this influx of people were large enough to alter dramatically the demographic characteristics of the Anotolian population. A rough calculation indicates, for example, that under the assumption of equal rates of growth for the immigrating population and the indigenous population, the direct descendants of the immigrants of the nineteenth century made up no less than 30 per cent of the Turkish population in 1970.[12]

It is not surprising, therefore, that the funds brought in by the immigrants constituted a not insignificant item in the balance of payments. In order to estimate these inflows, we first developed estimates of per capita inflows of funds, which varied according to the time of migration and the country of departure. Table A6.1 summarizes our estimates for annual immigration into the Ottoman Empire for each major population group. The average amount of funds brought in by the immigrants depended above all on the conditions under which immigrants moved. Per capita funds brought in were substantially lower during periods of war when literally hundreds of thousands of people were forced to migrate at short notice, in comparison to periods when migration took place under more peaceful circumstances. Moreover, there were substantial variations in the economic well-being of average immigrants, depending upon the country of departure. It is clear, for example, that Jewish immigrants into Palestine brought in higher amounts of per capita funds than immigrants from Crimea.

Table A6.1. *Estimates for nineteenth-century immigration into the Ottoman Empire*
Annual averages

Years	Crimean	Circassian	Jewish	From the Balkans
1856–8	30,000			
1859–60	30,000	30,000		
1861–3	50,000	30,000		
1864	75,000	450,000		
1865–6	20,000	150,000		
1867–76	4,000	10,000		
1877–9	4,000	35,000		320,000
1880–9	4,000	10,000	1,000	25,000
1890–9	4,000	10,000	1,500	
1900–9	4,000	10,000	2,250	
1910–12	4,000	10,000	3,000	
1913	4,000	10,000	3,000	120,000

Sources: In preparing these estimates, we relied primarily on the sources utilized by K. Karpat in his unpublished article, 'Migration and its Effects upon the Transformation of the Ottoman State in the Nineteenth Century', submitted to the Conference on the Economic History of the Near East, Princeton University, Spring 1974. A revised version of this study has recently appeared as chapter 4 of Karpat (1985). In addition, for Jewish immigration, Cuinet (1896), Bachi (1967) and U.S. Department of State Archives (1910–13) were used. As these sources make it clear, the above figures cannot be considered precise, but they provide reasonably good estimates of the orders of magnitudes involved.

We used this qualitative information, together with the estimates provided by North and Simon regarding per capita funds brought into the United States by European immigrants of different national origins throughout the nineteenth century.[13] North estimates the average per capita immigrants' funds at $75 (£16) for the period before 1840 irrespective of the country of origin. For 1840–60 the figure is £20 per capita for German immigrants, £5 for the Irish and £16 for the others, including the English immigrants. Similarly, Simon cites estimates for the 1890s that show large differences between the per capita funds brought in by the immigrants from the 'Old' countries – France, Wales, England and Germany – and those from the 'New' countries – Italy, Poland and Hungary. The per capita figures were around £9 for the former group and around £5 for the latter. Hence, the North and Simon studies provide a good yardstick for the orders of magnitude involved in our estimation problem.

There is little information regarding the economic well-being of the Crimean and Circassian immigrants. However, considering the level of economic development of the region they left in comparison with both the 'New' and 'Old' countries of Europe and the fact that an overwhelming majority of these immigrants were given land in various parts of Anatolia in accordance with government settlement plans where they started farming, it is reasonable to assume that per capita funds brought in by these two groups of immigrants were lower than those brought in by the immigrants from 'New' countries to the United States. Consequently, we adopted three levels for the per capita funds brought in by these groups: £3 for the war years or years of forced emigration (1861–4 for Crimean immigrants and 1864–6 for Circassian immigrants); £5 for the years of 'moderate' crisis, when migration was still heavy but not at the levels of the periods cited above (1856–60 and 1865–6 for Crimean immigrants and 1859–63 for Circassian immigrants); and £8 for migration at other times. There is very little information regarding the level of immigration per year for the period before 1856. Evidence indicates, though, that there had been continuous but relatively lower levels of immigration from these regions since the 1780s, but it is difficult to be more specific. Therefore, our estimates of the funds brought in by the immigrants before 1856 are necessarily even more crude.

By comparison with both the Crimean and Circassian immigrants and with European immigrants into the United States, the Jewish and some of the German immigrants into Palestine were economically better off. In contrast to the Crimeans and Circassians, immigrants into Palestine were able to purchase land in the region and, with the help of funds sent from abroad, were able to establish prosperous colonies in a relatively short period of time. Hence we chose a figure of £50 per capita for the funds brought in by this group of immigrants.

Finally, there is the large immigration from the Balkans as a consequence of the Ottoman defeats in the wars of 1877–8 and 1912–13 to consider. Since heavy migration that took place during and after these two wars can be considered as the movement of people and their funds within the same economy, there is no reason to include these funds in the balance of payments accounts. The only exception would be the funds brought in by the immigrants during 1880–9. Those immigrants should be considered to have come from 'abroad'. Not all of the immigrants from the Balkans were poor. For example, some of them joined the ranks of the commercial bourgeoisie in Istanbul within a short period, yet there is reason to expect that the relatively wealthy left the Balkans early, most probably during the war. Therefore, we adopted the figure of £10 per capita for the funds brought in by the immigrants from the Balkans during 1880–9, which is somewhat higher than the figure for the Crimean and Circassian immigrants arriving under normal circumstances. Our estimates for the total inflow of funds for each year are presented in table A6.4.

Incoming money orders

Paralleling the rise in Jewish immigration into Palestine, funds sent from Europe to this region increased very rapidly. For the years immediately preceding World War I, Ruppin estimates total inflows into the Syrian region from abroad to be £1,600,000 per year; of this amount, £1,200,000 was sent to Lebanon, and the rest to Palestine.[14] While some of these funds went into immediate consumption and to increases in the standards of living, a not insignificant amount must have provided the basic capital for the development and expansion of the Jewish communities in the region. Nonetheless, because of their special nature, we did not consider these funds as part of foreign capital inflows proper. We assumed that annual inflows of these funds followed a pattern similar to that of the growth of revenues from tourism in the Syrian region, namely, they were proportional to the square of the number of cumulative immigrants arriving in the region since 1880.

Money orders arriving elsewhere in the Empire must be added to these figures. The most well known among the latter are funds sent by Armenian immigrants in the United States to their relatives in Eastern Anatolia. Eldem estimates the magnitude of these flows to be around £1,000,000 per year, so that, together with Ruppin's estimates for the Syrian region, total incoming funds from money orders reach £2,700,000 for the year 1913.[15] However, on the basis of some scanty evidence available in the U.S. consular reports regarding the magnitude of money orders sent by Armenians in the United States, we found Eldem's estimate rather high and adopted a lower figure for all incoming money orders arriving at regions other than Syria. (See table A6.4 for the annual estimates of incoming money orders.)

Tributes, war indemnities

For the period 1841–1913, the annual tribute payment from Egypt constituted a major source of revenue for the much-troubled Ottoman Treasury. During the first wave of Ottoman public borrowing, the tribute was shown as a guarantee towards the payment of the loans of 1855 and 1871. After the foundation of the Ottoman Public Debt Administration, the Egyptian tribute was sent directly to Europe and primarily to England, where most of the bonds from these emissions had been purchased. It is not surprising, therefore, that even after the British occupation of Egypt, the British colonial administration did not stop the payment of the tribute. Even though the tribute never reached the Ottoman Treasury in this later period, we considered it a credit item in the balance of payments since the corresponding debt payments were entered as a debit item in the calculations of the payments flows arising from Ottoman state borrowing. The tribute started in 1841 at approximately £275,000 per year; it was raised to approximately £397,000 around 1856 and finally to £675,000 in 1866, at which level it remained roughly unchanged until 1913.[16] The other tribute payments entering the Ottoman Treasury were relatively unimportant. They included those from Wallachia (£18,000 per year), Moldavia (£9,000) and Serbia (£18,000), all until 1878; those from Eastern Roumeli (£45,000 on average) and Cyprus (£94,000), both for the period 1878–1908; and those from the islands of Sisam (Chios) (£3,600) and Aynaroz (Evia) (under £1,000 per year), both of which continued from the early nineteenth century to 1913.[17]

The Ottoman Empire paid war indemnities to Russia in accordance with the 1829 Treaty of Edirne and the 1878 Treaty of Berlin. The former payment amounted to a total of 800,000 Ottoman Liras or £1,100,000 at the existing rate of exchange. This sum was paid to Russia within a short period of time.[18] The latter was originally scheduled to last for a hundred years at an annual amount of £318,000. However, the Ottoman government rarely paid this amount in full, and this issue was a continuous source of friction between the two states. The remaining payments were finally cancelled in 1908 in exchange for the cancellation of the tribute of Eastern Roumeli.[19]

On the credit side is the war indemnity the Greek government was forced to pay as a result of its defeat in the war of 1897. The full amount was £3.6 million;[20] however, we have not come across any information on whether this amount was ever paid in part or in full. Considering both the history of the post-1878 indemnity payments to Russia and the frequent interference by European powers in these issues, we assumed that the actual payments amounted to half the initially established sum.

A6.3 On the internal consistency of the estimates

We have emphasized that due to the unavailability of data the estimates for some of the invisible items in the preceding section are rather crude. Specifically, estimates for net revenues from tourism, incoming money orders and immigrants' funds are not as reliable as other estimates presented in this appendix. However, estimation of these invisible items with accuracy was not the sole purpose of our study. We also undertook this reconstruction in order to check the reliability and accuracy of our estimates for the three major items, foreign trade, all funds flows arising from state external borrowing and all funds flows arising from direct foreign investment. In this section, we will argue that our estimates of invisible items, on the one hand, and our estimates regarding foreign trade and payments flows arising from foreign investment, on the other, are mutually consistent within the framework of an external payments account.

In what follows we will compare the size of the cumulative balance of payments surplus indicated by our estimates with the net inflows of bullion and specie into the Ottoman Empire as approximated from figures on the minting of new gold coins by the Ottoman Treasury from bullion and foreign specie between 1844 and 1913.

The logic of balance of payments accounts is well known. By definition, the accounts are in balance at all times. According to the terminology adopted for this reconstruction, a balance of payments surplus implies net inflows of bullion and specie, and a balance of payments deficit indicates net outflows of the same. Our estimates, presented in table A6.4, indicate that between 1844 and 1910 the Ottoman balance of payments showed a cumulative surplus of approximately £40 million. Our estimates do not indicate a cumulative surplus or deficit for 1830–44. On the other hand, the unusually large trade deficits of the early 1910s shown in these accounts were apparently financed by short- and medium-term commercial credits that were not included in our calculations. For this reason, the balance of payments deficits of the 1910s shown in table A6.4 do not necessarily imply bullion and specie outflows of the same magnitude. The deficits of 1910–13 will be excluded from the comparison below.[21]

According to the available data, the amount of gold coinage in circulation in the Ottoman Empire during the year 1844 was around £11–12 million. An estimate is available because in that year all gold and silver coins in circulation were collected and their precious metal content readjusted by the Treasury.[22] The statistics of the Istanbul Mint summarized in table A6.2 indicate that the value of gold coins minted after 1844 and until 1913 was around 50 million Ottoman Liras, the equivalent of £45 million. These coins were minted primarily from bullion and from European coins. The reminting of Ottoman gold coins remained very limited according to these statistics. Therefore, 50 million Liras can be taken as a crude approximation of the total amount of gold inflows into the Empire during this period. On the other hand, according to Biliotti, who worked in the Ottoman Bank early in this century, the amount of gold outflows from the Empire was very limited.[23] Consequently, we are inclined to accept the equivalent of 40 to 50 million Ottoman Liras as an approximation of the net inflows of gold into the Empire during 1844–1913. The same statistics of the Istanbul Mint

Table A6.2. *Value of gold coinage minted by the Ottoman Treasury from 1844 (Tashih-i Sikke) to 1913*

In thousands of Ottoman Liras

Years /during the reign of 1	Total 1	From Ottoman Liras 2	Net total 3 = 1 − 2	From bullion 4	From pounds sterling 5	From French francs and other 6
Abdulmecid (1844–60)	14,481	?				
Abdulaziz (1861–75)	14,971	?				
Murad V (1876)	13	?				
1876–89	2,860	94	2,766	730	2,019	17
1890–9	2,439	189	2,250	208	2,042	
1900–9	13,081	153	12,928	2,727	9,433	768
1910–13	14,322	280	14,052	5,021	8,700	331
Total (1844–1913)	62,177					

1.10 Ottoman Lira = 1.00 British pound sterling.
Source: Hasan Ferid (1914–18), vol. I, p. 371, based on the statistics of the Istanbul Mint.

indicate that inflows of silver were around one-tenth of this figure during the same period.[24]

In other words, both the results of our reconstruction and the statistics of the Mint point to a cumulative surplus of 40 to 50 million Liras in the Ottoman balance of payments. At first glance, the coexistence of large trade deficits and a virtually permanent fiscal crisis with cumulative trade surpluses may seem paradoxical. However, it should be emphasized that the Ottoman economy grew to some as yet unknown extent during the nineteenth century. Perhaps more important, the rate of monetization was steadily rising during this period. On the other hand, the economy remained *de facto* linked to the gold standard after 1862, and, with the exception of the war years of 1877–8, the printing of paper currency was very limited until 1914.[25] Under these circumstances, a long-term increase in the money stock was necessary for the functioning of the economy.[26] Since the volume of paper money did not expand considerably, this requirement had to be met by net inflows of bullion and specie, in other words by cumulative surpluses in the balance of payments. In short, despite varying degrees of uncertainty associated with some of our estimates, one major result emerging from our reconstruction, a long-term cumulative surplus in the balance of payments, is consistent with both the requirements of the Ottoman economy and the observed increases in the money stock in circulation.

This conclusion, in turn, implies that our estimates of Ottoman foreign trade and of payments flows arising from foreign investment are consistent with our estimates of the invisible items within the framework of an external payments account.

A6.4 An overview of the results

Having estimated each item separately for each year, we are now in a position to establish the long-term trends, or long swings, in the Ottoman international balance of payments. Towards that end, we present in table A6.3 a periodization of the nineteenth-century Ottoman balance of payments. The discussion below will focus on this summary picture rather than on the detailed results given in table A6.4. For our summary analysis we grouped items of the external payments account under three headings: (a) the trade balance; (b) funds flows arising from foreign investment; (c) other invisible items. Under the second heading we have included capital inflows arising from state external borrowing and from direct foreign investment, along with all debt payments and profit transfers. In present-day balance of payments accounting, interest payments and profit transfers are treated as part of the current account, separate from the capital account. However, for our purposes here and elsewhere in the book we chose to treat all funds flows arising from foreign investment together.

The third heading, other invisibles, includes all items discussed earlier in section A6.2, freight income, tourism revenues, rent income from land held abroad, incoming money orders, immigrants' funds, tributes and indemnity payments. The items grouped under this heading are associated more with the special characteristics of the Ottoman Empire than with its relations with the industrialized center economies. Among these items, especially rent income from land owned abroad, immigrants' funds and tribute income reflect the fact that the nineteenth-century Ottoman state was the continuation of an Empire that covered a vast geographical area for centuries. On the other hand, tourism revenues and incoming money orders are related primarily to Jewish immigration into Palestine.

On the basis of the summary presented in table A6.3, the following features of the nineteenth-century Ottoman balance of payments, in addition to the existence of cumulative surpluses discussed above, appear to be of particular importance:

(1) External trade showed a virtually permanent deficit throughout the century. The size of the deficit was subject to long-term fluctuations.

(2) For the 83-year period as a whole, inflows of foreign capital (state

Table A6.3. *A periodization of the Ottoman balance of payments,*
1830–1913

Annual averages in millions of British pounds sterling

Years		External trade balance 1	Net funds flows arising from foreign investment 2	Other items 3
I	1830–1853	− 0.9	—	+ 0.9
II	1854–1875	− 3.1	+ 1.9	+ 1.8
IIA	1854–1868	− 3.0	+ 1.2	+ 1.5
IIB	1869–1875	− 3.3	+ 3.4	+ 2.4
III	1876–1887	− 0.3	− 1.2	+ 2.4
IIIA	1876–1881	− 0.9	− 0.6	+ 1.9
IIIB	1882–1887	+ 0.3	− 1.8	+ 2.9
IV	1888–1896	− 1.6	+ 0.6	+ 2.4
V	1897–1913	− 4.5	− 2.1	+ 5.5
VA	1897–1903	0.0	− 4.1	+ 4.4
VB	1904–1913	− 7.7	− 0.6	+ 6.2
	1830–1913	− 2.2	0.0	+ 2.4

Notes: The columns of this summary table correspond to the following rows of table 6.4 given in parentheses:
1. External trade balance = f.o.b. exports − c.i.f. imports (3 = 1 − 2).
2. Net funds flows arising from foreign investment = net capital inflows arising from state external borrowing and direct foreign investment − debt payments and profit transfers (16 + 18 − 11 − 12).
3. Other items = freight receipts, tourism revenues, rent income from land held abroad, incoming money orders, immigrants' funds and tributes and war indemnities (4 + 5 + 6 + 7 + 8 + 9).
Source: Table A6.4.

debt and direct investment) were approximately equal to the outflows of funds arising from these investments. The direction of net funds flows arising from foreign investment also showed long-term fluctuations. Until 1875 capital inflows exceeded debt payments and profit transfers. After 1875, with the exception of the period 1888–96, the amount of funds transferred by foreign capital to the center countries exceeded new capital inflows. In other words, our calculations show that the trade deficits after 1875 could not have been financed with net inflows of funds arising from foreign investment.

(3) Therefore, the trade deficit, along with debt payments and profit transfers net of new capital inflows, was balanced after 1875 by certain special revenue items of the Empire and, after the 1890s, primarily by the funds inflows related to Jewish migration into Palestine.[27]

Having summarized the most basic features of the balance of payments picture, we can now examine briefly each of the sub-periods presented in table A6.3.[28]

I – 1830–53: A relatively small trade deficit was balanced primarily by rent incomes from land held in Egypt and by the Egyptian tribute. With the exception of some short-term private borrowing from Europe, which ultimately went towards the financing of the state deficit, foreign capital inflows can be considered negligible until 1854.

II – 1854–75: In this period of expansion for the world economy, the most important characteristic of the balance of payments was a large wave of state external borrowing and net funds inflows arising from this process. Both external borrowing and net funds inflows showed a distinct acceleration after 1869. As a result, the size of the trade deficits was substantially larger in comparison to both earlier and later periods. Funds flows arising from direct foreign investment remained limited. Rent income from land held abroad and the Egyptian tribute continued to be the most important items among the other invisibles.

III – 1876–87: With the beginning of the Great Depression and the cessation of capital exports to the periphery, the Ottoman state announced its inability to continue payments on its external debt. With the establishment of the Ottoman Public Debt Administration in 1881, European lenders began to control some of the major sources of fiscal revenue and reversed the direction of net funds flows. The most important characteristic of this sub-period was that debt payments transferred to Europe exceeded by far new borrowing, which remained limited. Paralleling this change, the trade deficit disappeared, and a small trade surplus emerged. Net revenues obtained from other invisibles continued to be substantial.

IV – 1888–96: The most important wave of direct foreign investment in the Empire occurred during this period, mostly in the form of railroad building. As a result, during these nine years total capital inflows remained above profit transfers and payments towards the external debt. The trade account began to show a deficit again, at least in part because of railroad construction by foreign capital. The effects on the balance of payments of Jewish migration into Palestine can be observed during these years, but they did not reach important magnitudes until later.

V – 1897–1913: In this sub-period of expansion for the world economy, the Ottoman balance of payments exhibits different characteristics before and after 1903. The pattern until 1903 resembles closely that of the years 1876–87 and especially of the years 1881–7. Debt payments and profit transfers arising from direct foreign investment were relatively large and, not independently of these outflows, the deficit in the trade account disappeared. Foreign capital as a whole transferred abroad more than it brought during these years. The difference roughly equalled net revenues from the other invisible items. This pattern changed after 1903 with the acceleration of state external borrowing. A new balance appeared after this date between capital inflows on the one hand and debt payments and profit transfers on the other. At the same time, our estimates point to rapid increases in tourism revenues and various funds flows into Palestine. Paralleling these changes, the Ottoman trade deficit reached levels unprecedented during the previous century. In the early 1910s, an important part of the large trade deficit was financed by short-term commercial credits from supplying countries.

Table A6.4. Estimates for the balance of payments of the Ottoman Empire, 1830–1913

In millions of British pounds sterling

	1830-9 (ann. av.)	1840-9 (ann. av.)	1850	1851	1852	1853	1854	1855	1856	1857	1858	1859	1850-9 (av.)
1. Commodity exports	4.2	6.0	7.8	8.8	9.8	9.8	9.3	9.7	12.5	10.0	10.0	10.4	9.8
2. Commodity imports	5.1	6.9	8.9	8.7	10.8	11.3	10.7	19.2	18.4	12.0	11.9	10.6	12.3
3. Balance of trade (1 − 2)	−0.9	−0.9	−1.1	+0.1	−1.0	−1.5	−1.4	−9.5	−5.9	−2.0	−1.9	−0.2	−2.5
4. Freight income	0.05	0.05	0.08	0.08	0.08	0.08	0.08	0.08	0.08	0.08	0.08	0.08	0.08
5. Tourism receipts	0.2	0.2	0.3	0.3	0.3	0.3	0.3	0.3	0.3	0.3	0.3	0.3	0.3
6. Rent from land abroad	0.4	0.4	0.4	0.4	0.4	0.4	0.4	0.4	0.4	0.4	0.4	0.4	0.4
7. Incoming money orders	—	—	—	—	—	—	—	—	—	—	—	—	—
8. Immigrants' funds	0.05	0.05	0.1	0.1	0.1	0.1	0.1	0.1	0.1	0.1	0.1	0.1	0.1
9. Tribute, indemnities	0.0	0.33	0.45	0.45	0.45	0.45	0.45	0.45	0.45	0.45	0.45	0.45	0.45
10. Total unilateral payments (7 + 8 + 9)	0.05	0.35	0.55	0.55	0.55	0.55	0.55	0.55	0.55	0.55	0.55	0.55	0.55
11. Interest payments on state borrowing	—	—	—	—	—	—	—	0.2	0.4	0.4	0.4	0.6	0.2
12. Profit transfer on direct foreign investment	—	—	—	—	—	—	—	—	—	—	—	—	—
13. Balance on current account (3 + 4 + 5 + 6 + 10 − 11 − 12)	−0.17	+0.06	+0.2	+1.4	+0.3	−0.2	−0.1	−8.4	−5.0	−1.1	−1.0	+0.5	−1.3

14. State borrowing (acc. to the date of signature of the loans)	—	—	—	—	—	—	2.3	5.1	—	—	3.4	—	1.1
14A. State borrowing (acc. to the date of actual flows)	—	—	—	—	—	—	2.3	5.1	—	—	1.7	1.7	1.1
15. Principal payments on the state debt	—	—	—	—	—	—	—	0.03	0.03	0.03	0.03	0.1	0.02
16. Net capital movements due to state borrowing (14A − 15)	—	—	—	—	—	—	2.3	5.1	0.0	0.0	1.6	1.6	1.1
17. Net payments flows arising from the state debt (16 − 11)	—	—	—	—	—	—	2.3	4.9	−0.4	−0.4	1.3	1.6	1.1
18. Direct foreign investment net of repatriation	—	—	—	—	—	—	—	—	—	—	—	1.0	0.9
19. Net payments flows arising from direct foreign investment (18 − 12)	—	—	—	—	—	—	—	—	—	—	—	1.2	0.1
20. Balance on capital account (16 + 18)	—	—	—	—	—	—	2.3	5.1	0.0	0.0	1.6	2.8	1.2
21. Balance of payments (13 + 20) or net flows of specie and bullion	−0.17	+0.06	+0.2	+1.4	+0.3	−0.2	+2.2	−3.3	−5.0	−1.1	+0.6	+3.3	−0.16
22. Cumulative balance (1830 = 0)		−1.1										−2.7	

	1860	1861	1862	1863	1864	1865	1866	1867	1868	1869	1860–9 (av.)
1. Commodity exports	11.1	12.3	13.7	15.8	16.7	15.6	15.5	14.9	19.7	18.9	15.4
2. Commodity imports	13.7	12.0	13.1	17.5	19.9	19.4	20.4	19.8	22.8	24.0	18.3
3. Balance of trade (1−2)	−2.6	+0.3	+0.6	−1.7	−3.2	−3.8	−4.9	−4.9	−3.1	−5.1	−2.9
4. Freight income	0.08	0.08	0.08	0.08	0.08	0.08	0.08	0.08	0.08	0.08	0.08
5. Tourism receipts	0.3	0.3	0.3	0.3	0.3	0.3	0.3	0.3	0.3	0.3	0.3
6. Rent from land abroad	0.5	0.5	0.5	0.5	0.5	0.5	0.5	0.5	0.5	0.5	0.5
7. Incoming money orders	—	—	—	—	—	—	—	—	—	—	—
8. Immigrants' funds	0.3	0.3	0.3	0.3	0.3	0.3	0.3	0.3	0.3	0.3	0.3
9. Tributes, indemnities	0.73	0.73	0.73	0.73	0.73	0.73	0.73	0.73	0.73	0.73	0.73
10. Total unilateral payments (7+8+9)	1.0	1.0	1.0	1.0	1.0	1.0	1.0	1.0	1.0	1.0	1.0

	1860	1861	1862	1863	1864	1865	1866	1867	1868	1869	1860–9 (av.)
11. Interest payments on state borrowing	0.7	0.8	0.8	1.2	1.7	1.7	2.2	2.1	2.4	2.3	1.6
12. Profit transfer on direct foreign investment	—	—	—	0.2	0.3	0.2	0.3	0.3	0.4	0.4	0.2
13. Balance on current account (3+4+5+6+10−11−12)	−1.4	+1.4	+1.7	−1.2	−3.3	−3.8	−5.5	−5.4	−4.0	−5.9	−2.7
14. State borrowing (acc. to the date of signature of the loans)	1.2	—	5.2	5.0	—	5.5	—	3.0	—	11.6	3.2
14A. State borrowing (acc. to the date of actual flows)	0.6	0.6	2.6	5.1	2.5	4.6	0.9	3.0	—	5.8	2.6
15. Principal payments on the state debt	0.1	0.2	0.2	0.3	0.5	0.6	0.7	0.8	0.8	0.9	0.5
16. Net capital movements due to state borrowing (14A−15)	0.5	0.4	2.4	4.8	2.0	4.0	0.2	2.2	−0.8	4.9	2.1
17. Net payments flows arising from the state debt (16−11)	−0.2	−0.4	1.6	3.6	0.3	2.3	−2.0	0.1	−3.2	2.6	0.5
18. Direct foreign investment net of repatriation	—	—	0.1	2.8	—	1.4	0.2	0.4	—	1.8	0.7
19. Net payments flows arising from direct foreign investment (18−12)	—	—	0.1	2.6	−0.3	1.2	−0.1	0.1	−0.4	1.4	0.5
20. Balance on capital account (16+18)	0.5	0.4	2.5	7.6	2.0	5.4	0.4	2.6	−0.8	6.7	2.7
21. Balance of payments (13+20) or net flows of specie and bullion	−0.9	+1.8	+4.2	+6.4	−1.3	+1.6	−5.1	−2.8	−4.8	+0.8	0.0
22. Cumulative balance (1830=0)	−2.7									−2.8	

	1870	1871	1872	1873	1874	1875	1876	1877	1878	1879	1870–9 (av.)
1. Commodity exports	17.4	20.7	20.2	19.2	21.1	19.0	23.0	17.4	13.2	15.0	18.6
2. Commodity imports	22.5	21.4	23.2	22.4	23.3	22.1	19.6	16.4	18.0	18.9	20.8
3. Balance of trade (1 − 2)	−5.1	−0.7	−3.0	−3.2	−2.2	−3.1	+3.4	+1.0	−4.8	−3.9	−2.2
4. Freight income	0.08	0.08	0.08	0.08	0.08	0.08	0.08	0.08	0.08	0.08	0.08
5. Tourism receipts	0.4	0.4	0.4	0.4	0.4	0.4	0.4	0.2	0.2	0.2	0.3
6. Rent from land abroad	0.6	0.6	0.6	0.6	0.6	0.6	0.6	0.2	0.2	0.2	0.5
7. Incoming money orders	—	—	—	—	—	—	—	—	—	—	—
8. Immigrants' funds	0.1	0.1	0.1	0.1	0.1	0.1	0.3	0.3	0.3	0.3	0.2
9. Tributes, indemnities	0.7	0.7	0.7	0.7	0.7	0.7	0.7	0.7	0.7	0.7	0.7
10. Total unilateral payments (7 + 8 + 9)	0.8	0.8	0.8	0.8	0.8	0.8	1.0	1.0	1.0	1.0	0.9
11. Interest payments on state borrowing	3.6	4.6	4.9	5.2	7.8	9.6	0.5	0.6	0.5	0.7	3.8
12. Profit transfer on direct foreign investment	0.3	0.4	0.4	0.3	0.4	0.3	0.2	0.2	0.2	0.5	0.3
13. Balance on current account (3 + 4 + 5 + 6 + 10 − 11 − 12)	−7.1	−3.8	−6.4	−6.8	−8.5	−11.1	+4.8	+1.7	−4.0	−3.6	−4.5
14. State borrowing (acc. to the date of signature of the loans)	11.0	4.0	4.7	25.4	15.1	—	—	2.6	—	—	6.3
14A. State borrowing (acc. to the date of actual flows)	12.1	11.1	7.8	12.7	14.8	7.5	—	—	2.6	—	6.9
15. Principal payments on the state debt	1.2	1.3	1.5	1.5	1.9	2.0	0.1	0.1	0.1	0.1	1.0
16. Net capital movements due to state borrowing (14A − 15)	10.9	9.8	6.3	11.2	12.9	5.5	−0.1	−0.1	2.6	−0.1	5.9
17. Net payments flows arising from the state debt (16 − 11)	7.3	5.2	1.4	6.0	5.1	−4.1	−0.6	−0.7	2.1	−0.8	2.1
18. Direct foreign investment net of repatriation	0.3	0.3	1.5	0.8	—	1.0	—	—	0.1	0.0	0.4
19. Net payments flows arising from direct foreign investment (18 − 12)	0.0	−0.1	+1.1	+0.5	−0.4	0.7	−0.2	−0.2	−0.2	−0.5	+0.1
20. Balance on capital account (16 + 18)	11.2	10.1	7.8	12.0	12.9	6.5	−0.1	−0.1	2.7	−0.1	+6.3
21. Balance of payments (13 + 20) or net flows of specie and bullion	+4.1	+6.3	+1.4	+5.2	+4.4	−4.6	+4.7	+1.6	−1.3	−3.7	+1.8
22. Cumulative balance (1830 = 0)	−2.8									+15.3	

	1880	1881	1882	1883	1884	1885	1886	1887	1888	1889	1880–9 (av.)
1. Commodity exports	14.3	15.4	15.9	16.3	16.7	16.9	16.3	14.0	13.2	16.3	15.5
2. Commodity imports	15.8	15.2	15.2	15.3	15.0	15.8	16.5	16.6	16.0	18.5	16.0
3. Balance of trade (1 − 2)	−1.5	+0.2	+0.7	+1.0	+1.7	+1.1	−0.2	−2.6	−2.8	−2.2	−0.5
4. Freight income	0.1	0.1	0.1	0.1	0.1	0.1	0.1	0.1	0.1	0.1	0.1
	1880	1881	1882	1883	1884	1885	1886	1887	1888	1889	1880–9 (av.)
5. Tourism receipts	0.4	0.4	0.6	0.6	0.6	0.6	0.6	0.6	0.6	0.6	0.6
6. Rent from land abroad	0.8	0.8	0.8	0.8	0.8	0.8	0.8	0.8	0.8	0.8	0.8
7. Incoming money orders	0.3	0.3	0.3	0.3	0.3	0.3	0.3	0.3	0.3	0.3	0.3
8. Immigrants' funds	0.3	0.3	0.3	0.3	0.3	0.3	0.3	0.3	0.3	0.3	0.3
9. Tributes, indemnities	0.7	0.7	0.7	0.7	0.7	0.7	0.7	0.7	0.7	0.7	0.7
10. Total unilateral payments (7 + 8 + 9)	1.3	1.3	1.3	1.3	1.3	1.3	1.3	1.3	1.3	1.3	1.3
11. Interest payments on state borrowing	0.7	0.7	2.4	2.2	2.3	2.1	2.0	2.3	2.5	2.5	2.0
12. Profit transfer on direct foreign investment	0.5	1.0	1.0	0.8	0.7	0.6	0.6	0.6	0.6	0.7	0.7
13. Balance on current account (3 + 4 + 5 + 6 + 10 − 11 − 12)	−0.1	+1.1	+0.1	+0.8	+1.5	+1.2	0.0	−2.7	−3.1	−2.6	−0.4
14. State borrowing (acc. to the date of signature of the loans)	—	—	—	—	—	—	5.9	—	1.1	—	0.7
14A. State borrowing (acc. to the date of actual flows)	—	—	—	—	—	3.6	3.0	—	1.1	—	0.8
15. Principal payments on the state debt	0.1	0.1	0.3	0.3	0.2	0.3	0.3	0.4	0.3	0.4	0.3
16. Net capital movements due to state borrowing (14A − 15)	−0.1	−0.1	−0.3	−0.3	−0.2	+3.3	+2.7	−0.4	+0.8	−0.4	+0.5
17. Net payments flows arising from the state debt (16 − 11)	−0.8	−0.8	−2.7	−2.5	−2.5	+1.2	+0.7	−2.7	−1.7	−2.9	−1.5
18. Direct foreign investment net of repatriation	0.6	0.1	0.1	0.2	—	0.5	0.4	0.6	2.1	3.5	0.8
19. Net payments flows arising from direct foreign investment (18 − 12)	+0.1	−0.9	−0.9	−0.6	−0.7	−0.1	−0.2	0.0	+1.5	+2.8	+0.1
20. Balance on capital account (16 + 18)	0.5	0.0	−0.2	−0.1	−0.2	+3.8	3.1	0.2	2.9	3.1	+1.3
21. Balance of payments (13 + 20) or net flows of specie and bullion	+0.4	+1.1	−0.1	+0.7	+1.3	+5.0	+3.1	−2.5	−0.2	+0.5	+0.9
22. Cumulative balance (1830 = 0)	+15.3									+24.6	

	1890	1891	1892	1893	1894	1895	1896	1897	1898	1899	1890–9 (av.)
1. Commodity exports	17.1	17.6	19.1	17.7	15.7	17.1	17.6	19.9	17.3	17.6	17.6
2. Commodity imports	19.4	18.7	19.4	19.3	20.5	17.4	16.3	17.6	19.8	18.0	18.6
3. Balance of trade (1−2)	−2.3	−1.1	−0.3	−1.6	−4.8	−0.3	+1.3	+2.3	−2.5	−0.4	−1.0
4. Freight income	0.13	0.13	0.13	0.13	0.13	0.13	0.13	0.13	0.13	0.13	0.13
5. Tourism receipts	0.7	0.7	0.7	0.7	0.8	0.8	0.9	0.9	1.0	1.0	0.8
6. Rent from land abroad	0.9	0.9	0.9	0.9	0.9	0.9	0.9	0.9	0.9	0.9	0.9
7. Incoming money orders	0.4	0.4	0.5	0.5	0.6	0.6	0.8	0.8	1.0	1.0	0.7
8. Immigrants' funds	0.1	0.1	0.1	0.1	0.1	0.1	0.1	0.1	0.1	0.1	0.1
9. Tributes, indemnities	0.9	0.9	0.9	0.9	0.9	0.9	0.9	0.9	0.9	0.9	0.9
10. Total unilateral payments (7+8+9)	1.4	1.4	1.5	1.5	1.6	1.6	1.8	1.8	2.0	2.0	1.7
11. Interest payments on state borrowing	2.7	2.5	2.6	2.6	2.5	2.6	2.5	2.5	2.6	2.6	2.6
12. Profit transfer on direct foreign investment	0.9	1.0	1.2	1.4	1.4	1.7	1.6	1.8	2.1	2.0	1.5
13. Balance on current account (3+4+5+6+10−11−12)	−2.8	−1.5	−0.9	−2.4	−5.3	−1.2	+0.9	+1.7	−3.2	−1.0	−1.6
14. State borrowing (acc. to the date of signature of the loans)	3.9	1.3	—	0.6	1.6	—	2.5	—	—	—	1.0
14A. State borrowing (acc. to the date of actual flows)	2.0	3.2	—	0.6	1.0	—	2.5	—	—	—	0.9
15. Principal payments on the state debt	0.4	0.9	0.8	0.8	0.8	0.9	0.9	1.0	1.0	1.0	0.8
16. Net capital movements due to state borrowing (14A−15)	1.6	2.3	−0.8	−0.2	−0.2	−0.9	1.6	−1.0	−1.0	1.0	+0.1
17. Net payments flows arising from the state debt (16−11)	−1.1	−0.2	−3.4	−2.8	−2.3	−3.5	−0.9	−3.5	−3.6	−3.6	−2.5
18. Direct foreign investment net of repatriation	2.0	5.2	4.9	0.4	10.8	4.4	1.7	0.2	0.1	0.3	3.0
19. Net payments flows arising from direct foreign investment (18−12)	1.1	4.2	3.7	−1.0	9.4	2.7	0.1	−1.6	−2.0	−1.7	+1.5
20. Balance on capital account (16+18)	3.6	7.5	4.1	0.2	11.0	3.5	3.3	−0.8	−0.9	−0.7	+3.1
21. Balance of payments (13+20) or net flows of specie and bullion	+0.8	+6.0	+3.2	−2.2	+5.7	+2.3	+4.2	+0.9	−4.1	−1.7	+1.5
22. Cumulative balance (1830=0)	+24.6									+39.7	

	1900	1901	1902	1903	1904	1905	1906	1907	1908	1909	1900–9 (av.)
1. Commodity exports	19.5	20.1	21.2	22.5	22.3	24.1	26.0	26.6	23.1	24.5	23.0
2. Commodity imports	18.4	21.9	20.6	21.6	27.6	26.1	30.8	31.3	28.8	33.3	26.0
3. Balance of trade (1 − 2)	+1.1	−1.8	+0.6	+0.9	−5.3	−2.0	−4.8	−4.7	−5.7	−8.8	−3.0
4. Freight income	0.13	0.13	0.13	0.13	0.13	0.13	0.13	0.13	0.13	0.13	0.13
5. Tourism receipts	1.25	1.25	1.5	1.5	1.75	1.75	2.0	2.0	2.25	2.25	1.75
6. Rent from land abroad	1.0	1.0	1.0	1.0	1.0	1.0	1.0	1.0	1.0	0.8	1.0
7. Incoming money orders	1.2	1.2	1.4	1.4	1.6	1.6	1.8	1.8	2.0	1.0	1.6
8. Immigrants' funds	0.25	0.25	0.25	0.25	0.25	0.25	0.25	0.25	0.25	0.25	0.25
9. Tributes, indemnities	0.66	0.66	0.66	0.66	0.66	0.66	0.66	0.66	0.66	0.66	0.66
10. Total unilateral payments (7 + 8 + 9)	2.1	2.1	2.3	2.3	2.5	2.5	2.7	2.7	2.9	2.9	2.5
11. Interest payments on state foreign borrowing	2.5	2.6	2.7	3.1	3.2	3.5	3.4	3.3	3.4	3.9	3.2
12. Profit transfer on direct foreign investment	1.7	2.2	2.3	2.2	2.3	2.5	2.7	2.9	2.9	3.0	2.5
13. Balance on current account (3 + 4 + 5 + 6 + 10 − 11 − 12)	+1.4	−2.1	+0.5	+0.4	−5.4	−2.6	−5.1	−5.1	−5.7	−9.7	−3.4
14. State borrowing (acc. to the date of signature of loans)	—	—	1.5	5.3	2.0	4.2	—	—	12.6	6.3	3.2
14A. State borrowing (acc. to the date of actual flows)	1.0	2.4	0.7	3.6	2.9	3.4			6.3	12.5	3.2
15. Principal payments on the state debt	1.0	1.0	1.1	0.9	0.7	0.8	0.9	1.1	1.1	1.3	1.0
16. Net capital movements due to state borrowing (14A − 15)	−1.0	1.4	−0.4	2.7	2.2	2.6	−0.9	−1.1	5.2	11.2	+2.2
17. Net payments flows arising from the state debt (16 − 11)	−3.5	−1.2	−3.1	−0.4	−1.0	−0.9	−4.3	−4.4	1.8	7.3	−1.0
18. Direct foreign investment net of repatriation	0.8	2.1	0.8	—	0.1	2.7	2.9	1.3	0.7	1.7	1.3
19. Net payments flows arising from direct foreign investment (18 − 12)	−0.9	−0.1	−1.5	−2.3	−2.2	0.2	0.2	−1.6	−2.2	−1.3	−1.2
20. Balance on capital account (16 + 18)	−0.2	3.5	0.4	2.7	2.3	5.3	2.0	0.2	5.9	12.9	3.5
21. Balance of payments (13 + 20) or net flows of specie and bullion	+1.2	+1.4	+0.9	+3.1	−3.1	+2.7	−3.1	−4.9	+0.2	+3.2	+0.1
22. Cumulative balance (1830 = 0)	+39.7									+41.3	

	1910	1911	1912	1913	1910–13 (av.)
1. Commodity exports	26.0	27.1	27.6	28.4	27.3
2. Commodity imports	39.3	40.4	35.2	39.4	38.6
3. Balance of trade (1 − 2)	− 13.3	− 13.3	− 7.6	− 11.0	− 11.3
4. Freight income	0.15	0.15	0.15	0.15	0.15
5. Tourism receipts	2.5	2.8	2.8	2.8	2.7
6. Rent from land abroad	0.8	0.8	0.8	0.8	0.8
7. Incoming money orders	2.2	2.2	2.2	2.2	2.2
8. Immigrants' funds	0.25	0.25	0.25	0.25	0.25
9. Tributes, indemnities	0.8	0.8	0.8	0.8	0.8
10. Total unilateral payments (7 + 8 + 9)	3.25	3.25	3.25	3.25	3.25
11. Interest payments on state borrowing	4.0	4.3	4.4	4.3	4.3
12. Profit transfer on direct foreign investment	3.1	3.2	3.3	3.2	3.2
13. Balance on current account (3 + 4 + 5 + 6 + 10 − 11 − 12)	− 13.7	− 13.8	− 8.3	− 11.5	− 11.9
14. State borrowing (acc. to the date of signature of the loans)	1.4	9.6	9.8	9.4	7.6
14A. State borrowing (acc. to the date of actual flows)	—	11.0	9.8	9.4	7.6
15. Principal payments on the state debt	1.5	1.6	1.5	1.7	1.6
16. Net capital movements due to state borrowing (14A − 15)	− 1.5	9.4	8.3	7.7	6.0
17. Net payments flows arising from the state debt (16 − 11)	− 5.5	5.1	3.9	3.4	1.7
18. Direct foreign investment net of repatriation	3.4	1.7	1.6	1.4	2.0
19. Net payments flows arising from direct foreign investment (18 − 12)	0.3	− 1.5	− 1.7	− 1.8	− 1.2
20. Balance on capital account (16 + 18)	1.9	11.1	9.9	9.1	8.0
21. Balance of payments (13 + 20) or net flows of specie and bullion	− 11.8	− 2.7	+ 1.6	− 2.4	− 3.9
22. Cumulative balance (1830 = 0)	+ 41.3			+ 26.0	

Notes

1 Introduction

1. Landes (1969); Hobsbawm (1968); Hanson (1980); also Saul (1960) and Lewis (1978) for the later period.
2. The significant exception is mining, where a considerable amount of capital was invested. See Paish (1914); Jenks (1927); Feis (1930); Hall (1968); Cottrell (1975).
3. Amin (1947); Bradby (1975); Hymer and Resnick (1969).
4. See, for example, O'Brien (1983).
5. Hymer and Resnick (1969); Resnick (1970).
6. Amin (1974); Bradby (1975); McEachern (1976); Wallerstein (1974); also Foster-Carter (1978).
7. Gallagher and Robinson (1953, 1961). Also see Louis (1976).
8. For studies of the economic policies pursued by colonial administrations, see Wolff (1974); Birnberg and Resnick (1975); Arrighi (1970).
9. See, for example, Graham (1972); Ferns (1960).
10. For example, Hoffman (1964); Forbes (1978).
11. The case of Egypt provides one of the most prominent examples of pre-emptive annexation in the nineteenth century. It should be added, however, that the class structure in Egypt differed considerably from those of Latin American countries.
12. For a comparison of the nineteenth-century Ottoman and Chinese Empires from this perspective, see Keyder (1983).
13. Owen (1975); Owen (1981), pp. 1–23.
14. Keyder (1980).
15. Issawi (1980a), p. 1; Owen (1981), pp. 7–8.
16. Barkan (1970a); Çizakca (1980); Braude (1979).
17. Svoronos (1956), Masson (1911); Paris (1957), pp. 370ff; Davis (1970), p. 202; Owen (1981), pp. 6–7.
18. Genç (1975).
19. Owen (1977); for a recent view of the long-term trends in the Ottoman economy during the eighteenth century, see Genç (1984).
20. See the sources cited in note 17 above; also Issawi (1966), pp. 30–1 and chapter 2 of this volume.
21. Owen (1981), p. 52.
22. Paris (1957); Svoronos (1956).

23. Wallerstein and Kasaba (1981); for the role of merchant capital in the struggle for Greek independence, see Stoianovich (1960); also Sadat (1972).
24. Owen (1981), pp. 6–7; Paris (1957), pp. 437–66; Veinstein (1976).
25. İnalcık (1977).
26. Stoianovich (1953); for a more careful assessment, see McGowan (1981); also İnalcık (1983).
27. Veinstein (1976).
28. Karpat (1972).
29. For the political history of the relations between the Ottoman Empire and the European powers and the rivalry amongst the latter, see Anderson (1966); Shaw and Shaw (1977).
30. Our periodization of the long-term fluctuations in the industrialized economies follows Kondratieff (1979) and Mandel (1980).
31. These generalizations are based on a large number of case studies of external trade and received foreign investment of the countries in the periphery. See, for example, the sources cited in Hanson (1980) and Cottrell (1975).
32. Footnotes will not be provided in this overview. For details see the relevant chapters of this volume.

2 Long-term fluctuations in Ottoman foreign trade, 1830–1913

1. The Ottoman Empire signed the first Treaty with Britain in 1838. This was followed by similar treaties with other European countries during the next three years. Whenever we refer to the Treaty in this chapter, we mean the series of Treaties signed during 1838–41. For a detailed and insightful study of the Treaty of 1838, see Puryear (1935). Also, Kütükoğlu (1976); Issawi (1966), pp. 38–41.
2. For studies of British overseas trade during the nineteenth century, see Davis (1979); Cain (1980); Hobsbawm (1968).
3. Puryear (1935).
4. See, for example, Urquhart (1833).
5. Until the 1870s, the foreign policy of Britain favored the territorial integrity of the Ottoman Empire against intrusions from the north. See Puryear (1935); Anderson (1966), chapter 4; and Temperley (1933). For a study of the importance of Ottoman markets and raw materials for Britain and their impact on British policy towards the Ottoman Empire and Russia until the Crimean War, see Bailey (1942). We will return to this theme in chapter 4.
6. For the concerns and reluctance of the Ottoman bureaucracy towards starting to borrow in the European financial markets, see Rodkey (1958); also chapter 4 of this volume.
7. İnalcık (1971); Gibb and Bowen (1957), vol. I, part II, pp. 12–15.
8. See, for example, Issawi (1966), pp. 38–41; Köymen (1971). For a view questioning the unfavorable effects of the Free Trade Treaties, see Kurmuş (1983).
9. Toprak (1982), chapter 5.

10. The official foreign trade statistics were re-published in 1939 along with a discussion of their methodology and shortcomings. When we refer to the official Ottoman trade statistics in this volume, we will be utilizing the figures provided in Aybar (1939).

11. Contemporary observers were aware of this problem. See, for example, Rougon (1892), pp. 266–7; U.S. Department of Commerce, *Commercial Relations of the United States*, 'Commercial Report from Turkey for the Year 1907', p. 518, 'Commercial Report from Turkey for the Year 1909', p. 325; Great Britain, *Parliamentary Papers, Accounts and Papers* (1903), vol. 79, 'Commercial Report from Constantinople for the Year 1902'; Eldem (1970), pp. 138–88.

12. For our reconstruction, we were able to gather the foreign trade statistics and particularly the statistics relating to imports from and exports to the Ottoman Empire of the following countries for the indicated periods: United Kingdom (1830–1913), France (1830–1913), Germany (1880–1913), Austria (1830–1913), United States (1830–1913), Russia (1830–1913), Italy (1852–1913), Belgium (1831–1913), Netherlands (1846–1913), Switzerland (1885–1913), Serbia (1878–1913), Greece (1857–76 and 1888–1913), Romania (1871–1913), Bulgaria (1880–1913), Egypt (1874–1913) and Iran (1902–13).

13. Because of the instability of the Ottoman Lira during the first half of the nineteenth century and since the British pound sterling was the most widely used currency before World War I, we will present all trade values in this volume in pounds sterling.

14. For the implicit price deflators on Ottoman exports and imports for the period 1854–1913, see chapter 3 and appendix 2. For the period before 1854, we utilized Imlah's price indices of British exports and imports in order to approximate the price levels for Ottoman imports and exports respectively. See Imlah (1958), pp. 94–7.

15. For estimates of the population of the Empire in 1840 within the borders defined in map 1, see Issawi (1980a), p. 17, and *Parliamentary Papers, Accounts and Papers* (1843). For the 1913 population of the Empire, we relied on the extrapolations undertaken by Eldem based upon official Ottoman figures supplied by the Ministry of Commerce and Agriculture. See Eldem (1970), pp. 61–2. Eldem provides an estimate of 13.5 million for the 1913 population of the Anatolian provinces of the Empire. In a recent study, J. McCarthy has presented new estimates which revise the earlier estimates for the 1913 population of the Anatolian provinces upwards by about 25 per cent to 17.5 million. McCarthy states that he has reached his estimates by correcting the official figures in the censuses and in provincial yearbooks (salnames) for undercounting in certain age groups and in women. See McCarthy (1983).

16. Let us consider the following stylized numerical example. We assume that: (a) in 1840, the population of the Empire was divided evenly between those areas that seceded before 1913 and those areas that remained part of the Empire in 1913 (each with a population of 10 million); (b) in 1840, the total

exports of the Empire were also divided evenly between these two areas (each area had an export index of 100; a total of 200 for the Empire as a whole); (c) in 1840, the volume of trade between these two areas of the Empire equalled 20.

We now turn to the picture in 1913. We assume that (d) total population of the Empire is now 20 million and (e) total exports from the Empire are 1,000. However, (f) 10 per cent or 100 of the last figure is due to exports to those countries which were part of the Empire in 1840.

As a result, 200 to 1,000, or a fivefold increase in the total exports of the Empire, understates the rate of growth of exports of the areas remaining within the Empire in 1913 (which actually increased from 100 + 10 = 110 to 1,000 or about ninefold). On the other hand, the same fivefold increase overstates by a smaller margin the rate of expansion of per capita exports from those areas within the 1913 borders since those per capita exports grew from an index of 110/10 or 11 to 1,000/20 or 50, about four-and-a-half-fold increase between 1840 and 1913.

17. Hanson (1980), p. 21. On the other hand, Rostow's estimates yield slightly lower rates of growth for world exports. See Rostow (1978), pp. 67, 669.
18. Bairoch (1973), p. 10; Bairoch (1974), p. 558.
19. Hanson (1980), p. 21.
20. Based on Bairoch (1973, 1974).
21. All estimates other than those related to the Ottoman Empire are taken from Hanson (1980), pp. 21, 26–7. A comparison of the Ottoman case with individual countries in the periphery will be undertaken in chapter 7.
22. Eldem (1970), pp. 302–9, reprinted in Issawi (1980a), pp. 6–7.
23. Frequent loss of land and population by the Ottoman Empire makes estimations of this sort rather difficult and hazardous. Our results summarized in table 2.2 indicate that the volume of Ottoman exports grew at an average annual rate slightly exceeding 3 per cent between 1880 and 1913, after adjustments are made for the loss of territory in 1912–13. The annual rate of growth of population remained below 1.0 per cent, close to 0.8 per cent during this period. (See Issawi (1980a), p. 18; Eldem (1970), pp. 49–65.) On the basis of our results, we estimate that per capita exports from the Empire, measured in constant prices, increased by more than 200 per cent between 1840 and the early 1870s.
24. See the discussion on the commodity composition of Ottoman foreign trade in appendix 1.
25. V. Eldem has estimated that in 1913 agriculture accounted for about half Empire GNP. This means that close to a quarter of the total agricultural product was exported in that year. We also know that towns with populations over 20,000 accounted for approximately 22 per cent of the total population of the Empire in 1912. See Issawi (1980a), p. 35. Therefore, it can be crudely estimated that, along with towns of smaller size, urban markets created demand for close to at least another 25 per cent of total agricultural production. This latter estimate takes into account imports of foodstuffs which accounted for close to one-third of all imports. For the composition of Ottoman foreign trade, see appendix 1.

26. Owen (1981), pp. 45–56, correctly emphasizes this point.
27. See tables 2.3 and 2.4 below, based on the results of our reconstruction.
28. See tables 2.3 and 2.4.
29. See appendix 6 for a study of nineteenth-century Ottoman balance of payments.
30. For the mid-century boom in Europe see, for example, Church (1975).
31. Masson (1911); Paris (1957); Owen (1981), chapter 3.
32. Puryear (1941), chapter 1; Owen (1981), chapter 3.
33. Wood (1935), chapter 10; unpublished foreign trade statistics of the United Kingdom, Public Record Office, Customs 8 and Customs 10 Series.
34. Imlah (1958), pp. 94–7.
35. Public Record Office, Customs 8 and Customs 10 Series.
36. In our estimation of the volume of Ottoman–European trade in 1730 and 1780, we relied on Issawi (1966), p. 30, and Paris (1957), pp. 572–7.
37. For recent estimates of the rates of growth of world trade during the nineteenth century, see Hanson (1980), p. 14, and Rostow (1978), pp. 67, 669.
38. Based on the foreign trade statistics of the respective countries. For full references, see the bibliography.
39. Based on the foreign trade statistics of Russia. These publications provide separate statistics for Russian trade with European and Asiatic provinces of the Ottoman Empire. For full references, see the bibliography.
40. Foreign trade statistics of Austria; for full references see the bibliography. Also, *Parliamentary Papers, Accounts and Papers*, 'Commercial Reports' from Venice, Trieste and Fiume for the years 1855–91; U.S. Department of Commerce, *Commercial Relations of the United States with Foreign Countries*, Annual Reports from Venice, Trieste and Fiume for the years 1855–80; Ubicini (1856), pp. 355–8.
41. Pamuk (1984); Rosenberg (1943); Musson (1959); Saul (1969); Mandel (1980).
42. See chapter 3. Also see chapter 4, pp. 33–4 and Pamuk (1984) for a discussion of the impact of the 'Great Depression' on the Ottoman economy and state finances.
43. Regional estimates for per capita levels of income in 1907, 1913 and 1914 are available in Eldem (1970), pp. 304–6.
44. Rates of growth of world trade are from Hanson (1980), p. 14, which also presents the estimates by W. W. Rostow (1978).
45. See chapter 3.
46. See chapter 4 for a more detailed discussion.
47. Quataert (1977); Novichev (1966).
48. Hoffman (1964).
49. Based on foreign trade statistics of Germany. For full references, see the bibliography.
50. Economic aspects of the rivalry between Britain, France and Germany over the Ottoman Empire are discussed in chapter 4, pp. 77–81.
51. Hasan (1970).
52. See chapter 6 and appendix 5. A more detailed discussion of Ottoman foreign

trade with major European countries and the United States during the nineteenth century remains outside the borders of the present study. For Ottoman trade with Britain, see Kütükoğlu (1976); Issawi (1980a), pp. 86–100; for Ottoman trade with Germany, see Önsoy (1982); for trade with Austria, Bogert (1976); for trade with the United States, Gordon (1931) and Turgay (1982); for trade with France and Russia, Issawi (1980a), pp. 134–43. We might also point out that the role of native and particularly foreign merchant houses in the expansion of Ottoman foreign trade constitutes an important area of investigation that is beginning to be explored. See Mears (1924), chapter 15; Issawi (1980a), pp. 100–2; Owen (1981), pp. 88–9.

53. Based on unpublished foreign trade statistics of the United Kingdom. For full references, see the bibliography.
54. Based on France, Affaires Etrangères, *Correspondance Commerciale*, Smyrne for 1819–52 and on Great Britain, *Parliamentary Papers, Accounts and Papers*, 'Commercial Reports from Smyrne', for the years after 1863. For annual estimates of the imports and exports of Izmir based primarily on these sources, see Issawi (1980a), pp. 110–12.
55. See chapter 5.
56. We follow here the approach developed by Maizels (1969).
57. Based on published foreign trade statistics of the United Kingdom and France. For full references, see the bibliography.
58. Aybar (1939); also see section A1.1 of appendix 1.
59. See the discussion on pp. 23–7 above and also pp. 83–5.
60. See notes 23 and 25 above.
61. Shaw (1975).
62. See chapter 6.
63. Pamuk (1984).
64. See Eldem (1970), p. 308, who based his calculations primarily on official tax revenue data. While we agree that there was an increase in per capita income levels during this period, we are inclined to treat estimates based on tax revenue figures with caution due to problems associated with this type of data. For a discussion of the latter point, see Pamuk (1984), pp. 115–17.

3 Ottoman terms of trade against industrialized countries, 1854–1913

1. United Nations (1949). The principal author of this anonymous U.N. staff publication was Hans Singer. See Spraos (1980), p. 107.
2. Prebisch (1950) and Singer (1950). Prebisch argued on the basis of the British net barter terms of trade data published in United Nations (1949) that the total deterioration in the terms of trade of primary products between 1876–80 and 1938 was 41 per cent, or an average annual rate of 0.9 per cent.
3. See, among others, Ellsworth (1961); Kindleberger (1956); Morgan (1963); Spraos (1980). At the end of the 1960s, Emmanuel introduced a new dimension to the debate by arguing, within the framework of the labor theory of value, that to the extent that the wage gap between the center and the periphery was wider than the corresponding gap in the levels of productivity,

the resulting *level* of the terms of trade led to the transfer of surplus value towards the center countries. However, it does not follow from this argument of 'unequal exchange' that the terms of trade would also *move* against the periphery over time. For that position, Prebisch's argument regarding the asymmetry in wage increases between the center and the periphery is still necessary. See Emmanuel (1972); Amin (1974), pp. 64–90.

4. Spraos (1980), p. 120.

5. *Ibid.*, pp. 119–21.

6. This point is emphasized by Hymer and Resnick (1969) and Resnick (1970).

7. A striking example is the arrival of the Anatolian Railway at the Ankara and Konya provinces of Central Anatolia in the early 1890s. The British consul at Ankara credited the railroad with raising agricultural production by 50 per cent and prices 50 to 100 per cent between 1892 and 1895, an estimate generally substantiated by the scant statistics available. See Quataert (1973), chapter 8, p. 190; also Quataert (1977).

8. British Consular Commercial Reports are the best source for the developments in rural Anatolia during this period. See especially the reports from Izmir and Aleppo in *Parliamentary Papers, Accounts and Papers*, 'Commercial Reports' from Turkey for the years 1860–6. Also, 'Circular to Her Majesty's Consuls in the Ottoman Dominions Regarding Cotton Cultivation; Together with a Summary of their Replies', *Accounts and Papers* (1865), vol. 57; Sandford (1862); Kurmuş (1974), pp. 77–89; Owen (1981), pp. 111–12.

9. For the only previous study of the Ottoman terms of trade based on the official statistics after 1878, see Sönmez (1970).

10. See appendix 1 for details.

11. Separate price indices for Ottoman trade with each of these five countries were prepared as part of this study, although they are not presented in appendix 2.

12. See appendix 2, section A2.1. For shares of each of these countries in Ottoman trade with industrialized center countries and in total Ottoman foreign trade, see also chapter 2, tables 2.3 and 2.4.

13. See chapter 2, tables 2.3 and 2.4, for the share of Russia in Ottoman exports and imports during the nineteenth century.

14. The index drift problem discussed in appendix 2 was quite severe in the case of Ottoman–Russian price indices. Since the net barter terms of trade measured by Laspeyres price indices and that measured by Paasche price indices moved in opposite directions for the period 1830–1913 as a whole, it became impossible to state unambiguously in which direction the terms of trade moved. (See note 16 below for Laspeyres and Paasche indices.) This problem was due to the nature of the data and to the fact that Ottoman–Russian trade was overwhelmingly in agricultural commodities subject to violent fluctuations in prices and quantities. In addition, the Russian trade statistics were probably not free of the so-called exchange rate problem until 1897.

15. Spraos (1980), pp. 116–17.

16. While Laspeyres price indices use weights of the base period, (Q_0P_1/Q_0P_0), Paasche is based on current period weights, (Q_1P_1/Q_1P_0). The Fisher Ideal Price index equals the square root of their product.

17. In annually linked chain indices, the initial period and end periods, and possibly the number of commodities included in the indices, change every year.

18. Samuelson and Swamy (1974).

19. See chapter 2, tables 2.3 and 2.4.

20. For example, our calculations indicate that the share of freight and insurance in c.i.f. prices of Ottoman imports from the United Kingdom declined from 7.3 per cent in 1860 to 4.5 per cent in 1913. Similarly, the ratio of freight and insurance costs to f.o.b. prices of Ottoman exports to the same country declined from 15.0 per cent in 1860 to 9.8 per cent in 1913. For details see appendix 1. Also Spraos (1980), pp. 108, 115–16.

21. The regression results can be summarized as follows:
    (a) For the period 1854–1913:
       $ln\ TT = 4.688 - 0.00183t$ where
       $ln\ TT$ = natural logarithm of the Fisher terms of trade index
       t = time variable:
       Taking the antilogarithm of the constant term gives $TT = 108.6$ for the year 1853 (1880 = 100.0). The standard error for the time trend coefficient is 0.000866. Therefore, the time trend coefficient is statistically significant at the 2 per cent level.
       $R^2 = 0.072$
    (b) For the period 1858–1913:
       $ln\ TT = 4.616 - 0.0000963t$
       Taking the antilogarithm of the constant term gives $TT = 101.1$ for the year 1857. The standard error for the time trend coefficient is 0.000824. Hence, the time trend coefficient is not statistically significant at the 10 per cent level.
       $R^2 = 0.000253$

22. This is the same as pointing out that the classical measure of gains from trade and of changes in productivity, the double factoral terms of trade, moved strongly in favor of the center countries during the nineteenth century. For similar arguments, see Kindleberger (1956), p. 240; Amin (1974), pp. 79–85.

23. Imlah (1958), pp. 208–15.

24. Based on commodity price data for Turkish opium, madder root, olive oil and raw silk kindly supplied by A. J. Schwartz. These time-series data were used for the construction of the well-known Gayer–Rostow–Schwartz indices of British domestic prices for the first half of the nineteenth century. See Gayer, Rostow and Schwartz (1953).

25. Imlah (1958), pp. 94–7. The results of a study of the terms of trade between the United Kingdom and the Kingdom of Two Sicilies, an agriculture-based Mediterranean economy the composition of whose trade with the United Kingdom might be expected to resemble that of the Ottoman–U.K. trade, point to a similar conclusion: net barter terms of trade of the United

Kingdom declined by about 40 per cent between 1819–21 and 1849–51. See Glazier and Bandera (1972), pp. 24–7.

26. Based on an examination of the published foreign trade statistics of the respective countries and on the unpublished foreign trade statistics of the United Kingdom in the Public Record Office, Customs 8 and Customs 10 Series.

27. See the discussion in Imlah (1958), pp. 20–5. If detailed data for the earlier years were available, an earlier year might possibly emerge as a more appropriate year for the beginning of this sub-period.

28. For example, Church (1975).

29. See chapter 2, tables 2.1 and 2.2.

30. The impact of the Crimean War conjuncture on the Ottoman economy is described in detail in the British Consular Reports. See *Accounts and Papers*, 'Commercial Reports' from Turkey for the years 1854–7.

31. Imlah (1958), pp. 208–10.

32. *Ibid.*, p. 96.

33. For a study of the Egyptian economy with special reference to cotton during the American Civil War, see Owen (1969), chapter 4.

34. See chapter 2, tables 2.1 and 2.2.

35. For a recent recapitulation of the evidence in this respect, see Lewis (1978), appendices I and II. Also, Mitchell (1975).

36. See chapter 2, tables 2.1 and 2.2.

37. Kindleberger (1956), pp. 150–3.

38. *Ibid.*, pp. 53–4; Imlah (1958), pp. 94–7.

39. For a discussion of the case of cotton textiles in rural areas see chapter 6, pp. 123–6.

40. This may be a good place to compare briefly our results with those of the only study on Ottoman external terms of trade (Sönmez 1970). Despite the problems of coverage and pricing and other problems associated with the official Ottoman foreign trade statistics, in terms of short-term fluctuations, the results obtained by Sönmez for the period 1878–1913 are fairly close to those of the present study for the same period. Sönmez's calculations also indicate a rapid deterioration of the external terms of trade during the second half of the 1880s and a rapid improvement during 1890–1900. However, the magnitudes of these fluctuations differ considerably between the two studies.

   The absence of data for the period before 1878, especially for 1871–7, apparently led Sönmez to search for a single long-term trend for 1878–1913. As a result, he reached the conclusion that the Ottoman external terms of trade improved during this period. In contrast, we have emphasized in this study the importance of long-term fluctuations in the world economy. Consequently, rather than attempting to examine 1878–1913 as a whole, we showed that 1871–96 was a period of long-term deterioration and that 1896–1913 was a period of long-term improvement in Ottoman external terms of trade.

41. Based on official Ottoman statistics for the period after 1878 and on the statistics of other countries for the earlier years. See Aybar (1939).

42. These issues are discussed in greater detail in chapter 5.
43. Aybar (1939).
44. Eldem (1970), pp. 133–4; Verney and Dambmann (1900), pp. 183–4; Issawi (1966), pp. 60–2; for an important recent work on the Regie, see Quataert (1983), chapter 2.
45. 'The immediate effect of the creation of the Ottoman Régie was to diminish considerably tobacco cultivation in Asiatic Turkey. This is a phenomenon that has been observed in several centers: in Beirut, Lebanon, Haifa, Mosul, Latakia and Smyrna.' Verney and Dambmann (1900), pp. 183–4; also cited in Issawi, (1966), p. 60.
46. Issawi (1966), p. 61.
47. Eldem (1970), p. 134b; Issawi (1980a), pp. 252–3; Pech (1911); Corporation of Foreign Bondholders, Annual Reports for the years 1885–1913.
48. A brief history of the Ottoman customs duties during the nineteenth century is given in chapter 2.

4 Foreign capital in the Ottoman Empire, 1854–1913

1. Long-term fluctuations in Ottoman foreign trade and external terms of trade were examined in chapters 2 and 3.
2. See, for example, Blaisdell (1929); Morawitz (1902); du Velay (1903); Roumani (1927); Ducruet (1964); Yeniay (1964); also Suvla (1966); Owen (1981), chapter 4.
3. For example, in the Berlin Congress of 1878, when the Ottoman delegation argued that the war indemnity payments to Russia should be kept low because of the financial difficulties of the central government, the Russian side responded by claiming that only one-third of the tax revenues actually entered the Ottoman Treasury and the remaining two-thirds were expropriated by various intermediaries and provincial elements. See Milgrim (1975), pp. 301–2.
4. Lewis (1961), pp. 110–11; Issawi (1980a), pp. 329–31.
5. For a discussion of the financial difficulties and crises of the period before the formal start of external borrowing and their impact on the economy, see du Velay (1903). On attempts to print and circulate paper money, see Davison (1980).
6. For the hesitancy of the Ottoman central bureaucracy regarding borrowing in European financial markets, see Rodkey (1958). Also, Owen (1981), p. 100; Anderson (1964).
7. Also, Yeniay (1964); Suvla (1966).
8. See, for example, Yeniay (1964); Suvla (1966).
9. In order to calculate the effective rate of interest on Ottoman external borrowing, we solved the following equation for r for each new bond issue:

$$\text{Amount received by the Ottoman Treasury} = \sum_{j=1}^{n} \frac{(\text{Interest and principal payments})_j}{(1 + r)^j}$$

10. Wynne (1951), vol. II; Winkler (1933).
11. As a result of these purchases, the Ottoman navy became the third largest of its kind in Europe during the third quarter of the century. Davison (1963), pp. 264–6.
12. Annual figures for interest and principal payments on the outstanding debt are presented in tables A3.1 and A3.2 of appendix 3. For Ottoman budgets of the late 1860s, which include projected revenues, see *Accounts and Papers* (1870b). Estimated tax collection figures for the early 1870s are based on Shaw (1975). Estimates for annual Ottoman exports are presented in chapter 2 and appendix 1.
13. Blaisdell (1929), chapter 3.
14. Shaw (1975), p. 451. Since one important objective of these early budgets was to facilitate additional borrowing in European financial markets, these estimates probably exaggerated actual collections of the Treasury.
15. The cessation of capital exports from industrial Europe to the periphery can be seen clearly in the estimates prepared by Bloomfield. See Bloomfield (1968), pp. 42–4.
16. The early 1820s and the 1870s are regarded as the two periods with the highest number of defaults on government borrowing during the century preceding World War I. Honduras, Costa Rica, Santo Domingo, Paraguay, Spain, Bolivia, Guatemala, Liberia, Uruguay, Egypt and Peru also defaulted or obtained rescheduling between 1872 and 1875. See Borchard (1951), vol. I, pp. xx–xxi; Jenks (1938). The case of Egypt is examined at length in Landes (1958).
17. On the Ottoman Public Debt Administration, see the sources cited in note 2 above.
18. For the calculation of the effective rate of interest on Ottoman external borrowing, see note 9.
19. Similarities between the two periods can be extended to the Ottoman balance of payments picture. See appendix 6, particularly section 6.4 and tables A6.3, A6.4.
20. Based on our study of Ottoman external terms of trade; see chapter 3 and appendix 2 for details. Since we have a different base year for each sub-period in this calculation, total decline since 1855 (based on price levels in 1855) is less than the sum of percentage declines for the two sub-periods.
21. Chapter 3 and appendix 2, table A2.1.
22. Pech (1911). We might add that a large majority of the joint-stock companies operating in the Ottoman Empire before World War I were owned by foreign capital. See the discussion in Toprak (1982), pp. 39–40.
23. Our choice of the year 1888 was due to the fact that large amounts of German capital began to enter the Ottoman Empire in that year. See below, pp. 72–81.
24. Estimates arrived at by Vedat Eldem in his study of the sectoral and country of origin distribution of the foreign capital stock in 1914 are in basic agreement with our estimates for that year. Eldem utilized most of the sources used in this study, including Pech, though it is difficult to determine

whether his results were based on firm-level data. See Eldem (1970), pp. 190–1.

25. No study has been undertaken until now to estimate the over-time magnitudes and sectoral and country of origin distributions of foreign capital *flows*.

The only other estimate for the sectoral and country of origin distribution of the foreign capital stock in 1914 is that of İ. Hüsrev Tökin (1934). Novichev adopted these estimates (1937) and they have been recently quoted by Issawi (1966). However, there appear to be major problems with Tökin's estimates, not the least of which is his assertion that Germany was the leading investor, with France a distant second (compare with table 4.3). Tökin offers no explanation as to how he reached his estimates. His estimates can perhaps be taken as representing the 1914 distribution of foreign investments inside the 1923 borders of Turkey rather than in the Ottoman Empire as a whole. See Tökin (1934), p. 132.

Both the estimates by Eldem and Tökin and our estimates here include only paid-in capital and outstanding bonds in the calculation of foreign capital stock. It is quite possible that these firms undertook new investments by reducing dividends rather than increasing paid-in capital, particularly in sectors with high rates of profitability. For this reason, the figures provided on tables 4.2 and 4.3 do not reflect the stock market value or the cost of production of direct foreign investment.

The results of our reconstruction of Ottoman foreign trade presented in chapter 2 point to large trade deficits for the Empire for the period 1904–13. As we show in appendix 1, the actual deficits were smaller than the magnitudes indicated by the official Ottoman foreign trade statistics, but the question remains: how can we explain, within a balance of payments framework, the coexistence of large trade deficits along with a long-term trend where outflows of funds arising from foreign investment exceeded new inflows of capital? In order to answer this question and in order to check the reliability of our estimates regarding foreign trade and foreign investment, we attempted to reconstruct the Ottoman international balance of payments by estimating each item separately for each year. The results of this attempt are presented in appendix 6. They indicate that net revenues from some of the invisible items of the Ottoman balance of payments reached quite large magnitudes after the turn of the twentieth century. In addition, part of the trade deficits of the early 1910s were financed by short-term commercial credits. For details, see appendix 6 and tables A6.3 and A6.4.

26. For a discussion of the failure of foreign investment in Ottoman agriculture, see chapter 5, p. 102.

27. Paish (1914); Simon (1967).

28. Moulton and Lewis (1925), p. 21.

29. The sectoral distribution of German investment abroad was calculated from the following sources: Hoffman (1965); Börsen-Enquete Kommission (1893); Deutsche Reich (1907), p. 231; Deutsche Reich (1915), vol. I, pp. 117–18.

30. For a comparative study of the economic impact of railroads built by European capital in the Ottoman Empire and elsewhere in the periphery of the world economy, see Kaynak (1982).

31. For the Izmir–Aydin Railway, see Kurmuş (1974); the economic impact of the Anatolian Railway is examined in Quataert (1973, 1977). Also see Novichev (1966); Earle (1924).

32. Feis (1930), pp. 342ff.

33. See chapters 2 and 3.

34. See pp. 56–62 above and appendix 3; also Shaw (1975); Akarlı (1976), appendices for Ottoman Treasury revenues.

35. The fiscal difficulties and crises during the reign of Abdülhamid, as well as the search for solutions, are examined in Akarlı (1976).

36. Quataert (1977).

37. For a discussion of the importance the Ottoman bureaucracy and various contemporary observers of the Ottoman economy attached to the domestic production of wheat, see Parvus Efendi (1977), pp. 139–46; Akarlı (1976), chapter 3; also Kaynak (1982).

38. Eldem (1970), p. 152; Quataert (1973), p. 16 and appendices.

39. Quataert (1977), p. 153; also Rey (1913).

40. Eldem (1970), p. 290.

41. See table 4.1 and figure 4 above.

42. Du Velay (1903). See also Anderson (1964).

43. Kurmuş (1974).

44. The most important example of this withdrawal is the history of the Izmir–Kasaba Railroad Company. This firm was established by British capital in 1863. It was sold to a group of French and Belgian investors in 1894 when its paid-in capital amounted to £640,000. See Pech (1911).

45. See, for example, Owen (1981), p. 195. Also, Thobie (1977).

46. See tables 4.2 through 4.5. For the penetration of German capital into the Ottoman Empire, see Verney and Dambmann (1900); Earle (1924); Henderson (1948); Ortaylı (1981), chapters 1 and 2.

47. Our use of the terms 'formal' and 'informal' empire are derived from but do not coincide completely with Gallagher and Robinson (1953, 1961). See the discussion in chapter 1.

48. For changing shares of major European countries in Ottoman exports and imports, see tables 2.3 and 2.4 in chapter 2. We showed in that chapter that the British share in Ottoman external trade declined and the German share increased rapidly after 1880. However, in 1913 the United Kingdom continued to hold the largest shares in both Ottoman exports and imports.

49. Bailey (1942); also Temperley (1933); Anderson (1966), chapters 4–7.

50. Platt (1968).

51. Jenks (1927), chapter 10.

52. Blaisdell (1929).

53. It has been argued in a comparative study of British policy in China, Persia and Turkey that in the years preceding World War I the Foreign Office actively intervened in support of British investors in the Ottoman Empire.

Foreign Office support of the National Bank of Turkey is provided as a case in point. See McLean (1976). The evidence presented here shows that even if the case of the National Bank of Turkey was representative of Foreign Office policy during 1908–13, this support came too late. In fact, the failure of the bank in 1913 supports our thesis that British capital was unable to survive in this environment of inter-imperialist rivalry.

54. There is an extensive literature on German economic penetration into the Balkans and the Middle East. See, for example, Meyer (1951–2, 1955), Flaningam (1954–5); Feis (1930), chapters 14 and 15. British–German trade rivalry in the Ottoman Empire is examined by Hoffman (1964). British concern about German economic penetration into the Ottoman Empire and the sharp contrast between British and German methods can also be followed from a number of contemporary pieces such as Anonymous (1907).

55. See, for example, Platt (1968); Feis (1930), chapters 1–6, 14 and 15.

56. Verney and Dambmann (1900); Pech (1911); Earle (1924).

57. Keyder (1976), pp. 124–5.

58. Moulton and Lewis (1925), p. 20.

59. Ortaylı (1981), chapter 2.

60. Feis (1930), chapter 14.

5 Commodity production for world markets and relations of production in agriculture, 1840–1913

1. By 'core' areas we do not claim to make an analytical distinction between different areas of the empire. Rather, with the exception of the provinces of Syria and Iraq, we are referring to those areas that remained part of the Empire until the 1910s.

2. See chapter 2, pp. 23–7.

3. Issawi (1980a), pp. 80–2, indicates that total exports from the five major ports of Northern Greece and Anatolia increased from £2,185,000 in the 'early 1840s' to £13,200,000 in 1910–12. The rate of expansion of exports from these areas was actually higher due to the emergence of secondary ports in the late nineteenth and early twentieth centuries. Moreover 1911–12 were war years and export volumes were considerably higher in 1913. For the relative importance of different Anatolian ports in 1890, see Maliye Tetkik Kurulu (1970) and Cuinet (1891–4).

4. See appendex 1, section A1.1, for the commodity composition of Ottoman exports.

5. It should be stressed that increases in tithe collections or assessments do not necessarily indicate increases in the volume of agricultural production. More precisely, the expansion of agricultural production probably remained well behind increases in tithe revenues of the Ottoman Treasury during this period. This was primarily due to the increasing effectiveness of the state in reducing the share accruing to the tax collectors and other middlemen. In interpreting year-to-year changes in tithe revenues it should also be noted that the rate of taxation out of the gross agricultural product

did not remain constant: it was raised above 10 per cent to as much as 15 per cent during periods of crisis for the state Treasury (see note 36 below). Our estimate for the increase in agricultural production attempts to take these factors into account in a rather crude way.

The following data provided the bases for our estimate:

(a) Tithe assessments for the entire Empire increased by 61 per cent between 1863 and 1874 (source: Shaw (1975), p. 452). This was a period of roughly constant prices for Ottoman agricultural commodities.

(b) After the War of 1877–8, within the smaller boundaries of the Empire, tithe assessments for the Empire increased by 71 per cent and tithe collections rose by 69 per cent between 1887 and 1910 (source: Shaw (1975), pp. 452–3). The prices of the Ottoman agricultural mix were probably slightly lower in 1910 than they were in 1887, primarily due to the significant decline in wheat prices.

(c) V. Eldem estimates, on the basis of region by region tithe assessment figures, that gross agricultural production of the Empire, measured in constant 1913 prices, increased by 44 per cent between 1889 and 1911 (source: Eldem (1970), p. 308).

(d) Tithe collections in the Anatolian provinces of the Empire increased by approximately 45 per cent between 1882 and 1902 (source: Quataert (1973), appendix A, table B).

6. Based on gross national product and net agricultural production estimates given in Eldem (1970), pp. 302, 283.

7. See chapter 2 for long-term fluctuations in Ottoman foreign trade and how they were associated with long-term fluctuations in the levels of economic activity in the industrialized center countries during the nineteenth century.

8. The Anatolian Railway was an exception to this pattern as a large part of the cereal shipments from Central Anatolia was consumed in the Istanbul area. Quataert (1977).

9. Issawi (1980a), pp. 34–5.

10. Quataert (1977).

11. Consider the following simple and admittedly crude calculation:

(a) Let us assume that agricultural production of the areas considered in this study doubled between 1840 and 1912 (based on tithe revenue figures: see p. 83 for text and note 5).

$Q_{1840} = 100 \qquad Q_{1912} = 200$

(b) We know that approximately 25 per cent of Q_{1912} was exported.

$X_{1912} = 50.$

(See text above and note 6.)

(c) Volume of agricultural commodity exports from the core areas of the Empire increased tenfold between 1840 and 1912.

$X_{1840} = 5$

(d) Considering the dependence of Istanbul on imported foodstuffs, the share of domestic markets in the domestically consumed portion of the agricultural production is close to the share of urban population in total population:

$D_{1840} = 0.17 \ (Q_{1840} - X_{1840}) = 16$

$D_{1912} = 0.22 \ (Q_{1912} - X_{1912}) = 33$

    (e) Then, the aggregate rate of marketization in agriculture is

$M_{1840} = (D_{1840} + X_{1840}) / Q_{1840} = 0.21$

$M_{1912} = (D_{1912} + X_{1912}) / Q_{1912} = 0.42$

    (f) Therefore, approximately three-fourths of the expansion in commodity production in agriculture that occurred between 1840 and 1912 was induced by world market demand:

$$(X_{1912} - X_{1840}) / ((D_{1912} + X_{1912}) - (D_{1840} + X_{1840})) = 45 / 62 = 0.73$$

12. Ottoman Empire, Orman ve Maadin ve Ziraat Nezareti (1910) and (1911); agricultural statistics for 1907 and 1909, cited in Güran (1978).

13. Aybar (1939), reprint of official Ottoman foreign trade statistics for 1878–1913. Based on *Accounts and Papers*, 'Commercial Reports'. Quataert (1980), p. 40, states that nine agricultural commodities (cereals, grapes, tobacco, figs, raw cotton, valonia, opium, hazelnuts and olive oil) accounted for 70 per cent of total exports from the major ports in Anatolia around 1900. This figure is not inconsistent with the official Ottoman statistics, since wheat, barley and other cereals are aggregated as one commodity, and exports from the entire Empire should be expected to be more diversified than exports from major Anatolian ports. See also appendix 1, section A1.1.

14. Based on *Accounts and Papers* (1860–76), 'Annual Statement of the Trade of the United Kingdom'.

15. The specific economic form, in which unpaid surplus labor is pumped out of direct producers, determines the relationship of rulers and ruled. It is always the direct relationship of the owners of the conditions of production to the direct producers . . . which reveals the innermost secret, the hidden basis of the entire social structure, and with it the political form of the relation of sovereignty and dependence, in short, the corresponding specific form of the state. (K. Marx (1967), p. 791)

16. For a recent statement on this point, see Boratav (1980), pp. 12–15.

17. Veinstein (1976). In an important recent work B. McGowan reaches a similar conclusion for the Balkans during the seventeenth and eighteenth centuries. Paralleling the conclusions of Veinstein's work, McGowan's findings 'demote the importance of investigating *chiftlik* agriculture, and at the same time . . . reassert the importance of the fiscal struggle between Imperial center and the periphery'. McGowan (1981), p. 171. See also Lampe and Jackson (1982), chapters 1, 3 and 5.

18. Lewis (1968), pp. 90–2; *Accounts and Papers* (1870a), 'Report on Land Tenure in Turkey', p. 282; Steeg (1924), p. 238; Issawi (1980a), p. 202. For the impact of the confiscation measures on Eastern Anatolia, see selections in Issawi (1980a), pp. 220–4; *Accounts and Papers*, 'Commercial Report' from Diyarbakır for the year 1856; on the Black Sea region, see *Accounts and Papers*, 'Commercial Reports' from Trabzon for the year 1867.

19. For legal aspects of Ottoman land tenure system in the nineteenth century, see Steeg (1924); also Barkan (1940); Issawi (1980a), p. 202; Eldem (1970), p. 70.

20. Issawi (1980a), p. 1.
21. *Ibid.*, pp. 17–19. For the annual estimates of nineteenth-century immigration into the Ottoman Empire from different outlying areas, see appendix 6, table A6.1. For immigration into the core areas of the Empire, see Eren (1966); Karpat (1974) and Karpat (1985).
22. *Accounts and Papers*, 'Commercial Reports' from Ankara, Konya and Antalya for the years 1893–1913.
23. *Accounts and Papers*, 'Commercial Reports' from Adana for the years 1873–1913.
24. *Accounts and Papers*, 'Commercial Reports' from consuls in Anatolia, Thrace and Northern Greece, 1854–1913. Also see Ubicini (1856), pp. 325–8; Köy ve Ziraat Kalkınma Kongresi (1938), pp. 96–146, 204–10.
25. For a sampling of reports on the availability of large amounts of uncultivated land and 'excessive' land–labor ratios in different parts of the Empire, see *Accounts and Papers*, 'Commercial Reports' for Monastir 1854, Bursa 1854–7, Diyarbakır 1856, 1862, 1863, Aleppo 1874, Edirne 1889, Ankara 1895. Also Güran (1978), pp. 4–9; Nickoley (1924), p. 291; Ubicini (1856); Köy ve Ziraat Kalkınma Kongresi (1938).
26. Nickoley (1924), p. 291; Güran (1978), p. 37.
27. Issawi (1980a), pp. 206–7.
28. For the magnitudes of increases in area under cultivation and total agricultural production between 1909–10 and 1914–15, see Ottoman Empire, Orman ve Maadin ve Ziraat Nezareti (1910) and (1911), summarized in Güran (1978), p. 5; Eldem (1970), pp. 69–87; Nickoley (1924), pp. 284–5, 291–2.
29. *Accounts and Papers*, 'Commercial Reports' from Izmir, Adana and Salonica. For the Izmir–Aydın area, see also Quataert (1973), chapter 7; Kurmuş (1974).
30. Chayanov (1966); Friedman (1978), pp. 559–64.
31. Tithe revenues that actually entered the Ottoman Treasury rose from 4.25 million Ottoman Liras in 1887–8 to 7.18 million in 1910–11 (1 British pound = 1.11 Ottoman Liras). Tithe revenues made up 27.1 per cent of all tax revenues in 1887–8 and 25.0 per cent of all tax revenues in 1910–11. Animal tax (*ağnam*) collections added 11.5 and 7.6 per cent respectively. Shaw (1975), pp. 451–3. It is not clear what part of this substantial increase in tithe revenues was due to increases in agricultural production, and what part was due to more effective control of the tax collections and tax collectors by the state.
32. *İltizam*, year-to-year or short-term tax-farming system, was increasingly replaced by the *malikane*, lifetime tax-farming system during the eighteenth century. See Genç (1975).
33. Shaw (1975); Quataert (1973), chapter 1.
34. During the late 1860s, when the budgetary deficits of the state could not be eliminated by large volumes of external borrowing, the tithe rate was raised to 15 per cent in 1868 and to 12.5 per cent during 1869–72. The rate was 12 per cent during 1873 and 1874 when the worst famine of the century hit

Central Anatolia. The rate was raised again to 11.75 per cent during the 1880s as the Great Depression of the world economy and large debt payments to the Ottoman Public Debt Administration intensified the fiscal crisis of the state.

35. *Accounts and Papers* (1870a), p. 283. For a detailed list of the different forms of taxes paid by the rural classes see *Accounts and Papers*, 'Commercial Report' from Trabzon for the year 1868. For road tax which could be paid either in cash or in labor services in road building, *Accounts and Papers*, 'Commercial Reports' from Trabzon 1867, 1872, 1883, Salonica 1868; *Accounts and Papers* (1884), 'Special Report on Road Building in Turkey'. Also, Shaw (1975), pp. 432–3, 457.

36. For the tax burden of the small peasantry, see Aktan (1966); Köy ve Ziraat Kalkınma Kongresi (1938), pp. 65–70, 206 and *passim*. For the arbitrary rule of tax collectors, *Accounts and Papers*, 'Commercial Report' from Aleppo for the year 1874.

37. Güran (1978), pp. 133ff. For a sampling of the rates of interest charged by usurers, see Issawi (1980a), pp. 341–3. *Accounts and Papers*, 'Commercial Report' from Aleppo for the year 1874.

38. For a detailed description of the living conditions of Anatolian peasants, see *Accounts and Papers* (1871), 'Condition of the Industrial Classes in Foreign Countries', pp. 735–44.

39. Estimates indicate that urbanization in Northern Greece and Anatolia as a whole remained limited during the nineteenth century. The size of both the total population in the core areas of the Empire approximately doubled between 1830 and 1912. The share of the urban population in the total is estimated to have increased from 17 to 22 per cent during the same period. Issawi (1980a), pp. 34–5.

40. Barkan (1940); Güran (1978), p. 136; *Accounts and Papers*, 'Commercial Reports', *passim*.

41. For example, *Accounts and Papers*, 'Commercial Report' from Trabzon 1880.

42. *Accounts and Papers*, 'Commercial Reports' from Diyarbakır 1856, Kavala 1858, Monastir 1859, Trabzon 1867, Ankara 1894.

43. *Accounts and Papers* (1870a), 'Report on Land Tenure in Turkey', pp. 276–92.

44. *Ibid.*, p. 286.

45. *Ibid.*, pp. 285–7. For a region by region distribution of farm size in Northern Greece, Thrace and some parts of Anatolia in 1863, see the table prepared by Issawi (1980a), p. 203. For more detailed descriptions of the basic forms of tenancy, see appendix 4.

46. Eight hectares for a household with one pair of oxen, according to Palgrave. See *Accounts and Papers* (1870a), 'Report on Land Tenure in Turkey'.

47. These middle peasants would, in effect, be bringing in their capital. In other words, in this case the sharecropper was not only a laborer but was also his own capitalist. See Marx (1967), vol. III, p. 803.

48. Chayanov (1966); Boratav (1980).

49. On this issue see, amongst others, Kurmuş (1974), *passim*.
50. Boratav (1980), pp. 84–9.
51. *Accounts and Papers*, 'Commercial Reports', *passim*.
52. *Accounts and Papers* (1870a), 'Report on Land Tenure in Turkey', p. 284. This portion of the report has been reprinted in Issawi (1980a), pp. 223–4.
53. For regional variations in sharecropping arrangements, see *Accounts and Papers* (1870a), 'Report on Land Tenure in Turkey', dispatches from consuls in Istanbul, Edirne, Çanakkale, Trabzon, Monastir, Salonica, pp. 273–312. A summary is available in Issawi (1980a), pp. 217–18. For an example of different forms of tenancy coexisting in a given area, see *Accounts and Papers*, 'Commercial Report' from Trabzon for the year 1880. Also Güran (1978), pp. 133–4. Also see appendix 4 for a detailed description of one case.
54. *Accounts and Papers* (1870a), 'Report on Land Tenure in Turkey', p. 289.
55. *Accounts and Papers*, 'Commercial Reports' from Izmir, Adana and Salonica, 1896–1913. Also see appendix 4.
56. Issawi (1980a), pp. 202, 220–3; *Accounts and Papers* (1870a), 'Report on Land Tenure in Turkey', pp. 282–4.
57. The inclusion of Syria and Iraq in Palgrave's survey could not have biased his estimates in the direction of small holdings since we would expect that distribution of land ownership was more unequal in these provinces of the Empire.
58. Boratav (1980), pp. 22–4.
59. For changing patterns of land ownership and tenancy in other areas of the Ottoman Empire, in Syria and the Fertile Crescent, see Smilianskaya (1958); Warriner (1944); Baer (1962, 1983).
60. *Accounts and Papers*, 'Commercial Reports' from Diyarbakır, Aleppo, Erzurum, Van, for the years 1900–13.
61. *Accounts and Papers*, 'Commercial Reports' from Diyarbakır and Van, various years.
62. *Accounts and Papers*, 'Commercial Reports' from Harput, various years.
63. *Accounts and Papers* (1870a), 'Report on Land Tenure in Turkey'; Issawi (1980a), pp. 220–1; *Accounts and Papers*, 'Commercial Report' from Diyarbakır for the year 1856. For the experience of the Balkan areas of the Empire during the nineteenth century, see Lampe and Jackson (1982), chapter 8; Todorov (1971, 1980).
64. The analysis of the patterns of land ownership is inevitably complicated by the presence of large numbers of nomads in the region. According to one estimate, which appears rather high, the nomadic population in the provinces of Erzurum and Diyarbakır exceeded 600,000 at the end of the 1860s. This, if true, would mean that the nomads comprised as much as half of the total population of these two provinces at the time. See *Accounts and Papers* (1870c), 'Condition of the Industrial Classes in Foreign Countries', dispatch from the consul in Diyarbakır.
65. Barkan (1940); *Accounts and Papers*, 'Commercial Report' from Diyarbakır for the year 1863.

66. *Accounts and Papers*, 'Commercial Report' from Diyarbakır 1863.
67. *Accounts and Papers*, 'Commercial Report' from Diyarbakır 1863, 1867, 1884, Van 1884.
68. For the observations of young Ziya Gökalp who grew up in the region, see Beysanoğlu (1956). For a collection of cases of land ownership disputes during the twentieth century which throws considerable light on the past, see Yalman (1971).
69. *Accounts and Papers*, 'Commercial Reports' from Erzurum, Harput; Issawi (1980a), pp. 216–18, 224. While examining patterns of land ownership and tenancy during the late 1920s and early 1930s, İ Hüsrev Tökin points to a similar ethnic distinction, without the Armenians, between the Kurdish settlements of the Southern tier where lord–peasant bonds were very strong and the small and middle holdings in the Turkish villages in Erzurum. Tökin (1934), pp. 176–86. Also see Sussnitzki (1966).
70. *Accounts and Papers*, 'Commercial Reports' from Erzurum 1906, Van 1879, 1906, Aleppo 1902, Diyarbakır 1907; Issawi (1980a), pp. 216–20; Quataert (1973), chapter 7.
71. Svoronos (1956); Masson (1911); Paris (1957); Veinstein (1976); Ülker (1974).
72. See chapter 2.
73. Nickoley (1924), pp. 286–91; Quataert (1980), pp. 40–2; Issawi (1980a), pp. 236–68.
74. Eldem (1970), pp. 164–5; Issawi (1980a), pp. 103–5, 108–11.
75. Issawi (1980a), p. 203.
76. *Ibid.*
77. Mouzelis (1978), pp. 17–22.
78. *Accounts and Papers*, 'Commercial Report' from Monastir for the year 1859.
79. Issawi (1980a), p. 203.
80. *Ibid.*, p. 202.
81. İnalcık (1973).
82. See, for example, evidence cited in *Accounts and Papers* (1870a), 'Report on Land Tenure in Turkey', dispatches by consuls in Monastir and Salonica.
83. Also, see Güran (1978), p. 86. For levels of agricultural wages, see Issawi (1980a), pp. 204, 37–43.
84. *Accounts and Papers* (1870a), 'Report on Land Tenure in Turkey', p. 284.
85. *Ibid.*
86. Rougon (1892), pp. 73–4.
87. Chapter 3 and appendix 2.
88. For long-term fluctuations in land prices, see Issawi (1980a), pp. 206–7.
89. See sources cited in note 42.
90. *Accounts and Papers*, 'Commercial Reports' from Salonica, Izmir, Adana, Konya. Quataert (1973), chapter 7; Kurmuş (1974), pp. 112–19.
91. Kurmuş (1974), pp. 102–3.
92. The British were not alone in their hopes and attempts at colonization of Anatolia. For the little-known case of a full-fledged German colony in the Amasya region, see *Accounts and Papers* (1871), 'Condition of the Industrial Classes in Foreign Countries', p. 733.

93. Issawi (1970, 1980a), pp. 124–6.
94. *Accounts and Papers*, 'Commercial Reports' from Trabzon, Samsun.
95. *Accounts and Papers*, 'Commercial Report' from Trabzon for the year 1867.
96. Issawi (1980a), p. 203.
97. *Accounts and Papers*, 'Commercial Report' from Antalya for the years 1897–9.
98. Ener (1961), pp. 200–17.
99. United States, Bureau of Foreign Commerce, *Commercial Relations of the United States with Foreign Countries*, Commercial Report from Adana for the year 1862.
100. *Accounts and Papers*, 'Commercial Reports' from Adana for the years 1871, 1872 and 1874.
101. *Accounts and Papers*, 'Commercial Report' from Adana for the year 1872; Ener (1961); for a study of the settlement policies of the state in this region, see Gould (1973).
102. Novichev (1966); Quataert (1973), chapter 2; Pamuk (1979).
103. Bruck (1919); Novichev (1966); Quataert (1973), chapter 2.
104. Quataert (1973), p. 168; Novichev (1966), p. 69. For cotton cultivation in the plain of Adana, see Bruck (1919), reprinted, in part, in Issawi (1980a), pp. 242–5, *Accounts and Papers* (1908), 'Special Report on Cotton Cultivation in Anatolia'; Novichev (1966).
105. *Accounts and Papers*, 'Commercial Report' from Ankara for the year 1873.
106. Quataert (1977); Novichev (1966), pp. 66–8.
107. Quataert (1977), p. 151.
108. Quataert (1973), appendices.
109. Novichev (1966), p. 66. However, in view of the limited reliability of the other figures cited by Novichev, these statistics should be treated with caution.
110. Quataert (1977), p. 149.
111. *Accounts and Papers*, 'Commercial Reports' from Ankara, Konya.
112. *Accounts and Papers*, 'Commercial Report' from Ankara, 1895; Issawi (1980a), pp. 230–1; Eren (1966).
113. Issawi (1980a), pp. 230–1; *Accounts and Papers*, 'Commercial Reports' from Ankara, Konya, various years.
114. H. Friedman makes a similar argument in explaining why commodity-producing households began replacing large capitalist farms employing wage laborers in wheat production during this period, especially in the North American plains. She also argues that the direction of technical progress did not favor capitalist farms during this period. See Friedman (1978), pp. 559–71.
115. *Ibid.*, pp. 574–8.
116. Quataert (1973), chapter 2; Issawi (1980a), pp. 229–31.
117. Quataert (1973); Kurmuş (1974); Güran (1978); Issawi (1980a).

6 The decline and resistance of Ottoman cotton textiles, 1820–1913

1. D. H. Thorner was one of the first scholars to examine the alleged phenomenon of de-industrialization. He implicitly defined de-industrialization as a decline in the proportion of the working population engaged in secondary industry or a decline in the proportion of total population dependent on secondary industry. See Thorner (1962); also Bagchi (1976). For a sampling of recent case studies, see Resnick (1970); Feuerwerker (1970); Issawi (1982), chapter 8; Twomey (1983). For the relevant employment and production figures in the case of British textiles, see Deane and Cole (1964), pp. 282ff.
2. Bagchi (1976), pp. 148ff; Owen (1984).
3. Deane (1965), pp. 84–99.
4. Todorov (1969); *Accounts and Papers* (1867–8), vol. 68, 'Commercial Report' from Edirne for the year 1867.
5. Faroqhi (1979).
6. Based on Svoronos (1956); Paris (1957); Masson (1911). Total domestic consumption is based on our estimates presented in table 6.1.
7. İnalcık (1981).
8. In this respect eighteenth-century Ottoman cotton textiles manufacturing cannot be compared with its flourishing counterpart in India, whose products were being kept out of the British market only by strongly protectionist measures. Alavi (1980).
9. Stoianovich (1960); Issawi (1982), chapter 8.
10. As we state elsewhere, this discussion excludes Egypt.
11. For example, compare the woolen textiles production and trade in Bulgaria, as analyzed in Todorov (1969), with textiles manufacturing in Syria, as described by Novichev (1937), reprinted in Issawi (1980a), pp. 300–3, and in *Accounts and Papers*, 'Commercial Reports' from Aleppo and Damascus, *passim*.
12. Novichev (1937), reprinted in Issawi (1980a), pp. 300–3.
13. As late as 1889, an official commission on 'industrial reform' recommended that the state attempts at industrialization should be based not on the factory system but on the existing guilds. Ortaylı (1979). See also Issawi (1980a), pp. 303–5.
14. Around Diyarbakır in the 1850s, the merchants gave peasant women 9 pounds of raw cotton in exchange for 6 pounds of hand-spun yarn. *Accounts and Papers* (1857), Second Session, vol. 38, 'Commercial Report' from Diyarbakir.
15. Direct and explicit references to the putting-out system in weaving in the 'Commercial Reports' of the British Consuls during the sixty-year period preceding World War I are very few in number. The most detailed reference, a report from Erzurum in 1870, indicates that in the weaving of standard coarse cotton cloth putting-out was quite widespread in the Erzurum–Diyarbakir area. The report estimates that there were 1,560 urban and 8,240 part-time, rural weavers of whole cotton cloth in that area.

Accounts and Papers (1871), vol. 68, 'Report from Erzurum on the Condition of the Industrial Classes'.

One area where the putting-out system was the dominant form was the weaving of Oriental carpets organized by European capital after the 1880s. However, since the very definition of the commodity precludes the adoption of more advanced technology, this case is of limited relevance for our purposes. See Kurmuş (1974), pp. 128–35; Issawi (1980a), pp. 306–9.

16. Before the middle of the century, production of cotton in these areas of the Empire was intended, to an important extent, for local consumption and it was quite dispersed. This pattern changed substantially with the disappearance of hand spinning and the concentration of cotton cultivation for export markets in a few areas.

17. For per capita consumption levels of woolen and cotton textiles in the 1820s, see table 6.1 below and section A5.2 of appendix 5. Also Urquhart (1833), p. 149. For early nineteenth-century Britain, see Deane and Cole (1964), pp. 182–201.

18. This account is based on a detailed study of the British Consular Reports from the Ottoman Empire during the 1850s and 1860s. *Accounts and Papers*, 'Commercial Reports' from Turkey, *passim*.

19. Based primarily on Issawi (1980a), pp. 17–36; see also table 5.3 in chapter 5.

20. See chapter 5 on the commercialization of Ottoman agriculture.

21. Sarc (1940), pp. 432–3, considers the Industrial Revolution as the basic cause of Ottoman de-industrialization. He cites the Free Trade Treaties as a secondary factor. Kurmuş goes as far as questioning the link between the Treaties and Ottoman de-industrialization. See Kurmuş (1981, 1983).

22. Shaw (1975).

23. *Accounts and Papers* (1859), Second Session, vol. 30, 'Commercial Report' from Bursa for the years 1858 and 1862; vol. 59, 'Commercial Report' from Aleppo for the year 1861; Puryear (1935), p. 127. Shaw (1975) gives the inland duty – Karagümrük – as 8 per cent; *Accounts and Papers* (1890), vol. 77, 'Commercial Report' from Aleppo for the year 1889.

24. Urban weavers began to use imported yarn at an early stage. If we assume that about two-thirds of the total value of cotton cloth was added at the weaving and finishing stages, the effective rate of taxation on the domestic weaving and finishing activities for cotton cloth transported within the Empire can be calculated from the standard formula

$$E_T = \frac{0.12 - \frac{1}{3}(0.05)}{\frac{2}{3}}$$

as being slightly over 15 per cent (12 per cent is the rate of taxation of exports and inland trade of finished cloth, and 5 per cent is the rate of taxation of imported yarn). In contrast, imported cloth was subject to 5 per cent duty until 1861 and to only 8 per cent until 1907.

25. A large compilation of these observations can be derived from Sarc (1940); Issawi (1980a); Issawi (1982), chapter 8; Ubicini (1856). A much more comprehensive account of the short- and long-term fluctuations in the

number of looms in operation in Syria and to a lesser extent in Eastern Anatolia after the 1840s is available from the annual reports of the British Consuls. *Accounts and Papers*, 'Commercial Reports' from Aleppo, Damascus, Diyarbakır, Erzurum and elsewhere.

26. The period 1820–2 was chosen in order to assess the situation in the aftermath of the Napoleonic Wars and at the beginning of the offensive by British manufactures. The period 1840–2 reflects the state of affairs when the Free Trade Treaties were signed and at the beginning of three decades of rapid integration of the Empire into world markets. The picture in 1840–2 is also important for determining the extent to which imports had invaded the domestic market before the Treaties were signed. The period 1870–2 signals the end of the mid-century boom for the world economy, a critical turning point for the Ottoman Empire, since the rate of growth of foreign trade during the three decades until 1873 was not matched until World War I.

The interval 1880–2 facilitated comparison with the later period, since the Empire lost a substantial amount of territory and population after the Russian War of 1877–8. Because of the secession of a considerable amount of population and territory from the Empire after the Balkan Wars of 1912–13, we have been forced to choose an early cut-off date, 1909–11. It is clear from the available data that 1912 and especially 1913 were years of exceptionally high rates of growth of total imports and imports of textiles in the remaining areas of the Empire. For further details regarding this periodization of Ottoman foreign trade, see chapter 2.

27. Ottoman Empire, Ticaret ve Ziraat Nezareti (1917), edited and reprinted by A. G. Ökçün, 1970, pp. 131–40, 148–53.

28. The estimates for the domestic factories' production levels of cotton yarn and cloth were based on a detailed study of their history. We briefly deal with this issue in pp. 126–7 below. In addition, the Ottoman Industrial Census of 1913 provides production figures for the factories in the Marmara and Izmir regions. See Ottoman Empire, Ticaret ve Ziraat Nezareti (1917).

29. Estimating the volume of hand spinning of cotton yarn, a relatively minor component of identity (1), proved more difficult. Evidence cited in the British Consular Reports indicates that most, but not all, hand spinning bf cotton yarn had been destroyed by competition from imports by the early 1870s. See *Accounts and Papers*, 'Commercial Reports' from Turkey, *passim*. A recent study of handicrafts weaving in the Denizli province of Western Central Anatolia cites 1872 as the approximate date until which hand spinning of cotton yarn dominated in this interior province. Cillov (1949), p. 75. On the other hand, a Consular Report from Van in 1903 indicated that hand spinning continued to survive in that remote area. See *Accounts and Papers* (1904), vol. 101, 'Commercial Report' from Van for the year 1903. We adopted an estimate of 3,000 tons for the early 1870s. Taking into account the long-term rhythms of commercialization of the rural areas, and rates of commercialization as discussed in the main text, we assumed that the level of hand spinning of cotton yarn was reduced to 1,000 tons by 1909–11.

Our estimate for the size of the domestic market in 1909–11, which is given in table 6.1, is very close to the statistic cited in the Ottoman Industrial Census of 1913. The latter gives total consumption figures for a smaller area and population after the Balkan Wars of 1912–13, but we also know that 1913 witnessed a sharp increase in the level of imports, by far the most important component of cotton textiles consumption. See Ottoman Empire, Ticaret ve Ziraat Nezareti (1917), the 1970 reprint by Ökçün, pp. 148–53. Also Eldem (1970), p. 41.

30. Eldem (1970), p. 308.

31. Income and price effects, respectively, as the determinants of demand for cotton textiles.

32. See chapter 2 and appendix 1.

33. Boratav, Ökçün and Pamuk (1985).

34. Data on increases in per capita cotton textile consumption levels in nineteenth-century industrialized economies can provide only limited guidance in this respect, since they reveal substantially higher rates of growth of per capita income. Our crude estimates indicate that in Britain per capita consumption of cotton cloth increased by as much as tenfold between 1805 and 1860, from 0.6 kg. to 6.0 kg. per person per year; only to decline to 3.5 kg. by 1900 as woolen textiles gained some of their relative share back. According to our estimates, per capita consumption of woolen textiles increased from 1.8 kg. in 1805 to 3.3 kg. in 1860 and to 5.5 kg. in 1900. These estimates are based on Deane and Cole (1964), pp. 182–98. These calculations exclude imports into Britain, which might have been relatively important for cotton cloth early in the century. In Japan, per-capita consumption of cotton cloth increased by more than 250 per cent between 1870 and 1910. M. Yasuzawa (1982), pp. 45–6. In sharp contrast, per capita consumption of cotton cloth appears to have increased only marginally in China between 1871–80 and 1901–10. Information based on A. Feuerwerker (1970).

35. Urquhart (1833), pp. 149–50; the emphasis is ours.

36. Since each ton of imported yarn corresponds to an equal volume of domestic weaving, in calculating the approximate share of imports in the domestic market we added to the imports of cloth half of the volume of imports of yarn and divided the sum by the estimated total consumption given in Alternative II.

37. Available information from contemporary observers points in the same direction. Reports of the beginning of European competition can be traced to the 1820s and even earlier, but most observations of decline and destruction come after the mid-1840s. See sources cited in notes 39 and 40, especially Sarc (1940). It should be noted that these observers were concerned primarily with urban manufacturing activity. As a result, little can be extracted from their reports regarding the disappearance of hand spinning of yarn, which was an overwhelmingly rural activity of rural production for the immediate consumption of the household. An important exception is Urquhart (1833), pp. 142–53.

38. These changes might have affected our estimates in a number of ways. There were considerable differences in the clothing habits of the population

between the seceding and remaining areas of the Empire, which were in effect differences in the levels of per capita consumption of cotton, woolen and other textile products. It is also possible that the migration of approximately 1 million people to Anatolia after the War of 1877–8 led to changes in the patterns of consumption of textiles in the remaining areas of the Empire, or that the consumption patterns had not yet recovered by 1880–2 from the effects of the war.

39. Urquhart (1833), p. 150; the Ottoman Commission on Industrial Reform, founded in 1866, traces the beginnings of decline in the Istanbul area to 30 to 40 years before that date. Sarc (1940), p. 428, citing Nuri (1922).

40. See observations cited in Issawi (1980b), p. 470; also Sarc (1940), *passim.*

41. *Accounts and Papers*, 'Commercial Reports' from Diyarbakır, Erzurum and Ankara, various years.

42. See chapter 5 of this volume.

43. Feuerwerker (1970), p. 375; Deane (1965), p. 86. Also see note 47.

44. Feuerwerker (1970), pp. 366, 375; *Accounts and Papers* (1887), vol. 86, 'Commercial Report' from Erzurum for the year 1885.

45. This is the way Thorner (1962) posed the problem.

46. In that case, the amount of 'full-time' employment provided by cotton textiles would have been 75,500 in 1820–2, with 57,500 in spinning and the rest in weaving (see table 6.1 and the average production coefficients cited in the text). For 1820–2, the population of the Empire within its 1911 borders is estimated at 13.5 million. In 1870–2, Ottoman cotton textiles provided 'full-time' employment for 103,750 people (see table 6.2 below). The population of the same areas is estimated at 18.5 million for that interval.

47. A shift in the clothing habits of the population implies, of course, that the invasion of Ottoman markets by cotton textiles imports also led to the decline of domestic woolen textiles.

48. Urquhart (1833), p. 149.

49. Imports of yarn expanded by 6,050 tons, and the output of domestic mills not industrially woven by 3,500 tons, while the volume of hand-spun yarn declined by 1,000 tons.

50. Until the last decade of the century, British yarn dominated the Ottoman market, on average accounting for about three-fourths of all imports. Starting in the late 1890s, cheaper imports from Italy and India expanded their share of the market. For details, see table A5.2 in appendix 5.

51. Imported British yarn was available in Sivas in 1835. Issawi (1980a), p. 298. On the other hand, hand-spun yarn was still important in the city of Diyarbakır in the second half of the 1850s. In remote Van, which, aside from exporting a limited amount of wool, remained isolated from long-distance markets, home spinning survived until after the turn of the century because of access to raw cotton from Iran. *Accounts and Papers* (1857), Second Session, vol. 38, 'Commercial Report' from Diyarbakır for the year 1856; (1904), vol. 101, part 1, 'Commercial Report' from Van for the year 1903.

52. A Western observer made the following comment on rural home weaving at the beginning of the twentieth century: 'weaving has *spread* to the entire

country and is the primary form of family industry. Handlooms can be seen even in the most remote villages.' Duckerts (1904), p. 119, cited by Sarc (1940).

53. British Consular Reports are replete with detailed descriptions of the patterns of cloth produced by the local manufacturing establishments. Frequently, samples were mailed to London.

54. *Accounts and Papers* (1862), vol. 59, 'Commercial Report' from Aleppo for the year 1861; (1906), vol. 129, 'Commercial Report' from Aleppo for the year 1905.

55. *Accounts and Papers*, 'Commercial Reports' from Turkey, *passim*; Eldem (1970), pp. 144–5.

56. *Accounts and Papers*, 'Commercial Reports' from Aleppo, various years. For studies of Syrian handicrafts and their resistance, see Chevalier (1962, 1963).

57. As a result, year-to-year fluctuations in production levels were quite substantial. For example, the number of handlooms in operation in the city of Aleppo fluctuated from 5,560 in 1855 to 4,000 in 1859, and 6,000 in 1860; from 4,000 in 1861 to 800 in 1866 and 3,000 in 1867; from 5,000 in 1871 to 6,000 in 1872, 2,400 in 1875, and 700 in 1876. See *Accounts and Papers*, 'Commercial Reports' from Aleppo, various years. The manufacturing establishments and the workforce were able to withstand these sharp fluctuations only because a large number of the workers still had ties with agriculture. For many weavers, men and women, wage income from seasonal employment in urban manufacturing represented a supplement to their rural incomes.

58. *Accounts and Papers*, 'Commercial Reports' from Aleppo, various years. For long-term fluctuations of Ottoman foreign trade, see chapter 2. The impact of the Great Depression of 1873–96 on the Ottoman economy is examined in Pamuk (1984).

In the longer term, however, the stage was set. The European textile industry achieved steady increases in labor productivity and cloth prices continued to decline until the 1880s while the pre-industrial technology of the small-scale manufacturing establishments remained unchanged. Under conditions of general decline, this form of production afforded little potential for capital accumulation. In the face of relentless competition from imports, their survival was accomplished only at the expense of declining wages for the workers. By the turn of the twentieth century, weavers were organizing strikes against owners' attempts to cut wages. See *Accounts and Papers* (1902), vol. 110, 'Commercial Report' from Damascus for the year 1901.

59. We believe, for this reason, that the timing of the observation by Duckerts (1904), emphasizing the importance and widespread nature of hand weaving by peasant households, was not coincidental. See note 52 above.

60. See chapter 5 of this volume.

61. This trend is in line with the theoretical argument put forth by Hymer and Resnick (1969). Also see Resnick (1970).

62. Clark (1974) provides a detailed account of this unsuccessful attempt.

However, one can hardly agree with his characterization of this process as an 'Industrial Revolution'.

63. Clark (1974), p. 75, citing MacFarlane (1850), vol. II, p. 453. Among the surviving factories were the cotton spindles and looms at Bakırköy, Istanbul, which continued to manufacture for the military, without undergoing any improvement, for more than half a century.

64. The first Industrial Encouragement Act was passed by the Union and Progress Administration in 1913. See Ökçün (1975). The earlier 'concessions' granted by the government to establish industrial enterprises offered very little support against the guilds or the imports. See Ökçün (1972). For the case of a successful resistance by the guilds against a cotton spinning mill in Antakya, see *Accounts and Papers* (1873), vol. 72, 'Commercial Report' from Aleppo for the year 1872.

65. *Accounts and Papers* (1883), vol. 72, 'Commercial Report' from Salonica for the years 1879–81.

66. It is reported that, by the end of the 1880s, the share of imports was reduced to a quarter of the total consumption of cotton yarn in Macedonia. *Accounts and Papers* (1890–1), vol. 88, 'Commercial Reports' from Salonica for the year 1889. However, in 1888, in the absence of other mills, these two mills could only meet less than one-tenth of the consumption of cotton yarn in the Empire. See table 6.1 for details.

67. The disparity between these figures and those given in the Ottoman Industrial Census of 1913 is primarily due to the exclusion of the Salonica and Adana regions from the official statistics. See Ottoman Empire, Ticaret ve Ziraat Nezareti (1917), the 1970 reprint by Ökçün, pp. 131–40, 148–53. In 1909, before its secession, the Salonica region accounted for more than half of the industrial production of cotton yarn in the Empire, with 10 mills, 60,200 spindles and an annual production capacity of about 3,500 tons. *Accounts and Papers* (1910), vol. 103, 'Commercial Report' from Salonica for the year 1909.

68. In 1909–11, the shares of cloth imports and handicrafts production were 73 per cent and 26 per cent respectively in the total domestic consumption of cotton cloth (see table 6.1).

69. Based on Ottoman Empire, Ticaret ve Ziraat Nezareti (1917).

70. See Twomey (1983); Feuerwerker (1970).

71. A comparison between the Ottoman Empire, with a population of 25 million, and China, with a population of about 450 million, immediately comes to mind. In the early 1900s, per capita consumption of cotton textiles appears to have been more than twice as high in the Ottoman Empire. Also in the Ottoman Empire the share of imports in total domestic consumption of cotton cloth was over 70 per cent, and about 65 per cent of the domestically woven cotton cloth used imported yarn. By comparison, in China in the early 1900s the share of imports in total domestic consumption was around a quarter and about 50 per cent of the domestically woven cotton cloth used imported yarn. Because of climatic and other reasons, we may not be able to

compare levels of per capita consumption meaningfully. However, it is clear that the degree of penetration of imports was much more limited in China on the eve of World War I (figures based on table 6.1 of this chapter and Feuerwerker (1970), tables 5 and 6, pp. 357–71).

72. See section A5.2 of appendix 5.
73. Since income elasticity of cotton textiles was relatively high, these figures should not suggest that per capita incomes also rose by 150 per cent during this period. Furthermore, part of the increase in the consumption of cotton textiles was due to the substitution of cotton for woolen cloth. See our discussion, especially section 5.2 of appendix 5.
74. Consider the following simplified picture for 1909–11 based on table 6.1:
    (a) 70 per cent of total consumption of cotton cloth was imported, the rest pre-industrially woven;
    (b) per capita consumption levels were about a quarter higher in the urban areas (e.g. urban areas with 25 per cent of the population accounting for 30 per cent of total consumption);
    (c) production levels of urban and rural handicrafts weaving were about equal, each accounting for 15 per cent of total consumption;
    (d) two-thirds of the production of urban manufacturing establishments was consumed in the urban areas, the rest in rural areas (e.g. 10 and 5 per cent of total consumption respectively);
    (e) all rural household weaving was consumed rurally;
    (f) then, the components of rural consumption (70 per cent of total consumption) were rural weaving, urban weaving and imports, with shares of 15 per cent, 5 per cent and 50 per cent in total consumption respectively;
    (g) the share of imported cloth in total rural consumption was 50 per cent divided by 70 per cent, or over 70 per cent.

This estimate for the 1910s notwithstanding, we should emphasize that rural household production for consumption within the village was the most important form of production of cotton textiles during the nineteenth century. What the contemporary observers, entirely native urban or Western, noticed with respect to this form was only the tip of the iceberg. That story of cotton textiles production by rural households remains to be written.

7 The Ottoman case in comparative perspective

1. See chapter 2.
2. *Ibid.*
3. See chapter 4 for further details.
4. See chapter 5. All British and German attempts to establish European settlements in the Ottoman Empire ended as failures.
5. Any comparative exercise of this kind inevitably leads to the question of economic growth. The relationship between the degree of penetration of world capitalism or integration into the world economy on the one hand and economic growth on the other is a complex one. The causality can run in both

directions. Moreover, it would be simplistic to suggest that economic growth or its absence can be explained solely in terms of the degree of integration into the world economy. For a brief discussion on this point see pp. 144–6 below.

6. Below we provide evidence in this direction for our group of medium-sized countries in the Third World. See sources cited in notes 7 and 9.

7. The estimates for per capita GNP are based on Maddison (1983) and Crafts (1983).

8. Based on McEvedy and Jones (1978) and Zimmerman (1962).

9. Based on Maddison (1983), Bairoch (1979) and Issawi (1962), appendix.

10. *Ibid.*

11. *Ibid.* The only estimate for Ottoman Empire GNP on the eve of World War I was prepared by V. Eldem. See Eldem (1970), pp. 302–8.

12. In addition, it is not clear whether this line of inquiry will provide major insights into the comparative position of the Ottoman Empire.

13. The rivalry category can be empirically distinguished from the category of informal empire by examining the country distribution of foreign trade and foreign investment. If the trade and capital flows into a country in the periphery are dominated by one imperialist power, the country in question will be considered in the category of informal empire. In the case of rivalry the foreign trade and received foreign investment of the country in the periphery will be more evenly distributed between two or more imperialist powers. For the country distribution of Ottoman foreign trade and foreign capital in the Ottoman Empire, both of which reflected the conditions of rivalry, see chapters 2 and 4 respectively.

14. As in the earlier reference, this discussion excludes Argentina.

15. Egypt became a *de facto* British colony after 1882. A large part of its external debt, however, was accumulated during the third quarter of the nineteenth century.

16. This point has recently been argued by Hanson (1980).

Appendix 1 The reconstruction of Ottoman foreign trade, 1830–1913

1. The official Ottoman foreign trade statistics have been republished by Aybar (1939). A limited part of these statistics has also been published in McCarthy (1982). For detailed discussion of their shortcomings, see Aybar (1939) and Sönmez (1970). Also see section A1.2 below. Full references for the official trade statistics of other countries are provided in the bibliography.

2. Aybar (1939).

3. Great Britain, *Parliamentary Papers, Accounts and Papers* (1860–76), 'Annual Statement of the Trade . . . of the United Kingdom', annual publication; *Accounts and Papers*, 'Commercial Reports' from Smyrna for the years 1864 and after; Kurmuş (1974).

4. Aybar (1939).

5. For the contribution of wheat from Central Anatolia to the provisioning of Istanbul after the construction of the Anatolian Railway and for a discussion

of the cereal and flour supplies of Istanbul around the turn of the century, see Quataert (1977, 1973).

6. The following discussion is based on Aybar (1939).

7. Some contemporary observers, as well as present-day researchers, have been aware of this problem. See the references cited in note 11 of chapter 2; also Kurmuş (1974), p. 265.

8. Eldem (1970), p. 187. For a detailed discussion of the 1861 Treaty and its comparison with the 1838 and 1850 Treaties, see Kütükoğlu (1976).

9. See chapter 3 and appendix 2.

10. Eldem (1970), p. 187. For complaints by British merchants regarding the wide divergence between the official list prices and the actual market prices of British manufactures, which resulted in effectively higher rates of customs duties on these imports, see *Accounts and Papers* (1879–80).

11. U.S. Department of Commerce, *Commercial Relations of the United States*, 'Commercial Report' from Turkey for the year 1907, p. 518, and 'Commercial Report' from Turkey for the year 1909, p. 323.

12. Aybar (1939).

13. Eldem (1970), p. 184.

14. U.S. Department of Commerce, *Commercial Relations of the U.S.*, 'Commercial Report' from Turkey for the year 1909, p. 324.

15. Eldem (1970), pp. 180ff, citing Biliotti (1909). Also see Mears (1924), chapter 15, pp. 334–5.

16. See, for example, Bateman (1899); Don (1968); Degreve (1976); Allen and Ely (1954). Also Morgenstern (1963), part II, chapter 9.

17. Imlah (1958).

18. U.S. Department of Commerce, *Commercial Relations of the U.S.*, and Great Britain, *Parliamentary Papers, Accounts and Papers*, 'Commercial Reports', various years.

19. Comparison with the freight charge indices provided by Cairncross (1953), p. 176.

20. Cairncross (1953), p. 176; North (1958, 1960, 1968, 1969).

21. Simon (1960).

22. We have relied on the following sources in determining the prevailing gold standard exchange rate of various currencies *vis-à-vis* the British pound sterling:

For 1830–58, *Tate's Modern Cambisit. A Manual of Foreign Exchanges and Bullion*, second, third, fourth and ninth editions.

For 1857–1913, Great Britain, *Parliamentary Papers, Accounts and Papers*, 'The Statistical Abstract for the Principal and Other Foreign Countries', annual publication.

For the exchange rate of the Ottoman Lira against the pound sterling during the nineteenth century, a rate that was not utilized in our reconstruction attempt, see Issawi (1980a), pp. 326–31.

23. Eldem (1970), pp. 186–93.

Appendix 2 Price indices for Ottoman foreign trade, 1854–1913

1. For a study of the Ottoman terms of trade utilizing official Ottoman statistics, see Sönmez (1970). Sönmez discusses the limitations of the data at length, although he could not determine the extent of the undervaluation problem with respect to exports. For further details see the discussion in appendix 1.
2. The low level of Ottoman imports from the United States for most of 1830–1913 and of Ottoman exports to the same country until 1896, as well as the poor coverage of U.S. statistics, did not make it worthwhile including them in our price indices. For full references for these statistics, see appendix 1.
3. Considering the fact that the early researchers in this field, Fabricant and Kuznets, considered 40 per cent coverage as a minimum, the level of our coverage is satisfactory for a study of the Ottoman terms of trade with the center countries. Also see Hansen (1976).
4. Imlah (1958), chapter 2, and Lipsey (1963).
5. See the discussion in appendix 1.
6. See appendix 1 for the sources used in the determination of prevailing exchange rates for each year of the period 1854–1913.
7. Given the Laspeyres price index, $[\Sigma Q_0 P_1 / \Sigma Q_0 P_0]$, and Paasche price index, $[\Sigma Q_1 P_1 / \Sigma Q_1 P_0]$, the Fisher Ideal price index is the geometric mean of the two, the square root of their product.
8. Hansen (1976).
9. Samuelson and Swamy (1974).

Appendix 4 Relations of production in agriculture and standards of living of the peasantry in the 1870s

1. *Accounts and Papers* (1870a), vol. 67, 'Report on Land Tenure in Eastern (Asiatic) Turkey', p. 279.
2. *Accounts and Papers* (1871), vol. 68, 'Report on the Condition of Industrial Classes (in Turkey)', p. 740.
3. *Accounts and Papers* (1870c), vol. 66, 'Report on the Condition of Industrial Classes (in Turkey)', pp. 242–3.
4. Peasants who cultivate their own land are not included in this classification.
5. *Accounts and Papers* (1871c), vol. 68, 'Report on the Condition of Industrial Classes (in Turkey)', pp. 809–10.
6. *Ibid.*, pp. 816–17.
7. *Ibid.*, pp. 736–9.
8. *Accounts and Papers* (1870b), vol. 65, 'Taxation in Turkey', Report by Mr Barron, Her Majesty's Secretary of the Embassy, pp. 173–239. See also chapter 5 of this book.
9. Detailed calculations on this point are presented in subsequent sections of the same report.
10. *Accounts and Papers* (1870c), vol. 66, 'Report on the Condition of Industrial Classes (in Turkey)', p. 244.

Appendix 5 The reconstruction of Ottoman textile imports, 1820–1913

1. See appendix 1.
2. See appendix 1 for details of the process and the difficulties encountered.
3. See table A5.2 below. The problem is more pronounced for imports of woolen textiles. See table A5.3 below.
4. Ottoman Empire, Ticaret ve Ziraat Nezareti (1917), the 1970 reprint by Ökçün, p. 150.
5. Great Britain, Public Record Office, Customs 8 and Customs 10 Series (1820–53); Great Britain, 'Annual Statement of the Trade of the United Kingdom . . .' (1854–1913).
6. The official figures were taken from the Industrial Census of 1913, which cites the official foreign trade statistics of the Empire. See Ottoman Empire, Ticaret ve Ziraat Nezareti (1917), the 1970 reprint by Ökçün, p. 150. It should be noted that our estimates refer to the Gregorian calendar year, whereas the Ottoman fiscal year ran from April to March.
7. Our attempt to estimate imports from Britain in units of weight produced coefficients of 15.4 yards per kilogram of cotton cloth and 4.9 yards per kilogram of woolen cloth.
8. According to the definition of the Empire employed in our reconstruction of its foreign trade in chapter 2, Wallachia and Moldavia seceded in 1856; Bosnia, Herzegovina and Bulgaria after 1878; and Northern Greece in 1912.
9. For the importance of the *aba* (woolen cloth) trade between Bulgaria and the rest of the Empire, see Todorov (1969).
10. All population figures for 1820–2, 1840–2 and 1870–2 are based on Issawi (1980a, 1982), pp. 18–19. The population estimates for the later period are taken from Eldem (1970), pp. 49–65, who based his calculations on the estimates supplied by the Ottoman Ministry of Commerce and Agriculture. Eldem provides an estimate of about 13.5 million for the 1913 population of the Anatolian provinces of the Empire. In a recent study, J. McCarthy has presented new estimates which revise the earlier estimates for the 1913 population of the Anatolian provinces upwards by about 25 per cent to 17.5 million. McCarthy states that he has reached his estimates by correcting the official figures in the censuses and provincial yearbooks (Salnames) for undercounting in certain age groups and in women. See McCarthy (1983).
11. Based on Ottoman Empire, Ticaret ve Ziraat Nezareti (1917), the 1970 reprint by Ökçün, pp. 154–63, Eldem (1970), pp. 127–30, and Dalsar (1960).

Appendix 6 An essay on the international balance of payments of the Ottoman Empire, 1830–1913

1. For a study of long swings in balance of payments, see Williamson (1964).
2. Biliotti (1909); Eldem (1970), pp. 189–93.
3. See studies by White (1933); Imlah (1958); North (1960); Simon (1960); Gregory (1979). Also see the discussion in Morgenstern (1963), part II, chapter 9.

4. The details of this estimation procedure are discussed in chapter 4. Appendix 3 presents the results for each year.
5. Biliotti (1909); Eldem (1970).
6. Eldem (1970), p. 191.
7. Biliotti (1909); Eldem (1970), p. 191.
8. Biliotti (1909).
9. Ruppin (1917), as cited by Eldem (1970), p. 192.
10. Simon (1960), pp. 668–72.
11. Based on Cuinet (1896), Bachi (1967) and the U.S. Department of State, Division of Near Eastern Affairs (1923).
12. Kazgan (1974); also see Karpat (1974) and Karpat (1985).
13. North (1960), pp. 611–15; Simon (1960), pp. 672–80.
14. Ruppin (1917), cited by Eldem (1970), p. 192.
15. Eldem (1970), p. 192.
16. *Ibid.*, pp. 256–7.
17. *Ibid.*
18. Temperley (1936), p. 32, and Erim (1953), pp. 275–89. For the rate of exchange of the Ottoman Lira *vis-à-vis* British sterling at the beginning of the 1830s, see Issawi (1980a), pp. 329–31.
19. For a history of this war indemnity, see Milgrim (1975, 1978).
20. Erim (1953), pp. 433–45.
21. Contemporary observers emphasized the active role played by German banks in the financing of German exports to the Ottoman Empire. However, it appears that the volume of credit became too large in the years preceding World War I:

    British and American banks were not interested in granting long commercial credits; therefore, their national customers were confronted with the alternative of assuming the risks themselves, of using the facilities of German banks which they largely did, or of neglecting the Turkish market entirely. That Germany was unwise in adopting a too liberal credit policy seems fairly well established. Not only did she induce her customers to overstock, but also many accounts on behalf of her nationals will remain open for generations to come. (Mears (1924), p. 343)

22. This process, which was undertaken in an attempt to end the virtual chaos in the monetary system, was called 'Tashih-i Sikke' (correction of coinage). See Eldem (1970), p. 225; du Velay (1930), p. 72; Biliotti (1909), p. 95; Hasan Ferid (1914–18), vol. I, pp. 371–7.
23. Biliotti (1909), pp. 100–3; also Eldem (1970), pp. 226–9. However, this does not necessarily mean that the volume of gold coinage in circulation reached 60 million Ottoman Liras by 1913. It is possible that some of these gold coins remained in the areas that seceded from the Empire during the nineteenth century and were reminted by the new governments. At the same time, hoarding of gold coins undoubtedly reached very high proportions. Using a variety of sources, Eldem estimates the volume of hoarded gold coins at 30 million Ottoman Liras and of gold coins in actual circulation at 32 million, a total of 62 million Liras, figures that are not inconsistent with the Mint

statistics of 1844–1913 or with our argument here, since there must have been some hoarding in 1844.

24. Biliotti (1909), pp. 102–4; Eldem (1970), p. 229. Minting of silver coinage ended in 1884. See Biliotti (1909), p. 103.

25. With the founding in 1863 of the Ottoman Bank, owned jointly by French and British capital, the power to print paper currency within the Empire was transferred to it. The only exceptions came during periods of war. When the Ottoman Bank refused to lend additional funds, Ottoman central authorities created paper currency in order to finance the War of 1877–8; they did the same during World War I. In 1913, the volume of paper currency issued by the Ottoman Bank stood at 12.7 million Liras, only 20 per cent of the total outstanding money stock. See Eldem (1970), p. 229.

26. There is some evidence for occasional crises of liquidity in different parts of the Empire. See, for example, Chevalier (1968) and also Gerber (1980). The reluctance of the Ottoman Bank to issue paper currency must have had unfavorable consequences for the economy. On the other hand, the increases in the volume of gold coinage in circulation that we have estimated must have met, at least partly, the growing requirements of the economy.

27. It should be emphasized that there are important differences between the balance of payments of a nineteenth-century economy linked to the gold standard and without a significant volume of paper currency, such as the Ottoman Empire, and that of an underdeveloped country in the twentieth century that has its own paper money and adopts various controls on foreign exchange. In the former case, the reserves of the country included, at least potentially, the stock of gold and silver coins in circulation. As a result, it might appear that such an economy was capable of sustaining deficits in its balance of payments for longer periods of time than could the twentieth-century economy described above. However, the resulting outflow of gold had depressing effects on the level of economic activity. In other words, the effects of deficits in external payments accounts could not be shielded from the domestic economy. Similarly, as we point out above, in the absence of increases in the volume of paper currency, such an economy had to show surpluses in its balance of payments in order to meet the growing requirements for money.

28. The details of each sub-period are discussed at greater length in chapters 1, 2, 3 and 4.

Bibliography

This bibliography includes only works cited in the text. For a general bibliography on the nineteenth-century economic history of the Ottoman Empire with special emphasis on the areas comprising present-day Turkey, the interested reader can refer to Erdal Yavuz, Orhan Kurmuş and Şevket Pamuk, '19. YY. Türkiye İktisat Tarihi Kaynakları; Bir Bibliyografya Denemesi', *Middle East Technical University, Studies in Development* (1979–80), Special Issue on Turkish Economic History, pp. 329–72. Also see the bibliographies in Issawi (1980a), Owen (1981) and Issawi (1966).

Unpublished documents

France, Affaires Etrangères, *Correspondance Commerciale*, Smyrne, Trebizonde, Alep, Tarsus, 1819–52.
United States, Department of State Archives (1923) 876/602, Microfilm No. 56, Department of State, Division of Near Eastern Affairs, *Foreign Interests and Concessions in Turkey*, April
(1910–13) 867/5, Microfilm No. 62, Correspondence from the U.S. consul in Harput relating to economic matters
Great Britain, Public Record Office, *Customs 4*, *Customs 8*, and *Customs 10* series, 1816–53, annual volumes

Published foreign trade statistics
(All annual publications unless otherwise noted.)
Austria, *Holkammer Ausweise über den Handel von Österreich*, 1830/1840–57, 1861
Bundesministerium für Finanzen Rechnungsdepartement, *Ausweise über den Auswartigen Handel*, 1858–60
Österreichisches Statistisches Zentralamt, *Ausweise über den Auswartigen Handel*, 1858–60
Österreichisches Statistisches Zentralamt, *Österreichische Statistik*, 1882–90
Statistisches Departement, *Statistik des Auswartigen Handels*, 1891–1913
Belgium, Ministère de l'Intérieur, *Tableau Générale de Commerce de la Belgique*, 1831/1834–1913
Bulgaria, Bureau Statistique de la Principauté de Bulgarie, *Commerce de la Principauté de la Bulgarie avec les Pays Etrangers*, 1880–94
Bureau Statistique de Royaume Bulgarie, *Statistique du Commerce du Royaume Bulgarie avec les Pays Etrangers*, 1895–1913

Egypt, Customs Administration, *Le Commerce Extérieur de l'Egypt*, 1874/8–1913

France, Direction Générale des Douanes, *Tableau Générale du Commerce de la France*, 1830–1913

Germany, *Statistisches Jahrbuch für das Deutsche Reich*, 1880–1913

Greece, Ethnike, Statistike Hyperesia, *Commerce Extérieur de la Grèce*, 1857–76, 1888–1913

Great Britain, *Parliamentary Papers, Accounts and Papers*, 'Annual Statement of the Trade . . . of the United Kingdom', 1854–1913

Iran, Administration des Douanes, *Tableau de commerce avec les Pays Etrangers*, 1902/3–1913/14

Italy, Direzione Generale delle Dogane, *Movimento Commerciale*, 1852–1913

Netherlands, Ministeries van Financien, *Statistiek van den handel ende Scheepvaart in hetkoningrijk der Nederlanden*, 1846–76
    Ministeries van Financien, *Statistieck van den in- uit en doorvoer over het jaar*, 1877–1913

Romania, Directiunea Varnilor si statisticel financiera, *Commerciul exterior al Roumanici*, 1871–1913

Russia, Departement tamozhennykh shorov, *Obzor Vnieshnei Torgovli Rossi*, 1830–1913, annual publication, title varies for 1830–69

Serbia, la Direction des Douanes au Ministère des Finances, *Statistique du Commerce Extérieur du Royaume de Serbia*, 1913, summary information for 1879–1913

Switzerland, Zollverwaltung-Oberzolldirektion, *Statistik des Waarenverkehrs der Schweiz mit dem Auslande*, 1885–1913

United States, Treasury Department, *Commerce and Navigation of the United States*, 1830–1913

Other official publications, documents, statistics

Deutsche Reich (1907) *Statistisches Jahrbuch für das Deutsche Reich*
    (1915) *Vierteljahrshefte zur Statistik des Deutschen Reichs*, vol. I
    Marineleitung, Die Marine-Vorlage (1906) 'Die Entwicklung der deutschen Seenterressen im Letzten Jahrzehnt', Berlin

Great Britain, *Parliamentary Papers, Accounts and Papers* (1855–1914), 'Commercial Reports' from consular offices in Turkey and elsewhere, annual publication

Other documents published in Great Britain, *Parliamentary Papers, Accounts and Papers*:
    (1843) 'Commercial Tariffs and Regulations', part VIII, Ottoman Empire
    (1865) 'Circular to Her Majesty's Consuls in the Ottoman Dominions Regarding Cotton Cultivation', vol. 57
    (1870a) 'Report on Land Tenure in Turkey', vol. 67
    (1870b) 'Taxation in Turkey', vol. 65

(1870c, 1871) 'Report on the Condition of Industrial Classes (in Turkey)', 1870, vol. 66, and 1871, vol. 68

(1884) 'Special Report on Road Building in Turkey'

(1908) 'Report on Agriculture in Asia Minor with Special Reference to Cotton Cultivation' by Professor W. Duncan, vol. 107

Commissioners of Inland Revenue (1872–1914) 'Annual Reports'

'The Statistical Abstract for the Colonial and Other Possessions of the United Kingdom' (1857–1913) annual publication

'The Statistical Abstract for the Principal and Other Foreign Countries' (1857–1913) annual publication

Ottoman Empire, Orman ve Maadin ve Ziraat Nezareti, Istatistik Idaresi (1910 / 1326) *1323 Senesi Avrupay-i Osmani Ziraat Istatistigi*, Istanbul

Orman ve Maadin ve Ziraat Nezareti, Istatistik Subesi (1911 /1327) *1325 Senesi Asya ve Afrika-i Osmani Ziraat Istatistigi*, Istanbul

Ticaret ve Ziraat Nezareti (1917 /1333), *1328, 1331 Seneleri Sanayi Istatistigi*, Istanbul; reprinted by A. G. Ökçün in 1970

An edited collection of the Ottoman trade statistics can be found in Celal Aybar (1939) *Osmanh Imparatorluğunun Ticaret Muvazenesi, 1878–1913*, Ankara. Also see Block (1906); Erim (1953); McCarthy (1982); Meray (1972); Ökçün (1970).

United States (1852–1914) Department of Commerce or Bureau of Foreign Commerce, *Commercial Relations of the United States with Foreign Countries*, Commercial Reports from U.S. consuls in the Ottoman Empire and elsewhere

Books, articles, unpublished dissertations, unpublished papers

Akarlı, Engin (1976) 'The Problem of External Pressures, Power Struggles and Budgetary Deficit under Abdülhamid II, 1876–1909: Origins and Solutions', Princeton University, unpublished Ph.D. dissertation

Aktan, Reşat (1966) 'The Burden of Taxation on the Peasants', in Issawi (1966), pp. 107–13

Alavi, Hamza (1980) 'India: Transition from Feudalism to Colonial Capitalism', *Journal of Contemporary Asia*, vol. 10, no. 4

Allen, R. G. D. and Ely, J. E. (eds.) (1953) *International Trade Statistics*, New York

Amin, Samir (1974) *Accumulation on a World Scale: A Critique of the Theory of Underdevelopment*, 2 vols., New York and London

Anderson, M. S. (1966) *The Eastern Question 1774–1923*, London and New York

Anderson, Olive (1964) 'Great Britain and the Beginnings of the Ottoman Public Debt, 1854–55', *Historical Journal*, vol. 7, pp. 47–63

Anonymous (1907) 'German Finance in Turkey', *National Review*, London, vol. 48, January, pp. 868–80

(1919) *Les Interêts Financiers dans l'Empire Ottoman*, Paris

Arrighi, Giovanni (1970) 'Labor Supplies in Historical Perspective: A Study of the Proletarianization of the African Peasantry in Rhodesia', *Journal of Development Studies*, vol. 6, no. 3

Bachi, R. (1967) 'Immigration into Israel', in J. H. Adler (ed.), *Capital Movements and Economic Development*, New York

Baer, Gabriel (1962) *A History of Landownership in Modern Egypt, 1800–1950*, London

   (1983) 'Landlord, Peasant and the Government in the Arab Provinces of the Ottoman Empire in the 19th and 20th Centuries', in Jean-Louis Bacqué-Grammont and Paul Dumont (eds.), *Economie et Sociétés dans l'Empire Ottoman (Fin du XVIIIe – Début du XXe Siècle)*, Paris, pp. 261–74

Bagchi, A. K. (1976) 'De-industrialization in India in the Nineteenth Century: Some Theoretical Implications', *Journal of Development Studies*, vol. 12, pp. 135–64

Bailey, Frank Edgar (1942) *British Policy and the Turkish Reform Movement*, Cambridge, Mass.

Bairoch, Paul (1973) 'European Foreign Trade in the XIX Century: The Development of the Value and Volume of Exports (Preliminary Results)', *Journal of European Economic History*, vol. 2, no. 1

   (1974) 'Geographical Structure and Trade Balance of European Foreign Trade from 1800 to 1970', *Journal of European Ecomomic History*, vol. 3, no. 3

   (1979) 'Ecarts Internationaux des Nivaux de Vie avant la Révolution Industrielle', *Annales: Economies, Sociétés, Civilisations*, vol. 34, pp. 145–71

Barkan, Ömer Lütfi (1940) 'Türk Toprak Hukuku Tarihinde Tanzimat ve 1274 (1858) Tarihli Arazi Kanunnamesi', in *Tanzimat*, Istanbul

   (1945) 'Çiftlik', *İslam Ansiklopedisi*, vol. 3

   (1970) 'XVI. Asrın Ikinci Yarısında Türkiye'de Fiyat Hareketleri', *Belleten*, vol. 34, pp. 557–607; for an abridged translation see Ö. L. Barkan, 'The Price Revolution of the Sixteenth Century: A Turning Point in the Economic History of the Near East', *International Journal of Middle East Studies*, vol. 6, 1975, pp. 3–28

Bateman, A. E. (1899) 'Comparability of Trade Statistics of Various Countries', *Bulletin de l'Institut International de Statistique*, vol. 11, St Petersburg

Beysanoğlu, Şevket (1956) *Ziya Gökalp'in İlk Yazı Hayatı*, Istanbul

Biliotti, A. (1909) *La Banque Imperiale Ottomane*, Paris

Birnberg, T. B. and Resnick, S. A. (1975) *Colonial Development: An Econometric Study*, New Haven and London

Blaisdell, Donald C. (1929) *European Financial Control in the Ottoman Empire*, New York

Block, A. (1906) 'Memorandum Respecting Franco-German Economic Penetration (into Turkey)', in G. P. Gooch and H. W. V. Temperley (eds.), *British Documents on the Origins of the War 1898–1914*, ? vols., London, vol. v, pp. 175–84

Bloomfield, A. I. (1968) *Patterns of Fluctuation in International Investment before 1914*, Princeton Studies in International Finance, no. 21

Bogert, E. J. (1976) 'Austro-Hungarian Maritime Trade with the Ottoman Empire, 1873–1895: A Commercial History', 2 vols., unpublished Ph.D. dissertation

Boratav, Korkut (1980) *Tarımsal Yapılar ve Kapitalizm*, Ankara

Boratav, Korkut, Ökçün, A. Gündüz and Pamuk, Sevket (1985) 'The Ottoman Wages and the World Economy, 1839–1913', *Review*, Fernand Braudel Center, vol. 8, no. 3, pp. 379–406

Börsen-Enquête Kommission (1893) *Statistische Anlagen der Borsen-Enquete Kommission*, Berlin

Bradby, Barbara (1975) 'The Destruction of Natural Economy', *Economy and Society*, vol. 4, no. 2

Braude, Benjamin (1979) 'International Competition and Domestic Cloth in the Ottoman Empire, 1500–1650: A Study in Development', *Review*, Fernand Braudel Center, vol. 2, no. 3, pp. 437–51

Bruck, W. F. (1919) *Die turkisch-Baumwollwirtschaft*, Jena

Cain, P. J. (1980) *Economic Foundations of British Expansion Overseas 1815–1914*, London

Cairncross, A. K. (1953) *Home and Foreign Investment, 1870–1913*, Cambridge

Chaudhuri, K. N. (1978) *The Trading World of Asia and the English East India Company, 1660–1760*, Cambridge

Chayanov, A. V. (1966) *The Theory of Peasant Economy*, translated from Russian and edited by D. Thorner *et al.*, Homewood, Ill.

Chevalier, Dominique (1962) 'Les Tissus Ikates d'Alep et de Damas: Un Example de Résistance Technique de l'Artisanat Syrien aux XIXe et XXe Siècles', *Syria*, vol. 39, pp. 300–24.

(1963) 'A Syrian Craft: The Ikat Weaves', *Middle East Forum*, Summer, pp. 25–31

(1968) 'Western Development and Eastern Crisis in the Mid-Nineteenth Century', in William R. Polk and Richard L. Chambers (eds.), *Beginnings of Modernization in the Middle East: The Nineteenth Century*, Chicago

Church, R. A. (1975) *The Great Victorian Boom 1850–1873*, London

Cillov, Haluk (1949) *Denizli'de El Dokumacılığı Sanayii*, Istanbul

Çizakça, Murat (1980) 'Price History and the Bursa Silk Industry: A Study in Ottoman Decline 1550–1650', *Journal of Economic History*, vol. 40, pp. 533–50

Clark, E. (1974) 'The Ottoman Industrial Revolution', *International Journal of Middle East Studies*, vol. 5, pp. 65–76

Corporation of Foreign Bondholders (1882–1919) *Annual Reports*, London

Cottrell, P. L. (1975) *British Overseas Investment in the Nineteenth Century*, London

Crafts, N. F. R. (1983) 'Gross National Product in Europe 1870–1910, Some New Estimates', *Explorations in Economic History*, vol. 20, pp. 387–401

Cuinet, V. (1891–4) *La Turquie d'Asie*, 4 vols., Paris

(1896) *Syrie, Liban et Palestine*, Paris

Dalsar, Fahri (1960) *Bursa'da İpekçilik*, Istanbul

Davis, Ralph (1970) 'English Imports from the Middle East, 1580–1780', in M.

Bibliography

A. Cook (ed.), *Studies in the Economic History of the Middle East*, London
  (1979) *The Industrial Revolution and British Overseas Trade*, Leicester
Davison, Roderic H. (1963) *Reform in the Ottoman Empire, 1856–1876*, Princeton
  (1980) 'The First Ottoman Experiment with Paper Money', in O. Okyar and
  H. İnalcık (eds.), *Türkiyenin Sosyal ve Ekonomik Tarihi 1071–1920*, Ankara,
  pp. 243–51
Deane, Phyllis (1965) *The First Industrial Revolution*, Cambridge
Deane, Phyllis and Cole, W. A. (1964) *British Economic Growth 1688–1959*,
  Cambridge
Degreve, D. (1976) 'Une Critique des Donnes du Commerce Extérieur Belge: La
  Comparison Inter-pays', paper submitted to the International Symposium
  on L'Evolution de l'Economie d'Entreprise et Contributions Récentes à
  l'Histoire Economique de la Belgique'
Don, Yehuda (1968) 'Comparability of International Trade Statistics: Great
  Britain and Austria-Hungary before World War I', *Economic History
  Review*, vol. 21
Duckerts, M. (1904) *Turquie d'Asie*, Brussels
Ducruet, J. (1964) *Les Capitaux Européens au Proche-Orient*, Paris
Earle, E. M. (1923) *Turkey, the Great Powers and the Baghdad Railway*, New
  York
Eldem, Vedat (1970) *Osmanlı İmparatorluğunun İktisadi Şartları Hakkında Bir
  Tetkik*, Istanbul
Ellsworth, P. T. (1956) 'The Terms of Trade between Primary Producing and
  Industrial Countries', *Inter-American Economic Affairs*, vol. 10, pp. 47–65
Emmanuel, Arrighi (1972a) *Unequal Exchange: A Study of the Imperialism of
  Trade*, New York and London
  (1972b) 'White Settler Colonialism and the Myth of Investment Imperialism',
  New Left Review, no. 73, May–June, pp. 35–57
Ener, K. (1961) *Tarih Boyunca Adana Ovasına Bir Bakış*, Istanbul
Eren, A. C. (1966) *Türkiye'de Göç ve Göçmen Meseleleri*, Istanbul
Erim, Nihat (ed.) (1953) *Devletlerarası Hukuku ve Siyasi Tarih Metinleri, Cilt I:
  Osmanlı İmparatorluğunun Andlaşmaları*, Ankara
Faroqhi, S. (1979) 'Notes on the Production of Cotton and Cotton Cloth in
  XVIth and XVIIth Century Anatolia', *Journal of European Economic
  History*, vol. 8, no. 2, pp. 405–17
Feis, Herbert (1930) *Europe, the World's Banker 1870–1914*, New Haven, Conn.
Ferns, H. S. (1960) *Britain and Argentina in the Nineteenth Century*, Oxford
Feuerwerker, A. (1970) 'Handicraft and Manufactured Cotton Textiles in China,
  1871–1910', *Journal of Economic History*, vol. 30, pp. 338–78
Flaningam, M. L. (1954–5) 'German Eastward Economic Expansion, Fact and
  Fiction', *Journal of Central European Affairs*, vol. 16, pp. 319–33
Forbes, I. L. D. (1978) 'German Informal Imperialism in South America before
  1914', *Economic History Review*, vol. 31, no. 3
'La Fortune Française à l'Etranger' (1902) *Bulletin de Statistique et de Legislation
  Comparée*, October, Paris

Foster-Carter, Aidan (1978) 'The Modes of Production Debate', *New Left Review*, no. 107, January–February, pp. 47–77

Friedman, Harriet (1978) 'World Market, State and Family Farm: Social Bases of Household Production in the Era of Wage Labor', *Comparative Studies in Society and History*, vol. 20, pp. 545–86

Gallagher, J. and Robinson, R. E. (1953) 'Imperialism of Free Trade', *Economic History Review*, vol. 6

(1961) *Africa and the Victorians*, London

Gayer, A., Rostow, Walt Whitman and Schwartz, Anna J. (1953) *The Growth and Fluctuations of the British Economy, 1790–1850*, 2 vols., London

Genç, Mehmet (1975) 'Osmanlı Maliyesinde Malikane Sistemi', in Ünal Nalbantoğlu and Osman Okyar (eds.), *Türkiye İktisat Tarihi Semineri, Metinler, Tartışmalar*, Ankara, pp. 231–91

(1984) 'Osmanlı Ekonomisi ve Savaş', *Yapıt*, Ankara, No. 4 and No. 5, April–May and June–July, pp. 52–61, 86–93

Gerber, H. (1980) 'Inflation and Deflation in Syria', *Journal of Economic History*, vol. 40

Gibb, H. A. R. and Bowen, Harold (1957) *Islamic Society and the West*, 2 vols., vol. I, part II, London

Glazier, I. A. and Banderra, V. I. (1972) 'Terms of Trade between South Italy and the United Kingdom, 1817–1869', *Journal of European Economic History*, vol. I, pp. 7–36

Gordon, Leland James (1932) *American Relations with Turkey, 1830–1930*, Philadelphia

Gould, A. G. (1973) 'Pashas and Brigands: Ottoman Provincial Reform and its Impact on the Nomadic Tribes of Southern Anatolia, 1840–1885', unpublished Ph.D. dissertation, University of California, Los Angeles

Graham, R. (1972) *Britain and the Onset of Modernization in Brazil 1850–1914*, Cambridge

Gregory, P. R. (1979) 'The Russian Balance of Payments, the Gold Standard and Monetary Policy: A Historical Example of Foreign Capital Movements', *Journal of Economic History*, vol. 39, pp. 379–99

Güran, Tevfik (1978) 'Osmanlı Tarım Ekonomisine Giriş, 1840–1910', unpublished Ph.D. dissertation, University of Istanbul

Hall, A. R. (ed.) (1968) *The Export of Capital from Britain 1870–1914*, London

Hansen, Bent (1976) 'On the Biases in Foreign Trade Indices', Working Paper No. 4, Institute of International Studies, University of California, Berkeley

Hanson, John R. II (1980) *Trade in Transition: Exports from the Third World, 1840–1900*, New York

Hasan, Ferit (1914–18) *Nakit ve İtibar-ı Milli*, 4 vols., vol. I, Istanbul

Hasan, Mohammed Salman (1970) 'The Role of Foreign Trade in the Economic Development of Iraq 1864–1964: A Study in the Growth of a Dependent Economy', in M. A. Cook (ed.), *Studies in the Economic History of the Middle East*, London, pp. 346–72

Bibliography

Helfferich, K. (1913) 'Die Turkische Staatsschuld und die Balkanstaaten', *Bankarchiv*, Berlin

Henderson, W. O. (1948) 'German Economic Penetration of the Near East, 1870–1914', *Economic History Review*, vol. 18, pp. 54–64

Hirschman, Albert O. (1945) *National Power and the Structure of Foreign Trade*, Berkeley

Hobsbawm, E. J. (1968) *Industry and Empire*, London

Hoffman, R. J. S. (1964) *Great Britain and the German Trade Rivalry, 1875–1914*, New York

Hoffman, W. G. (1965) *Das Wachstum der deutschen Wirtschaft seit der Mitte des 19. Jahrhunderts*, Berlin

Hymer, S. H. and Resnick, S. A. (1969) 'A Model of an Agrarian Economy with Non-Agricultural Activities', *American Economic Review*, vol. 59, pp. 493–506

Imlah, A. (1958) *Economic Elements in the Pax Britannica*, New York

İnalcık, Halil (1970) 'The Ottoman Decline and Effects upon the Reaya', Report to the Second International Congress of Studies on South-East Europe, Athens

(1971) 'Imtiyazat: The Ottoman Empire', *Encyclopedia of Islam*, 2nd edn, Leiden, vol. III, pp. 1179–89

(1973) 'The Application of Tanzimat', *Archivum Ottomanicum*, vol. I

(1977) 'Centralization and Decentralization in Ottoman Administration', in Thomas Naff and Roger Owen (eds.), *Studies in Eighteenth Century Islamic History*, Philadelphia, pp. 27–52

(1981) 'Osmanlı Pamuklu Pazarı, Hindistan ve İngiltere: Pazar Rekabetinde Emek Maliyetinin Rolü', *Middle East Technical University, Studies in Development*, 1979–80, Special Issue on Turkish Economic History, Ankara, pp. 1–65

1983) 'The Emergence of Big Farms, Giftliks: State, Landlords and Tenants', in Jean-Louis Bacqué-Grammont et Paul Dumont (eds.), *Contributions à l'Histoire Economique et Sociale de l'Empire Ottoman*, Leuven, pp. 105–26

İslamoğlu, Huri and Keyder, Çağlar (1977) 'Agenda for Ottoman History', *Review*, Fernand Braudel Center, vol. I, pp. 31–55

Issawi, Charles (1966) *The Economic History of the Middle East, 1800–1914*, Chicago

(1968) 'Asymmetrical Development and Transport in Egypt, 1800–1914', in W. R. Polk and R. L. Chambers (eds.), *Beginnings of Modernization in the Middle East: The Nineteenth Century*, Chicago, pp. 383–400

(1970) 'The Tabriz-Trabzon Trade, 1830–1900: Rise and Decline of a Route', *International Journal of Middle East Studies*, vol. I, pp. 18–27

(1980a) *The Economic History of Turkey, 1800–1914*, Chicago

(1980b) 'De-industrialization and Re-industrialization in the Middle East since 1800', *International Journal of Middle East Studies*, vol. 12

(1982) *An Economic History of the Middle East and North Africa*, New York

Jenks, L. H. (1927) *The Migration of British Capital to 1875*, New York

Karpat, Kemal (1972) 'The Transformation of the Ottoman State, 1789–1908', *International Journal of Middle East Studies*, vol. 3, pp. 243–81

(1974) 'Migration and its Effects upon the Transformation of the Ottoman State in the Nineteenth Century', paper presented to the Conference on the Economic History of the Near East, Princeton University

(1985) *Ottoman Population 1830–1914, Demographic and Social Characteristics*, Madison, Wis.

Kaynak, Muhteşem (1982) 'Demirolları ve Ekonomik Gelişme: XIX. Yüzyıl Deneyimi', unpublished Ph.D. dissertation, Gazi University, Ankara

Kazgan, Gülten (1974) 'Milli Türk Devletinin Kuruluşu ve Gögler', *Istanbul Üniversitesi İktisat Fakültesi Mecmuası*, vol. 30

Keyder, Çağlar (1980) 'Ottoman Economy and Finances, 1881–1918', in Okyar and İnalcık (eds.) (1980), pp. 323–8

(1981) 'Proto-industrialization and the Periphery: A Marxist Perspective', *Insurgent Sociologist*, vol. 70, pp. 51–7

(1983) 'Dünya Ekonomisi İçinde Çin ve Osmanlı İmparatorluğu; Kolonyal Olmayan Periferileşmeye İki Örnek', in Çağlar Keyder, *Toplumsal Tarih Galışmaları*, Ankara, pp. 153–70

Kindleberger, Charles P. (1956) *The Terms of Trade: A European Case Study*, Cambridge, Mass.

Kondratieff, N. D. (1979) 'The Long Waves in Economic Life', *Review*, Fernand Braudel Center, vol. 2, no. 4, pp. 519–62; first published in 1926

Köy ve Ziraat Kalkınma Kongresi (1938) *Türk Ziraat Tarihine Bir Bakış*, Istanbul

Köymen, Oya (1971) 'The Advent and Consequences of Free Trade in the Ottoman Empire', *Etudes Balkaniques*, vol. 2

Kurmuş, Orhan (1974) *Emperyalizmin Türkiye'ye Girişi*, Istanbul, based on the author's Ph.D. dissertation, 'The Role of British Capital in the Economic Development of Western Anatolia, 1850–1913', University of London 1974

(1981), 'Some Aspects of Handicrafts and Industrial Production in Ottoman Anatolia, 1800–1915', *Asian and African Studies*, vol. 15, pp. 85–101

(1983), 'The 1838 Treaty of Commerce Re-examined', in Jean-Louis Bacqué-Grammont and Paul Dumont (eds.), *Economie et Sociétiés dans l'Empire Ottoman*, Paris, pp. 411–17

Kütükoğlu, Mübahat S. (1976) *Osmanlı İngiliz İktisadi Münasebetleri, Cilt II (1838–1850)*, Istanbul

Lampe, John R. and Jackson, Marvin R. (1982) *Balkan Economic History, 1550–1950*, Bloomington, Ind.

Landes, David (1958) *Bankers and Pashas: International Finance and Economic Imperialism in Egypt*, Cambridge, Mass.

(1969), *The Unbound Prometheus*, London

Latham, A. J. H. (1978) *The International Economy and the Underdeveloped World 1865–1914*, London

Lewis, Bernard (1961) *The Emergence of Modern Turkey*, London

Lewis, W. Arthur (1978) *Growth and Fluctuations 1870–1913*, London

Bibliography

Lipsey, R. E. (1963) *Price and Quantity Trends in the Foreign Trade of the United States*, National Bureau of Economic Research, Princeton

Louis, William Roger (ed.) (1976) *Imperialism: The Robinson and Gallagher Controversy*, New York

McCarthy, Justin (1982) *The Arab World, Turkey and the Balkans: A Handbook of Historical Statistics*, Boston

(1983) *Muslims and Minorities: The Population of Ottoman Anatolia and the End of the Empire*, New York

McEachern, D. (1976) 'The Mode of Production in India', *Journal of Contemporary Asia*, vol. 6

McEvedy, Colin and Jones, Richard (1978) *Atlas of World Population History*, Harmondsworth, Middlesex

MacFarlane, C. (1850) *Turkey and its Destiny*. X vols.; vol. II, London

McGowan, Bruce (1981) *Economic Life in Ottoman Europe: Taxation, Trade and Struggle for Land 1600–1800*, Cambridge

MacGregor, J. (1847), *Commercial Statistics*, 4 vols., London

McLean, D. (1976) 'Finance and 'Informal Empire' before the First World War', *Economic History Review*, vol. 29, pp. 291–305

Maddison, Angus (1983) 'A Comparison of GNP per Capita in Developed and Developing Countries, 1700–1980', *Journal of Economic History*, vol. 43, no. 1

Maizels, Alfred (1969) *Industrial Growth and World Trade*, Cambridge

Maliye Tetkik Kurulu (1970) *Osmanlı İmparatorluğunda XIX. Yüzyılın Sonunda Üretim ve Dış Ticaret*, Ankara

Mandel, E. (1980) *Long Waves of Capitalist Development: The Marxist Interpretation*, Cambridge

Marx, Karl (1967) *Capital*, vol. III, New York, International Publishers; first published in 1894

Masson, P. (1911) *Histoire du Commerce Français dans le Levant au XVIIIe siècle*, Paris

Mears, E. G. (ed.) (1924) *Modern Turkey: A Politico-Economic Interpretation, 1908–1923*, New York

Meray, Seha, (tr.) (1972) *Lozan Barış Konferansı Tutanaklar, Belgeler*, Ankara

Meyer, Henry Cord (1951–2) 'German Economic Relations with Southeastern Europe, 1870–1914', *American Historical Review*, vol. 62, pp. 77–90

(1955) *Mitteleuropa in German Thought and Action*, The Hague

Milgrim, Michael R. (1975) 'The War Indemnity and Russian Commercial Investment Policy in the Ottoman Empire: 1878–1914', in Okyar and Nalbantoğlu (eds.), (1975), pp. 297–371

(1978) 'An Overlooked Problem in Turkish–Russian Relations: The 1878 War Indemnity', *International Journal of Middle East Studies*, vol. 9, pp. 519–37

Mitchell, B. R. (1975) *European Historical Statistics 1750–1970*, London

Morgan, T. (1963) 'Trends in Terms of Trade and their Repercussions on Primary Producers', in R. Harrod and D. Hague (eds.), *International Trade Theory in a Developing World*, London, pp. 52–72

268

Morgenstern, Oscar (1963) *On the Accuracy of Economic Observations*, second edition, Princeton, N.J.

Moulton, H. and Lewis, C. (1925) *The French Debt Problem*, New York

Mouzelis, N. P. (1978) *Modern Greece*, London

Musson, A. E. (1959), 'The Great Depression in Britain, 1873–1896: a Reappraisal', *Journal of Economic History*, vol. 19

Neymarck, A. (1908) 'Les Capitaux Français Engagés en Turquie', *Bulletin de l'Institut International de Statistique*

Nickoley, E. F. (1924) 'Agriculture', in Mears (1924) pp. 280–301

North, D. (1958) 'Ocean Freight Rates and Economic Development', *Journal of Economic History*, vol. 18

(1960) 'The United States Balance of Payments 1790–1860', in *National Bureau of Economic Research Studies in Income and Wealth*, Princeton, vol. 24

(1968) 'Sources of Productivity Change in Ocean Shipping', *Journal of Political Economy*, vol. 82

(1969) 'Transportation in North America', *Les Grandes Voices Maritimes dans le Monde*, Paris

Novechev, A. D. (1973) *Ocherki ekonomiki Turtsii*, Moscow–Leningrad

(1966) 'The Development of Agriculture in Anatolia', in Issawi (1966), originally published in Novichev (1937)

Nuri, Osman (1922) *Mecellei Umuru Belediye*, vol. I, Istanbul

O'Brien, P. K. (1983) *Railways and the Economic Development of Europe, 1830–1914*, London

Ocampo, José-Antonio (1981) 'Export Growth and Capitalist Development in Colombia in the Nineteenth Century', in Paul Bairoch and Maurice Levy-Leboyer (eds.), *Disparities in Economic Development since the Industrial Revolution*, New York, pp. 98–109

Ökçün, A. Gündüz (ed.) (1970) *Osmanlı Sanayii: 1913, 1915 Yillari Sanayi İstatistiki*, Ankara

(1972) 'XIX. Yüzyılın İkinci Yarısında İmalat Sanayii Alanında Verilen Ruhsat ve İmtiyazların Ana Çizgileri', *Ankara Üniversitesi Siyasal Bilgiler Fakültesi Dergisi*, vol. 27, pp. 135–66

Okyar, Osman and İnalcık, Halil (eds.) (1980) *Social and Economic History of Turkey*, papers presented to the First International Congress on the Social and Economic History of Turkey, Ankara

Okyar, Osman and Nalbantoğlu, Ünal (eds.) (1975) *Türkiye İktisat Tarihi Semineri, Metinler, Tartışmalar, Haziran 1973*, Ankara

Önsoy, R. (1982) *Türk-Alman İktisadi Münasebetleri (1871–1914)*, Istanbul

Ortaylı, İlber (1979) 'Osmanlı İmparatorluğu'nda Sanayileşme Anlayışına Bir Örnek: Islah-ı Sanayi Komisyonu' Olayı', *Middle East Technical University, Studies in Development*, 1978 Special Issue on Turkish Economic History, Ankara, pp. 123–30

(1981) *İkinci Abdülhamit Döneminde Osmanlı İmparatorluğu'nda Alman Nüfuzu*, Ankara

Owen, E. R. J. (1969) *Cotton and the Egyptian Economy, 1820–1914*, Oxford
  (1975) 'The Middle East in the Eighteenth Century – an "Islamic" Society in Decline: A Critique of Gibb and Bowen's *Islamic Society and the West*', *Review of Middle East Studies*, vol. 1, pp. 101–11
  (1977) 'Introduction', Nafand Owen (eds.), *Studies in Eighteenth-Century Islamic History*, pp. 133–51
  (1981) *The Middle East in the World Economy, 1800–1914*, London
  (1984) 'The Study of Middle Eastern Industrial History: Notes on the Interrelationship between Factories and Small-Scale Manufacturing with Special References to Lebanese Silk and Egyptian Sugar 1900–1930', *International Journal of Middle East Studies*, vol. 16, pp. 475–87
Paish, G. (1914) 'Export of Capital and the Cost of Living', *The Statist*, February, Supplement
Pamuk, Şevket (1984) 'The Ottoman Empire in the "Great Depression" of 1873–1896', *Journal of Economic History*, vol. 44, pp. 107–18
Paris, R. (1957) *Histoire du Commerce de Marseille, Tome V. 1660 à 1789, Le Levant*, Paris
Parvus Efendi (pseudonym for Alexander Israel Helphand) (1977) *Türkiye'nin Mali Tutsaklığı*, Istanbul; first published in 1914
Pech, E. (1911) *Manuel des Sociétés Anonymes Fonctionnant en Turquie*, fifth edition, Constantinople
Platt, D. C. M. (1968) *Finance, Trade and Politics: British Foreign Policy, 1815–1914*, London
Prebisch, Raul (1950) *The Economic Development of Latin America and its Principal Problems*, published by United Nations Economic Commission for Latin America; reprinted in *Economic Bulletin for Latin America*, vol. 7, 1962, pp. 1–22
Puryear, V. J. (1935) *International Economics and Diplomacy in the Near East*, Stanford, Cal.
  (1941) *France and the Levant from the Bourbon Restoration to the Peace of Kutaia*, Los Angeles
Quataert, Donald (1973) 'Ottoman Reform and Agriculture in Anatolia, 1876–1908', unpublished Ph.D. dissertation, University of California, Los Angeles
  (1977) 'Limited Revolution: The Impact of the Anatolian Railway on Turkish Transportation and the Provisioning of Istanbul, 1890–1908', *Business History Review*, vol. 51, pp. 139–61
  (1980) 'The Commercialization of Agriculture in Ottoman Turkey, 1800–1914', *International Journal of Turkish Studies*, vol. 1, pp. 38–55
  (1983) *Social Disintegration and Popular Resistance in the Ottoman Empire, 1881–1908: Reactions to European Economic Penetration*, New York and London
Resnick, Steven (1970) 'The Decline of Rural Industry under Export Expansion: Burma, Philippines and Thailand, 1870–1938', *Journal of Economic History*, vol. 30, pp. 51–73
Rey, A. (1913) *Statistique des Principaux Résultants de l'Exploitation des Chemins*

de Fer de l'Empire Ottoman pendant l'Exercise 1911, Constantinople

Rodkey, F. S. (1958) 'Ottoman Concern about Western Economic Penetration in the Levant, 1849–1856', *Journal of Modern History*, vol. 30, pp. 348–53

Rosenberg, H. (1943) 'Political and Social Consequences of the Great Depression of 1873–1896 in Central Europe', *Economic History Review*, vol. 13

Rostow, Walt Whitman (1978) *The World Economy: History and Prospect*, Austin

Rougon, F. (1892) *Smyrne, Situation Commerciale et Economique*, Paris

Roumani, A. (1927) *Essai Historique et Technique sur la Dette Publique Ottomane*, Paris

Ruppin, A. (1917) *Syrien als Wirtschaftsgebiet*, Berlin

Sadat, Deena R. (1972) 'Rumeli Ayanları: The Eighteenth Century', *Journal of Modern History*, vol. 44, pp. 346–63

Samuelson, Paul A. and Swamy, S. (1974) 'Invariant Economic Index Numbers and Canonical Duality: Survey and Synthesis', *American Economic Review*, vol. 64, no. 4

Sandford, W. (1862) *On Cotton Growing in Turkey and Smyrna*, London

Sarc, Celal Ömer (1940) 'Tanzimat ve Sanayiimiz', in *Tanzimat*, Istanbul, pp. 423–40; translated and reprinted in part in Issawi (1966), pp. 48–59

Saul, S. B. (1960) *Studies in British Overseas Trade, 1870–1914*, Liverpool
(1969) *The Myth of the Great Depression, 1873–1896*, London

Shaw, S. J. (1975) 'The Nineteenth Century Ottoman Tax Reforms and Revenue System', *International Journal of Middle Eastern Studies*, vol. 6

Shaw, S. J. and Shaw, E. K. (1977) *History of the Ottoman Empire and Modern Turkey, Vol. II, Reform, Revolution and Republic, The Rise of Modern Turkey, 1808–1975*, Cambridge

Simon, M. (1960) 'The United States Balance of Payments, 1861–1900', in *National Bureau of Economic Research Studies in Income and Wealth*, vol. 25, Princeton
(1967) 'The Enterprise and Industrial Composition of New British Portfolio Investment 1865–1914', *Journal of Development Studies*, vol. 3

Singer, H. (1950) 'The Distribution of Gains between Investing and Borrowing Countries', *American Economic Review*, vol. 40, pp. 473–85

Smilianskaya, I. M. (1966) 'From Subsistence to Market Economy (Syria in the 1850's)', in Issawi (1966), pp. 226–47

Sönmez, Atilla (1970) 'Ottoman Terms of Trade, 1878–1913', *Middle East Technical University, Studies in Development*, no. 1, Ankara, pp. 111–48

Spraos, J. (1980) 'The Statistical Debate on the Net Barter Terms of Trade between Primary Commodities and Manufactures', *Economic Journal*, vol. 90, pp. 107–28

Steeg, L. (1924) 'Land Tenure', in Mears (1924), pp. 238–64

The Stock Exchange Official Intelligence (1908–9) London

Stoianovich, T. (1953) 'Land Tenure and Related Sectors of the Balkan Economy', *Journal of Economic History*, vol. 13, pp. 398–411
(1960) 'The Conquering Balkan Orthodox Merchant', *Journal of Economic History*, vol. 20, pp. 234–313

Stone, Irving (1977) 'British Direct and Portfolio Investment in Latin America

Before 1914', *Journal of Economic History*, vol. 37, pp. 690–722

Sussnitzki, A. J. (1966) 'Ethnic Division of Labor (in Turkey)', reprinted in Issawi (1966), pp. 115–25

Suvla, Refii-Şükrü (1966) 'Debts during the Tanzimat Period', in Issawi (1966) pp. 95–106

Svedberg, Peter (1978) 'The Portfolio–Direct Composition of Private Foreign Investment in 1914 Revisited', *Economic Journal*, vol. 88, pp. 763–77

Svoronos, N. G. (1956) *Le Commerce de Salonique au 19e Siècle*, Paris

Tate's Modern Cambisit, a Manual of Foreign Exchanges and Bullion, second edition (1831), third edition (1836), fourth edition (1842), ninth edition (1858), London

Temperley, Harold (1933) 'British Policy towards Parliamentary Rule and Constitutionalism in Turkey, 1830–1914', *Cambridge Historical Journal*, vol. 4, pp. 156–91

(1936) *England and the Near East: The Crimea*, London

Tengirşenk, Yusuf Kemal (1940) 'Tanzimat Devrinde Osmanli Devleti'nin Harici Ticaret Siyaseti', in *Tanzimat*, Istanbul, pp. 289–320

Tezel, Yahya S. (1972) 'Notes on the Consolidated Foreign Debt of the Ottoman Empire: The Servicing of the Loans', in *Milletlerarası Münasebetler Türk Yıllığı*, University of Ankara, Faculty of Political Sciences

Thobie, Jacques (1977) *Interêts et Imperialisme Français dans l'Empire Ottoman (1895–1919)*, Paris

Thorner, D. H. (1962) 'De-industrialization in India, 1881–1939', in D. H. Thorner and A. Thorner, *Land and Labour in India*, Bombay

Todorov, Nikolay (1969) '19. Yüzyılın İlk Yarısında Bulgaristan Esnaf Teşkilatında Bazı Karakter Değişmelerı', *Istanbul Üniversitesi İktisat Fakültesi Mecmuasi*, vol. 27, no. 1–2

(1971) 'The First Factories in the Balkan Provinces of the Ottoman Empire', *Middle East Technical University, Studies in Development*, vol. 1, no. 2

(1980) 'La Révolution Industrielle et l'Empire Ottoman', in Okyar and İnalcık (eds.) (1980), pp. 253–61

Tökin, İsmail Hüsrev (1934) *Türkiye'de Köy Iktisadiyatı*, Istanbul

Toprak, Zafer (1982) *Türkiye'de 'Milli İktisat' (1908–1918)*, Ankara

Turgay, A. Üner (1982) 'Ottoman–American Trade during the Nineteenth Century', *Osmanlı Arastırmaları*, vol. 3, pp. 189–246

Twomey, Michael J. (1983) 'Employment in Nineteenth Century Indian Textiles', *Explorations in Economic History*, vol. 20, pp. 37–57

Ubicini, A. (1856) *Letters on Turkey*, London

Üller, Necmi (1974) 'The Rise of Izmir, 1688–1740', unpublished Ph.D. dissertation, University of Michigan

United Nations (1949) *Relative Prices of Imports and Exports of Underdeveloped Countries*, U.N., 11.B.3, Geneva

Urquhart, David (1833) *Turkey and its Resources*, London

Uzunçarşılı, İsmail Hakkı (1951) 'Kanun-i Osmani Mefhum-i Defteri Hakani', *Belleten*, vol. 15

Veinstein, G. (1976) 'Ayan de la Région d'Izmir et Commerce du Levant (Deuxième Moitié du XVIIIe Siècle)', *Etudes Balkaniques*, Sofia, vol. 12, pp. 71–83

du Velay, A. (1903) *Essai sur l'Histoire Financière de la Turquie*, Paris

Verney, N. and Dambmann, G. (1900), *Les Puissances Etrangères dans le Levant en Syrie et en Palestine*, Paris

Wallerstein, Immanuel (1974) *The Modern World-System*, New York

Wallerstein, Immanuel and Kasaba, Reşat (1981) 'Incorporation into the World-Economy: Change in the Structure of the Ottoman Empire 1750–1839', *Middle East Technical University, Studies in Development*, vol. 8, no. 1–2, pp. 537–69

Warriner, Doreen (1944) 'Land Tenure in the Fertile Crescent', reprinted in Issawi (1966), pp. 72–8

White, H. D. (1933) *The French International Accounts, 1880–1913*, Cambridge, Mass.

Wiedenfeld, K. (1915) *Die deutsch-turkischen Wirtschaftsbeziehung*, Munich and Leipzig

Williamson, Jeffrey G. (1964) *American Growth and the Balance of Payments 1820–1913*, Chapel Hill, N.C.

Winkler, M. (1933) *Foreign Bonds: An Autopsy*, Philadelphia

Wolff, R. D. (1974) *The Economics of Colonialism: Britain and Kenya, 1870–1930*, New Haven

Wood, Alfred C. (1935) *A History of the Levant Company*, Oxford

Wynne, W. H. (1951) *State Insolvency and Foreign Bondholders*, vol. II, New Haven

Yalman, Nur (1971) 'On Land Disputes in Eastern Turkey', in G. L. Tikku (ed.), *Islam and its Cultural Divergence*, Urbana, Ill.

Yasuzawa, M. (1982) 'The Changes of Lifestyle: Changing Consumption Patterns in Meizi Japan', in *Eighth International Economic History Congress, Budapest, printed papers of Session B-4: Types of Consumption, Traditional. and Modern*, Budapest, pp. 41–50

Yeniay, H. (1964) *Yeni Osmanlı Borçları Tarihi*, second edition, Ankara

Zimmerman, L. J. (1962) 'The Distribution of World Income 1860–1960', in É. De Vries (ed.), *Essays on Unbalanced Growth*, The Hague, pp. 39–54

Index

CPSIA information can be obtained
at www.ICGtesting.com
Printed in the USA
FSHW011257230321
79775FS